NEW PERSPECTIVES ON MUSIC AND GESTURE

SEMPRE Studies in The Psychology of Music

Series Editors

Graham Welch, *Institute of Education, University of London, UK*
Adam Ockelford, *Roehampton University, UK*
Ian Cross, *University of Cambridge, UK*

The theme for the series is the psychology of music, broadly defined. Topics will include: (i) musical development at different ages, (ii) exceptional musical development in the context of special educational needs, (iii) musical cognition and context, (iv) culture, mind and music, (v) micro to macro perspectives on the impact of music on the individual (such as from neurological studies through to social psychology), (vi) the development of advanced performance skills and (vii) affective perspectives on musical learning. The series will present the implications of research findings for a wide readership, including user-groups (music teachers, policy makers, parents), as well as the international academic and research communities. The distinguishing features of the series will be this broad focus (drawing on basic and applied research from across the globe) under the umbrella of SEMPRE's distinctive mission, which is to promote and ensure coherent and symbiotic links between education, music and psychology research.

Other titles in the series

Sociology and Music Education
Edited by Ruth Wright

The Musical Ear: Oral Tradition in the USA
Anne Dhu McLucas

Infant Musicality
New Research for Educators and Parents
Johannella Tafuri

New Perspectives on
Music and Gesture

Edited by

ANTHONY GRITTEN
Middlesex University, UK

and

ELAINE KING
University of Hull, UK

ASHGATE

Published by
Ashgate Publishing Limited
Wey Court East
Union Road
Farnham
Surrey, GU9 7PT
England

Ashgate Publishing Company
Suite 420
101 Cherry Street
Burlington
VT 05401-4405
USA

www.ashgate.com

British Library Cataloguing in Publication Data
New perspectives on music and gesture. – (SEMPRE studies in the psychology of music)
   1. Music – Psychological aspects. 2. Gesture in music.
   I. Series II. Gritten, Anthony. III. King, Elaine, 1974–
   IV. Society for Education, Music and Psychology Research.
   781.1'1-dc22

Library of Congress Cataloging-in-Publication Data
New perspectives on music and gesture / [edited by] Anthony Gritten and Elaine King.
     p. cm. – (SEMPRE studies in the psychology of music)
   Includes index.
   ISBN 978-0-7546-6462-8 (hardcover : alk. paper) – ISBN 978-1-4094-2517-5 (ebook)
1. Music–Psychological aspects. 2. Gesture in music. 3. Performance practice (Music)
I. Gritten, Anthony. II. King, Elaine
   ML3838.N49 2011
   781'.1–dc22

2010042013

ISBN 9780754664628 (hbk)
ISBN 9781409425175 (ebk)

Bach musicological font developed by © Yo Tomita

MIX
Paper from
responsible sources
FSC
www.fsc.org   FSC® C018575

Printed and bound in Great Britain by the
MPG Books Group, UK

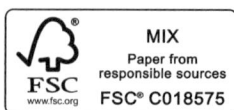

To Adèle and Gabriel
To Andrew and Sarah

Contents

List of Figures

List of Tables

List of Music Examples

Notes on Contributors

Martin Clayton is Professor of Ethnomusicology at the University of Durham. He has written extensively on Indian music and on issues relating to rhythm, metre and entrainment; gesture in musical performance; the history of comparative musicology; and musical encounters between India and the West. His publications include the books *Time in Indian Music* (Oxford University Press, 2001), *The Cultural Study of Music* (Routledge, 2003), *Music, Time and Place* (B. R. Rhythms, 2007) and *Music and Orientalism in the British Empire, 1780s–1940s* (Ashgate, 2007).

Jonathan Delafield-Butt is a Research Fellow at the Copenhagen University Babylab, and at the Perception Movement Action Research Centre at the University of Edinburgh. He obtained his PhD in neurobiology and has crossed fields to study the principles of animal movement in human psychological contexts. His research extends an animate movement science to study the coordination of conscious, expressive movement through voice, limb and hand within the developing infant–adult relation. He is in clinical training at the Scottish Institute of Human Relations.

Phillip Murray Dineen is a Professor in the School of Music at the University of Ottawa. His research interests stretch from Adorno to Zarlino. He is currently at work on the relationship of music and ethics, Schoenberg's theories of harmony and leftist musical thought in Central Europe between the world wars. An article on the ethics of musical performance appeared in the *International Review of the Aesthetics and Sociology of Music* 40/2 (2009). Recent work on Schoenberg and Adorno has appeared in the online periodical *Culture Unbound* (2009), in a collection of essays entitled *Schoenberg's Chamber Music, Schoenberg's World* (Pendragon, 2009), and in *Music Theory Spectrum* 31/2 (2009). A book entitled *Friendly Remainders: Essays in Music Criticism after Adorno* will be published by McGill-Queens' University Press in 2011.

Mine Doğantan-Dack is a Research Fellow in Music at the University of Middlesex, London. She is a pianist (BM, MM The Juilliard School) and a music theorist (MA Princeton University; PhD Columbia University). She also holds a BA in Philosophy (Bosphorus University, Istanbul). She regularly performs as a soloist and chamber musician, and is the recipient of the William Petschek award for piano performance. She is the founder of the Marmara Piano Trio and recently received an AHRC award for her research in chamber music performance. She has published articles on the history of music theory, expressivity, phenomenology of performing and affective responses to music. Her books include *Mathis Lussy: A Pioneer in Studies of Expressive Performance* (Peter Lang, 2002) and the edited volume *Recorded Music: Philosophical and Critical Reflections* (Middlesex University Press, 2008). She was awarded Dozency in 2002 and Professorship in 2008 by the Turkish Ministry of Education. She has taught at Columbia, New York and Yeditepe Universities. Mine is an Associate of the AHRC-funded Centre for Musical Performance as Creative Practice (CMPCP), and the founder of the Marmara Piano Trio (www.marmaratrio.com).

Gina A. Fatone is Associate Professor of Music at Bates College in Lewiston, Maine. Her research interests include the cognitive psychology of musical experience and intercultural music transmission. She completed her PhD in Ethnomusicology at UCLA in 2002 with a dissertation on vocal-to-motor transfer in the transmission of instrumental music. Her article on intermodal imagery in Scottish classical bagpiping transmission appears in *Ethnomusicology* (Fall 2010). She performs as a keyboardist and directs the Bates College Gamelan Orchestra.

Jane Ginsborg is Associate Dean of Research and Enterprise, and Director of the Centre for Music Performance Research at the Royal Northern College of Music, Manchester. She is a musician and a psychologist, with degrees from the University of York, the Open University and Keele University, and an Advanced Diploma from the Guildhall School of Music and Drama. She won the British Voice Association's Van Lawrence Award in 2002 for her PhD research on the interaction of words and melody in singers' memory for songs, and has published widely on topics including musicians' practice, memorizing strategies and long-term recall for music, musicians' health and well-being, and collaborative rehearsal and performance. She is Managing Editor of the online journal *Music Performance Research* and serves on the editorial boards of the *Journal of Interdisciplinary Musicology* and *Musicae Scientiae*.

Rolf Inge Godøy is Professor of Music Theory at the Department of Musicology, University of Oslo. His research is centered on phenomenological approaches to music theory, with a focus on the theoretical work of Pierre Schaeffer and related experience-based explorations of musical features. A natural extension of this research has been the study of music-related movement based on the belief that the experience of musical sound is closely linked with sensations of body movement (for more information, see www.fourms.uio.no).

Nicolas Gold is a Senior Lecturer in Computer Science at University College London, having previously worked at King's College London, the University of Manchester Institute of Science and Technology (UMIST) and the University of Durham. He received his PhD in software engineering from the University of Durham in 2000. His research interests encompass digital humanities, in particular computational musicology, and software maintenance. He has published many international conference and journal papers and has led or participated in research projects funded by the UK Engineering and Physical Sciences Research Council

(EPSRC), European Union (EU) and industry. He is a member (and former deputy-director) of the Centre for Research in Evolution, Search, and Testing (CREST), and led the EPSRC Service-Oriented Software Research Network.

Roger Graybill is on the Music Theory Faculty at New England Conservatory in Boston, Massachusetts. Between 2002 and 2011 he also served as Chair of the Music Theory Department at that school His research has focused on rhythm and gesture, the music of Brahms and theory pedagogy, and his work has appeared in *Music Theory Spectrum*, *Theory and Practice*, *Journal of Musicological Research*, *Journal of Music Theory Pedagogy*, *Theoria*, and the book *Engaging Music: Essays in Music Analysis* (edited by Deborah Stein, Oxford University Press, 2004). He is also co-author (with Stefan Kostka) of the *Anthology of Music for Analysis* (Prentice-Hall, 2003). A member of the Executive Board of the Society for Music Theory (SMT) between 1998 and 2001, he also served as chair of the programme committee for the national joint AMS/SMT meeting in 1997. In addition to his work as a theorist, Graybill has extensive experience as a church organist.

Anthony Gritten is Head of the Department of Performing Arts, Middlesex University, UK. He is contracted to co-edit *Music and Value Judgement* (with Mine Doğantan-Dack). His essays have appeared in the journals *Performance Research*, *Musicae Scientiae*, *Dutch Journal of Music Theory*, and *British Journal of Aesthetics*, and in various edited collections in English and German, as well as in philosophy books and artists' exhibition catalogues. A Fellow of the Royal College of Organists, he performs across the UK, Europe, and Canada, and has a close working relationship with the organist-composer Daniel Roth, several of whose recent works he has premiered.

Elaine King is Senior Lecturer in Music at the Department of Drama and Music, University of Hull. She has published widely on aspects of solo and ensemble performance, including gestures, breathing, rehearsal strategies and social interaction. She co-edited the first volume of *Music and Gesture* (with Anthony Gritten) and is currently co-editing *Music and Familiarity* (with Helen Prior). She is an ordinary member of Council for the Royal Musical Association (RMA) and Conference Secretary for the Society for Education, Music and Psychology Research (SEMPRE). She is an active cellist, pianist and conductor, performing regularly in chamber and orchestral ensembles.

Ole Kühl is a Postdoctoral Researcher in the Musicology Department of Oslo University. He is currently working on the project 'Music, Motion and Emotion'. He has spent most of his life working as a musician-cum-composer in the area of improvised music in areas such as jazz, fusion and world music. He turned to the academic field around 2000, where he has specialized in a cognitive approach to musicology. His PhD dissertation (2007) focused on the question of a musical semantics.

Laura Leante is a Lecturer in Music at the University of Durham. She was awarded her PhD in ethnomusicology at the University of Rome in 2004 for research on issues of meaning and cross-cultural reception of music in British Asian repertories. Her research interests range over Indian classical and folk music, music of the South Asian diaspora, music and globalization, and popular music. Since 2005 Laura has been involved in an AHRC-sponsored project 'Experience and Meaning in Music Performance', studying processes of meaning construction in music through the analysis of imagery and gesture and performance of Hindustani classical music. She is currently directing an AHRC-funded project on 'The Reception of Performance in North Indian Classical Music'.

Geoff Luck is an Academy of Finland Research Fellow in the music department of the University of Jyväskylä. He has a background in music psychology and movement analysis, and, as a member of the Finnish Centre of Excellence in Interdisciplinary Music Research, currently focuses on kinematic and dynamic aspects of musical communication. He uses a combination of motion-capture, computational, and statistical techniques to examine the role of movement in basic synchronization processes and musical activities such as conducting, singing and dancing.

Matt Rahaim is currently Assistant Professor of Ethnomusicology at the University of Minnesota, and has taught in the departments of Religious Studies, Asian Studies, and Music at Berkeley, Stanford, and St. Olaf College. Other research and teaching interests include early Gregorian chant notation, the politics of tuning systems, Sufi-Bhakti musical syncretism, acoustic ecology, and speech melody. He recently was studying oud performance and Arabic language in Damascus, Syria, funded by an ACM-Mellon Post-Doctoral fellowship. His articles have appeared in *World of Music, Gesture, The Brill Encyclopedia of Hinduism* and *Journal of Asian Studies*. His current book project focuses on the transmission of melodic knowledge through generations of Indian vocalists via hand gesture. He has been studying Hindustani vocal music (Gwalior gayaki) with Vikas Kashalkar of Pune, India, since 2000.

John Rink is Professor of Musical Performance Studies at the University of Cambridge. His books include *The Practice of Performance: Studies in Musical Interpretation* (Cambridge University Press, 1995), *Musical Performance: A Guide to Understanding* (Cambridge University Press, 2002), and (with Christophe Grabowski) *Annotated Catalogue of Chopin's First Editions* (Cambridge University Press, 2010). He directs the AHRC Research Centre for Musical Performance as Creative Practice as well as Chopin's First Editions Online (CFEO) and the Online Chopin Variorum Edition (OCVE). He was an Associate Director of the AHRC Research Centre for the History and Analysis of Recorded Music, in which he led a project on 'Analysing Performance Motif'. He is an experienced pianist and holds the Concert Recital Diploma (*Premier Prix*) of the Guildhall School of Music & Drama.

Benjaman Schögler is a member of the Perception–Movement–Action Research Centre, University of Edinburgh, UK, and a director of Skoogmusic Ltd (skoogmusic.com). A professional jazz musician, he is interested in music-making, communication and the practicalities of being a performer. As a founding member of Skoogmusic Ltd he is currently engaged in creating new technologies that make playing music more accessible to children and adults of all abilities.

Neta Spiro was a member of the UK-based CHARM project on 'Motive in Performance' in which, together with John Rink and Nicolas Gold, she explored the relationships between music theory, performance and perception. Previously, Neta studied for her BA at St Edmund Hall, Oxford (1997–2001), and Master's in Cognitive Science and Natural Language at the University of Edinburgh (2001–02). Her PhD was on the perception of phrasing, which she explored under the joint supervision of Rens Bod (University of Amsterdam) and Ian Cross (Centre for Music and Science, University of Cambridge). She is currently a Post-Doctoral Fellow in the Department of Psychology at The New School of Social Research in New York, and is working on musical interaction.

Colwyn Trevarthen is Professor (Emeritus) of Child Psychology and Psychobiology at the University of Edinburgh, where he has taught since 1971. He trained as a biologist, has a PhD in psychobiology from Caltech and was a Research Fellow at the Centre for Cognitive Studies at Harvard, where his infancy research began. His published work covers brain development, infant communication and child learning, and emotional health. He has recently edited, with Stephen Malloch, an authoritative book on *Communicative Musicality: Exploring the Basis of Human Companionship* (Oxford University Press, 2009).

W. Luke Windsor has been researching and teaching psychological, aesthetic, analytical and semiotic aspects of music since the mid-1990s. In particular he has published on rhythm and timing in performance, the sources and modelling of musical expression, and ecological approaches to the perception and production of musical performances. He has supervised doctoral work on a range of music-psychological and practice-led topics including musical improvisation, an area he is currently looking to for fresh inspiration. Luke is currently Deputy Head of the School of Music, University of Leeds, and Deputy Director of its Interdisciplinary Centre for Scientific Research in Music (ICSRiM) having previously worked and studied at City University, London, the University of Sheffield, and Radboud University in the Netherlands.

Lawrence M. Zbikowski is Associate Professor of Music in the Department and of the Humanities in the College at the University of Chicago. His research focuses on the application of recent work in cognitive science to various problems confronted by music scholars, including the nature of musical syntax, text–music relations, the relationship between music and movement, and the structure of theories of music. He is the author of *Conceptualizing Music: Cognitive Structure, Theory, and Analysis* (Oxford University Press, 2002), which was awarded the 2004 Wallace Berry prize by the Society for Music Theory. He recently contributed chapters to *The Cambridge Handbook of Metaphor and Thought* (Cambridge University Press, 2008), *Communication in Eighteenth Century Music* (Cambridge University Press, 2008), and *Music and Consciousness* (Oxford University Press, forthcoming). He was co-chair, with David Huron, of the 2009 Mannes Institute on Music and the Mind, at which he also served as a member of the Faculty.

Series Editors' Preface

There has been an enormous growth over the past three decades of research into the psychology of music. SEMPRE (the Society for Education, Music and Psychology Research) is the only international society that embraces an interest in the psychology of music, research and education. SEMPRE was founded in 1972 and has published the journals *Psychology of Music* since 1973 and *Research Studies in Music* Education since 2008, both now in partnership with SAGE (see www.sempre.org.uk). Nevertheless, there is an ongoing need to promote the latest research to the widest possible audience if it is to have a distinctive impact on policy and practice. In collaboration with Ashgate since 2007, the 'SEMPRE Studies in The Psychology of Music' has been designed to address this need. The theme for the series is the psychology of music, broadly defined. Topics include (amongst others): musical development at different ages; musical cognition and context; culture, mind and music; micro to macro perspectives on the impact of music on the individual (such as from neurological studies through to social psychology); the development of advanced performance skills; musical behaviour and development in the context of special educational needs; and affective perspectives on musical learning. The series seeks to present the implications of research findings for a wide readership, including user-groups (music teachers, policy makers, parents), as well as the international academic and research communities. The distinguishing feature of the series is its broad focus that draws on basic and applied research from across the globe under the umbrella of SEMPRE's distinctive mission, which is to promote and ensure coherent and symbiotic links between education, music and psychology research.

Graham Welch
Institute of Education, University of London, UK
Adam Ockelford
Roehampton University, UK
Ian Cross
University of Cambridge, UK

Acknowledgements

We wish to thank the other authors for their contributions to this volume. We should also like to thank Heidi Bishop at Ashgate for her valuable help and continual enthusiasm towards this project as well as the members of the production team for their assistance in the delivery of the book, notably Sarah Price and Barbara Pretty, and Tom Norton, who prepared the index. We are grateful to the SEMPRE Series Editors, particularly Adam Ockelford, for their support and guidance in this project too.

Introduction

Anthony Gritten and Elaine King

In recent years there has been a veritable explosion of work on aspects of the music–gesture interface. Research continues to develop the foundations laid by Lidov (1987), Hatten (1982, 1994, 2004) and others, many in non-musical disciplines, whose seminal activity remains a touchstone for new projects. Hatten's definition of human gesture as 'any energetic shaping through time that may be interpreted as significant' (2006: 1) provides a central starting point for researchers. Musical gestures may be conceived, produced, experienced and interpreted by individuals in various ways, whether aurally, visually, physically, conceptually or otherwise, and the functions of those gestures depends upon the contexts within which they arise. Research has already begun to shed some light upon the different types, functions, sizes, intensities and experiences of gestures as they relate to music, musicians and music-making, and the present volume aims to contribute further to the development of this knowledge and wisdom.

Musical Gesture Studies

Disciplines as varied as musicology, human movement studies, psychobiology, cognitive psychology, cognitive linguistics, anthropology, ethnology, music technology and performance studies have produced important work on musical gesture that has fed our broadening and deepening understanding of the subject. Most of this work has circulated around two interrelated areas (sometimes in tension): one comprises the musical body; the other comprises music cognition. The former has emerged as musicologists have worked through positivist tendencies and heritages of Modernism, while the latter has developed as the technological infrastructure of scholarship has embraced the opportunities afforded by digital technology for analysis and rationalization.

Representative examples of work on the musical body include: the use of cognitive feedback to increase the effectiveness and efficiency of musicians' movements (Juslin & Laukka 2000); books by prize-winning performers on the embodied status of gestures (Le Guin 2005); studies of the relationships between performing and T'ai Chi (David 1996); research into visual perception of body movements (Dahl & Friberg 2007); and long-term interdisciplinary research council-funded projects on the relationships between sound and movement in ballet (Jordan 2000, 2007). Representative examples of work on music cognition include: bridging music theory and general cognition by emphasizing how music is embedded in the world and how understanding it requires a battery of basic mental capacities (Zbikowski 2002); pedagogical interventions into the practice of performance that mediate cognitive and scientific advances into the looser languages, rhetorics and pragmatic 'strategies' of the performer (Parncutt & McPherson 2002; Williamon 2004); and work being produced out of the systematic 'fourMs' project at the University of Oslo on 'Music, Mind, Motion, Machines', which continues the earlier work of the 'Musical Gestures Project' (for example, Godøy & Jørgensen 2001; Godøy & Leman 2009).

Research continues both to widen in scope and to broaden in appeal, as ideas and methodologies are extended and new lines of enquiry are formed and tested. Of particular note is the influence of other scholarly disciplines, and the rich pickings that have been afforded as a result. There is, for example, an International Society of Gesture Studies based in the USA, with its own conferences since 2002 and a journal, of which music is but one contributory strand of activity. There have been Master's level courses on music and gesture (NNIMIPA 2010) and many doctoral students working on gesture and its cognates. For some scholars, Musical Gesture Studies is already an academic discipline with cross-disciplinary tendencies and a fertile community of scholars contributing to its development; it certainly becomes closer to one with every advance in the use of digital technologies to document, study and model musical gestures of all types – real, virtual, imagined, manipulated.

Considered as a whole, it might be noted that scholarship on musical gesture continues to strive for further, and sometimes better, ways to negotiate a fundamental set of distinctions that cuts across virtually all intellectual traditions and methodological biases, being related to the cliché concerning 'the two cultures': between acoustic sound and musical gesture, between physical and expressive gestures, and so on. All work seems to be heading towards a general understanding of why the concept of gesture is both all-embracing and all-important across virtually all forms of human music-making. Not only is gesture tied up in issues of agency and intention in musical practice, and not only is it figured within the concept of creativity (whether or not the product is tangible physically), but it is the site and vehicle for the crucial flow of energy between domains, and, as such, is the entropic loophole of music-making – that event through which, at which point, and by means of which music happens, and in consequence of which we are afforded and enjoy all those luxurious and multifarious activities that we describe as 'musical', whether compositional, performative, perceptual, critical, or all of the above.

Overview of *New Perspectives on Music and Gesture*

The first volume of essays on *Music and Gesture* (Gritten & King 2006) worked through a few of the fundamental strands of research in Musical Gesture Studies. During and since the preparation of that volume it became clear that there was a need to revisit the subject with the aforementioned developments in mind, and to showcase the continuing expansion of work on the subject. The rationale for this sequel volume entitled *New Perspectives on Music and Gesture* was thus twofold: first, to clarify the way in which the subject was continuing to take shape, by highlighting both central and developing trends, as well as popular and less frequent areas of investigation; second, to provide alternative insights into particular areas of the subject as articulated in the first volume.

About two-thirds of the material selected for inclusion in this volume was drawn from work presented and discussed at the Second International Conference on Music and Gesture held at the Royal Northern College of Music, Manchester UK, in July 2006. About half of the chapters are from authors based in the UK, a quarter come from North America, and a quarter represent work conducted in Scandinavia.

The 13 chapters in this volume reflect research in the key areas of Musical Gesture Studies outlined above. The volume is structured as a broad narrative trajectory moving from theory to practice in the following areas: psychobiology (Chapter 1), perception and cognition (Chapters 2–4), philosophy and semiotics (Chapters 5–6), conducting (Chapters 7–8), ensemble work (Chapters 9–11) and solo piano playing (Chapters 12–13). Alongside this broad spine, various alternative groupings of chapters provide an idea of the multiplicity of current directions in Musical Gesture Studies and the motifs recurring across the book, including: movement (Chapters 7–9, 12–13), semiotics (Chapters 3, 6–7), real and virtual gestures (Chapters 3, 7–9), socio-cultural meanings of gestures (Chapters 6–7, 10), attending to gestures (Chapters 3–5, 8), and the acoustic signals within gestures (Chapters 1–2, 8, 13). Some of the chapters represent areas of work not explicitly included in the first volume, notably psychobiology (Chapter 1), conducting (Chapters 7–8), ensemble work (Chapters 9–11), ethnomusicology (Chapter 10) and the study of sound recordings (Chapter 13).

In Chapter 1 ('Psychobiology of Musical Gesture: Innate Rhythm, Harmony and Melody in Movements of Narration'), Colwyn Trevarthen, Jonathan Delafield-Butt and Benjaman Schögler base their work on the idea that there is an essential coherence of purpose to musical gesture and our use of gesture to interact with our parents and children. Their research explores the musicality of mother–infant interactions and the narratives that emerge from these co-performances through analysis of facial, hand and verbal discourse. Furthermore, they suggest that the perceptual segmentation of gestures draws on innate capacities that underpin and ground musically specific tasks.

The issue of perception is exploited further in Chapter 2 ('Gestures in Music-making: Action, Information and Perception') as W. Luke Windsor considers ecological and psychological theories in his discussion of the analysis, perception and production of musical gestures. Focussing on performer's bodily gestures and data from Schubert's G♭ Impromptu for solo piano, he notes that the relationship between movement and sound is not necessarily fixed, and makes a useful heuristic separation of music from gesture. Windsor also writes about the many available definitions of gesture and reminds us that what 'gesture' is taken to mean and how musically significant information about performing or listening is extracted from raw data depends on which musical agent (performer, listener, acousmatic composer) is in question.

In Chapter 3 ('Co-articulated Gestural-sonic Objects in Music), Rolf Inge Godøy considers the ways in which continuous streams of sound or movement are divided (segmented) into coherent chunks. Through the analysis of visual and auditory events using motion capture and other sound imaging technology, Godøy argues that the notion of co-articulation can be fundamental to our understanding of human movement and sound perception.

That musical gestures are immediate in perception and rely on a basic level of human perception and performance is further underlined by Lawrence Zbikowski in Chapter 4 ('Musical Gesture and Musical Grammar: A Cognitive Approach'). He focuses on the ways in which gestures are basic to musical grammar and explains how the gestures that accompany speech are closely linked to our understanding of the dynamic processes of music. He uses psycholinguistic theory to support his discussion of sonic analogues and musical sequences, looking closely at Fred Astaire's performance of the Kern/Field number 'The Way You Look Tonight' to illustrate his discussion.

In Chapter 5 ('Distraction in Polyphonic Gesture'), Anthony Gritten investigates the multi-modal phenomenon of 'distraction' within the perception of gestures. He identifies the polyphonic basis of a gesture in Stravinsky's Violin Concerto as it resonates with material by Bach, Brahms and Tchaikovsky, showing how what such a gesture is and how it might be perceived vary according to the particular occasion of listening, and how changes of attention, or perceptual shifts of focus, mobilize the gesture and transform our understanding of it.

By contrast, a semiotic perspective on musical gesture is provided in Chapter 6 ('The Semiotic Gesture') by Ole Kühl. He argues that music is a holistic semiosphere, that its internal worldliness and external relations to the wider world are important to our interpretations of musical gesture. Kühl notes that gestures communicate at a more basic level than words and describes gesture as a matter of expressive sharing, focussing on the semiotic mapping from sound to body.

Our physical engagement with music is detailed more closely in the ensuing chapters of the volume as the focus moves towards conducting, ensemble playing and solo piano performances. In Chapter 7 ('Gestural Economies in Conducting'), Phillip Murray Dineen analyses conducting gestures on the basis of the belief that gestures support rather than contradict each other, and that together they express a unified conception and elicit a unified outcome in music-making. His work explores the interactive nature of gestures through analysis of the relationship between the conductor and the orchestra (including the interaction between shadow ensemble and the rest of the players). There is further awareness of the links between musical gestures and other human pursuits in the detailed cross-comparison of conducting and ice hockey. Dineen also compares the speed at which gestures establish a performative interpretation with the much slower revealing of an interpretation through words, similar to the semiotic assumption put forward by Kühl (Chapter 6).

In a complementary approach to studying gestures in conducting, Geoff Luck investigates how the beat is communicated by a conductor using empirical procedures from music psychology. Chapter 8 ('Computational Analysis of Conductors' Temporal Gestures') discusses three main areas of research: computational feature extraction techniques, the kinematics of conductors' gestures, and musician–conductor synchronization. Luck argues that the perception of temporal events draws on a set of fundamental perceptual processes. He asserts that the ability to interact and make the most of those signals (for example, synchronization cues) is a necessary skill for expert performance.

An empirical approach is also adopted in Chapter 9 ('Gestures and Glances: Interactions in Ensemble Rehearsal') as Elaine King and Jane Ginsborg investigate issues of familiarity and expertise between musicians in ensemble rehearsal. They study the gestures and glances produced by singers and pianists as they work with their regular duo partners and in new combinations. After coding the performers' physical gestures and eye contact, they conclude that the performers used physical gestures to a greater extent when rehearsing with familiar and same-expertise partners than new or different-expertise partners. Also, a wider range of gestures was produced in rehearsals with familiar partners.

In Chapter 10 ('Imagery, Melody and Gesture in Cross-Cultural Perspective'), Gina Fatone, Martin Clayton, Laura Leante and Matt Rahaim present case studies of gestures occurring in non-Western music performances. They emphasize the cross-modal interactions of physical gesture and its implication in communication between individuals and groups of musicians. They discuss the ways in which mimetic gestures accompanying melodic material complement and sometimes modify aural information, and how physical gestures often precede the melodic movements with which they are associated. They note that knowing music is three-dimensional and that the constituent moments are integrated into unified meaningful actions.

In Chapter 11 ('Whose Gestures? Chamber Music and the Construction of Permanent Agents'), Roger Graybill attends to the nuanced interactions between the virtual agents that are constructed in the discourse of chamber music. In his case study of Brahms's String Quartet in C Minor, Op. 51 No. 1, he reveals the ways in which agency theory may assist in the creation of vivid – literally 'life-like' – listening experiences.

Moving away from the arena of chamber music and ensemble playing, the last two chapters in the book focus on solo pianists. In Chapter 12 ('In the Beginning was Gesture: Piano Touch and the Phenomenology of the Performing Body'), Mine Doğantan-Dack explores the nature of pianistic touch in terms of the indivisibility of phoronomic experience. In her phenomenological account, she articulates the 'living body' of the pianist by describing the sensation of the initiatory gesture as the 'singing hand' prepares to strike the keys. Her study complements the material in Chapter 13 ('Motive, Gesture and the Analysis of Performance') which focuses more specifically on the significance of analysing sonic gestures in piano playing. John Rink, Neta Spiro and Nicolas Gold explore the expressive micro-patterns of selected performance parameters through detailed analysis of the motivic gestures produced in sound recordings of Chopin's Mazurka, Op. 24 No. 2. They offer a detailed appraisal of Rubinstein's performance, highlighting the way in which musical features of the dance genre underpin his interpretation. Furthermore, they show how the interpretations and strategies of different performers are based on recurrent patterns across a wide stylistic range of actual performance practices.

Ideological and Methodological Issues

A number of general assumptions are shared by the chapters as described above, tying them together at a basic level in terms of their aesthetic ideology. Some of the more significant deserve note: gestures operate holistically and there are overlaps between musical gestures and other human or 'worldly' gestures; gestures are immediate in perception and form an innate part of the human musical toolkit; interaction is an important component of gesture; and musical gestures are necessarily cross-modal phenomena. Indeed, all of the chapters are grounded in the premise that musical gestures are cross-modal and that gestures include non-sounding physical movements as well as those that produce sound.

Alongside these recurrent general assumptions concerning aesthetic ideology, a number of broad epistemological issues concerning scholarly methodology run through this volume. These can be grouped together under three broad headings: ethnography, information retrieval and rule-following.

Several authors note that ethnographic techniques are useful in order to retain the rich detail of performing data within the scholarly purview. Trevarthen et al. (Chapter 1), for example, note the importance of folk psychology in both performing and perceiving musical gesture, and what Dineen (Chapter 7) calls 'belief complexes' are also important to the investigations of King and Ginsborg (Chapter 9), Fatone et al. (Chapter 10) and Doğantan-Dack (Chapter 12), which present thick descriptions of what it is like to engage with music gesturally.

Issues of information retrieval are common to the methodological reflections of Windsor (Chapter 2), who notes that the retrieval of gestures from performance by listeners is an open-ended activity, Zbikowski (Chapter 4), King and Ginsborg (Chapter 9) and Luck (Chapter 8), in whose chapters cue extraction is an important issue prior to the interpretation of gestural data. Luck's focus is the creation of algorithms for generating and describing movements in performance. King and Ginsborg, Zbikowski, and Windsor are concerned with how gestures are coded and categorized.

Rule-following arises as a methodological focus in several chapters focussing on the mechanics of perceptual segmentation. The bases of segmentation are explored by Trevarthen et al. (Chapter 1) in terms of intentional plots and gesture complexes, by Godøy (Chapter 3) in terms of chunking (both through music notation and in terms of auditory scene analysis), by Gritten (Chapter 5) in terms of the fluid relationships – 'smearing' – between auditory and virtual chunks, by Dineen (Chapter 7) in terms of the various economies of conducting, and by Graybill (Chapter 11) in terms of agency theory and the structural congruence of musical patterns with those of real-life agents. More generally, several chapters uncover the invariant rules by which musical gestures work, taking their various modes as, broadly speaking, a matter of rule-following. Windsor (Chapter 2) takes expression to be rule-like, while Zbikowski (Chapter 4) focuses on gesture and grammar, Luck (Chapter 8) calculates algorithms that ground musically significant features of performance, and Rink et al. (Chapter 13) use digital technology to compare multiple data sets.

Perhaps this shows one clear way towards the future, as we come to terms with the extraordinary potential of digital technology to work for us and to resurrect the hard empirical study of creative practice − as Kühl (Chapter 6) says, to economically and effectually process information. Several of the chapters in this volume show that digital technology provides a powerful new prosthetic limb for Musical Gesture Studies, while also functioning as a catalyst to the renewed attention to the creation of impact-focussed bridges between music and science. As we renew the search for rules underlying musical gesture, employing technology to help us make our reflective judgements as both musicians and scholars, we do well to reflect on Windsor's (Chapter 2) ecological approach to the flow of information, which, like the smearing between chunks that Godøy theorizes (Chapter 3) and the relationships between expenditure and outcome that Dineen discusses (Chapter 7), leads us to the concept of energy – that which is channelled, focussed, and articulated by and through musical gesture.

The Way Ahead

On the basis of this picture of scholarship on musical gesture and the broad commonalities shared between the chapters in the present volume, it can be proposed that the concept of gesture has become increasingly useful to scholarship because it has contributed to a constellation of interrelated concepts that has included, *inter alia*, voice, authenticity, freedom, subjectivity, expression, autonomy, organicism and interiority. Of particular note is the extraordinary quality of achievements that has been afforded to scholarship on the back of committed, intense and sometimes apparently irreversible investments in this constellation of concepts, alongside equally imaginative insights set in motion by broadly deconstructive critiques of these same concepts. Noting in passing that there has been an essentially Modernist quality to this approach to musical gesture, it has become necessary to consider how these satellite concepts provide an appropriate image and model for musical practice in our digital world of the twenty-first century; the essays in this volume and the first book on *Music and Gesture* contribute to this process of reflection and development.

As gesture continues to provide a hook upon which scholars can mount their research, or at least a heuristic for future explorations, we can turn to some of the wider implications of this volume concerning what Musical Gesture Studies needs in order to ensure that provocative and creative work continue to be produced. Some might propose that a peer-reviewed journal is needed to formally cement the subject into the institutional and intellectual framework of musical scholarship, and that cyberspace provides a brilliant medium for the multi-media, multi-dimensional dissemination of such a collective enterprise. Others might request or wish to offer a regular international conference on the subject in order to showcase work-in-progress and to provide a platform for emerging scholars; the Third International Conference on Music and Gesture took place at McGill University in Montreal in March 2010. Others may wish that the innovative creative work of artists such as Stelarc and others working with prosthetics and virtual technologies be assimilated into the field, and that the creative practices of artists such as Trent Reznor and Radiohead be examined for models of music production, distribution and reception in which property and propriety lack the tight grip upon theorizing gesture that they have within Western Classical music traditions. Many will seek to embed scholarship on musical gesture into the broader discourses of the Performing Arts, and to consider whether there is such a thing as an essentially or specifically 'musical' gesture; whether, that is, the word and concept of 'gesture' can be extracted from its theatrical origins. Everyone will, looking back on *Music and Gesture*, ask for continuing clarification of the very meaning of the term 'musical gesture', in order to be able to compare and contrast research on the subject. In terms of local, specific formulations of particular projects that are needed in order to complete or extend previous work or to test hypotheses and make connections between different theories and repertoires, lists could be drawn up in each of the areas of work represented in this volume, and will be determined by the personal interests and ideological bases of the value judgements that each and every musician, whether performer, scholar, or music lover (or all three), commits to as part of his or her ongoing musical practice.

Whatever specific ideas and research topics are eventually proposed, evaluated, funded, explored, disseminated, debated, improved and (most importantly) implemented by musicians within their practices, the future of Musical Gesture Studies is bright.

References

Dahl, S. & Friberg, A. (2007). Visual Perception of Expressiveness in Musicians' Body Movements. *Music Perception* 24: 433–54.

David, C. (1996). *The Beauty of Gesture: The Invisible Keyboard of Piano and T'ai Chi.* Berkeley: North Atlantic Books.

Godøy, R. I. & Jørgensen, H. (eds.) (2001). *Musical Imagery*. Lisse, Holland: Swets & Zeitlinger.

Godøy, R. I. & Leman, M. (eds.) (2009). *Musical Gestures: Sound, Movement, and Meaning*. New York: Routledge.

Gritten, A. & King, E. (eds.) (2006). *Music and Gesture*. Aldershot: Ashgate.

Hatten, R. (1982). *Toward a Semiotic Model of Style in Music: Epistemological and Methodological Bases*. PhD dissertation, Indiana University.

— (1994). *Musical Meaning in Beethoven: Markedness, Correlation, and Interpretation*. Bloomington: Indiana University Press.

— (2004). *Interpreting Musical Gestures, Topics, and Tropes: Mozart, Beethoven, Schubert*. Bloomington: Indiana University Press.

— (2006). A Theory of Musical Gesture and Its Application to Beethoven and Schubert. In A. Gritten & E. King (eds.), *Music and Gesture* (pp. 1–23). Aldershot: Ashgate.

Jordan, S. (2000). *Moving Music: Dialogues with Music in Twentieth-Century Ballet*. London: Dance Books.

— (2007). *Stravinsky Dances: Re-Visions across a Century*. Alton: Dance Books.

Juslin, P. & Laukka, P. (2000). Improving Emotional Communication in Music Performance through Cognitive Feedback. *Musicae Scientiae* 4: 151–83.

Le Guin, E. (2005). *Boccherini's Body: An Essay in Carnal Musicology*. Berkeley: University of California Press.

Lidov, D. (1987). Mind and Body in Music. *Semiotica* 66: 69–97.

NNIMIPA (2010). Nordic Network for the Integration of Music Informatics, Performance and Aesthetics, Master's course on 'Music, Meaning and Gesture', University of Southern Denmark at Odense, 22–26 March 2010 (http://www.nnimipa.org/MMG.html/; accessed March 2010).

Parncutt, R. & McPherson, G. (eds.) (2002). *The Science and Psychology of Music Performance: Creative Strategies for Teaching and Learning*. Oxford: Oxford University Press.

Williamon, A. (ed.) (2004). *Musical Excellence: Strategies and Techniques to Enhance Performance*. Oxford: Oxford University Press.

Zbikowski, L. (2002). *Conceptualising Music: Cognitive Structure, Theory, and Analysis*. Oxford: Oxford University Press.

Chapter 1

Psychobiology of Musical Gesture: Innate Rhythm, Harmony and Melody in Movements of Narration

Colwyn Trevarthen, Jonathan Delafield-Butt and Benjaman Schögler

After the pleasures which arise from gratification of the bodily appetites, there seems to be none more natural to man than Music and Dancing. In the progress of art and improvement they are, perhaps, the first and earliest pleasures of his own invention; for those which arise from the gratification of the bodily appetites cannot be said to be his own invention. (Adam Smith 1982[1777]: 187)

Time and measure are to instrumental Music what order and method are to discourse; they break it into proper parts and divisions, by which we are enabled both to remember better what has gone before, and frequently to foresee somewhat of what is to come after: we frequently foresee the return of a period which we know must correspond to another which we remember to have gone before; and according to the saying of an ancient philosopher and musician, the enjoyment of Music arises partly from memory and partly from foresight. (Adam Smith (1982[1777]: 204)

Culture is activity of thought, and receptiveness to beauty and humane feeling. Scraps of information have nothing to do with it. (Alfred North Whitehead 1929)

In this chapter we explore the *innate sense of animate time in movement* – without this there is no dance, no music, no narrative, and no teaching and learning of cultural skills. We interrogate the measured 'musicality' of infants' movements and their willing engagement with musical elements of other persons' expressive gestures. These features of human natural history are still mysterious, but they are clearly of fundamental importance. They indicate the way we are built to act to express ideas and tell stories with our bodies, and out of which all manner of musical art is created, how our experience of the meaning of our actions is passed between persons, through communities and from generations to generation.

The communicative gestures of human bodies may become elaborately contrived, but they do not have to be trained to present the rhythm and harmony of what minds intend. Our movements communicate what our brains anticipate our bodies will do and how this will feel because others are sensitive to the essential control processes of our movements, which match their own. Gestures, whether seen, felt or heard, indicate the motivating force and coherence of central neural plans for immanent action in present circumstances. They have a desire to tell stories by mimesis, and may allude to imaginary adventures over a scale of intervals of time, in rhythmic units from present moments to lifetimes measured in the brain. They can imitate thoughts about circumstances that lie away from present practical reality somewhere in the imagined future or the remembered past, assuming responsibility for a sensible fantasy that wants to be shared. In this way music is heard as sounds of the human body moving reflectively and hopefully, with a sociable purpose that finds pride in the telling of 'make believe'.

The Natural Process that Makes Music, and Makes it Communicative

Music moves us because we hear human intentions, thoughts and feelings moving in it, and because we appreciate their urgency and harmony. It excites motives and thoughts that animate our conscious acting and appraising of reality. It appeals to emotions that measure the effort and satisfactions, advantages and dangers of moving in intricate repetitive ways. Evidently a feeling for music is part of the adaptations of the human species for acting in a human-made world; part, too, of how cultural symbols and languages are fabricated and learned (Gratier & Trevarthen 2008; Kühl 2007).

Sensations in the body of the moving Self and its well-being, proprioceptive and visceral, are perceived as metaphors for effective action, feeling 'how' or 'why' the act is made without actually having to say 'what' the object is (Damasio 1999; Gallese & Lakoff 2005; Lakoff & Johnson 1980, 1999). When we hear another's voice their intentions and affective qualities are powerfully conveyed because our organ of hearing is designed to appreciate the energy, grace and narrative purpose of mouths moving as human breathing is made to sound through the actions of delicately controlled vocal organs (Fonagy 2001). Vocalizations reflect the motives and effects of the whole body in action. We hear how inner and outer body parts may come into action in harmonious combination under the control of motives and experience, or fall into clumsy disorder. Thus we can cry out or sing gestures of hope and fear, of love and anger, peace and violence, moving one another with the power of the voice so we can participate in one another's feelings (Panskepp & Trevarthen 2009).

Human hands are also gifted with the mimetic ability to accompany these vocal images of action (Kendon 1980, 1993), richly illustrating the messages of the voice in chains of action that may be sounded as melodies on musical instruments to accompany song, or take its place. Music and dance exhibit how we plan the moving of where to go and what to know, and they appeal immediately to the imaginations of others. They are poetry without words about roles for acting in community. They are the matter and energy that dramatists, composers and choreographers transform in the creation of what the philosopher Adam Smith

(1982[1777]) calls the 'imitative arts', activities that express 'pleasures of man's own invention'.

Music communicates the mind's essential *coherence of purpose*, a wilfulness that holds its elements in a narrative form through phenomenal, experienced, time (Malloch & Trevarthen 2009). Every gesture in music feels with the whole Self of a performer, an imaginary actor or dancer, whether the stepping body with its full weight and strong attitudes, or only the subtle flexions of a hand, or the lifts and falls that link tones of voice in melody with expressive movements of the eyes and face. The different parts share an intrinsic pulse and tones ordered in *polyrhythmic sequences* – harmonious or beautiful because they convey the making of well-formed thoughts and sensitively compounded feelings, or unharmonious and ugly, not because they are out of control, but because they struggle to keep hold of and rein in forces that would pull them to pieces. Every piece of music, even the smallest melody, is made with sociable purpose. That is what distinguishes a musical action from an action that is purely practical, to get something done.

Research on infants' gestures and their sensitivity for responsive company reveals that these properties of the embodied human spirit, and the programme of their development in human company, are innate (Trevarthen 1986). It indicates, also, how music expresses an inborn human skill for cultural learning that seeks to know traditional stories in body movement. Human gestures are communicative, creative and inquisitive, seeking to imitate new forms.

Natural Causes and Functions of Gestures and Gesture Complexes

For this chapter we define a *unit gesture* as *expression of intention by a single movement*. Any body movement can be an expression with potential to communicate, but the expression most often meant when we speak of a human gesture is a movement of the hands. Single gestures do not 'mean' in isolation from meaningful situations and activities that are contrived with the intentions and awareness of the subjects that perform them. They are components of *intentional plots* – sequences or *gesture complexes* that express the flow and invention of movement and awareness in the mind. When gestures are defined as artificial symbols comparable to words they are said to derive meaning from the 'context' in which they are performed, but the context of any expression is not a static, or objective, state of affairs. A context of meanings, for all kinds of expression including symbols, is the field of intentions and awareness in which the expressions are generated. It is something psychologically invented.

It is important that all communicative gestures of animals – head bobbing and hand waving of lizards, singing of whales or nightingales, cries of migrating geese, squeaking of mice, grunts of baboons – are both *self-regulatory* (felt within the body or guided by interested subjective attention to objects and events in the world) and adapted for *social communication,* intersubjectively (Darwin 1872; Panksepp & Trevarthen 2009; Porges 2003; Rodriguez & Palacios 2007). They are for transmitting purposes and feelings through a community. They manifest intentions in forms that can be sensed by other individuals as signs or symptoms of the motives that generate them. They serve cooperative life, including adaptive engagements between species, be they predatory or mutually beneficial.

Human gestures function in the creation of a unique cultural world where motives are shared in *narrations of movement expressive of inventions in thinking and acting* – organized sequences of actions that convey original thoughts, intentions, imaginary or remembered experiences – that are made, not only with logical order to perform some action in the world, but *with feeling for the drama of changing experience* (Gratier & Trevarthen 2008). Gestural expressions, with their innate timing and combination in narrations, are the foundation for learning all the forms and values of the elaborate cultural rituals and the conventions of art and language (Gentilucci & Corballis 2006). Their motive processes expressed in sound are the primary matter of music (Gritten & King 2006; Trevarthen 1999a).

Many kinds of movements of a person can communicate psychological or physiological experiences and purposes, and this has made for confusion in discussions by psychologists and linguists about what is a gesture (Hatten 2006). Attention focused on an *a priori* categorization of the multifarious special uses or products of gestures, according to contrived grammatical and semantic rules and symbols, leaves the motivating source of timing, form and feeling obscure. The movements and sounds we make with our bodies, both when reflecting to ourselves on experience or in live dialogue with others, are not just learned conventions. They arise as spontaneous acts of vitality, more or less artfully contrived, all of which reveal motive states and experiences of the Self that others may appreciate.

Works of art require the intimate cultivation of gestures as more or less elaborate confections of ritual and technique that enable a community to share identified beliefs, dreams and memories. They are coloured by innate *aesthetic and moral emotions* that regulate their motive source, and, as Whitehead (1929) says, that guide cultural thinking. Musical art cultivates gestures of the voice, or of sound made by skilled action of hands or bodies on resonant matter. While it may be compared, in its basic social functions, to sound-making activities by which animals enliven their encounters and sustain relationships in community, human music has much more ambitious narrative content and make-believe.

Gestures are embodied intentional actions that signal three kinds of moving experience, in three different domains of consciousness. They can sense, show and regulate the state of the *body* of the person who makes them; they can manifest and direct interests to the *objective world* of physical 'things'; and they can convey the purposes of communication with *other persons*, or any combination of these three (Figure 1.1). Every gesture is an outward expression of the vitality of the subject's dynamic 'state of mind'', the feeling of how motive energy flows in the muscles of the body through a controlled time. It shows the purpose or project that prompts moving in that way and with that rhythm and effort. By a unique process of sympathetic resonance of motives and narratives of feeling, which need not be regulated by any conscious intention to communicate or any technique

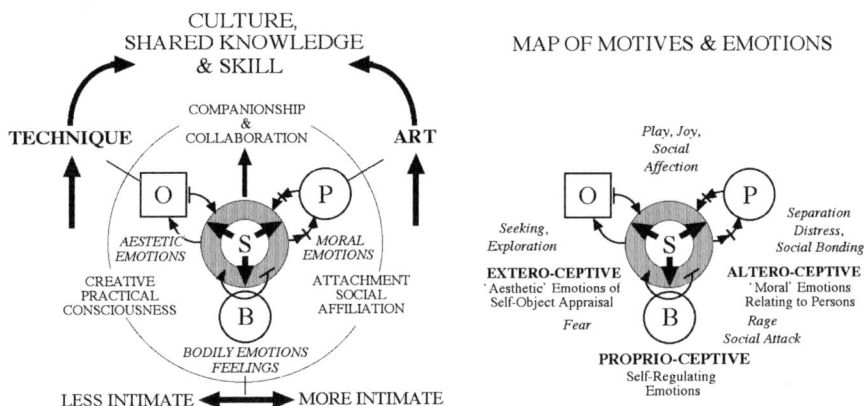

Figure 1.1   *Left*: Three ways in which the Self (S) regulates intentions to move: within the body (B), in accommodation to objects (O) and in communication with persons (P). All three participate in the collaborations of companionship and shared meaning.
Right: A map of motives and emotions – affects regulating intentions of the Self in different circumstances (after Panksepp 1998; Panksepp & Trevarthen 2009)

of rational organization, it can function to transmit vitality states or motives to another or to many others, intersubjectively, mediating companionship in agency.

Contemporary brain science is helping us realize that intersubjective communication of intentions and emotions is part of our cerebral physiology (Gallese 2003; Gallese, Keysers & Rizzolatti 2004). Nevertheless, while it is clear that gestures function by engaging brain activity between persons, the primitive 'generative' process of *sympathy*, by which the motive and affective regulation of a movement in one embodied animal mind may engage with and affect the stream of intentions and feelings of mind and body in another individual, remains a mystery. We cannot explain how the gestural motive evolving in the brain of one being becomes a message that motivates another brain to pick up the process in a particular imitative way. Presumably it is by sensitivity to parameters of the control processes of our individual self-awareness, revealed by our moving bodies, that others become aware of that control and can participate in it.

In social life, the distinction between a movement or posture made 'in communication' and therefore a 'gesture', as opposed to one not intended for communication but entirely for individual purposes is unclear. It would appear to depend on the abilities of one individual to 'feel with' the motives that cause and direct any kind of action of the other. The process will gain direction and subtlety by learning in real-life communication, but this learning itself would appear to require adaptations for an innate intersubjective awareness that is active from the start of life with others (Beebe et al. 2005; Trevarthen 1987, 1998, 1999b; Zlatev et al. 2008).

A Theory of Expressive Movement: Levels of Regulation of Action

Motives give form and prospective control to movements, and emotions expressed in the tempi and qualities of movement are the regulators of the power and selectivity of motives. They carry evidence of the Self-regulated flow of energy in motor actions – of the *proprio-ceptive regulation* of the force and grace of moving, with prospective emotional assessment of risks and benefits. Movements must be adjusted to the external realities of the environment and therefore have to submit to *extero-ceptive regulation* of awareness of the configurations, motions and qualities of places and things. Motives and emotions are communicated between persons by an immediate sympathetic perception of their dynamic features – i.e. by assimilation of their proprioceptive feelings and exteroceptive interests by others into *altero-ceptive regulation* (Figure 1.1). This interpersonal regulation in the moment of communicating opens the way to further and more enduring levels or fields of regulation for actions, their manners and goals. What may be called *socio-ceptive regulation* of actions in relationships and communities leads to development of collective ways of behaving that become an environment of common understandings or a 'habitus' for cooperative life. Further elaboration of conventional customs, rituals, structures, tools, institutions, symbols and beliefs, and languages, gives cooperative works trans-generational meaning in an *icono-ceptive regulation* of human cultural behaviour.

These distinctions of how actions are regulated for different purposes are important in the sharing of the creativity and exuberance of art, and in any educational or therapeutic practice designed to strengthen the participation of persons, children or adults, in affectionate and meaningful relationships with others. All art and therapy depends on respect for altero-ceptive and 'higher', more contrived forms of regulation. When a learner experiences difficulties in understanding and practice of a culturally valued behaviour, such as appropriate social manners, speech or performance of sport or music, it is not sufficient to identify a fault and try to treat it as if the affected individual were a physical system or a form of life without human sympathies. 'Intent participation' in new experience with a teacher is required (Rogoff 2003).

Because human minds naturally seek to live in relationships, disorders of motives and emotions, and therefore of learning, thinking and communicating with or without language are disorders of processes *between* persons, in a 'system' of engagements (Sander 1983; Tronick 2007). Dealing with a diagnosed fault in an individual leads to recognition that the effect of the fault is between that person and others. Emotion is not simply the regulating of states of arousal, nor just the building of schemas for objects, but the regulating of acting with intentions that have both defined goals and creativity of interpretation. Actions are evaluated by the emotions that accompany their motives as forces within the human psyche, which learning of language and other cultural skills channel and elaborate.

All these functions of human gesture are evident in the first two years of life before a child can speak with the special shared intelligence of language (Stern 2000 [1985]). They show their beginnings before birth, and after birth they create, in collaboration with sympathetic companions, what we have called a 'communicative musicality' (Malloch & Trevarthen 2009).

Innate Intersubjectivity and Second Person Psychology

Human life, from its beginnings, depends on the regulation of cooperative vital functions in active ways, by motivated processes and emotionally qualified movements. Foetuses, living in intimate symbiosis with their mother's body, practice expressive gestures that assist formation of their bodies and minds (Figure 1.2(a)), and newborn infants show a wealth of self-satisfying or action-exploring 'creative' movements that are ready to engage the affections of a mother in intimate communication (Trevarthen & Aitken 2003; Trevarthen & Reddy 2007). The neonate's movements may attend to environmental events, orient to locate or track them, and focus to identify them (Figure 1.2(b)). More importantly, they become a discriminating part of communicative, intersubjective exchanges. Imitations by newborn infants offer surprising evidence that human gestural expressions can immediately seek engagement with contingent responses of a sympathetic other, and that they actively try to reciprocate in an intermodal matching of motives, taking the initiative to learn new marked forms or 'conventions' of movement by matching the body part, timing and expressive quality of the other's gestures (Nagy 2006; Nagy & Molnar 2004; Nagy et al. 2005; see Figures 1.2(b) and 1.2(c)).

Many scholars and scientists, convinced that all valuable or 'important' human meanings and conventions require higher cognitive representations far out of reach of an infant, have contended that these first human movements are not gestures, because they cannot contain volitional communicative content regulated by the semantics and grammar of a symbolic system. This point of view relies on an artificial sense of volition, a reductive theory of how the mind of a human person is taught to regulate and elaborate its experience through moving. It does not comprehend that natural 'biological' functions of gesture, with their creative motives for learning new ways of meaning, may be instinctively apparent to other persons.

The argument against sophisticated constructivism is beautifully set out in a recent text by Vasudevi Reddy (2008), who reviews, with skillful and systematically examined observations, the complex, engaging nature of human infants and their remarkable, hitherto largely unremarked, perceptive and intentional social awareness, rich in self-conscious humour. In her opening chapters, Reddy proposes that infants, as do adults, experience the subjectivity of another through 'second-person' interpersonal interaction. She sets out a clear logic that knowing the subjectivity, or mind, of another entails engaging with their expressions directly,

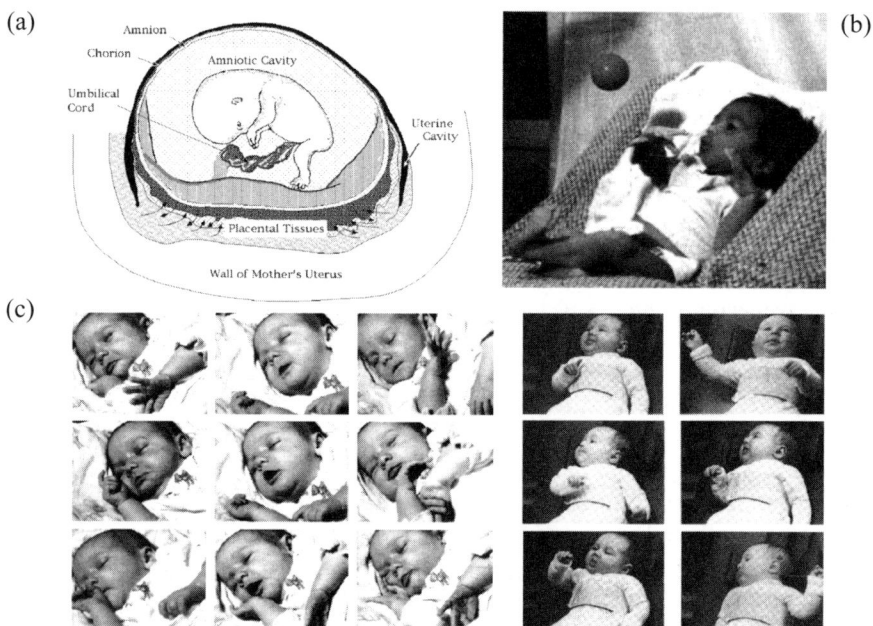

Figure 1.2   (a) The foetus *in utero*, showing adaptations of the body for
                coordinated gestures
                (b) Newborn in India, 30 minutes old, expressing interest with his
                whole body as he tracks a red ball moved by another person
                (c) Expressive gestures of a newborn in active sleep, and of a six-
                week-old, coordinating movements of head, eyes, face and hands

forming the so-called *second-person perspective*, i.e. one that is neither first-person
(from within an isolated individual mind) nor third-person (by an observing other,
empathically), but an engaging self-with-other, sympathetically.

From this position, neglected by developmental experts but shared by the
'folk' psychologies of mothers the world over, we can see that knowing and
sharing with another mind is not just about communicating with volitional
calculation, or what Whitehead describes as 'products of rational discernment'
(Whitehead 1929), but it is about awareness of another through direct, shared
experience of living, creatively and with passion. Felt intersubjective activity *is*
the knowing we have of one another. Perinatal care that confirms the intuitions of
new parents that their unsophisticated child is a conscious human person brings
great pleasure to them, and strengthens the bonds with their infant and with one
another (Brazelton 1993).

How Hand Gestures tell their Rich Stories, Complementing the Voice

The motor-intentional possibilities of human upper limbs, and therefore their demands for elaborate cerebral imaginative control, are very great, because the jointed lever system of arms, palms and fingers has many biomechanical 'degrees of freedom', and because the cerebral programming of the combinations of rotation about the many joints is, from birth, extremely refined and informed by many sensitive receptors. Hands of adults can be projected from the body with high velocity to transmit large forces, moved with exquisite temporal and spatial precision of guidance in an extensive reaching field, and rotated to contact surfaces of objects with accuracy in any direction while responding to light touch, modulating pressure. Fingers are extended or flexed in an infinite number of combinations to palpate, push, poke, punch, pat, etc. The two hands cooperate, performing complementary tasks in manipulation of objects and many expressive movements. These may be self-adjusting: carriage of food to the mouth, scratching of itches, removing of thorns, brushing off dirt, rubbing hot, cold or sore parts, pulling on or off clothes; and hands contribute to adjustment of body state through stroking, touching and holding, transmitting warmth and stimulating autonomic responses. Hands participate in postural balance and locomotion, but they are particularly adapted to reach out away from the body to grasp and manipulate objects. Thus they may show practical purposes for selecting, exploring and transforming elements of the environment.

But hands are adapted for more than practical or bodily tasks. They are a principal component of the intersubjective signalling system by which human minds share their states and ambitions. Research on conversational communication finds that gestural expression of the hands is a ubiquitous accompaniment in vocal communication, and that it plays an essential part in the regulation and transmission of thoughts, images and spoken language (Goldin-Meadow & McNeill 1999; Iverson & Goldin-Meadow 1998; McNeill 1992). Further, recent evolutionary theory of language origins is persuaded that gestural mimesis pre-dates verbal communication, that it was efficient for our hominid ancestors as it is for living primate cousins, and that this explains why it is of fundamental communicative importance, before speech, in the mastery of communication by human infants (Donald 2001; Gentilucci & Corballis 2006; Pollick & de Waal 2007).

Monkeys, apes and infants use hand movements to regulate their comfort and vital needs, and for social regulation and communication in a shared experience. Where one draws the line between a gestural movement intended to be communicative to an attentive other, and one that is self-serving, and not communicative at all, remains unclear. For this reason we find it simpler to consider infantile or ancestral gesture not across the problematic conscious–non-conscious divide, but to accept gesture and its communication as inherent attributes of a fundamentally social animal endowed with a single will to move complexly articulated head, face, eyes, hands and feet, and with feeling for the process and quality of the moving. The questions then raised are not whether gestures exist at some 'low', preconscious, proto-human level, but how the full repertoire of self-sensed bodily movements is used to communicate internal worlds into social worlds, no matter the age or evolutionary development of the individuals concerned.

We may classify human hand gestures into five kinds, differentiated by their psychological control and communicative potential (Trevarthen 1986). These define overlapping but reasonably clear classes of hand expression that communicate states of mind: *gratuitous* (given off in the course of manipulations, etc.), *self-regulatory*, *emotional*, *indicating* and *symbolic*. (1) *Gratuitous gestures* are self-regulatory, emotional, or object-oriented intentional actions made for the subject. They are not intended as communicative and may be done without any awareness of others, but they can provide 'stolen' psychological information for an observer. An attentive human observer and listener can pick up information from what another's hands are doing about their owner's intentions, attentions, interests and, importantly, about their vital affect, how the other feels about the activity. In principle, as a consequence of a mirroring of motivating states, all animal movements have the potential to communicate one-way as gratuitous gestures. Human hands are an exceptionally rich and versatile special case. (2) *Self-regulatory movements* of a person's hands comfort, protect or stimulate the body, or they may gate or modulate input to the special sense organs, as when the eyes are shaded or the ears blocked. They transmit information about motivation and the emotional regulation of the internal state of the person. Unintended 'regulator' movements effecting comfort or protection form an undercurrent to any deliberate referential communication by speech or gesture. (3) *Emotional movements* of the hands express emotion more explicitly to evaluate and control the interpersonal contact itself. They can show how the presence and behaviour of another is received. Hands move in specific ways with face expressions, eye movements and vocalizations to convey feelings that affect other persons, whether by imitation of conventional signs or in unconscious expression of innate coordinations in an integrated affective signalling system. (4) *Indicating gestures* are added to attentional orienting, the hands being deliberately extended and aimed to show another person an object or place of interest in their common environment. They direct attention and possibly action as well. (5) *Symbolic hand movements* may be formed in patterns and sequences to construct graphical representations of actions, events, objects or situations in a conventional code or language. A full language of hand signs may be learned to express infinite subtleties of purpose, knowledge and feeling in a conventional vocabulary and message-making syntax replacing speech. Though formed by arbitrary conventions, the latter signs of hand language are produced within a dynamic and spatial frame of hand activity that is shared with the spontaneous and universal or innate displays of motivation and emotion, and with the phrasing, prosody and rhythmic articulations of speech, especially in the less 'informative' emotive forms of poetry and song.

In natural conversation, and more systematically in hand sign language, all five levels of expression are combined. All are clarified and articulated together by syntactic processes of motivation that support the symbols which identify external referents, that hold together elements of skilled articulation and that mediate messages in the formal conventions of the language. The same kinds of expressive hand actions as are used in spontaneous sharing of company are variously combined in dance, drama and musical performance, but with particular attention to control of their motivation and emotional quality (Birdwhistell 1970). The narratives of art are concerned more with the interpersonal responsibilities of beauty and morality than with objective truth, and music particularly has a direct appeal to the spell of a 'floating intentionality' (Cross 1999; Cross & Morley 2009) and 'vitality affects' that attend to their own 'dynamic emotional envelopes' (Stern 1999). Art makes mundane events and objects 'special' (Dissanayake 1988). The timing, sequencing and syntactic modulations of gesture common to conversation and art are essential motivating forces deep within even the most formal or abstract language of philosophy, logic and mathematics.

Remarkably, these same parameters are possessed in subtle basic forms by infants, in ways that respond to and move the motives inherent in gestures of other attentive persons. As Ellen Dissanayake has explained, the arts arise from the kind of intimacy we see alive in talk between infants and their mothers (Dissanayake 2000, 2009). Before we examine the evidence of gestural 'musicality' in the behaviour of infants, we must review evidence that movements of all kinds are regulated in time and with respect to measures of vital energy.

The Biochronologic Scale of Movement: A Hierarchy of Rhythms of Body and Mind, with Internal Guidance that Generate Narrative Form

Gestures, being evolved for communication as well as self-regulation, have enhanced dynamic features of regulation or accentuated expression to facilitate transmission to a perceiver. They express distinctly the processes of the brain that anticipate and 'feel' the energy and power of moving and that connect immediately sensed events with future and past experiences of moving. The integrated motor images made evident in the harmony and orderly progress of movements animated by many body parts give evidence of a core regulatory mechanism that defines both the coordination and the emotional evaluation of movements. The neural mechanisms for this are identified as the Intrinsic Motive Formation (IMF), which guides the orientation and timing of moves in the body's field of action, with the Affective Nervous System, which attends to the needs and protections of vital processes in the body. Both are intricately involved in directing the cognitive processes and acquired skills that are mediated in cortical tissues of forebrain and cerebellum.

A remarkable biochronology or hierarchy of rhythmic processes governs all the movements of the body, including the slow energy-husbanding cycles of days and seasons. This is the temporal foundation of voluntary motor activity and of sympathetic engagements between communicating subjects (Trevarthen 1999a, 2009). Musical gestures and narratives explore the whole range of times, from the fastest accents through rhythms of dance to slow events that move mysteriously in memories and dreams with their hopes and fears (Osborne 2009). Some of this process of pacing movement and experience proves to be amenable to precise mathematical analysis and a universal law of gestures is made evident, at least for skeleto-muscular activities of the soma (Lee 2005). Visceral rhythms that determine the phases of a dramatic episode may obey different laws.

We appear to share narratives of gesture as a natural result of the way we coordinate movements of our multi-segmented bodies and because we are born with the desire to share the time of moving in creative ways with others. Human movements make manifest the regulatory process of the moving body – the 'motor images' (Bernstein 1967), 'serial ordering' (Lashley 1951) and 'prospective control' (Lee 1998) of sequenced actions. When we move with grace and purpose we integrate sensory information from the world outside our body with guiding information from within our nervous system by a process that aims to control the future experience of our behaviour in the world. This process is not just self-serving, it is naturally communicative by a process of sympathetic assimilation of its dynamic principles, which involves the transfer and management of action-related information between intra- and intersubjective realms. Gestures and their messages are, moreover, open to experience and adapted to increase their variety and effectiveness by learning. Learned complexes of gesture become habits of individual action and of cooperation in shared, cultural experience, including the imitative arts of music theatre and dance, which, with poetry and song, bring the referential communication of language back to its interpersonal foundations (Brandt 2009; Fonagy 2001).

Our narratives of all kinds evolve from the skilful sequencing of action complexes prospectively controlled in this way. The purposeful movements each of us makes as a coherently conscious Self involve a harmony of concurrent bodily activity composed with unconscious ease: for example, I am reaching for a pencil to make notes whilst reading this text. The intention guides the fingers of my hand in concert with the actions of the muscles of my arm, shoulder and torso, while what my hand does is monitored by movements of my eyes, head and neck. The principal effector is my hand and it is on this that my attention focuses. But the other movements of my body are also being controlled, in actions that have their own time course and dynamic form nested together in one 'narrative' of the whole pattern of movement. Hand and pencil are characters in the story, each playing their assigned part in the plot: 'take the pencil and write that thought'.

The essential process in all communicative narratives of gestural expression, and in all the products of work with instruments that function as agents for human action, is the guided uptake of information about the 'vitality' or 'energy in time' that our brains use to control our own bodies' actions. This information about energy dynamics is the same as that other bodies and minds need to sense what we are doing, and to join in collaborative activity with us.

Mathematical Analysis of Gymnastic Gestures Reveals Precisely how 'Narrative Complexes' of Sequential Movement are Controlled at High Speed and High Energy

Purposes in action or in thought can be viewed as the products of an essential natural motivating principle by which the brain coordinates and regulates movements of one's body. The example of a gymnast performing a somersault lasting less than a second may be used to illustrate how individually controlled elements of a moving body contribute to, and form part of, a larger performance of effective skill or control, a performance that may be perceived as an expressive narrative of human action.

To leap into a somersault from a trampoline and to land in balance on one's feet one must control the many elements of the performance while turning through the air. Crucially, after achieving the necessary lift, the speed of rotation of your body around its axis must be regulated so you will arrive in balance with feet on the ground in an upright posture. The principal goal or 'effector' of the flight is a correct angle of rotation, shown as angle θ in Figure 1.3. It is measured clockwise in the picture round the centre of rotation of the gymnast's body.

Figure 1.3   A gymnast's somersault

General *tau* (τ) theory (Lee 1998) provides a conceptual 'tool' to measure precisely how such an intention to move is achieved and regulated by sensory perception. A voluntary behaviour must aim a complex of muscular actions to reach a series of defined goals. It can be described, first, as a sequence of elementary moves to close 'motion gaps'. A 'motion gap' is defined as the difference between the current state of an effector in movement, such as a reaching hand, and its goal state. It is assumed that the prospective control or plan of any movement complex requires the controlled closure of a series of motion gaps. According to *tau* theory, the dynamic of a gap in any animal movement, the *manner* in which it is closed, is determined according to a mathematically defined relationship, which is named the 'τ function'. This is a measure of change in time of moving and can be applied to any perceived dimension that may be controlled to regulate a movement, such as *angular distance*, *force*, *pitch*, *loudness*, etc. The τ of a motion gap for any such dimension is 'the time it will take to close that gap at the current closure rate'. This measure will change according to how the movement is regulated through its course, i.e. according to its 'expression'.

A brain function named 'τ coupling' (Lee 1998) maintains proportionality between two changing streams of τ information for motor control (in two motion gaps) and controls a synchronous closure of the two gaps in a precisely determined way. For example, when a sportsman catches or hits a ball with skill he must control the τ functions of two motion gaps – that between the ball flying through the air and the point of interception, and the one between the moving hand or bat and the point of interception. Coupling the τ functions of these two gaps controls synchronous closure so hand and ball arrive at the same place at the same time.

General τ theory also helps understanding how self-paced complexes of voluntary movements are directed and controlled by coupling *perceptual information* for sensing the changing gap to be closed with *intrinsic motive information* generated from within the nervous system as a τ guide (τ–G). Controlled closure of each gap is achieved by coupling the perceptual τ to the intrinsic τ–G guide, keeping them in constant relationship. In the case of the gymnast's leap, the control of the rotation of the body (angle θ) obeys the equation: $\tau \theta = K \tau G$ (see Austad & Van der Meer 2007; Craig et al. 2000; Lee 2005).

Measures of the movements of a dancer and a drummer performing together demonstrate that they are generating and sharing τ guides, and the same coordination of prospective motor control is shown within a singer's body between the movements of her larynx and the gestures she makes with hands to accompany her song (Lee & Schögler 2009). Musical sounds and movements of dance or gesture in a well-made performance are in perfect sympathy.

For the gymnast rotating through the air in Figure 1.3, the motion gap to be closed is the gap of the angle of rotation of her body (θ) through 360 degrees, from standing to standing. Using high-speed motion capture equipment (500 Hz Qualisys) we measured this motion very accurately, and calculated the changing angle to track the gymnast's control of her movement using a *tau* analysis (as detailed by Lee 1998). The per cent of coupling derived from this analysis provides a measure of the degree of her control. Figure 1.4(a) shows, as a grey line, the changing angle *theta* (θ) measured relative to the vertical Y axis for one somersault recorded at 500 Hz. Vertical lines mark the take-off and landing of the gymnast, and the velocity or rate of change of θ is plotted by a black line. The angle increases and then decreases smoothly in a well-controlled skilled manner, and the measure of coupling for this movement is 94.7 per cent, which proves that the athlete was making a tightly controlled, coherent and unitary skilled activity.

But how can the gymnast achieve this smooth control of rotation while she somersaults through the air in defiance of gravity and out of touch with the earth? She controls the speed of rotation by controlling the opening and closing of her body. As she launches into the somersault her feet are tucked tight into her body increasing the speed of rotation, then extension and opening of the head-to-toe distance by extending her legs slows the rotation and affords a controlled and perfectly timed landing on her feet. This changing distance between feet and head was calculated from the motion capture output and is marked by dashed lines in Figure 1.4(b). The time scale for (a) and (b) in Figure 1.4 are the same and the dashed lines mark take off and landing in both. The smooth control of the changing rotational angle can be seen to consist of three sub-movements, each individually controlled with grace and purpose, the initial closing of the head to toe distance creates the acceleration in rotation, which is followed by a brief holding period before the gymnast applies a braking force to that rotation by opening her body, increasing the head-to-toe separation.

The analysis of these three movements proves that each is prospectively and smoothly controlled by the gymnast, as shown by the high per cent coupling values. The 'opening lift', 'holding' and 'closing fall' phases of this elegant performance function as players in the overall narrative of the rotation. Each is prospectively controlled, and each leads efficiently to the next. Such an intentionally made movement is perceptible and predictable by another human being, thus enabling engagement with that narrative of purpose and enjoyment of the athlete's skill. And most importantly all are nested within the scale of the overall skill or 'narrative' that is the controlled rotation of the body in flight ((a) in Figure 1.4), both the whole and the parts may be appreciated and perceived directly. A novice can gain appreciation of how to practice and learn a performance by watching a master, sympathizing with the flow of intrinsic control (Buccino et al. 2004). Such analyses demonstrate just how our active bodies are a rich seam of information when perceived by others and this forms the substrate or primordial gestural soup for all of our temporal skills.

Lee (2005) has demonstrated that principles of prospective control in movement have a crucial role in early development, when a baby is learning to control with skill such essential movements as sucking and swallowing milk, tracking an object with eyes and head, reaching and grasping, and standing and walking. The innate ability to coordinate how our bodies move naturally promotes the creation of narrative as the social manifestation of the experienced will of acting in the body. Angles, distances, pitches and timbres that change with gestures can all be

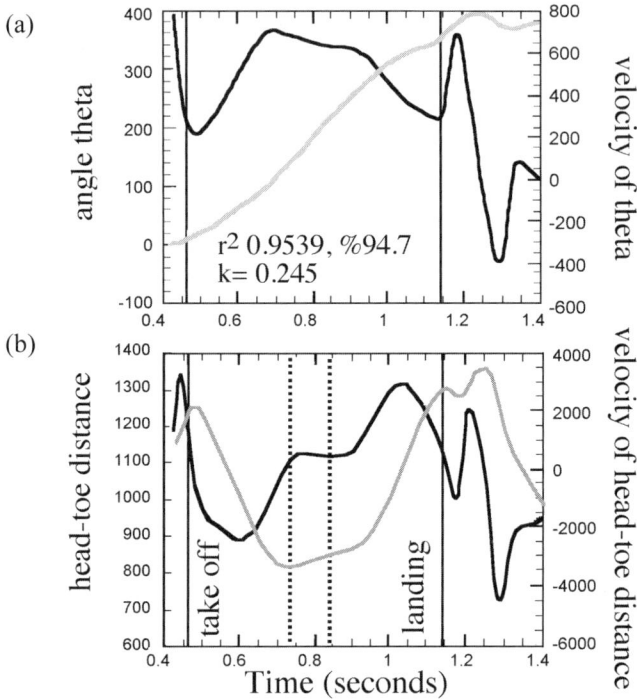

Figure 1.4　　Parameters of movement in the gymnast's somersault

combined and sequenced by the mind in a fluid stream of narrative purpose that we learn to coordinate and elaborate in sympathetic co-action with others of all ages. Infants and their family share time looking at one another, exchanging toe wiggles and heartfelt giggles telling stories with consciousness of their bodies.

Toddlers, in the exuberance of their dancing, singing life together, create an anarchic culture of their own (Bjørkvold 1992). When we are well coordinated, like the gymnast, the story is clear and easy to follow, a pleasure to perform to behold or, if we are able, to participate in. At times we may be poorly coordinated within ourselves, in stress or anxiety or due to dysfunction of the motor system, and then our body's narrative is hard to read and communication becomes problematic and may be crippled (Gratier & Apter-Danon 2009). But the need and ability to generate prospective control of moving is innate and deep seated. It can be brought to more effective life by moving forms of therapy or education that seek to collaborate with its purposes directly, in ways that sympathize with the imperatives of emotional regulation (Malloch & Trevarthen 2009).

The Infancy of Human Gesture and the Musicality of its Narrations

Infants, we have noted, make gestures from birth. These movements are expressions of self-regulation, but they are felt immediately to be communicative by a sympathetic partner, and they are ready from the start to learn new forms by imitation. They engage with 'contingent' gestures of other persons. Observations of interactions with infants in the first days prove that movements of head, eyes, face and hands, as well as simple vocalizations, may be negotiated with a partner and new forms acquired (Figure 1.5). The movements are affected by, and expressive of, emotions that powerfully regulate the intersubjective contact.

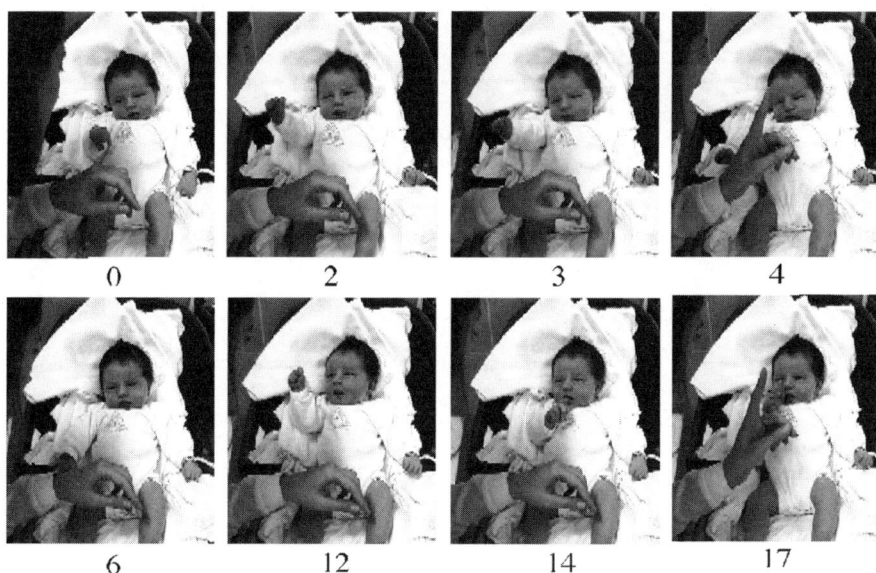

Figure 1.5   A newborn infant in dialogue with a researcher, who is inviting the infant to imitate. Numbers indicate successive seconds: 0–3 the infant is looking at movements of her own hand; 4 the researcher extends an index finger; 6 the infant looks at her for several seconds and then imitates (12). She then looks intently at the researcher (14) who responds by repeating the movement (17) [Stills from a video recorded by Dr Emese Nagy of the University of Dundee at an ICU in Szeged, Hungary (Nagy 2006; Nagy et al. 2005)]

The arms and legs of a baby move spontaneously in regular extensions and retractions, the form of the movements dependent on the internal state of the satiation or need. A more highly energetic movement signals an internal sense of unease. It can be said the infant tries to 'kick away' the uneasy feelings through the energy of the gesture. These kicks and arm punches, or more graceful waves and pointing movements, occur in rhythmic sequences with rises and falls in intensity, each individual gesture taking place in relation to the other. Within these arm rhythms exist smaller ones, employing different musculatures making subtler, but equally expressive movements. Prechtl (2001) calls these 'fidgety movements', and bases his diagnosis of infant neurological health on measures of their quality. They are made up of oscillations in the wrists and small rotations of the arms, usually occurring in rhythmic left/right asymmetry. The head, neck, eyes, mouth and trunk are also moving in time with the limbs. Remarkably, the concerted gesturing of even a newborn may respond in coordinated precision to the prosodic rhythm of an adult voice (Condon & Sanders 1974) as discussed below.

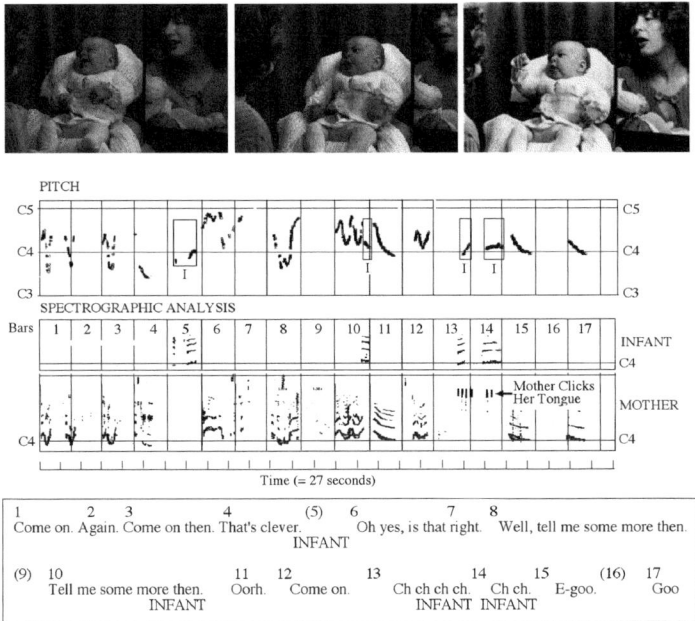

Figure 1.6   Protoconversation with a six-week old baby. *Above*: She looks at her mother speaking and smiles, coos and gestures with her right hand. Centre: Pitch plot and spectrographic analysis (Malloch 1999) showing the melody of the mother's voice and vocalizations of the infant, both based on middle C. Regular bars lasting approximately 1.5 seconds are numbered and marked by accented components of the mother's speech that serve to give timing to the infant's utterances. *Below*: Text of the mother's speech with the bar numbers placed in relation to the consonants that define them

Micro-analysis of recordings of young infants' movements show the infant is a highly receptive, mobile and finely tuned Self working with a dynamic neuro-musculature that interrelates all its parts into one coherent, connected activity – that expresses the baby's *rhythm of experience*. An attending adult cannot fail but to find it intended and meaningful behaviour, echoes of a past once lived and living again. Most scientific theories of the development of human sympathy and 'mind-sharing', including Freud's psychoanalytic theory and contemporary 'theory of mind', are not based on fine observation of early infancy, and they are sceptical as concerns infants' mental states, even denying that infants are conscious at all. They presume that 'other awareness' must be 'constructed' in experience, and explained in language. And yet, there is an old philosophical position that we have an immediate innate sympathy (Smith 1984[1759]), and Darwin (1872) believed that gestures of emotional expression are part of our sociable nature, permitting acquisition of shared wisdom. Contemporary brain science supports this less reductive, less rational theory in remarkable ways (Panksepp & Trevarthen 2009; Rizzolatti & Gallese 2003; Turner & Ioannides 2009) and advanced philosophical thought now recognizes the direct relation between social perceiving and social moving, i.e. gesturing, in what has been termed 'direct perception' (Gallagher 2008).

This is an important point, because it undercuts the need for so-called higher-order conscious cognitive processes in infant or adult moving with social meaning. Rather, these intersubjective acts of communication are driven by the feelings of the shared present moment (Stern 2004). Dyadic consciousness is generated (Tronick 2005). Developmental psychology has a rich history of findings from unprejudiced descriptive research that greatly expand ideas of the intuitive mental experiences and abilities of infants and young children, and especially their sociable abilities (Donaldson 1978, 1992; Reddy 2008; Stern 2000[1985]).

Prior to birth, the foetus is revealed by ultrasound recordings to be active, gesturing in ways that anticipate a different much larger world (e.g. Piontelli 1992; Zoia et al. 2007). The movements of mother and baby exhibit matching rhythms that may communicate, even while their mediation is restricted to the core proprioceptive senses, with touch and sound. In the last trimester the foetus uses feelings of its own body to regulate graceful actions of the hands, and can respond to the impulses transmitted by body movements of the mother, including heartbeat, breathing and uterine muscular activity. The baby's hearing can learn qualities that identify the mother's voice from 27 weeks. Then, at birth around 40 weeks, the infant is carried into a world where its physiological needs are not constantly met, but have to be strived for and provided by new sympathetic actions of engagement with another human being. The physiological intimacy between mother and infant is not broken at birth, but the mode of nurture and provision changes to one that requires the engagement of expressions in new ways. The co-consciousness of infancy opens the growing experience of the infant's mind to the habits and knowledge of another person and her family and community. For this more active and more aware existence, the infant comes well prepared. It is 'environment expectant' for human company.

The most obvious expressions of the young infant take place through its voice, movements of the hands, arms and legs, accompanied by many eye movements and delicate facial expressions. These manifold expressions, acting in concert, indicate to any attentive and sympathetic observer the internal states of the infant and their changes. Accurate measurements of neonatal expressions prove they are not simply reflex responses to stimuli, and they are not chaotic. They are intrinsically guided, and they communicate clear feelings of comfort and ease, or anxiety and stress. They indicate transforming feelings of contentment and joy or discomfort and pain. They express wants and needs, and importantly, these are wants and needs that call for provision by another human being, lest the infant will perish from lack of physical support, stress-relieving care and nourishment.

The Growing Purpose of Infant Gestures in a Cultural World, Guided by the Motive Forces of Communicative Musicality

These early infant movements, communicative at the most fundamental human level, develop quickly. They express psychological needs for other persons' interest, sympathy and love, and for sharing 'co-created' expressive performances. Infants' gestures are themselves 'interested' or outward-reaching and 'affectionate', acting to engage the other in a dialogue of shared experience or 'companionship' that will in coming weeks lead to the formulation of preferred narrative formats or games that Maya Gratier calls a 'protohabitus', after Bourdieu (1977).[1] The 'protoconversations' of early weeks can be playful and inventive, and mother and infant can collaborate in the co-creation of an entertaining ritual lasting tens of seconds (see Figure 1.6). They have the basic properties of intelligent art, which rewards and strengthens friendship in shared experience of beautiful movement. A six-month old infant can be a talented performer in the ritual of an action game to accompany a traditional baby song, showing pride in the responses of an appreciative audience, or shame when not understood by a stranger (Trevarthen 2002). It is not only teenagers who find an 'identity' or recognized role in a group by sharing conventional forms of rhythmic melodic stories. Similar, though generally more delicate, patterns of relating are as fundamental to the infant's first participation in family relationships as they are to the skilled adult's participation in powerful social groupings and institutions (Merker 2009).

In Figure 1.7, a newborn infant, recorded by a motion capture camera in the hospital at about 36 hours after birth, regulates the velocity of her arm movement (tangential velocity of the wrist) to 'track' the syllables of an adult voice. The

---

[1]   'Habitus comprises organized sets of dispositions that generate and regulate or "spontaneously and collectively orchestrate" social practices. [These dispositions are] historically rooted and they actively produce and shape newer dispositions ... . A central feature of "habitus" is that it is body-based, it is considered as a "second nature" or embodied social learning – a history that is forgotten and transformed into natural state. Habitus can be seen, for our purposes, as a non-verbally grounded embodied cultural knowing that is expressed in practice by people connected through time within real life communities (Gratier & Trevarthen 2008: 136–7).

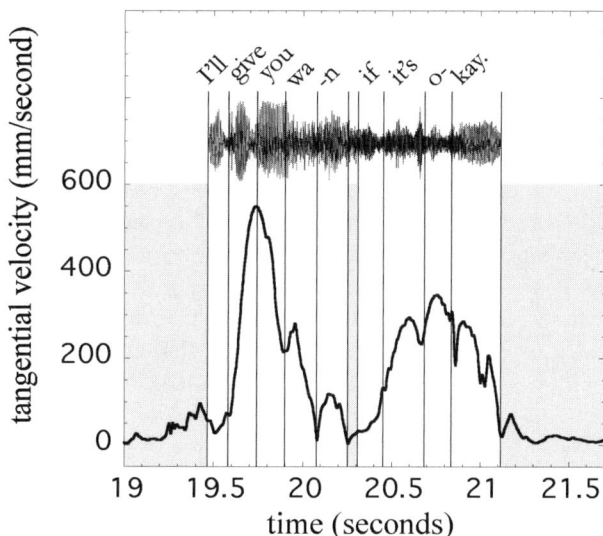

Figure 1.7   Arm movements of a newborn infant synchronize with an adult's speech (the microphone signal and vertical lines indicate the timing of syllables)

infant's arm lies at rest before and after the utterance. The infant moved as the experimenter approached to say, 'I'll give you one … if it's okay'. The two phrases make up a complete sentence with a gentle conclusion. The infant extended her left hand from a rest position with the hand flexed close to the head, down toward her waist, and then back again to a flexed resting position. The more rapid outward stretch matched the first phrase, 'I'll give you one'. There was a slight pause in the arm movement anticipating one in the speech (shaded) near 20.5 seconds before the conclusion, 'if it's okay', when the arm was brought back to flexion. Syllabic boundaries are marked in Figure 1.7 by vertical lines to show their correspondence with velocity shifts (the dark curve). The stresses in speech on 'give', 'one' and 'kay' are separated by approximately 500 milliseconds, which corresponds to *allegro moderato*.

The infant mind is alive as a coherent conscious whole, a fact immediately perceptible in the coordinated interrelations of all of its body activity as conveyed previously in Figure 1.2(b). The movements of lips, eyes, head, arm, hand and torso, for instance, are precisely coordinated in temporal pattern sharing common points of rest, starting and stopping of movement, not unlike an orchestral piece where the commencement and conclusion of instrumental sections fits into harmony with others in differing patterns to express different qualities (Condon & Sander 1974; our own data – see Figure 1.7). There is weighty evidence for the existence of an intrinsic expressive mechanism in the infant (and adult) brain that links oral, auditory, manual, and visual sensory and motor channels in such a way that they are complementary and equivalent for making ideas expressive in language (Trevarthen 2009). Young infants have elaborate facial and vocal expressions and they use these to regulate interactions with their caretakers or other persons from birth. When they are responding to their mothers, one- or two-month-old infants impulsively carry their hands up away from the body, often with one or more fingers extended and palm supine or facing forwards. The hand movements are made in tight coordination with other expressions, particularly lip and tongue movements and vocalizations (Trevarthen 1974, 1979) (see Figure 1.6 above).

The development of human communication with infants and young children proves that there are innate motives coordinating and giving vital emotional regulation to whole-body movements giving them intention, interest and feeling, and that these states of mind are adapted to be shared and complemented in engagements with other persons in a humanly contrived world. Children match the actions of adults with inherent measures of *rhythm* and *affective vitality* in movement, as well as defined features of body shape or *physiognomy*. A healthy newborn infant, although weak and inexperienced, is ready for the rhythms of intersubjective communication. They have the same fundamental Intrinsic Motive Pulse (IMP) and range of dynamic expressions of embodied feeling states as an adult (Trevarthen 1999a). They join in mutually regulated intimate exchanges with affectionate and responsive partners, dancing with their IMPs.

Within a few weeks these exchanges become finely attuned protoconversations in which reflective and assertive states of mind are exchanged and accepted with enjoyment in narrative patterns – as short 'stories' (see Figure 1.6 above). And these stories develop habits or 'tricks' and rituals of movement that are recognized by infant and parents with delight (see Figure 1.8). Then, with pleasurable support from their family, a happy baby displays a comical self-awareness based on their talents for collaboratively planned and memorable everyday activities in creative play with people to whom they are emotionally attached (Reddy 2008).

In Figure 1.8, Leanne (top: 4 months) enjoys taking part in her mother's rhythmic nonsense 'chant' with bouncing arm movements; at 5 months she is involved in the action song 'Round and round the garden'. Emma (middle: 6 months) is pleased to be able to share 'Clappa, clappa handies' with her mother. On the left she is watching herself perform in the camera window, which she mirrors herself. Unlike her mother, she claps with her left hand above her right, and she became strongly left-handed. At home, sitting on her father's knee, Emma (bottom left) proudly shows how clever she is when her mother, standing behind the camera, says, 'Show clap handies!' Other babies (bottom right) are shown sitting alone at home by Dr Katerina Mazokopaki of the University of Crete. They reveal their joy and need to participate with rhythmic gestures when a cheerful children's song comes on from an audio-player. Their rhythmic movements reflect their motor development. Georgos (5.5 months) is lying in his chair, he smiles and claps his hands; Katerina (9 months) waves her hands as if flying and moves them in the rhythm of the song; Panos (9 months) beats his hand and 'sings' after smiling a 'welcome' to the song; Anna (10 months) is

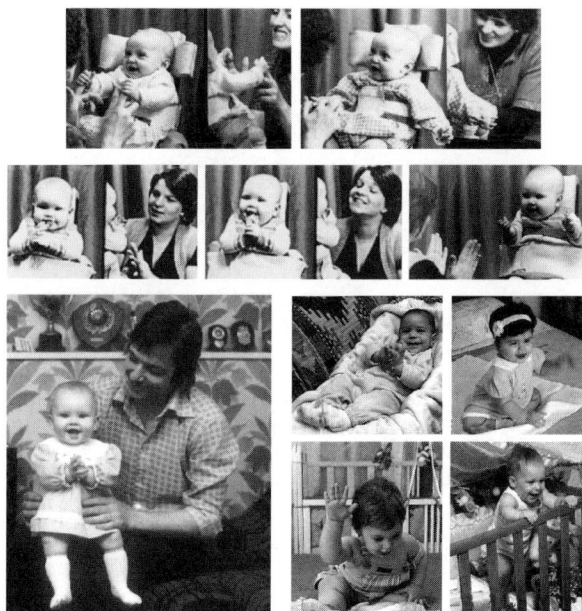

Figure 1.8   Infants picking up the rhythms of music and performing rituals to nursery rhymes

standing in her cot when she is surprised and pleased by the music. She gets in the rhythm with her whole body, bouncing, wiggling her hips, batting her hands and 'singing' (Mazokopaki & Kugimutzakis 2009).

Six-month-old babies want to create together, with people they know, games regulated by aesthetic and moral feelings that evaluate shared acts and shared experiences in favourite rituals. At one year, acts of meaning are shared in confident intimacy with or without words (Trevarthen & Hubley 1978; see Figure 1.9). In the next year or two the child masters many skills of culture – language, tools and many technical practices and arts – by 'intent participation' within cooperative groups of friends of different ages (Rogoff 2003). As they pass into this new level of human awareness of what may be communicated with others, and of the significance of their actions for the sharing of meaning, infants, about 7 to 9 months of age, are highly sensitive to the difficulties of sharing intentions and activities with unfamiliar persons. They express their mistrust and distress with graphic gestures of the whole body, moving to protect themselves from an unwanted human presence (see Figure 1.10).

In Figure 1.9, Emma (top left: 7 months) is too young to comprehend when her mother asks her to put wooden dolls in a toy truck. She looks at her mother who is repeating her request, but only explores the dolls for herself. For Basilie (right: 12 months), cooperating in this task is simple. She understands immediately what her mother's gestures and talking require of her. She takes the doll offered to her,

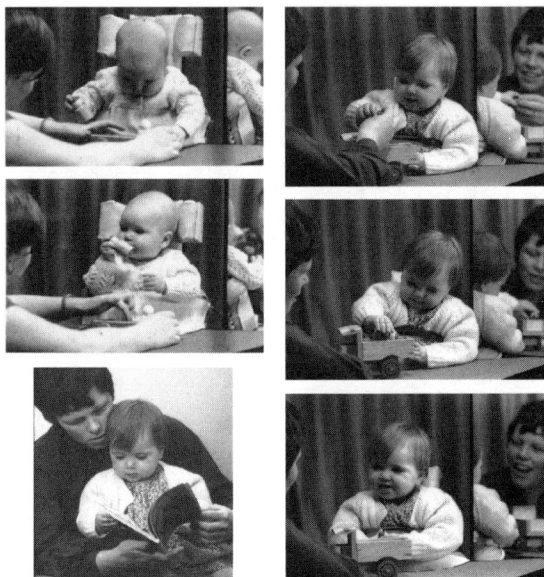

Figure 1.9   After 9 months, infants understand gestures of request and are eager
                to cooperate in meaningful activities with objects

immediately puts it in the truck then looks up with satisfaction when her mother says, 'Clever girl!'. A few minutes later, Basilie (bottom left) asks for a magazine and starts looking at the pictures.

In Figure 1.10, Emma (above: at 6 months), who was delighted and proud to show 'Clappa handies' to her mother, cannot communicate with confidence with a stranger. She is at first 'shy' and looks away from him touching the band supporting her; then she bravely offers to share her skill, but he makes a comment in a tone that shows he does not appreciate her ability; she touches her head protectively, then claps her hands to herself, looking away from him. Infant boys (middle left to right at 9 and 10 months) show unease and avoidance of the stranger, who is trying to be friendly, and one is about to cry. On the right, Emma clearly shows her avoidance of an unfamiliar lady. Other infants (below) are crying with the stranger. On the right, Emma is defiant and stares at him, and she is very angry with her mother who returns and tries to cheer her up.

Forces of Communicative Musicality Guide the Education of Human Cultural Impulses, Giving them Memorable Content in Narrative Form

Infants lack all external knowledge, of special or artificial cultural things, but have internal or intuitive knowledge, a feeling for what can be done and what things are useful. They have 'aesthetic' sensibilities. They sense tastes and odours that please

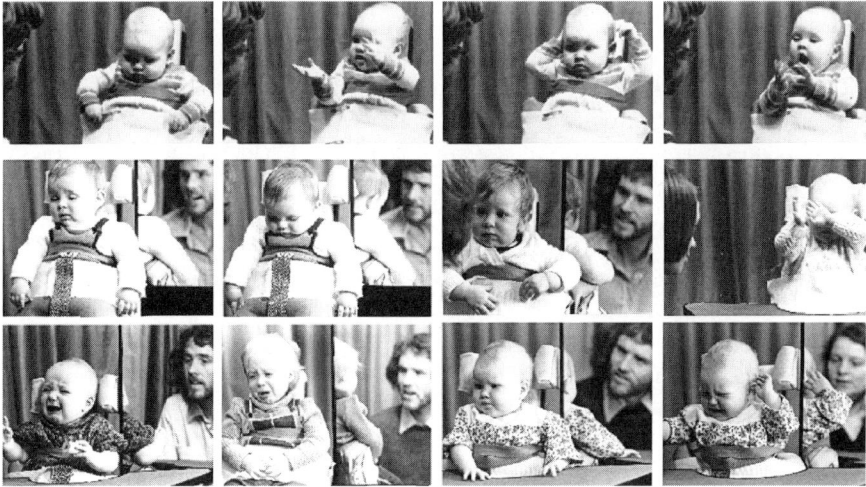

Figure 1.10   Dramatic gestures of older infants when with uncomprehending strangers

or offend, see brightness and colour in light or substance, hear pitch, loudness and timbre, feel soft or hard, hot or cold. They perceive form and space and measure change in time. Infants' perceptions of 'qualia' are also particularly sensitive to those 'moral' qualities that define the intimate 'presence' of another person, their kind of sympathy. Both aesthetic and moral feelings may be celebrated and remembered in vocal and gestural exchanges.

The hand movements of infants, as they shift with turns of the head and the directions of gaze, have gestural, story-telling fluency – distal and proximal parts are coordinated in sequences so their different rhythms form melody-like phrases – and the two hands may act in 'counterpoint', making 'dialogues of gesture as if they are two protagonists in an unfolding drama. These movements submit to the regulations of inner visceral processes that attempt to maintain well-being of the whole person. They 'flow' over an energy 'landscape' like the shadows of moving clouds, in cycles of action and conservation, of *assertions* into the prospects the body and the world offer, and *apprehensions* of different, changing circumstances, including surprises and emergencies. This is the nature of what Stern (1999) calls their 'vitality', which is controlled by 'dynamic affects' that make states of vitality sharable in 'narrative envelopes'. Thus infants show communicative musicality as part of their being – they have motives that move them in polyrhythmic, self-expressing ways – they have immediate, unreflected-upon messages, but they are open to the address of a companion who wishes to build a different story by engaging their different wills in new directions, blending their stories in exploration of a different landscape.

We reiterate, a human gesture is neither just in the present nor is it isolated in the motive stream while it occurs. It is never only of and for the Self. Its purposes and feelings are available, without translation, for Others through all times in episodes of experience. Musical gestures of voice and hands exploit both the acting and the emotive power for the interests and feelings of others – for their appreciation and appraisal. They grow in an innate narrative, time-telling intersubjectivity. Music makes narrations with innate significance, but with learned invention, so the stories are always new.

The Message of Gesture for Musicians, Music Teachers and Music Therapists

The teaching of musical art depends on communication with the natural musicality of the pupil, child or adult, who is seeking high-performance skill. All music learners want to master ways of celebrating the companionship of story-telling in sound. At the same time they must enjoy the experience within themselves of moving in ways that excite and test the voice or the agility of the hands and dancing body (Flohr & Trevarthen 2008). Highly skilled musical activities, obeying more or less complex conventions and traditions of execution, composition and interpretation, require concentration on the precision and harmony of effect in the moment of each gesture and through the construction of the narrative desired. This concentration on cognitive and rational or organizational properties of performance can lead awareness away from the personal and interpersonal experience, the affectionate and moral aspects of the musical drama. But the two aspects are inseparable in good 'authentic' learning and performance. They are complementary parts of an artist's work.

Over and over again great artists and the philosophers of musical art and aesthetics (Adam Smith, Stravinsky, Langer, Bernstein, Clynes, Frisse, Blacking, Deutsch, Nattiez, Meyer, Iyer, Kühl), including those particularly concerned with music teaching (Jaques-Dalcroze, Moorehead & Pond, Zimmerman, Bjørkvold, Hargraeves, Sloboda & Davidson, Gordon, Custodero, Rutkowski & Trollinger) have emphasized the importance of the living movement that communicates excellence and beauty in a message that has compelling human importance. A lyrical phrase in a folk song or the magnificent whole of a symphony or opera has to speak to a listener in anticipated and memorable ways. This power of music depends on the shared appreciation of the making of gestures in human bodies (Kühl 2007; Malloch & Trevarthen 2009). It is given value by innate human motives and emotions that first appear in the responses and expressions of infants to the affectionate sounds and sights of parents seeking their company.

Recently, teachers of music have drawn on the evidence that infants are musical creatures to support their understanding that intuitive motives are the source of the ability for learning music, and they warn of the inhibition of these motives by a method of instruction that is too didactic, that does not seek to lead out the pupil's natural eagerness to make music in ways that others will find moving and talented, can prevent or even suppress musical expression. Thus, a person who sang freely and with a clear sense of rhythm, harmony and tonality as a child in the playground may learn that they 'cannot sing' or are 'tone deaf'. Bannan and Woodward (2008) compare the principles of music teaching to the theory of instruction of Jerome Bruner, who would found the strategy of a teacher on the unfolding developmental impulses of the child and who characterizes humans as 'story-telling creatures'. For development of the highest levels of musical performance a similar respect for the initiative of the learner for discovery of the message that 'moves' in a piece of music to be mastered is again essential (Correia in Rodrigues et al. 2009). Imberty (2008) and Gratier (2008) develop the idea of music as 'narrative' that, in sympathetic negotiation with the responses of others, expresses the emotions of discovery with hope or dread, and also the systematic strategies of thought.

Therapists seeking to give support and to encourage more confident participation in relationships increasingly find benefits in the use of the appealing dynamics of music, dance and drama as an alternative or complement to the use of language and cognitive appraisals of life events and personal narrative histories. Music sensitively presented to engage the willing participation of a person who has difficulty relating and sharing life has been successfully used for premature newborns, autistic children, children who have been harmed by abuse, war traumatized adolescents, and old persons suffering from dementia. In every case the practice that is most effective is one that employs an enlivening and playful 'improvisation' in response to any attempts made to share action and experience in movement and sound. Most interesting is the evidence that participation in improvised musical performance can be beneficial to a whole community when the invention of musical pleasure is stimulated for a group, not just in a one-to-one dialogue.

References

Austad, H. & Van der Meer, A. L. (2007). Prospective Balance Control in Healthy Children and Adults. *Experimental Brain Research* 181: 289–95.

Bannan, N. & Woodward, S. (2009). Spontaneity in the Musicality and Music Learning of Children. In S. Malloch & C. Trevarthen (eds), *Communicative Musicality: Exploring the Basis of Human Companionship* (pp. 465–94). Oxford: Oxford University Press.

Beebe, B., Knoblauch, S., Rustin, J. & Sorter, D. (2005). *Forms of Intersubjectivity in Infant Research and Adult Treatment*. New York: Other Press.

Bernstein, N. (1967). *Coordination and Regulation of Movements*. New York: Pergamon.

Birdwhistell, R. (1970). *Kinesics in Context*. Philadelphia: University of Pennsylvania Press.

Bjørkvold, J-R. (1992). *The Muse Within: Creativity and Communication, Song and Play from Childhood through Maturity*. New York: Harper Collins.

Brandt, P. A. (2009). Music and How We Became Human—a View from Cognitive Semiotics: Exploring Imaginative Hypotheses. In S. Malloch &

C. Trevarthen (eds), *Communicative Musicality: Exploring the Basis of Human Companionship* (pp. 31–44). Oxford: Oxford University Press.

Brazelton, T. B. (1993). *Touchpoints: Your Child's Emotional and Behavioral Development.* New York: Viking.

Bourdieu, P. (1977). *Outline of a Theory of Practice.* Cambridge: Cambridge University Press.

Buccino, G., Vogt, S., Ritzl, A., Fink, G. R., Zilles, K., Freund, H. J., & Rizzolatti, G. (2004). Neural Circuits Underlying Imitation Learning of Hand Actions: An Event Related fMRI Study. *Neuron* 42: 323–34.

Condon, W. S. & Sander, L. S. (1974). Neonate Movement is Synchronized with Adult Speech: Interactional Participation and Language Acquisition. *Science* 183: 99–101.

Craig, C. M., Delay, D., Grealy, M. A. & Lee, D. N. (2000). Guiding the Swing in Golf Putting. *Nature* 405: 295–96.

Cross, I. (1999). Is Music The Most Important Thing We Ever Did? Music, Development and Evolution. In S. W. Yi (ed.), *Music, Mind and Science* (pp.10–39). Seoul: Seoul National University Press.

— & Morley, I. (2009). The Evolution of Music: Theories, Definitions and the Nature of the Evidence. In S. Malloch & C. Trevarthen (eds.), *Communicative Musicality: Exploring the Basis of Human Companionship* (pp. 61–81). Oxford: Oxford University Press.

Damasio, A. R. (1999). *The Feeling of What Happens: Body, Emotion and the Making of Consciousness.* London: Heinemann.

Darwin C. (1872). *The Expression of Emotion in Man and Animals.* London: Methuen.

Dissanayake, E. (1988). *What Is Art For?* Seattle: University of Washington Press.

— (2000). *Art and Intimacy: How the Arts Began.* Seattle: University of Washington Press.

— (2009). Root, Leaf, Blossom, or Bole: Concerning the Origin and Adaptive Function of Music. In S. Malloch & C. Trevarthen (eds.), *Communicative Musicality: Exploring the Basis of Human Companionship* (pp. 17–30). Oxford: Oxford University Press.

Donald, M. (2001). *A Mind So Rare: The Evolution of Human Consciousness.* London: Norton.

Donaldson, M. (1978). *Children's Minds.* Glasgow: Fontana.

— (1992). *Human Minds: An Exploration.* London: Allen Lane.

Flohr, J. & Trevarthen, C. (2008). Music Learning in Childhood: Early Developments of a Musical Brain and Body. In W. Gruhn & F. Rauscher (eds.), *Neurosciences In Music Pedagogy* (pp. 53–100). New York: Nova Biomedical Books.

Fonagy, I. (2001). *Languages within Language: An Evolutive Approach.* Foundations of Semiotics 13. Amsterdam: John Benjamins.

Gallagher, S. (2008). Direct Perception in the Intersubjective Context. *Consciousness and Cognition* 17: 535–43.

Gallese, V. (2003). The Roots of Empathy: The Shared Manifold Hypothesis and the Neural Basis of Intersubjectivity. *Psychopathology* 36/4: 171–80.

— & Lakoff, G. (2005). The Brain's Concepts: The Role of the Sensory-Motor System in Reason and Language. *Cognitive Neuropsychology* 22: 455–79.

—, Keysers, C., & Rizzolatti, G. (2004). A Unifying View of the Basis of Social Cognition. *Trends in Cognitive Sciences* 8: 396–403.

Gentilucci, M. & Corballis, M. C. (2006). From Manual Gesture to Speech: A Gradual Transition. *Neuroscience and Biobehavioral Reviews* 30: 949– 60.

Goldin-Meadow, S. & McNeill, D. (1999). The Role of Gesture and Mimetic Representation in Making Language. In M. C. Corballis & E. G. Lea (eds.), *The Descent of Mind: Psychological Perspectives on Hominid Evolution* (pp. 155–72). Oxford: Oxford University Press.

Gratier, M. (2008). Grounding in Musical Interaction: Evidence from Jazz Performances. *Musicae Scientiae, Special Issue: Narrative in Music and Interaction*: 71-110.

— & Apter-Danon, G. (2009). The Improvised Musicality of Belonging: Repetition and Variation in Mother–Infant Vocal Interaction. In S. Malloch & C. Trevarthen (eds.), *Communicative Musicality: Exploring the Basis of Human Companionship* (pp. 301–27). Oxford: Oxford University Press.

— & Trevarthen, C. (2008). Musical Narrative and Motives for Culture in Mother–Infant Vocal Interaction. *Journal of Consciousness Studies* 15/10–11: 122–58.

Gritten, A. & King, E., eds. (2006). *Music and Gesture*. Aldershot: Ashgate.

Hatten, R. S. (2006). A Theory of Musical Gesture and Its Application to Beethoven and Schubert. In A Gritten & E. King (eds.), *Music and Gesture* (pp. 1–23). Aldershot: Ashgate.

Imberty, M. (2008). Narrative, Splintered Temporalities and the Unconscious in 20th-century Music. *Musicae Scientiae, Special Issue: Narrative in Music and Interaction*: 129–46.

Iverson, J. M. & Goldin-Meadow, S., eds. (1998). *The Nature and Functions of Gesture in Children's Communications*. New Directions for Child Development 79 (pp. 89–100). San Francisco: Jossey-Bass.

Kendon, A. (1980). Gesticulation and Speech: Two Aspects of the Process of Utterance. In M. R. Key (ed.), *The Relationship of Verbal and Nonverbal Communication* (pp. 207–27). New York: Mouton.

— (1993). A Human Gesture. In T. Ingold & K. R. Gibson (eds.), *Tools, Language and Cognition* (pp. 43–62). Cambridge: Cambridge University Press.

Kühl, O. (2007). *Musical Semantics*. European Semiotics: Language, Cognition and Culture 7. Bern: Peter Lang.

Lakoff, G. & Johnson, M. (1980). *Metaphors We Live By*. Chicago: University of Chicago Press.

— (1999). *Philosophy in the Flesh: The Embodied Mind and Its Challenges to Western Thought*. New York, Basic Books.

Lashley, K. S. (1951). The Problems of Serial Order in Behavior. In L. A. Jeffress (ed.), *Cerebral Mechanisms in Behavior* (pp. 112–36). New York: Wiley.

Lee, D. N. (1998). Guiding Movement by Coupling Taus. *Ecological Psychology* 10/3–4: 221–50.

— (2005). Tau in Action in Development. In J. J. Rieser, J. J. Lockman & C. A. Nelson (eds.), *Action as an Organizer of Learning and Development* (pp. 3–49). Hillsdale, NJ: Erlbaum.

Lee, D. N. & Schögler, B. (2009). Tau in Musical Expression. In S. Malloch & C. Trevarthen (eds), *Communicative Musicality: Exploring the Basis of Human Companionship* (pp. 83–104). Oxford: Oxford University Press.

Malloch, S. (1999). Mothers and Infants and Communicative Musicality. *Musicae Scientiae, Special Issue: Rhythm, Musical Narrative and Origins of Human Communication*: 29–57.

— & Trevarthen, C., eds. (2009). *Communicative Musicality: Exploring the Basis of Human Companionship*. Oxford: Oxford University Press.

Mazokopaki, M. & Kugiumutzakis, G. (2009). Infant Rhythms: Expressions of Musical Companionship. In S. Malloch & C. Trevarthen (eds.), *Communicative Musicality: Exploring the Basis of Human Companionship* (pp. 185–208). Oxford: Oxford University Press.

McNeill, D. (1992). *Hand and Mind: What Gestures Reveal About Thought*. Chicago: University of Chicago Press.

Merker, B. (2009). Ritual Foundations of Human Uniqueness. In S. Malloch & C. Trevarthen (eds.), *Communicative Musicality: Exploring the Basis of Human Companionship* (pp. 45–60). Oxford: Oxford University Press.

Nagy, E. (2006). From Imitation to Conversation: The First Dialogues with Human Neonates. *Infant and Child Development* 15: 223–32.

— & Molnar, P. (2004). Homo Imitans or Homo Provocans? The Phenomenon of Neonatal Initiation. *Infant Behavior and Development* 27: 57–63.

—, Compagne, H., Orvos, H., Pal, A. P., Molnar, P., Janszky, I., Loveland, K. & Bardos, G. Y. (2005). Index Finger Movement Imitation by Human Neonates: Motivation, Learning and Left-hand Preference. *Pediatric Research* 58: 749–53.

Osborne, N. (2009). Towards a Chronobiology of Musical Rhythm. In S. Malloch & C. Trevarthen (eds.), *Communicative Musicality: Exploring the Basis of Human Companionship* (pp. 545–64). Oxford: Oxford University Press.

Panksepp, J. (1998). *Affective Neuroscience: The Foundations of Human and Animal Emotions*. New York: Oxford University Press.

— & Trevarthen, C. (2009). The Neuroscience of Emotion in Music. In S. Malloch & C. Trevarthen (eds), *Communicative Musicality: Exploring the Basis of Human Companionship* (pp. 105–46). Oxford: Oxford University Press.

Piontelli, A. (1992). *From Fetus to Child*. London: Routledge.

Pollick, A. S. & de Waal, F. B. M. (2007). Ape Gestures and Language Evolution. *Proceedings of the National Academy of Sciences* 104/19: 8184–9.

Porges, S. W. (2003). The Polyvagal Theory: Phylogenetic Contributions to Social Behavior. *Physiology and Behavior* 79: 503–13.

Prechtl, H. F. R. (2001). Prenatal and Early Postnatal Development of Human Motor Behaviour. In A. F. Kalverboer & A. Gramsbergen (eds.), *Handbook of Brain and Behavior in Human Development* (pp. 415–27). Dordrecht: Kluwer.

Reddy, V. (2008). *How Infants Know Minds*. Cambridge MA: Harvard University Press.

Rizzolatti, G. & Gallese, V. (2003). Mirror Neurons. In L. Nadel (ed.), *Encyclopedia of Cognitive Science* (pp. 37–42). London: Nature Publishing Group.

Rodrigues, H. M., Rodrigues, P. M. & Correia, J. S. (2009). Communicative Musicality as Creative Participation: From Early Childhood to Advanced Performance. In S. Malloch & C. Trevarthen (eds.), *Communicative Musicality: Exploring the Basis of Human Companionship* (pp. 585–610). Oxford: Oxford University Press.

Rodrıguez, C. & Palacios, P. (2007). Do Private Gestures have a Self-Regulatory Function? A Case Study. *Infant Behavior and Development* 30: 180–94.

Rogoff, B. (2003). *The Cultural Nature of Human Development*. Oxford: Oxford University Press.

Sander, L. W. (1983). Polarity, Paradox, and the Organizing Process of Development. In J. D. Call, E. Galenson & R. L. Tyson (eds.), *Frontiers of Infant Psychiatry* (pp. 333–45). New York: Basic Books.

Smith, A. (1982[1777]). Of the Nature of that Imitation which takes place in what are called the Imitative Arts. In W. P. D. Wightman & J. C. Bryce (eds.), with Dugald Stewart's account of Adam Smith (ed. I. S. Ross), D. D. Raphael & A. S. Skinner (General eds.), *Essays on Philosophical Subjects* (pp. 176–213). Indianapolis: Liberty Fund.

— (1984[1759]). *Theory of Moral Sentiments*, ed. D. D. Raphael & A. L. Macfie. Indianapolis: Liberty Fund.

Stern, D. N. (2000[1985]). *The Interpersonal World of the Infant: A View from Psychoanalysis and Development Psychology*. New York: Basic Books.

— (1999). Vitality Contours: The Temporal Contour of Feelings as a Basic Unit for Constructing the Infant's Social Experience. In P. Rochat (ed.), *Early Social Cognition: Understanding Others in the First Months of Life* (pp. 67–90). Mahwah, NJ: Erlbaum.

— (2004). *The Present Moment: In Psychotherapy and Everyday Life*. New York: Norton.

Trevarthen, C. (1974). The Psychobiology of Speech Development. In E. H. Lenneberg (ed.), *Language and Brain: Developmental Aspects. Neurosciences Research Program Bulletin* 12: 570–85. Boston: Neurosciences Research Program.

— (1979). Communication and Cooperation in Early Infancy: A Description of Primary Intersubjectivity. In M. Bullowa (ed.), *Before Speech: The Beginning of Human Communication* (pp. 321–47). Cambridge: Cambridge University Press.

— (1986). Form, Significance and Psychological Potential of Hand Gestures of Infants. In J-L. Nespoulous, P. Perron & A. R. Lecours (eds.), *The Biological*

Foundation of Gestures: Motor and Semiotic Aspects (pp. 149–202). Hillsdale, NJ: Erlbaum.

— (1987). Sharing Makes Sense: Intersubjectivity and the Making of an Infant's Meaning. In R. Steele & T. Threadgold (eds.), *Language Topics: Essays in Honour of Michael Halliday* 1 (pp. 177–99). Amsterdam: John Benjamins.

— (1998). The Concept and Foundations of Infant Intersubjectivity. In S. Bråten (ed.), *Intersubjective Communication and Emotion in Early Ontogeny* (pp. 15–46). Cambridge: Cambridge University Press.

— (1999a). Musicality and the Intrinsic Motive Pulse: Evidence from Human Psychobiology and Infant Communication. *Musicae Scientiae Special Issue*: 155–215.

— (1999b). Intersubjectivity. In R. Wilson & F. Keil (eds.), *The MIT Encyclopedia of Cognitive Sciences* (pp. 413–16). Cambridge MA: MIT Press.

— (2002). Origins of Musical Identity: Evidence from Infancy for Musical Social Awareness. In R. MacDonald, D. J. Hargreaves and D. Miell (eds.), *Musical Identities*. (pp. 21–38). Oxford: Oxford University Press.

— (2009). Human Biochronology: On the Source and Functions of 'Musicality'. In R. Haas & V. Brandes (eds.), *Music That Works: Contributions of Biology, Neurophysiology, Psychology, Sociology, Medicine and Musicology* (221–65). New York: Springer.

— & Aitken, K. J. (2003). Regulation of Brain Development and Age-Related Changes in Infants' Motives: The Developmental Function of 'Regressive' Periods. In M. Heimann (ed.), *Regression Periods in Human Infancy* (pp. 107–84). Mahwah, NJ: Erlbaum.

— & Hubley, P. (1978). Secondary Intersubjectivity: Confidence, Confiding and Acts of Meaning in the First Year. In A. Lock (ed.), *Action, Gesture and Symbol* (pp. 183–229). London: Academic Press.

— & Reddy, V. (2007). Consciousness in Infants. In M. Velman & S. Schneider (eds.), *A Companion to Consciousness* (pp. 41–57). Oxford: Blackwell.

Tronick, E. Z. (2005). Why is Connection with Others so Critical? The Formation of Dyadic States of Consciousness: Coherence Governed Selection and the Co-Creation of Meaning out of Messy Meaning Making. In J. Nadel & D. Muir (eds), *Emotional development* (pp. 293–315). Oxford: Oxford University Press.

— (2007). *The Neurobehavioral and Social Emotional Development of Infants and Children*. New York: Norton.

Turner, R. & Ioannides, A. (2009). Brain, Music and Musicality: Inferences from Neuroimaging. In S. Malloch & C. Trevarthen (eds.), *Communicative Musicality: Exploring the Basis of Human Companionship* (pp. 147–81). Oxford: Oxford University Press.

Whitehead, A. N. (1926). *Science and the Modern World*. Lowell Lectures (1925). Cambridge: Cambridge University Press.

— (1929). *The Aims of Education and Other Essays*. New York: Macmillan.

Zlatev, J., Racine, T. P., Sinha, C. & Itkonen, E., eds. (2008). *The Shared Mind: Perspectives on Intersubjectivity*. Amsterdam: John Benjamins.

Zoia, S, Blason, L., D'Ottavio, G., Bulgheroni, M., Pezzetta, E., Scabar, A. & Castiello, U. (2007). Evidence of Early Development of Action Planning in the Human Foetus: A Kinematic Study. *Experimental Brain Research* 176: 217–26.

Chapter 2

Gestures in Music-making:
Action, Information and Perception

W. Luke Windsor

This chapter will explore some issues related to the analysis, perception and production of gestures in music-making. Although it will touch on the most obvious modality through which gestures are viewed by audiences, the visual, it will take a more poietic (and perhaps neutral) approach to defining gestures themselves, rather than an esthesic approach (see Nattiez 1990 for an explanation of these distinctions): for the purposes of this chapter, gestures will be considered to be certain *movements made by musicians*. Such movements may complement or indeed express other kinds of 'gestures' (such as those a music analyst or performer might discover in a score) and may be perceived through a range of modalities and media.

The focus here will, therefore, be on the bodily gestures made by musicians, the nature of the traces these gestures leave on the environment, and how these traces might be picked up and interpreted by audiences. Throughout, the theoretical underpinnings of my arguments are drawn from perceptual psychology, in particular the work of the 'ecological' psychologist James Gibson (1966, 1979; see Heft 2001 for an attempt to integrate Gibson's work into a broader history of realist and pragmatic psychology and philosophy). This ecological approach has recently received interest from a small number of researchers of music who wish in different ways to integrate action and perception (e.g. Clarke 2005, 2007; Dibben 2001; Dibben & Windsor 2001; Windsor 1996, 2000), although they mainly focus on the perceptual side of this equation, with some attention paid to electroacoustic manipulation.

The Problem of Gesture in Performance

It has become commonplace to talk of gesture in music: that this volume exists at all is testament to the recent popularity of the term. For the purposes of this discussion a number of questions will be addressed, first in relation to the Western art music tradition of performance, then through an intentionally paradoxical turn to the performative nature of gesture in electroacoustic composition.

First, how are musical gestures perceived? Normally, gestures are considered to be visual signals, but in music it has become quite normal to talk about gestures being expressed through sound, sometimes independently of any visual complement. Both visual and auditory perception will therefore be considered. Second, what is a musical gesture made by a performer? Is it any movement they make (whether or not it results in sound), or only certain movements? This question necessitates some analysis of the kinds of movement performers make, and some reflection on conscious and unconscious intentionality. Third, how can gestures be audible? An everyday definition of a gesture is an expressive movement (like a shrug, wink or a hand-wave) that is seen: how are gestures heard, and what does it mean to say we hear a gesture? To address these questions requires attention to the actions performers make, the extent to which they can be perceived through different media, how they are perceived and what constraints limit their perception under different reception conditions.

Action in Music

Musicians engage in all kinds of actions, many of which result directly in the production of sound. The movements of our bodies can interact with objects and air columns to produce a wide variety of sounds. However, many of the movements made by musicians are not strictly necessary for producing sound. It is possible to play a woodwind instrument without making movements of the upper body which would be visible to a distant onlooker: the lungs need to be filled and emptied and the fingers need to operate the mechanism of the keys, but the visible swaying of a body, and resulting movement of a whole instrument is not a direct source of sound. Of course, such movements are made by musicians, and have been studied fairly extensively for the clarinet at least (e.g. Vines et al. 2006) and also for the piano (e.g. Davidson 1993, 1994, 1995). Some musicians are explicitly coached in making such movements, either early in their training (e.g. Dalcroze eurythmics) or when they become involved in opera or musical theatre. Davidson has looked at the way such movements can communicate meaning and expression in performance (Davidson 2001) and has also suggested that pianists have a repertoire of movements that may serve similar ends (Davidson 1995, 2002).

For the purposes of the ensuing discussion, musicians' movements can be categorized in two ways, both of which might be helpful in clarifying the gestural qualities of musical performance. First, actions can be categorized by their relative importance to sound production: they directly make sounds, they indirectly affect the making of sounds, or they supplement the making of sounds. In the first category would fall the movements of a pianist's fingers that are necessary to set the piano's hammers in motion, or the changes in embouchure made by a flautist changing octave, or the movements of a guitarist's hand to create vibrato. Note that although some of these movements do not initiate vibration, but modify it, all have a physical mapping from movement to acoustic consequence. In the second category would come cyclical movements such as foot tapping, head nodding or body sway, where these are phase-locked to the beat or tactus, or related to tempo change, dynamic shaping or the like. Similarly there are the punctual movements that accompany events of structural importance such as those discussed by Davidson (2002). Such movements play no necessary physical role in making the sound itself (indeed performers are often warned away from their excessive use as they can disturb the mechanics of performance) but they certainly accompany aspects of musical sound production in a potentially predictable manner and in many cases affect the sound that is produced, or at least seem to. Whether or not they have a truly causal relationship with aspects of musical performance is a question that will be returned to later in this chapter. Lastly, there are supplementary movements that appear to have no causal relationship with the sound (although this is an un-asked empirical question as yet) but certainly seem to play a huge role in the performance: the raised eyebrow of an opera singer to signal surprise, the closing of a pianist's eyes throughout a delicate passage.

The second manner of categorization is related to the first but does not beg questions of causality. Movements are either correlated to some acoustic parameter or not: such correlations can be determined empirically and do not require any appeal to cognitive psychology or philosophy. One can either measure movements and relate them to acoustic dimensions in more or less direct ways, or one can ask participants in experiments to make judgements about music and sound and see whether these judgements are correlated. What becomes important is whether sound and movement are potentially related, and whether such a relationship is detectable by an observer/listener. Focusing on this second type of categorization suits a more ecological approach to studying the perception of musical expression as it reflects a desire to discover what patterns of acoustic or visual structure determine our perceptions: movements (of objects) very closely specify the sound that results and it is argued that these predictable relationships are perceived according to a kind of ecological psychophysics (e.g. Freed 1990; Warren & Verbrugge 1984; Warren et al. 1987). In particular, temporal patterns of excitation are preserved in acoustic information and can be shown to have perceptual relevance (Warren & Verbrugge 1984). Similarly, the pressure and velocity with which a bow moves across a violin string (and the movements of the arm that holds the bow) has a physically predictable relationship with the resulting timbre, one that we can become sensitive to in a direct, rather than conventional, manner, and one that can be modelled in sound synthesis (e.g. Cadoz et al. 1984). In semiotic terms, such a relationship between what would be called expression and content is indexical, rather than symbolic, or, if one prefers Eco's terminology to that of Peirce, the sign function is 'motivated' rather than relying on a purely arbitrary and systemic basis (Eco 1979: 190–92).

Aural and Visual Perception of Performance

What then do observers perceive when they see and hear performance? The movements of performers create patterns in sound and light that are picked up by the visual and auditory systems of audience members. These patterns more or less clearly specify what the performer is doing. They do so in rather general terms in that certain patterns can only be produced by human organs: for example, the human voice is closely specified through a peculiar relationship between the vibration of the vocal chords and the resonances of the vocal cavities. Greater levels of specificity are achievable, however: the sounds as well as the visible movements of a pianist can specify the force with which the performer is depressing keys, the tempo of the music, even the degree of expressivity (Davidson 1993, 1994). Patterns that specify the magnitude and temporal structure of action reveal an enormous amount about what a performer is *doing* and are often cross-modal in that similar descriptions of structure can be found that specify sources in both visual and acoustic domains. This can be true of the patterns of a bouncing ball and their relationship with the ball's elasticity (Warren et al. 1987), or the patterns of movement that specify expressivity of a performance (Davidson 1993). If one is willing to take a radical ecological approach (i.e. Gibson 1979) then what is perceived is movement of a person (in interaction with an instrument), not sounds and light. Auditory and visual perception are processes of picking up information that specifies events and objects. In the case of music, the objects are people and instruments, the events are sets of movements that constitute musical performances (whether seen or heard, or both). This rather counter-intuitive view of musical performance may seem overly radical and seems to downplay a more typical focus on sonic descriptions of music. However, if we are to study movements, and that subset of movements we call gestures, then focusing on movement and how it is jointly perceived through sound and light rather than any metaphorically gestural quality of sound seems a sensible step. This is not to say that the 'structure as such' (Gibson 1966: 225) of sound is not of interest to psychologists or musicologists. However, if we wish to focus on actual rather than metaphorical gestures then sound plays the same role as light: it can tell us what movement another person makes and whether it was a gesture, or an accidental, insignificant or uncommunicative movement.

Other researchers may wish to focus on more metaphorical approaches to musical gestures, but here an attempt will be made to analyse visual and acoustic information and reveal how it specifies the kinds of movements and patterns of movements that are gestural in quality, whether more continuous in nature or more punctual. What do musicians do that is like the flowing continuous hand gestures that accompany speech and how do we perceive these gestures? What do they do that acts like a shrug, or a wink? Clearly the gestures that 'accompany' music may not play quite the same role as the non-verbal communicative movements that supplement other forms of communication nor may they be structured in the same way. However, they are potentially a primary manner in which an audience has direct contact with the performer: we cannot see what a performer thinks but we can hear and see them move, and this may provide us with useful information about their conception of the music they are playing, or at least allow us to form an interpretation of what we think this conception might be.

In order to exemplify the role that the perception of underlying movements may have in performance, two areas of musical activity will be considered. First, this chapter will examine expressive timing in music, along with its relationship to body movement. Some observations will be made about what performers do that we might consider gestural, how these gestures might be perceived by audiences and how gestural information can be recovered from the movements of performers for the purposes of analysis. Second, this chapter will turn from a focus on performers' gestures to compositional gestures, in an attempt to integrate two sides of musical production that are too easily portrayed as being at either end of a continuum between the practical and conceptual.

Gesture and Expressive Timing in Performance

A huge number of psychological studies attest to the expressive nature of musical performance, most of which focus at least in part on timing. These studies are largely concerned with the control of timing in performance (e.g. Shaffer 1981, 1984), what patterns of timing can tell us about cognitive representations of musical structure and vice-versa (e.g. Clarke 1988; Palmer 1989), and how timing might encode (or indeed communicate) mood or other interpretative intention (e.g. Juslin 2000). The concept of gesture is rarely used in such work, although possible relationships between patterns of expressive timing and movement have been explored in both theoretical and empirical studies (e.g. Friberg & Sundberg 1999; Shove & Repp 1995; Todd 1995). Of course, expressive timing in music is directly the result of patterns of movement that directly or indirectly create sound. Whether such movements are gestural in nature, and how they might be analysed if they are, will be explored below.

Most researchers on expressive timing agree that many patterns of rubato, durational accenting, fermata, voice asynchrony and articulation seem to be generated in a rule-like and predictable manner from an interpretation of musical structures (in particular metrical and phrase structure). One way of conceptualizing these rules is in terms of gesture: we move in a particular way to attempt to communicate something. The movements determined by the canonic demands of the score are supplemented by additional movements that may enhance the projection of certain musical elements, or even communicate elements that are to an extent independent of the canonic notation. Of particular interest might be the way in which such movements (whether visible or audible) work in parallel given the multi-modal nature of musical expression, and the notions of parallel, nested and hierarchical gestures will be addressed below through attention to empirical, computational and theoretical findings and methodological issues. First, however, a consideration of some definitions of and assumptions about gesture in performance and its relationship to movement are in order.

Gestures as Expressive Action in Performance

Outside of musicology, and in current definitions, gestures are considered to be body movements that are employed expressively to convey either thought or feeling. However, earlier usages are either broader than this (all bodily movements) or narrower (religious or oratorical postures or movements) and even include the historic usage 'to walk proudly' in verb form. Gesture has also become figuratively employed as will be familiar to all readers of this book: indeed the *Oxford English Dictionary* cites the compositional 'gestures' of new music as an example of this figurative usage (*Oxford English Dictionary*, n.d.). If one eschews figurative definitions then we might indeed come to the conclusion that gestures in musical performance are all expressive actions (or manners of inaction), whether visible or audible. Movements 'expressive of thought or feeling' might be thought to comprise all movements made by performers, although one might wish to distinguish between such expressive movements as called for by the score and those merely implied by it, or added by the performer. Such movements may be discrete, applying to a single time point in a musical performance, or across multiple time points. Just as the hand may be used to signal *stop* when the palm is displayed motionless, the same hand may describe a flowing gesture intended to signify rising emotional intensity. The movements of a performer might indicate a single event in a performance with a discrete movement such as depressing a key on the piano forcefully, or might gesture continuously when a series of key depressions vary in force.

In music, just as in other domains, gestures can occur in parallel. I might in response to a question both shake my head and shrug, or shake my head and frown. In the first instance I might be perceived to be negative but unsure, in the second, negative and displeased. In musical performance, because some very small movements and series of movements become audible the potential for parallel gestures becomes extremely rich. The combined audibility *and* visibility of gesture in musical performance creates a rich possibility for combining parallel gestures across or within modalities. Parallel gesturing may involve more than one modality: a performer might accompany a slowing of tempo with a waggle of the head, for example. It can also occur within a single modality: for example one might slow down and play more staccato. Within a single modality one might vary more than one expressive parameter, as in the case of getting louder and faster.

Moreover, multiple gestures can occur even where a single expressive parameter is involved: a continuous slowing of tempo can be accompanied by a pause of an agogic accent. To illustrate this, imagine playing a short melodic piece on a hand-cranked musical box. Given the same canonic structure, we can articulate at least two parallel strands of gestural timing, despite the constraints of the instrument. By turning the crank faster or slower, stopping or starting, or modulating the frequency with which the crank turns (following any kind of continuous or stepped function) one can produce a range of performances. Each of these performances is the result of performative actions or gestures that combine both sequentially and simultaneously. The tune might be played with a relatively static and fast tempo (roughly periodic rotation of the hand, high velocity), a slow tempo with much rubato (aperiodic rotation of the hand with continuously modulated velocity, average velocity low), a slow tempo with pauses (periodic rotation interrupted with zero velocity segments), or any combination of the above. The results reflect the additive combination of gestures. Interestingly it may be hard to separate out the contribution of each kind of gesture: a gradual deceleration in combination with a final cessation of movement could be perceived in combination as a stepped deceleration. Such problems will be returned to below when analysis techniques are explored.

Given that gestures may be parallel, it is worth noting that they can both complement and/or contradict one another. For example, a pause and a gradual ritardando can together signal the approach and arrival of a cadential figure, whereas an accelerando followed by a fermata has a very different flavour. Dynamic accents can mark individual onsets, but if they occur too close to the peak of crescendo, can be hard to discern as such (e.g. Clarke & Windsor 2000). Across modalities, movements can be intermodally related more or less strongly: tempo, along with the structure of bars and beats and other temporal markers may be correlated with head, torso or instrument positions and velocities and may contribute to our perception of form and its expression (Clarke & Davidson 1998; Vines et al. 2006; Windsor et al. 2003). For example, in Windsor et al. (2003) the head and shoulder movements of two pianists described a roughly oval continuous movement towards and away from the piano keyboard with a period of one or two bars. In contrast, a third pianist nodded his head at the beginning of each bar, the upper body and head remaining otherwise static.

In summary, the actions of performers can be viewed as thoroughly gestural in that they give character to a musical performance. They are available to audiences either through sound or light, or both, can be produced in parallel, can be more or less independent or complementary. In the following section the analysis of such gestures will be investigated, and in particular how one can separate out parallel gestures given only a single parameter, in this case expressive inter-onset timing.

Retrieving Expressive Gestures from Performance

Although thus far this chapter has focused on the actions of performers, the discussion will now turn to the traces such actions leave on the environment. In particular, expressive variability in tempo, dynamics and timbre within performance is information that can be picked up by the listener that can more or less unequivocally specify the gestures that create it. The processes that lead to such direct perception of action will be considered later in this chapter: here the focus will be on the structure of expressive inter-onset timing and how it can be decomposed to reveal the kinds of parallel and multiple patterns discussed in the previous section. It will be assumed that the structured patterns of timing discussed here are the basis for perceiving performative gestures through sound.

Many researchers have worked to extract and measure time-varying properties from acoustic or mechanical signals collected from performances. Such measurements are often represented numerically and/or visually, and attempts are made to model the predictable aspects of such signals (for a review, see Windsor 2008). However, if the processes that create such signals are multiple, it may not always be obvious how to extract such different expressive components. Here, the problems of parallel sources of expressive timing will be exemplified through a re-analysis of some data and model-fitting originally carried out by Windsor and Clarke (1997), and then some solutions will be explored, in particular a decomposition technique developed by Windsor et al. (2006).

Windsor and Clarke (1997) assessed the fit between an algorithmic model of expressive inter-onset timing (and dynamics) developed by Todd (1992) and an expert performance of an extract from a Schubert's Impromptu in G♭ (see Example 2.1). In this study the researchers optimized the fit between model and human performance separately for inter-onset timing and dynamics to minimize error. The best fit achieved by the model for timing was around 43 per cent of the variability observed in the human performance, which was highly significant given the number of inter-onset intervals modelled. However, despite this close relationship between model and performance, the residuals (the remainder of the variance after model fitting) show considerable structure. The model produces roughly polynomial patterns of tempo change, curves that have been observed in many empirical studies of timing in piano performance. After these have been accounted for, the remaining variability in onset timing seems to suggest either additional agogic accents and micro-pauses at the beginnings and ends of phrases in addition to the behaviour predicted by Todd's model, which accelerates continuously towards the middle of phrase then decelerates towards the phrase boundary, although this was only given as a speculative interpretation. Is this a case of parallel sets of gestures being combined additively?

Example 2.1   Schubert, Impromptu in G♭, bars 1–2

Taking the first 24 note onsets (the first bar) of the piece only and applying the same model settings as in the original study gives a fit of around 53 per cent. Figure 2.1 shows the durations of each inter-onset interval (IOI) in the performance (nominally equal events in the score) plotted alongside the output of the model. The qualitative lack of fit here is striking, especially for the initial and terminal events. Leaving aside the small-scale structure, can one fit these two events from the performance better in quantitative terms? A simply linear model that assumes only the first and last events vary in duration from the others, but does not predict by how much, fits the performance data to a much greater extent, without even attempting to match the small-scale detail (see Figure 2.2).

Unfortunately, simply combining these two models to account for both continuous and discrete modulation of timing is neither easy nor terribly logical. The two models are quite different in their conception: one is highly constrained and based on a complex and thorough set of theoretical predications about expressive timing, whilst the other is a thoroughly naïve and under-theorized approximation.

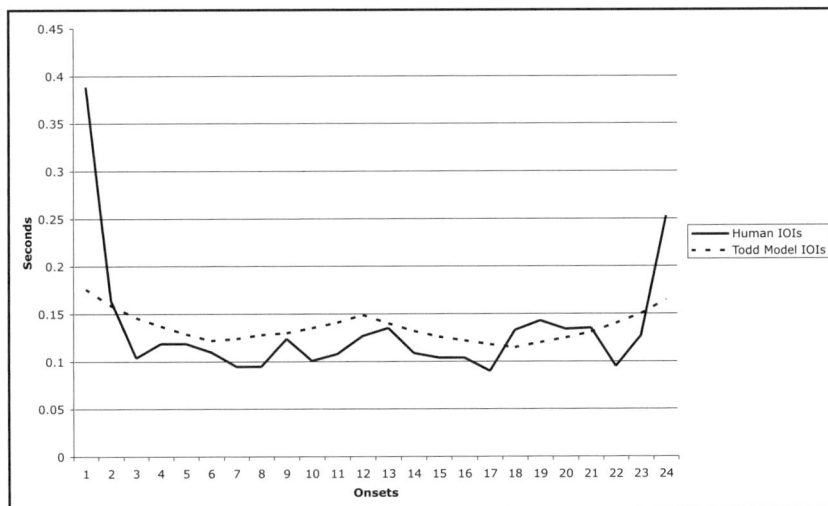

Figure 2.1   An overlay chart plotting the inter-onset timing of the first bar of Schubert's *Impromptu* in G♭ for a human performer and the optimized output of Todd (1992). Model fitting is as in Windsor and Clarke (1997)

The Todd model tests some clear predictions at least, whereas the better-fitting model simply says: the first and last notes in a phrase may be longer or shorter than the others. Moreover, the Todd model does not account for the residuals left behind by the other model, nor vice-versa. Although the simplistic model does capture some aspects of what Todd's model fails to capture, it does not do so comprehensively. This kind of ad-hoc, post-hoc attempt to fit data to a model is unsystematic and lacking in theoretical rigour. What is needed is an approach to expressive timing that *a priori* assumes that expression may have multiple sources that combine in an additive manner. Todd's model does assume that expression is additively combined across multiple hierarchical levels of phrase structure, but each level of timing determines each other level such that expressive timing follows a single underlying equation. Although this is an elegant idea, it is not

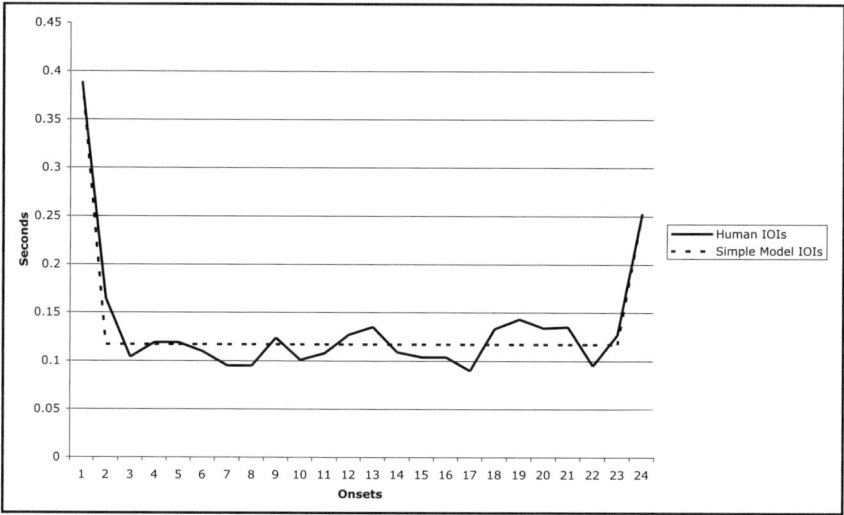

Figure 2.2   An overlay chart plotting the inter-onset timing of the first bar of
             Schubert's *Impromptu* in G♭ for a human performer (data from
             Windsor & Clarke 1997) and a simple linear model with an agogic
             accent at the first event and a final micro-pause

the only approach to combining expressive gestures. There are now a number of algorithmic approaches to combining different aspects of expressive performance, such as *Director Musices* (Friberg et al. 2000) and GERM (Juslin et al. 2002). Here, many rules interact with varying parameters to create a simulated performance that can be evaluated in relation to human performances or judgements. For example, optimizing these parameters to best fit with a set of real performances has been an approach taken by Sundberg et al. (2003) and Zanon and de Poli (2003a, 2003b).

An alternative to such rule-based approaches is to optimize the fit of a performance (or performances) to a model that has few assumptions about what form expressive gestures might take, only that they will be associated in a predictable fashion with structural features in the score. One such model is that of Windsor et al. (2006): here a hierarchical representation of musical structure is used to predict where expressive timing will occur, and a process of optimization finds the individual contributions of each pattern as well as the additively combined result, which should match a target performance closely, given that the musical structure chosen has some close relationship to that expressed through the performance. This process delivers an analysis of expressive timing that breaks down the performed timing into separate repeated gestures associated with different levels and types of structure: a single event may be associated with an accent and be lengthened, a phrase may accelerate, another phrase may accelerate then decelerate, and so on. Figure 2.3 shows an example of such an analysis of timing and Figure 2.4 the result of adding together each of these gestural layers alongside the original performance. The analysis reveals how different sources of expression combine, despite their different time-spans, shapes and structural types.

For example, the analysis shows that the largest phrasal division into one unit of 48 quavers, and two of 36, does not produce uniform timing strategy in the manner of models such as Todd (1992). The performer accelerates towards the end of the first phrase, then follows a romantic ebb and flow pattern across the next two phrases. The analysis also manages to capture the potentially distorting contribution of the fermata at the end of the second long phrase: the ritardando here is extremely deep, and in a more conventional analysis tends to conceal the fact that when it is removed the underlying pattern of rubato is actually quite repetitive. In Figure 2.4 it is much harder to see that there is a repeated pattern of timing, and a statistical analysis of the rubato would have similar problems without such decomposition. Note also the way in which two parallel patterns of timing interlock at the finest level of structure, one associated with metrical regularity, one with out-of-phase grouping structure. Finally, observe the way that this kind of analysis allows one to test whether continuous *and* discrete deviations from metronomic performance are working in parallel: the two leaps down from a grace note are associated with a slight delay that combines additively with all the other patterns to produce the combined model shown in Figure 2.4 (interestingly the other grace notes have no such effect on global timing).

Returning to the issue of gesture, how are these patterns of timing gestural? Each acceleration or deceleration, pause or agogic accent is generated by action, and as we will return to in the next section, the perceptual system is attuned to picking up information that specifies such actions. We do not perceive sound just for itself, but as a source of information about the various bodily gestures that create that sound. Whether each of the gestural layers in such an analysis presented above is perceptible, and whether some layers are perceptually (or motorically) distinct or not remains an empirical question, but decomposition of the expressive signal is a clear precursor to such questions.

The captions for Figures 2.3 and 2.4 (that appear overleaf) are as follows:

Figure 2.3   The decomposition of the expressive profiles: the x axis shows score position, the y axis the parameter values in quaver-note IOIs in seconds. The names of the structural units are displayed to the right of each profile. Score annotations as in Figure 2.4. Note that the x axis is warped to align with the musical notation, distorting the canonically regular shape of the profiles (from Windsor et al. 2006: 1188)

Figure 2.4   Observed and predicted IOIs plotted against a score annotated with phrase, bar and non-contiguous segments. L = leap; R = ritardando; C-R = chord-ritardando. Phrase segments are identified by their duration in score time measured in quavers. Note that the x axis is warped to align with the musical notation (from Windsor 2006: 1187)

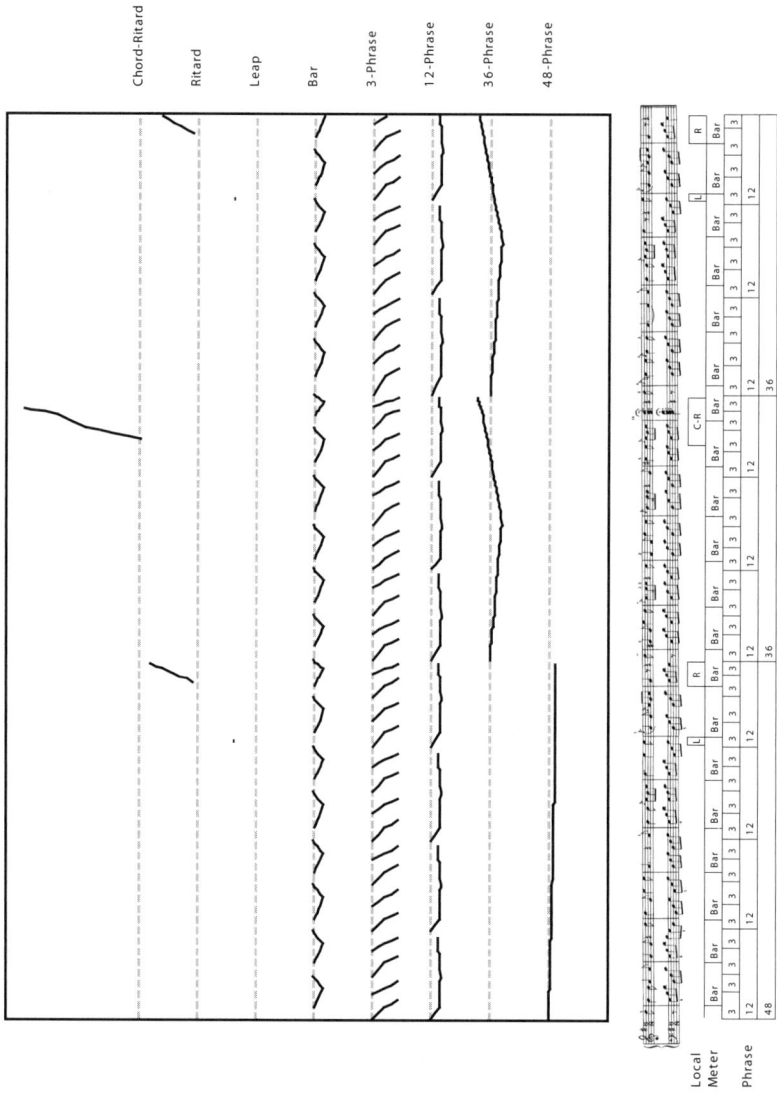

Figure 2.3

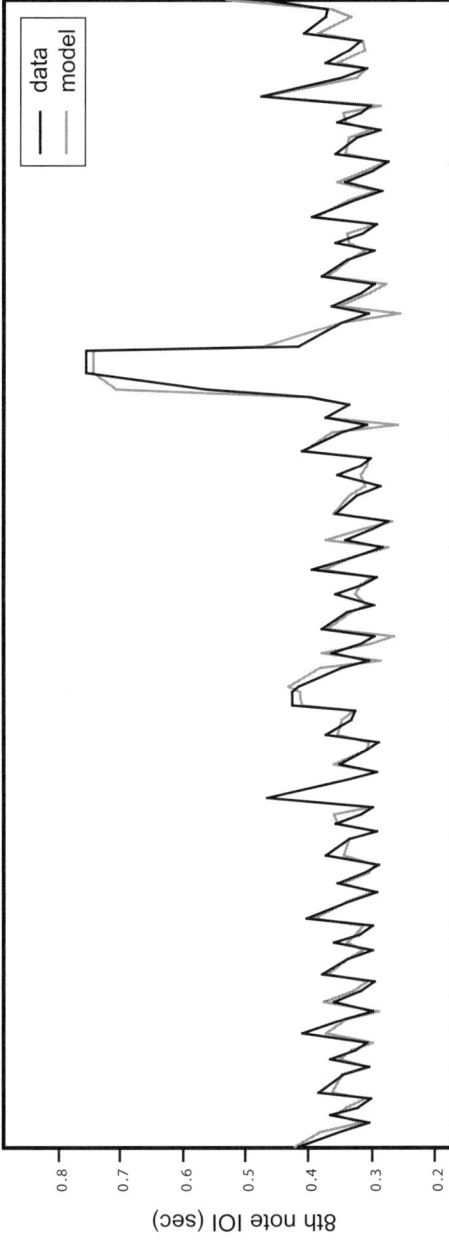

Figure 2.4

Gesture in Acousmatic Composition

A performance, as has been demonstrated above, may be made up of a complex combination of movements, which can be considered gestural in that they give character to a piece of music. Acousmatic music, composed for and performed by loudspeakers, and as conceived by Pierre Schaeffer (e.g. Schaeffer 1966), rests upon a theoretical disjunction between sound and source, the idea of reduced listening, a disjunction called into question by many of his successors. Schaeffer's theoretical approach to sound in acousmatic composition seems diametrically opposed to the Gibsonian approach to everyday perception (Gibson 1966, 1979), where sound is simply information for events and objects (see also Gaver 1993). Such a disjunction, if carried over into perception would place acousmatic music in clear contrast to acoustic performances where the relationship between sound and source is visible.

However, given that perceptual processes are peculiarly able to pick up information that specifies the origin of sounds (Gaver 1993) it has been argued that although acousmatic experience is 'impoverished' in relation to everyday perception, we still default to source identification as a primary manner of making sense of what we hear, and that the tension between the ambiguous and incomplete information about sources in acousmatic presentation and our tendency to ascribe them is precisely that which leads to much of acousmatic music's aesthetic richness (Windsor 2000; see also Windsor 2004). In order to form a richer view of gesture from the perspective of action this section will look for compositional gestures (as well as information for inanimate objects and events) in acousmatic music, or the traces of these gestures in the acoustic signal.

Musician versus Listener

Regardless of whether music is presented acousmatically or not, the listener's experience is impoverished in relation to the musician's experience of the music as they are making it. The listener can hear, possibly see (and very possible smell) what a musician is doing, but has no access to the haptic and proprioceptive experiences of the musician. Beyond this, however, the listener can perceive what a musician does to a great extent, although acousmatic presentation certainly widens the gap between making and listening, as much of the information used by a listener to figure out what a musician is doing is undoubtedly visual. This impoverishment of experience, however, is where music becomes interesting. Gibson (1966: 303) argues that in cases where our perceptual field is limited we act to do something about this uncertainty:

> More typical of life than absence of stimulation, however, is the presence of stimulation with inadequate information – information that is conflicting, masked, equivocal, cut short, reduced, or even sometimes false... With conflicting or contradictory information the overall perceptual system alternates

or compromises... ... but in lifelike situations a search for additional information begins, information that will reinforce one or the other alternative... If detection still fails, the system hunts more widely in space and longer in time.

Arguably, it is in this action that interpretation (as opposed to communication) begins when in a musical context (Windsor 2000). However, the listener is not entirely cut off from the actions of the musician: we can perceive events veridically even in degraded acousmatic, unimodal situations; indeed our ability to do so is well documented (Kendall 1991: 71):

> In everyday life, sound events arise from action, in fact, from the transfer of energy to a sounding object. The auditory system provides us with perceptual characterizations of the energy transfer and of the internal structure of the objects involved. Early in childhood one learns to recognize the occurrence of sound events and to relate them to physical events.

We can perceive the hardness of a mallet from the sound it makes on impact (Freed 1990) and the elasticity of a ball from the timing of its audible bounces (Warren et al. 1987); sonar operators can identify different kinds of ship and propeller from sound alone (Howard & Ballas 1983; Solomon 1958, 1959a, 1959b): such an ecological physics arguably underpins much of our everyday perceptual activity. Hence, it is not exactly a bold claim to suggest that the body's involvement in the production of many musical sounds is specified through predictable relationships between sound and action: such skills are the skills of the expert instrumental teacher who can diagnose deficits in technique through hearing a student. Although acousmatic presentation may make this harder, the traces of human activity are readily perceptible where such lawful relationships between sound and action are not obscured.

The 'Hand' of the Composer

Of course, a primary role of the acousmatic composer may be to obscure the actual origins of sounds, or deceive us about them. The acousmatic composer chooses sounds that specify events and objects more or less closely, sequences and aggregrates of sound objects that more or less resemble environmental 'lawfulness' (e.g. Howard & Ballas 1980): the more closely the real world is alluded to the easier it is for the listener to fall back on direct perception. Conversely, the less closely it is mimicked the more active and potentially imaginative our perception becomes, and paradoxically the 'hand' of the composer becomes audible. In more everyday listening situations we have access to the actions of musicians through the presence of acoustic correlates of action, but in many acousmatic situations the 'hand' of the composer is revealed by the absence of such correlates or the re-ordering or combination of sounds in such a way as to contradict their origins. We become aware of intentionality because the sounds we hear do not sound as if they were simply recorded and re-presented. Of course, many compositions also reveal the actions of their composers through the use of gestural interfaces, their own voices or instruments. What is interesting is that in both cases, the composer is perceivable through the traces he or she has left on the work, in the same way as a performer leaves an audible trail that identifies their contribution. An example where such different kinds of intentionality can be perceived is 'Toccata' from Francois Bayle's *camera oscura* (2000[1976]). This piece combines many allusions to the real, as well as the hyperreal and surreal. Bayle himself 'appears' as a *personnage sonore*: we hear the sounds of a real person interacting with the recorded environment, an environment that seems to sometimes obey everyday rules, and at other times its own internal logic.

To summarize this argument, we tend to hear the bodies of musicians as the primary 'cause' of sounds in instrumental music, whereas in acousmatic music our attention is shifted to more compositional causes. The acousmatic can act to conceal or distort the information we would normally use to identify the gestures made by musicians, but instead the gestures of the composer are highlighted through the traces such gestures leave behind. From an ecological standpoint such traces provide information that specifies the presence of human activity, and actions that communicate or signify character.

Gesture in Context: Action and Perception

In this final section an attempt will be made to integrate the preceding arguments. Gestures, it has been proposed in this context are actions, rather than abstract, figurative or metaphorical entities. Moreover, they are communicative or perceived as such. The central questions underlying this chapter are how musical gestures relate to physical actions by musicians, how such gestures can be recovered in analysis, and how their perception – and attempts to conceal their perception – affect our understanding of intentionality.

In phenomenological terms gestures are perceived through the traces they leave on the environment, whether immediately on their production or preserved over time, as in a recording. The ecological approach to perception adopted here gives a more precise understanding of how such traces betray their origins: patterns of sound and light lawfully specify events and objects including the details of their human origins: the trace of a gesture is the information that specifies a particular action. To conclude this chapter an attempt will be made to characterize the flow of information, perception and action that pertains when a single musician plays on their own, and when that musician is observed and heard by a single listener.

Action, Perception and Information in Performance

Figure 2.5 represents the flow of information that applies when a single musician (performer, improviser or composer) is at work. Actions here result in events that

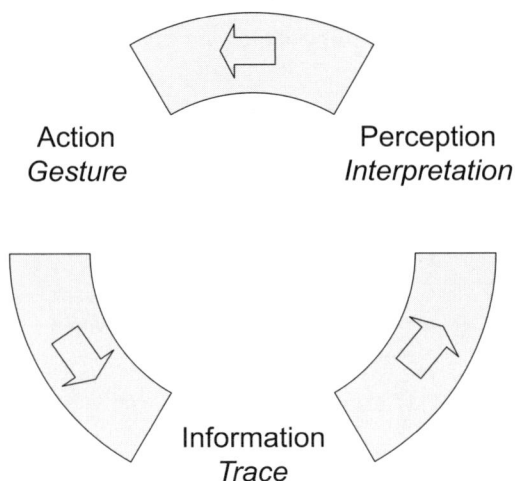

Action   Perception
Gesture   *Interpretation*

Information
Trace

Figure 2.5   Diagram representing the flow of perception and action for a single
musician

provide information for perception, which then guide further action. Actions here might be movements that create sound, or incidental movements that accompany sound production: the events they generate, whether sounding or not, are accessible to the musician because they provide information for the musician's perceptual systems to pick up. This information guides further actions, not only though providing feedback on the success of previous actions, but also guiding information further gathering movements.

Figure 2.6 shows what happens when a listener/observer breaks into this loop: the listener/observer acts to perceive by orienting their head towards the auditory and visual information that is being produced by the musician. The movements that are perceived through these sources of information more or less closely specify what the musician is doing, and the gestural character of this activity. What is perceived then generates further action on the part of the listener/observer, either immediate and exploratory, or deferred: one might focus on the hands of a pianist, or attend to a line in a polyphonic texture; or one might seek out an explanation of a detail from the pianist after the performance (or switch one's attention to the programme note). Of course, this situation becomes even more complex and interesting when the musician perceives the actions of listener/observer and modifies his or her actions accordingly.

The shared information about action available to the listener/observer might be thought of as being never as detailed as that available to the musician themselves, but in many ways the listener/observer can observe and listen to the body of the performer in much more detail and freedom, unconstrained by technical limitations and from a distant vantage point. The oddity of seeing and hearing oneself performing on video for the first time bears witness to the privileged viewpoint of the spectator.

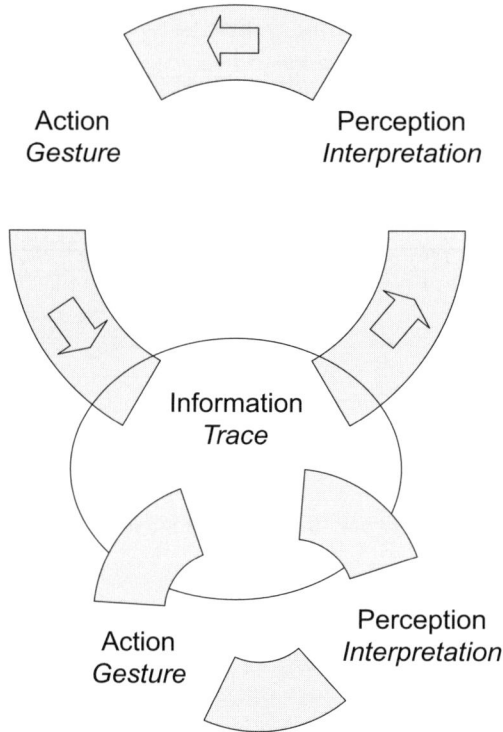

Figure 2.6   Diagram representing the flow of perception and action for a musician and listener/observer

Composers, however physically absent from a performance, still arguably leave a trace of their physical actions in the sounds that are produced, although this is far less specific, leaving much more to the listener/observer's interpretation.

Performance and Composition: Analysing Gesture

What this chapter has endeavoured to show is that it is possible to recover from musical signals traces that betray the gestural origins of sound. However, the empirical basis for many of the claims advanced here is relatively weak. It is one thing to show how a musical signal can be decomposed to reveal a nested hierarchy of temporal trajectories that originate in the gestures of the human body, quite another to detail the extent to which these are perceived. Similarly, although an attempt has been made to show how even in acousmatic composition the human presence of the composer can be detected, it is another thing to show the extent to which this occurs and identify the invariant properties of sound that specify such human causation.

However, the aim here has been to emphasize that any analysis of gesture in music has to consider the real actions of musicians and how these are perceived through the eyes and ears of the audience. Gestures are actions that musicians make, and the supreme virtue of music in this respect is that it can make audible gestures that are near invisible. Moreover, the potential for parallel strands of gesture within a performance also gives music a peculiar efficacy. Much work needs to be done to investigate the manner in which sound and light specify the actions of performers and how these give meaning to musical experience if we are to understand music and its gestural qualities.

References

Bayle, F. (1976/2000). *camera oscura*. Paris: Magison.

Cadoz, C., Florens, J-L. & Luciani, A. (1984). Responsive Input Devices and Sound Synthesis by Simulation of Instrumental Mechanisms: The CORDIS System. *Computer Music Journal* 8/3: 60–73.

Clarke, E. F. (1988). Generative Principles in Music Performance. In J. A. Sloboda (ed.), *Generative Processes in Music: The Psychology of Performance, Improvisation, and Composition* (pp. 1–26). Oxford: Clarendon Press.

— (2005). *Ways of Listening. An Ecological Approach to the Perception of Musical Meaning*. New York: Oxford University Press.

— (2007). The Impact of Recording on Listening. *Twentieth Century Music* 4/1: 47–70.

— & Davidson, J. W. (1998). The Body in Performance. In W. Thomas (ed.), *Composition, Performance, Reception: Studies in the Creative Process in Music* (pp. 74–92). Aldershot: Ashgate.

— & Windsor, W. L. (2000). Real and Simulated Expression: A Listening Study. *Music Perception* 17/3: 1–37.

Davidson, J. W. (1993). Visual Perception of Performance Manner in the Movements of Solo Musicians. *Psychology of Music* 21: 103–13.

— (1994). What Type of Information is Conveyed in the Body Movements of Solo Musician Performers? *Journal of Human Movement Studies* 6: 279–301.

— (1995). What does the Visual Information Contained in Music Performances Offer the Observer? Some Preliminary Thoughts. In R. Steinberg (ed.), *The Music Machine: Psychophysiology and Psychopathology of the Sense of Music* (pp. 105–13). New York: Springer Verlag.

— (2001). The Role of the Body in the Production and Perception of Solo Vocal Performance: A Case Study of Annie Lennox. *Musicae Scientiae* 5/2: 235–56.

— (2002). Understanding the Expressive Movements of a Solo Pianist. *Musikpsychologie* 16: 9–31.

Dibben, N. (2001). What Do We Hear When We Hear Music? Music Perception and Musical Material. *Musicae Scientiae* 5/2: 161–94.

— & Windsor, W. L. (2001). Constructivism in Nicholas Cook's Introduction to Music: Tips for a 'New' Psychology of Music. *Musicae Scientiae* 2: 43–50.

Eco, U. (1979). *A Theory of Semiotics*. Bloomington: Indiana University Press.

Freed, D. J. (1990). Auditory Correlates of Perceived Mallet Hardness for a Set of Recorded Percussive Sound Events. *Journal of the Acoustical Society of America* 87: 311–22.

Friberg, A., Colombo, V., Frydén, L. & Sundberg, J. (2000). Generating Musical Performances with Director Musices. *Computer Music Journal* 24/3: 23–9.

— & Sundberg, J. (1999). Does Music Performance Allude to Locomotion? A Model of Final Ritardandi Derived from Measurements of Stopping Runners. *Journal of the Acoustical Society of America* 105/3: 1469–84.

Gaver, W. W. (1993). What in the World Do We Hear? An Ecological Approach to Auditory Event Perception. *Ecological Psychology* 5/1: 1–29.

Gesture. *Oxford English Dictionary Online* (http://dictionary.oed.com; accessed August 2008).

Gibson, J. J. (1966). *The Senses Considered as Perceptual Systems*. London: Unwin Bros.

— (1979). *The Ecological Approach to Visual Perception*. New Jersey: Lawrence Erlbaum.

Heft, H. (2001). *Ecological Psychology in Context: James Gibson, Roger Barker and the Legacy of William James's Radical Empiricism*. Mahwah, NJ: Lawrence Erlbaum.

Howard, J. H. & Ballas J. A. (1980). Syntactic and Semantic Factors in the Classification of Nonspeech Transient Patterns. *Perception and Psychophysics* 28: 431–9.

— & Ballas, J. A. (1983). Perception of Simulated Propeller Cavitation. *Human Factors* 25/6: 643–55.

Juslin, P. N. (2000). Cue Utilization in Communication of Emotion in Music Performance: Relating Performance to Perception. *Journal of Experimental Psychology: Human Perception and Performance* 26: 1797–813.

—, Friberg, A. & Bresin, R. (2002). Toward a Computational Model of Expression in Performance: The GERM model. *Musicae Scientiae*, Special Issue (2001–02): 63–122.

Kendall, G. S. (1991). Visualisation by Ear: Auditory Imagery for Scientific Visualisation and Virtual Reality. *Computer Music Journal* 15/4: 70–73.

Nattiez, J-J. (1990). *Music and Discourse: Toward a Semiology of Music* (trans. C. Abbate). Princeton: Princeton University Press.

Palmer, C. (1989). Mapping Musical Thought to Musical Performance. *Journal of Experimental Psychology: Human Perception and Performance* 15/12: 331–46.

Schaeffer, P. (1966). *Traité des Objets Musicaux*. Paris: Seuil.

Shaffer, L. H. (1981). Performances of Chopin, Bach and Bartok: Studies in Motor Programming. *Cognitive Psychology* 13: 326–76.

— (1984). Timing in Solo and Duet Piano Performances. *The Quarterly Journal of Experimental Psychology* 36A: 577–95.

Shove, P. & Repp, B. H. (1995). Musical Motion and Performance: Theoretical and Empirical Perspectives. In J. Rink (ed.), *The Practice of Performance: Studies in Musical Interpretation* (pp. 55–83). Cambridge: Cambridge University Press.

Solomon, L. N. (1958). Semantic Approach to the Perception of Complex Sounds. *Journal of the Acoustical Society of America* 30/3: 421–5.

— (1959a). Search for Physical Correlates to Psychological Dimensions of Sounds. *Journal of the Acoustical Society of America* 31/4: 492–7.

— (1959b). Semantic Reactions to Systematically Varied Sounds. *Journal of the Acoustical Society of America* 31/7: 986–90.

Sundberg, J., Friberg, A. & Bresin, R. (2003). Attempts to Reproduce a Pianist's Expressive Timing with Director Musices Performance Rules. *Journal of New Music Research* 32/3: 317–25.

Todd, N. P. (1992). The Dynamics of Dynamics: A Model of Musical Expression. *Journal of the Acoustical Society of America* 91: 3540–50.

— (1995). The Kinematics of Musical Expression. *Journal of the Acoustical Society of America* 97: 1940–49.

Vines, B. W., Krumhansl, C. L., Wanderley, M. M. & Levitin, D. J. (2006). Cross-Modal Interactions in the Perception of Musical Performance. *Cognition* 101/1: 80–103.

Warren, W. H. & Verbrugge, R. R. (1984). Auditory Perception of Breaking and Bouncing Events: A Case Study in Ecological Acoustics. *Journal of Experimental Psychology: Human Perception and Performance* 10/5: 704–12.

—, Kim, E. K. & Husney, R. (1987). The Way the Ball Bounces: Visual and Auditory Perception of Elasticity and the Bounce Pass. *Perception* 16: 309–36.

Windsor, W. L. (1996). Perception and Signification in Electroacoustic Music. In R. Monelle & C. Gray (eds), *Song and Signification: Studies in Music Semiotics* (pp. 64–74). Edinburgh: Edinburgh University Faculty of Music.

— (2000). Through and Around the Acousmatic: The Interpretation of Electroacoustic Sounds. In S. Emmerson (ed.), *Music, Electronic Media and Culture* (pp. 7–33). Aldershot: Ashgate.

— (2004). An Ecological Approach to Semiotics. *Journal for the Theory of Social Behaviour* 34/2: 179–98.

— (2008). Measurement and Models of Performance. In S. Hallam, I. Cross & M. Thaut (eds), *Oxford Handbook of Music Psychology* (pp. 323–31). Oxford: Oxford University Press.

— & Clarke, E. F. (1997). Expressive Timing and Dynamics in Real and Artificial Musical Performances: Using an Algorithm as an Analytical Tool. *Music Perception* 15/2: 127–52.

—, Ng, K., Davidson, J. W. & Utley, A. (2003). Investigating Musicians' Natural Upper Body Movements. Paper presented at the First International Conference on Music and Gesture, University of East Anglia, UK, 28–31 August.

—, Desain, P. W. M., Penel, A. & Borkent, M. (2006). A Structurally Guided Method for the Decomposition of Expression in Music Performance. *Journal of the Acoustical Society of America* 119/2: 1182–93.

Zanon, P. & de Poli, G. (2003a). Time-varying Estimation of Parameters in Rule Systems for Music Performance. *Journal of New Music Research* 32/3: 295–316.

— (2003b). Estimation of Parameters in Rule Systems for Expressive Rendering in Musical Performance. *Computer Music Journal* 27/1: 29–46.

Chapter 3

Coarticulated Gestural-sonic Objects in Music

Rolf Inge Godøy

A longstanding issue in both music cognition research and in human movement research has been that of segmentation, that is, of how we divide continuous streams of sound or movement into units. In our research on musical gestures (University of Oslo, 2010), we talk of *gestural-sonic objects* in the sense of units based on the convergence of sound and movement into holistically perceived chunks (Godøy 2006). One of the main criteria for perceiving these gestural-sonic objects as coherent chunks is that they exhibit superordinate trajectory shapes of motion and sound, and that elements or 'atoms' of sound and movement that occur sequentially in the course of any chunk are subsumed under such superordinate trajectory shapes. This phenomenon of subsumption of atoms of sound and movement is known in linguistics and in movement sciences by the term *coarticulation*. Since we believe we may observe similar subsumptions in music-related gestures and sounds, I shall in this chapter speak of *coarticulated gestural-sonic objects in music*.

Such coarticulated gestural-sonic objects typically have durations in the range of a couple of seconds, similar to *sonic objects* in Schaeffer's theory (Schaeffer 1966; see also Godøy 2006). These coarticulated gestural-sonic objects are on the *meso-level*, or mid-level, between the *micro-level* of continuous sound and movement and the *macro-level* of sections, movements or whole works, and are found as various kinds of ornaments, motives, rhythmical figures and textural fragments. Coarticulated gestural-sonic objects are conceived of as units with regards to both perception and motor control, and thus concern basic issues of music perception, music cognition and movement science, in particular the relationship between continuity and discontinuity in our experiences of musical sound and gestures. It could thus be useful to first review some notions of chunking and of music-related gestures before having a closer look at coarticulation in the production and perception of musical sound.

Theories of Chunking

It is generally agreed that music may be segmented into units. This goes for more traditional approaches of *Formenlehre* or 'theory of form' (e.g. Schoenberg 1967) as well as for music cognition theories (e.g. Lerdahl & Jackendoff 1983) and data-driven pattern recognition studies (e.g. Cambouropoulos 2006). Common to these approaches is that they are notation-based; however, we have also seen work on segmentation based on continuous sound such as in Auditory Scene Analysis (Bregman 1990) and ongoing work in Music Information Retrieval (ISMIR, n.d.). Although there have been significant advances in such signal-based, bottom-up approaches, there seems to be a limit to how far this can go without also resorting to top-down schemas of various kinds (Leman 2008). Bregman's well-known distinction between *primitive* and *schema-based* components of Auditory Scene Analysis attests to the need for combined bottom-up and top-down processes where the bottom-up process relies on patterns in the signal (e.g. various Gestalt theory criteria for coherence) and the top-down process imposes schema-based interpretations on these low-level features.

Top-down elements in segmentation are basically *endogenous* in origin, meaning that it is the listener who 'from the inside out' is actively doing the segmentation. This implies regarding perception as an active process of incessant mental simulation of 'what is what' in listening. The point is that although events we perceive may contain various qualitative discontinuities potentially signalling points of segmentation (e.g. accents, silences, shifts in register, and so on), these *exogenous* cues may, or may not, trigger sensations of segment borders for the simple reason that there may be many and competing qualitative discontinuities in rapid succession, for example many note onsets, leaps, accents and figures. On the other hand, there is also evidence that we may impose endogenous segmentations on sounds that offer little or no qualitative discontinuities, such as imposing various kinds of meters on a steady, unaccented series of pulses (Fraisse 1982).

Another aspect of segmentation is that of how we perceive the content of a segment, that is of how a segment has some kind of 'meaning', or that a segment is not just an arbitrary cutting out of a sound fragment. This understanding of segments as significant units of musical sound means that any segment must be considered as a whole, as having some kind of autonomous status in spite of it being cut out of a larger context. For this reason, I shall from now on use the term *chunk* to denote segments of musical sound, and refer to the process of cutting up continuous musical sound into somehow meaningful units a *chunking*. My use of the term 'chunking' here is inspired by the seminal 1956 paper by Miller, where one of the main points was that in our perception there is a transformation or 're-coding' of complex sensory information into overviewable units, reducing the memory load and enhancing our ability to cope with large amounts of information. Basically, chunking concerns the relationship between continuity and discontinuity in our minds, a topic that has intrigued philosophers and cognitive scientists for a long time.

In phenomenological philosophy, we find an introspective yet very lucid analysis of the relationship between continuity and discontinuity in perception and cognition in Husserl's writings on temporal awareness (Husserl 1964). Husserl's main point is that if we are submerged in a continuous perception of the world, there simply cannot be awareness of anything, because everything just continuously passes through our minds as an amorphous, continuous stream. It is only by intermittently breaking out of this continuous stream that we will be able to make sense of whatever we perceive, implying that we have to think of events in a single flash of awareness, 'in a now', as a chunk that we overview 'all at once'. Husserl illustrates this with the example of a melody, stating that it is only possible to perceive the melody if we somehow withdraw ourselves from the flow of tones and think of the whole melody in one instant. Paul Ricoeur (1981) later advanced a similar idea by using the term 'interruption'; that we have to interrupt the sensory flow in order to make sense of it.

Interestingly, there seems to be similar notions of discontinuity in awareness in recent neurophysiological research, correlated to patterns in the electrical activity of the brain (Engel et al. 2001; Varela 1999). Similar ideas on discontinuity may be found in (Pöppel 1997), and here also with indications of a time interval of roughly 3 seconds as a common size of chunks both in perception and/or attention and in action. For sensory impressions significantly longer than 3 seconds, it is suggested that there will be a shift of attention, as in bi-stable Gestalt images where there typically will be a figure-ground reversal after approximately 3 seconds. Similar notions of chunks in the roughly 3-second range in short-term memory may be found in memory research, with shifts in memory strategy for sensory impressions significantly longer than that (Snyder 2000). Furthermore, there seems to be a preference for action chunks in the 3-second range in human action (Schleidt & Kien 1997), but this may also be related to biomechanical constraints.

To what extent movement is pre-planned as chunks has been debated in the human motor control literature since Woodworth's presentation of the notion of an initial impulse that determined much of the ensuing motion trajectory (Woodworth 1899); however, there seems now to be a consensus for a combination of pre-planning and continuous adjustment (Elliott et al. 2001). A related issue was raised by Lashley (Lashley 1951) who suggested that there had to be a pre-planning of movements because the serial order by so-called response chaining seemed just not fast enough to account for very many kinds of human movement. As argued in Rosenbaum et al. (2007), there is now considerable amount of evidence in favour of pre-planning of human motion by way of goal postures that is similar to the phenomenological idea of a 'snapshot' of past and/or future movements.

From a more specifically musical point of view, the argument in favour of discontinuity and chunking at the meso-level – at the level of roughly 3 seconds – is that chunks will typically have readily identifiable rhythmic, melodic, harmonic, timbral and stylistic features, making such chunks fairly robust in view of recognition and aesthetical signification. For segments significantly shorter, such identification may not be possible, and for segments significantly longer, there is good reason to be suspicious of claims from much traditional western music theory about the necessity of the composer's original order of things. As has been demonstrated by Eitan and Granot (2008), music may very well survive a re-editing of chunks in new orders, notably as long as the size of the chunks is right.

Finally, the idea of the chunk as the prime level of musical significance was strongly advocated in Schaeffer's theoretical work (Schaeffer 1966), in the form of the *sonic object*, meaning fragments of musical sound typically in the range of approximately 0.5 to 5 seconds (duration variable dependent upon both the nature and the context of the sonic object). Besides the argument that chunks of this size are most significant for music in general (similar to the preceding point), this also allowed for thinking of sonic objects as *shapes*, thus enabling quite extensive research on previously not well-conceptualized features of musical sound such as overall dynamical envelopes, overall envelopes for pitch evolution, timbral evolution, textural evolution and the evolution of all kinds of micro-level features (Godøy 2006).

All in all, we may find ideas in several different domains that shed light on chunking and the enigmatic relationship between continuity and discontinuity in experience, and I shall later try to show how principles of gestural coarticulation also may contribute to our understanding of chunking, but I shall now first mention some general points on sound–gesture relationships.

Gestural Schemas in Musical Sound

Obviously, there are innumerable close links between musical sound and gestures, as can be seen everywhere in musical performance, in dance, and in all kinds of everyday listening situations. We usually see some kind of synchrony between the music and the gestures that listeners make, but otherwise we may see great variations in the gestures that different people make to the one and same piece of music. In our context of musical sound and coarticulation, it may be of particular interest that listeners with very different levels of expertise seem to be able to play 'air instruments' quite well, meaning that even non-experts demonstrate quite detailed associations between musical sound and the corresponding sound-producing gestures (Godøy et al. 2006).

Some sound–motor couplings seem to be 'hard wired', that is, are due to direct neurophysiological connections in the brain (Kohler et al. 2002), but in general, it seems that we have a capacity for readily learning sound–motor couplings, as was claimed by the so-called *motor theory* of perception several decades ago (Liberman & Mattingly 1985), and which is now quite well supported by converging evidence from several different domains (Galantucci et al. 2006). The motor theory (with various variations) claims that perceiving sound is closely linked with mentally simulating the gestures that we believe have been made in the production of that sound. Some recent neurophysiological research suggests that perception and cognition in general is a matter of simulating the actions we assume are related to what we perceive: 'to perceive an action is equivalent to internally simulating it' (Gallese & Metzinger 2003: 383). And: 'This enables the observer to use her/his own resources to penetrate the world of the other by means of an implicit, automatic, and unconscious process of motor simulation' (: 383). In our context, this means that when listening to music (or even just imagining music with our 'inner ear') we may very well mentally simulate some of the sound-producing gestures that we have previously learned go with the music; for example, energetic movements of the arms with ferocious drum sounds, long protracted gestures with sustained string sounds, and so on.

These associations of musical sound with sound-producing gestures could be regarded as integral to music perception, leading to the idea that any sound will be included in some mental image of a gestural trajectory, which is what I previously have termed *motor-mimetic cognition* (Godøy 2003). From such a motor-mimetic perspective, it would hardly be possible to think of sound as not belonging to some gesture, and notably so, a gesture that is primordial to the sound: a piano sound would be included in a gesture involving movement of a finger, a hand, an arm, and even the torso; a violin sound would be included in the preparatory bow positioning before the start of the stroke as well as in the stroke itself. In cases of several sounds in succession as in a rapidly played ornament, all the sounds may be included in one superordinate gesture, a phenomenon that now brings us to the topic of coarticulation.

Principles of Coarticulation

As defined above, chunking musical sound means that several events, including note onsets, pitch changes and timbral evolutions, are fused into a larger unit. Typically, these individual events, events we for clarity's sake could call *atom events*, overlap with neighbouring events in a contextual 'smearing' and actually lose some of their individual features in favour of the emergent features of the chunk as a whole. Notably, exactly the same goes for atom events of sound production: individual key presses, drum stokes, string depressions and other such events are fused into larger action units. This fusion of atom events, both in sound and in sound-producing actions, is the essence of what we call *coarticulation*.

Speaking of atom events that are fused into coarticulated chunks may be misleading in terms of what comes first: the atom events, or the coarticulated chunk? One consequence of above-mentioned ideas on the primordial nature of sound-producing gestures is to turn our understanding here upside down, meaning that we really ought to regard coarticulated chunks as primordial to their atom events. Ontogenetically, we may guess that musical utterances in the form of phrases or 'sonic gestures' came before notions of individual tones, and in an ethnomusicological perspective, it is not obvious that atom events in the form of notes are primordial to phrases. In Western music history, it is interesting to remember that neume notation actually had elements of phrase notation and not only discrete pitches. Western music notation and music theory has (for good and bad) given individual notes an abstract status that has diverted attention away from the primordial role of sound producing gestures. The point now is to not regard coarticulation as something added to tones, but rather regard tones as something we abstract from coarticulated gestures.

In linguistics, there are very many publications concerned with coarticulation (see Hardcastle & Hewitt 1999 for an overview), and they are all essentially concerned with the way individual phonemes are fused, or assimilated in what is often referred to as 'continuous speech'. As an example:

> Look into a mirror and say (rather deliberately) the word *tulip*. If you look closely, you will notice that your lips round before you say 't', Speech scientists call this phenomenon *anticipatory lip rounding*. ... anticipatory lip rounding suggests that a plan for the entire word is available before the word is produced. If 'tulip' were produced in a piece-meal fashion, with each sound planned only after the preceding sound was produced, the rounding of the lips required of 'u' would only occur *after* 't' was uttered. (Rosenbaum 1991: 14)

Similarly, 'anticipatory lip rounding illustrates a general tendency that any theory of serial ordering must account for—the tendency of effectors to coarticulate' (Rosenbaum 1991: 15). The reference to serial ordering in this quote concerns the above-mentioned problem posed by Lashley and his suggested solution of anticipatory behaviour. Rosenbaum then goes on to give the following definition of coarticulation: 'The term *coarticulation* refers to the simultaneous motions of effectors that help achieve a temporally extended task' (1991: 15), and adds the comment that coarticulation is not restricted to speech and that, although coarticulation may be difficult to explain:

> It is a blessing for us as behaving organisms. Think about a typist who could move only one finger at a time. Lacking the capacity for finger coarticulation, the person's typing speed would be very slow. Simultaneous movements of the fingers allow for rapid responding, just as concurrent movements of the tongue, lips and velum allow for rapid speech. Coarticulation is an effective method for increasing response speed given that individual effectors (body parts used for movement) may move relatively slowly. (Rosenbaum 1991: 15)

Although linguistics clearly has dominated the topic of coarticulation, coarticulation is, as Rosenbaum stated, applicable to any domain of motion where there is a concatenation of otherwise distinct atom events. We have seen some examples of research on coarticulation in other areas such as facial animation (Cohen & Massaro 1993), fingerspelling (Jerde et al. 2003), as well as a few applications in music (see the references below). However, we are for the moment just barely starting to understand how coarticulation works in music, and there are some general principles here that I believe we should bear in mind:

- *Anticipatory cognition*, in the sense of both planning ahead and of actually moving effectors in place before they do their job, is an essential feature of coarticulation, and means that coarticulation works by considering whole chunks at a time, cf. the theories of chunking mentioned above.

- *Goal postures or keyframes*, in the sense of targets for the action trajectories, seem to be well supported in human movement science. This also implies a distinction between goal postures and the intervening trajectories, or between keyframes and interframes (Rosenbaum et al. 2007). The importance of key postures over intervening trajectories furthermore seems to be the case in imitative behaviour (Wohlschläger et al. 2003), something that we ourselves could observe in our air instrument studies (Godøy et al. 2006). In particular, it makes sense to see coarticulation in music in relation to goal postures in the form of targets for the action trajectories, either as accent points or as pitch contour peaks, or as combinations of these, and not just as a continuous, unbroken, even stream of effort. Sound-producing actions in music (as in spoken language) are usually constantly changing direction, constantly accelerating or decelerating, and constantly shifting between effort and relaxation, often making use of rebounds to conserve energy (Dahl 2006).

- *Contextual smearing*, meaning that the borders between the atom events are made unclear both in the gestures and in the sound, or both in the production and in the perception. This means that atom events lose many of their otherwise individual features and may become indistinct in favour of more prominent features of the chunk as a whole. This also means that the coarticulated chunk must be conceived (planned) as a whole and perceived (listened to) as a whole, and that all elements of the chunk will linger on for a while in short-term memory. Actually, this is similar to what happens in the perception of a single (isolated) tone or sound; the different stages of the envelope (attack, sustain, decay and various transients or fluctuations in the course of the sound) mutually influence each other (so that we could say time is bi-directional within the sound at this level of resolution).

- *Mass-spring models*, meaning that the energy involved in the sound production often is unevenly distributed, often having the form of peaks followed by decays, or impulses followed by rebounds, as is apparent in drumming, piano performance and probably other performances as well. The point is that event atoms may be included in such mass-spring actions, like in the rebound of the mallets in drumming or the rebound of the hands in piano performance. Such mass-spring types of excitatory gestures may occur even in cases where the effector is in contact with the instrument before the impact; for example, finger on the key, where the origin of the impulse is probably higher up (in the shoulder/torso) and travels outward to the effector (cf. the notion of whiplash action in Dahl 2006). With these elements of mass-spring systems and of contextual smearing, we could also extend our notion of coarticulation to include the phenomenon of multiple excitations with instruments that are capable of being excited repeatedly (for instance, struck, stroked or bowed), such as membranes, tubes, bells and piano (with depressed sustain pedal), where the sounds of successive excitations linger on and fuse into more composite sonic objects.

- *Coarticulation both in sound production and in sound perception*, meaning that what goes on in sound production also has consequences for sound perception, and that the contextual smearing is in fact a feature of sound. We shall now have a brief look at coarticulation, first as a phenomenon of sound production and then as an element in sound perception.

Coarticulation in Sound Production

Clearly, coarticulatory anticipation is readily observable in various instrumental performances. In one of the few studies of coarticulation in music that have been published so far, we can read the following on what was observed in cases of piano performance:

> The results of this study show that the motor apparatus controlling motion of the hand and fingers exhibits features similar to those characterizing the control of speech production. We have described the equivalent of the phenomenon of 'coarticulation' in speech for hand and finger movements. Such anticipatory modifications of the movement were found to be variable from piece to piece and from subject to subject, and it is likely that this phenomenon reflects the task demands of the different pieces and the capabilities and physical constraints (such as fingerspan) of each subject. In fact, we observed a continuum in the extent of anticipatory modifications of finger and hand kinematics, ranging from as much as 500 ms in advance of the time of the last common note to about 15 ms after the time of key-on of this note. (Engel et al. 1997: 198)

Coarticulation may also be found in the performance on string instruments in the form of anticipatory finger placement (Wiesendanger et al. 2006), as well as on wind instruments, where performers practice transitions in numerous constellations in order to achieve smooth transitions and as homogenous a quality of tone as possible (Jerde et al. 2006). We may also assume that coarticulation can be found in singing in similar ways to in phonemic transitions in spoken language. Furthermore, similar formantic transitions can be produced on some instruments, such as on brass instruments by moving the mutes or on string instruments by moving the bow position; in short, any timbral change that may be perceived as an action trajectory may also be understood as a kind of coarticulation because of the gradual change in the resonant features (as is the case with our vocal apparatus). In addition, such formantic transitions may be produced by digital sound synthesis and signal processing, for instance by different time-varying filters or by diphone synthesis. This is of course an artificial coarticulation, but the mental schema of coarticulation could still be useful in a perceptual perspective as what we could call an anthropomorphic projection.

On wind instruments, one may observe upper body and instrument movement called *ancillary gestures*, gestures that musicians make spontaneously and that are remarkably stable across repeated performances (Vines et al. 2006). Although these gestures are not indispensable (musicians can do without them when asked to), one might assume that these are some kind of facilitating coarticulatory gestures, shaping the performance on a higher level of motor control and musical intention. Also for other instruments, for example piano or strings, it may not always be clear what are strictly sound-producing coarticulatory gestures (that is gestures necessary because of biomechanical constraints), what are more expressive and sound-shaping gestures, and what are perhaps outright theatrical gestures by way of exaggerating what at the outset could have been more strictly necessary sound-producing coarticulatory gestures.

Furthermore, sound-producing gestures are goal directed in the sense that they both aim for *targets on the instrument* (or for a certain shape of the vocal apparatus in the case of singing) and *targets at certain points in time*. We can thus speak about goal postures, or keyframes, in time, and we find these typically at accented points, that is at downbeats (in metrically clear music) or other accent points (both in non-metrical and metrical music, in the latter case with accents that contradict the usual metrical accents), or salient points in melodic contours. We may typically also have trajectories to and from any key posture, trajectories we could call respectively *prefix* and *suffix* of any goal point; for example, an upbeat gesture to a downbeat point followed by a return to the initial position. In this sense, coarticulation is not just a matter of anticipatory finger movements as suggested in studies of piano playing (Engel et al. 1997; Jabusch 2006; Jerde et al. 2006; Palmer 2006), but concerns the energy distribution over an entire chunk, as suggested by the very early preparation of accented strokes in drumming (Dahl 2006). The energy distribution in the coarticulated chunk could also have consequences for other parts of the effector apparatus; for example, it could involve movements of the arms, shoulders, and even torso when performing on a piano and on other instruments. In our ongoing studies of coarticulation in piano performance, we can clearly see this involvement of other body parts in order to position the fingers in optimal positions for depressing the piano keys. In Figure 3.1 we see the movements of the right wrist, elbow and shoulder joints of a pianist in relation to the onsets of tones in a rapid triplet figure, and in the bottom part of Figure 3.1, we see the movements of the whole body in addition to the movements of the fingers.

Coarticulation should be understood as a naturally emergent phenomenon on the basis of our biomechanical and neurocognitive constraints, i.e. understood as an efficient way to carry out tasks with the effectors that we have, and at the same time increasing fluency and reducing energy cost and risk of strain injury. Similarly, there are some other emergent phenomena we may observe in musical performance such as in drumming (Dahl 2006) and in bowing (Rasamimanana et al. 2007) of so-called *phase transitions* in cases where fast movements are required, a phenomenon that is well known from dynamical theory (Haken et al. 1985).

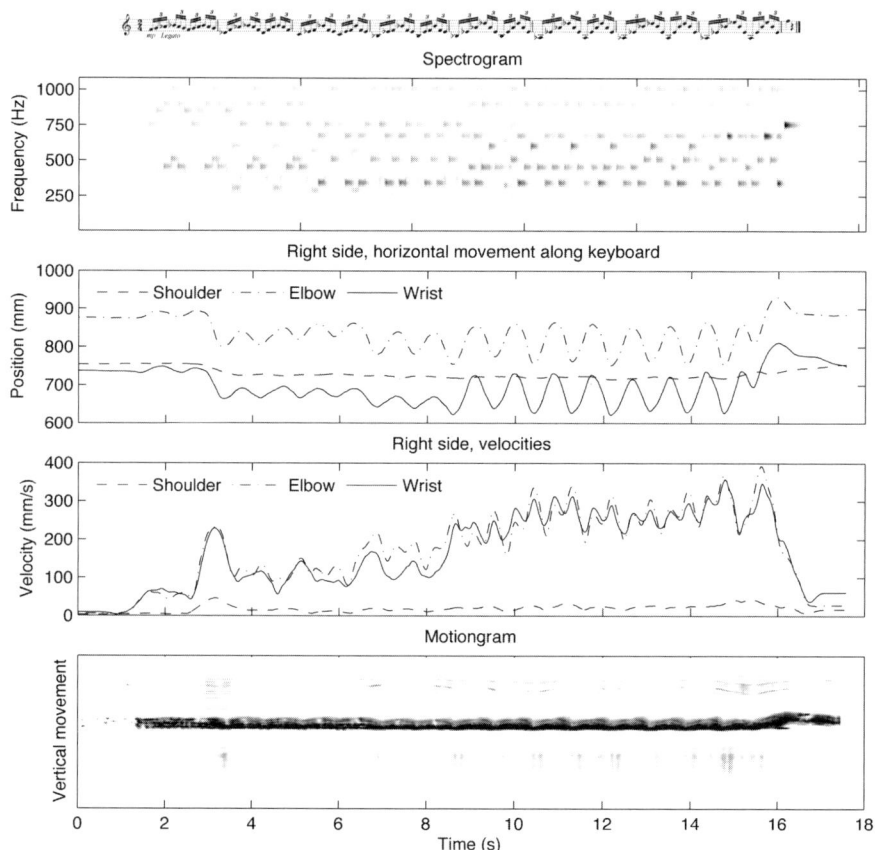

Figure 3.1   A pianist's performance of a rapid triplet figure on the piano with the right hand. The top of the figure shows the triplets in conventional notation, and below this, the spectrogram of the actual performance. The next box shows the horizontal movement (in relation to the keyboard) of the right wrist, elbow and shoulder (based on marker positions recorded by an infra-red motion capture system), and the next box shows the velocities of the same wrist, elbow and shoulder movements. Notice the increased velocities of wrist and elbow movements with increasing interval sizes in the triplet figure. The lower part of the figure shows a so-called *motiongram* of the fingers and the rest of the body of the pianist as seen from in front of the piano. Motiongrams are images made by compressing each frame of video to one line such as to display motion patterns over a certain extent of time in one still picture (see Jensenius 2007 for details)

These phase transitions may be understood as a way to solve a problem, that is in the case of fast drumming or bowing, by decreasing the amplitude of the movements in order to increase the speed, but it is not clear whether this is due to biomechanical or motor control constraints. It would not seem far-fetched to assume that we may find similar phase transitions based on effector speed and amplitude variables in coarticulation, and this is something that we presently are focussing on in our research.

Coarticulation in Sound Perception

Coarticulation forces us to have holistic perceptions of whole chunks of musical sound because of the contextual smearing of various features within the chunk. This means that the overall features of the chunk are important, such as its contour or shape and its evolution with respect to its internal features, or such as in its evolution in harmonic content, perceived pitch or intensity. Coarticulation consistently works on the level of the chunk, and once we appreciate this, we can see how coarticulated gestures can work as schemas in the perception of several important features of musical sound:

- *Rhythmic patterns*, where the atom events are fused into coarticulated chunks, are often centred on goal points in the form of accent points, either as downbeats or as other accents, and often with upbeat prefixes and rebound suffixes. This also means that cyclical patterns such as metre can be understood as instances of coarticulation where downbeats equal goal postures at goal times, upbeats equal prefixes, and rebounds equal suffixes. Such a coarticulation understanding of cyclical patterns may also accommodate various variations (for example, accented 2s and 4s, being slightly ahead or after the beat, and so on.), as variant trajectory shapes within the overall coarticulatory shape.
- *Textural fragments*, where there also may be motion at simultaneously different frequencies – for instance, fast repeated arpeggio figures together with slower displacements of the registers of the figures – may be understood as coarticulated movements with an overall slower trajectory containing faster sub-movements (cf. Figure 3.1 above).
- *Melodic motives and contours* may arise where several tones are fused into one superordinate gesture trajectory.
- *Tone semantic features*, meaning the emergent, contextual effects of sequentially presented tones fusing into a holistically perceived chunk having distinct modal flavours (Persichetti 1962), recognize that modal qualities reside in the holistic perception of a sequence of tones simultaneously present in short-term memory.
- *Timbral contours* may arise where there is a spectral change, such as in vowel transitions in language, various mute displacements in brass

instruments, or bow displacements in string instruments. An example of this can be seen in Figure 3.2 where there is a timbral change in a trumpet sound made by a time varying formantic filter.

• *Shapes, envelopes, and contours of any kind in any kinds of music*, be that instrumental, vocal or electroacoustic, may be identified as a matter of perhaps more metaphoric projection of coarticulatory schemas, as long as the sound is short enough to be perceived holistically as a chunk. An example of this from electroacoustic music can be seen in Figure 3.3 where the last sonic object of the figure is a fusion of the two first sonic objects.

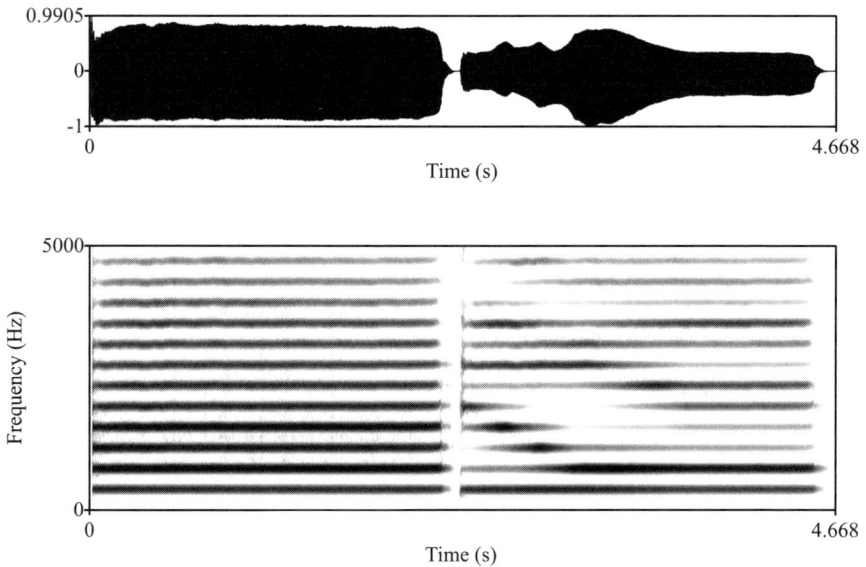

Figure 3.2   The waveform (top) and the spectrogram (bottom) of a trumpet sound in the left part of the figure and the same trumpet sound processed with a time-varying formantic filter so as to produce a sound that resembles the vowel transition o–e–u–i, hence is a timbral trajectory that can be perceived as a coarticulated sonic object

In general, we should remember that in spoken language, the coarticulatory smearing is just simply the way language works, usually unproblematic except for when trying to learn a foreign language, or when trying to make machines understand continuous speech. In music, the situation is similar in that we listen to and enjoy the music without worrying about there being a contextual smearing of sound due to coarticulation. In other words, coarticulation is a natural phenomenon in music, and the problem is rather that we have become so used to note atoms as the 'building blocks' of music that we have lost sight of this.

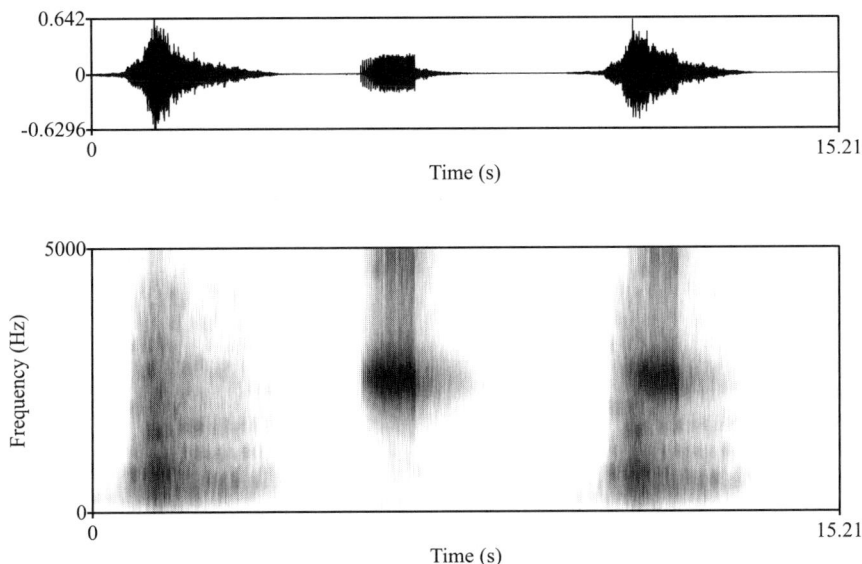

Figure 3.3   Here we see the waveform (top) and the spectrogram of a coarticulated
electroacoustic sonic object. The first two parts of the waveform and
the spectrogram are two separate sonic objects and the third part
of the waveform and spectrogram is the fused, coarticulated sonic
object made up of the two preceding sonic objects. This is what is
called a *composite sonic object* in Pierre Schaeffer's theory, and this
sound example may be found in Schaeffer (1998: CD3, tracks 2–3)

Conclusion

The main ideas of this chapter are summarized briefly below:

- Tones (or sonic events in general) are included in action trajectories.
- Sound-producing gestures are primordial to tones.
- Sound-producing gestures influence the chunking of musical sound.
- Coarticulation is a naturally emergent phenomenon of sound-producing actions.
- Contextual smearing and other emergent features are the result of coarticulation.
- Coarticulation is essential for coherence of melodic fragments.
- Coarticulation is essential for rhythmic grouping, articulation and expressivity.

Needless to say, we are presently only beginning to understand coarticulation
in music. It is hoped that future advances in technologies for motion capture as

well as for studying the neurophysiological components of sound production and sound perception will contribute here, as will also simulation and modelling of sound-producing actions. However, from what is already known about human movement and sound perception, there can be little doubt that coarticulation plays an important role in the generation and perception of musical sound, and that focussing on coarticulation will enhance our understanding of music as an embodied phenomenon.

References

Bregman, A. (1990). *Auditory Scene Analysis*. Cambridge, MA: MIT Press.

Cambouropoulos, E. (2006). Musical Parallelism and Melodic Segmentation: A Computational Approach. *Music Perception* 23: 249–69.

Cohen, M. M. & Massaro, D. W. (1993). Modeling Coarticulation in Synthetic Visual Speech. In N. Thalmann & D. Thalmann (eds), *Models and Techniques in Computer Animation* (pp. 139–56). Tokyo: Springer-Verlag.

Dahl, S. (2006). Movements and Analysis of Drumming. In E. Altenmüller, M. Wiesendanger & J. Kesselring (eds), *Music, Motor Control and the Brain* (pp. 125–38). Oxford: Oxford University Press.

Eitan, Z. & Granot, R. Y. (2008). Growing Oranges on Mozart's Apple Tree: 'Inner form' and Aesthetic Judgment. *Music Perception* 25: 397–417.

Elliott, D., Helsen, W. & Chua, R. (2001). A Century Later: Woodworth's (1899) Two-Component Model of Goal-Directed Aiming. *Psychological Bulletin* 127: 342–57.

Engel, A. K., Fries, P. & Singer, W. (2001). Dynamic Predictions: Oscillations and Synchrony in Top-Down Processing. *Nature Reviews Neuroscience* 2/10: 704–16.

Engel, K. C., Flanders, M. & Soechting, J. F. (1997). Anticipatory and Sequential Motor Control in Piano Playing. *Experimental Brain Research* 113: 189–99.

Fraisse, P. (1982). Rhythm and Tempo. In D. Deutsch (ed.), *The Psychology of Music* (pp. 149–80). New York: Academic Press.

Galantucci, B., Fowler, C. A. & Turvey, M. T. (2006). The Motor Theory of Speech Perception Reviewed. *Psychonomic Bulletin & Review* 13: 361–77.

Gallese, V. & Metzinger, T. (2003). Motor Ontology: The Representational Reality of Goals, Actions and Selves. *Philosophical Psychology* 13: 365–88.

Godøy, R. I. (2003). Motor-Mimetic Music Cognition. *Leonardo* 36: 317–19.

— (2006). Gestural-Sonorous Objects: Embodied Extensions of Schaeffer's Conceptual Apparatus. *Organised Sound* 11: 149–57.

—, Haga, E. & Jensenius, A. (2006). Playing 'Air Instruments': Mimicry of Sound Producing Gestures by Novices and Experts. In S. Gibet, N. Courty & J. F. Kamp (eds), *Gesture in Human–Computer Interaction and Simulation: Sixth International Gesture Workshop, Berder Island, France, 18–20 May 2005* (pp. 256–67). Springer-Verlag: Berlin.

Haken, H., Kelso, J. A. S. & Bunz, H. (1985). A Theoretical Model of Phase Transitions in Human Hand Movements. *Biological Cybernetics* 51: 347–56.

Hardcastle, W. & Hewlett, N. (eds) (1999). *Coarticulation: Theory, Data and Techniques*. Cambridge: Cambridge University Press.

Husserl, E. (1964). *The Phenomenology of Internal Time Consciousness* (trans. J. S. Churchill). Bloomington: Indiana University Press.

ISMIR (n.d.) ISMIR – The International Society for Music Information Retrieval (http://www.ismir.net/; accessed 18 November 2010).

Jabusch, H. C. (2006). Movement Analysis in Pianists. In E. Altenmüller, M. Wiesendanger & J. Kesselring (eds), *Music, Motor Control and the Brain* (pp. 91–108). Oxford: Oxford University Press.

Jensenius, A. R. (2007). *Action-Sound: Developing Methods and Tools to Study Music-Related Body Movement*. PhD dissertation, University of Oslo,.

Jerde, T. E., Santello, M., Flanders, M. & Soechting, J. F. (2006). Hand Movements and Musical Performance. In E. Altenmüller, M. Wiesendanger & J. Kesselring (eds), *Music, Motor Control and the Brain* (pp. 79–90). Oxford: Oxford University Press.

— , Soechting, J. F. & Flanders, M. (2003). Coarticulation in Fluent Fingerspelling. *Journal of Neuroscience* 23: 2383–93.

Kohler, E., Keysers, C., Umiltà, M. A., Fogassi, L., Gallese, V. & Rizzolatti, G. (2002). Hearing Sounds, Understanding Actions: Action Representation in Mirror Neurons. *Science* 297: 846–8.

Lashley, K. S. (1951). The Problem of Serial Order in Behavior. In L. A. Jeffress (ed.), *Cerebral Mechanisms in Behavior* (pp. 112–31). New York: Wiley.

Leman, M. (2008). Embodied Music Cognition and Mediation Technology. Cambridge, MA: MIT Press.

Lerdahl, F. & Jackendoff, R. (1983). *A Generative Theory of Tonal Music*. Cambridge, MA: MIT Press.

Liberman, A. M. & Mattingly, I. G. (1985). The Motor Theory of Speech Perception Revised. *Cognition* 21: 1–36.

Miller, G. A. (1956). The Magic Number Seven, Plus or Minus Two: Some Limits on our Capacity for Processing information. *Psychological Review* 63: 81–97.

Palmer, C. (2006). The Nature of Memory for Music Performance Skills. In E. Altenmüller, M. Wiesendanger & J. Kesselring (eds), *Music, Motor Control and the Brain* (pp. 39–53). Oxford: Oxford University Press.

Persichetti, V. (1962). *Twentieth Century Harmony*. London: Faber and Faber.

Pöppel, E. (1997). A Hierarchical Model of Time Perception. *Trends in Cognitive Science* 1: 56–61.

Rasamimanana, N., Bernardin, D., Wanderley, M. & Bevilacqua, F. (2007). String Bowing Gestures at Varying Bow Stroke Frequencies: A Case Study. In M. S. Dias and R. Jota (eds), *Proceedings of GW2007: Seventh International Workshop on Gesture in Human-Computer Interaction and Simulation, Lisbon, 2007* (pp. 62–3).

Ricoeur, P. (1981). *Hermeneutics and the Human Sciences*. Cambridge: Cambridge University Press.

Rosenbaum, D. A. (1991). *Human Motor Control*. San Diego: Academic Press.

Rosenbaum, D. A., Cohen, R. G., Jax, S. A., Weiss, D. J. & van der Wel, R. (2007). The Problem of Serial Order in Behavior: Lashley's Legacy. *Human Movement Science* 26: 525–54.

Schaeffer, P. (1966). *Traité des Objets Musicaux*. Paris: Éditions du Seuil.

— (1998). *Solfège de l'Objet Sonore*. Paris: INA/GRM.

Schleidt, M., & Kien, J. (1997). Segmentation in Behavior and What it can Tell us about Brain Function. *Human Nature* 8: 77–111.

Schoenberg, A. (1967). *Fundamentals of Musical Composition*. London: Faber & Faber.

Snyder, B. (2000). *Music and Memory: An Introduction*. Cambridge, MA: MIT Press.

University of Oslo (2010). fourMs - Music, Mind, Motion, Machines (http://fourms.uio.no; accessed 18 November 2010).

Varela, F. (1999). The Specious Present: The Neurophenomenology of Time Consciousness. In J. Petitot, F. J. Varela, B. Pachoud & J. M. Roy (eds), *Naturalizing Phenomenology* (pp. 266–314). Stanford: Stanford University Press.

Vines, B., Dalca, I. & Wanderley, M. (2006). Variation in Expressive Physical Gestures of Clarinetists. In M. Baroni, A. R. Addessi, R. Caterina & M. Costa (eds), *Proceedings of the Ninth International Conference on Music Perception & Cognition (ICMPC9), Bologna, 22–26 August 2006* (pp. 1721–2). Bologna: SMPC & ESCOM.

Wiesendanger, M., Baader, A. & Kazennikov, O. (2006). Fingering and Bowing in Violinists: A Motor Control Approach. In E. Altenmüller, M. Wiesendanger & J. Kesselring (eds), *Music, Motor Control and the Brain* (pp. 109–23). Oxford: Oxford University Press.

Wohlschläger, A., Gattis, M. & Bekkering, H. (2003). Action Generation and Action Perception in Imitation: An Instance of the Ideomotor Principle. *Philosophical Transactions of the Royal Society of London* B 358: 501–15.

Woodworth, R. S. (1899). The Accuracy of Voluntary Movement. *Psychological Review* 3: 1–119.

Chapter 4

Musical Gesture and Musical Grammar: A Cognitive Approach

Lawrence M. Zbikowski

A case could be made that our notion of musical gesture is a thoroughly metaphorical one. Physical gestures – pointing with one's hand, or nodding one's head – are typically soundless. Musical gestures, by contrast, are all about sound, or more specifically about *sequences* of sounds. And although musical gestures are often (although not exclusively) produced by physical actions, there may be no correlation between the gesture and the sound that produced it: an arch-like musical gesture, for instance, might well be produced by a decidedly lateral motion with no appreciable up and down component. Finally, physical gestures – and especially the sort of physical gestures on which I would like to focus – are often correlated with speech, as when the phrase 'The book is over there' is accompanied by the speaker pointing with their hand, or when the utterance 'That's a quite good idea' is accompanied by nodding. In both cases the gesture adds something crucial to communication: in the first case, an indication of the location of the book (that is, a specification of where 'there' is); in the second case, adding affirmation to the evaluation (the idea is not only a good one, but one with which the speaker agrees). To expand on this point just a bit, consider how our understanding would change if the statement 'That's a quite good idea' were accompanied by the speaker *shaking* their head. One interpretation of such behaviour might be that the speaker is both sharing their positive evaluation of the idea and wondering why they didn't think of it first. In all three cases the physical gestures add information that is not included in the linguistic constructions uttered by the speaker. The same, generally speaking, is not true of musical gestures – or at least is not true of musical gestures as we usually think of them.

On this evidence, it would seem that the notion of musical gesture is indeed a metaphorical one. We can add some particularity to this assessment through the framework provided by the contemporary theory of metaphor (Grady 2007; Lakoff 1993; Zbikowski 2008b): 'musical gesture', as it is conventionally construed, reflects a conceptual mapping in which knowledge from one domain of experience (namely, *physical gestures*) is used to structure another domain of experience (*sequences of musical materials*) with the goal of organizing our understanding of the second domain. According to this interpretation, when we describe the sequence of pitches E–F♯–G–F♯–E as an 'arch-like gesture' we are using our knowledge about physical gestures (specifically, those that trace the pattern of an arch) to characterize musical sounds. This mapping offers a visual analogue for the musical sounds (and here I would wish to set to one side the way the pitches are rendered in staff notation, which I regard as supporting but not necessary to their visualization) as well as a kinesthetic analogue: the pitches of the musical gesture 'rise and fall' (as does a physical gesture that traces an arch) *and* there is a sense of repose when, after this trajectory, the sequence of pitches returns to its starting point.

While I am perfectly comfortable with this perspective on musical gesture, and would agree that many descriptions of musical gesture are based on this sort of metaphorical mapping, in what follows I would like to explore the idea that the communicative function demonstrated by the physical gestures that accompany speech is one shared by sequences of musical materials. Here I should be a bit more specific about the physical gestures on which I wish to focus, which are somewhat different from deictic gestures such as pointing, or conventional gestures such as nodding. The gestures that are my concern are more spontaneous, created on the fly in the process of discourse. In one attested case, for instance, a speaker accompanied the utterance 'And he went up a winding staircase' by making a spiral motion with his index finger pointing upward, a gesture that made clear that the ascent was up a circular staircase (Iverson and Goldin-Meadow 1997: 458). Again, the information provided by the gesture is distinct from – and even of a different sort than – that provided by the utterance: where the linguistic construction gives us a general picture of the events (a person ascending a staircase) the gesture gives us a dynamic analogue for the actual process of ascent, from which we then infer the physical characteristics of the staircase. I would like to propose that the sequences of sound events proper to music can, in a similar fashion, provide analogues for dynamic processes. There are, however, two important differences between these two means of creating analogues for dynamic processes. First, where the physical gestures that accompany speech are closely linked to language, the sonic analogues of music are largely independent of language. Second, while it is generally recognized that the gestures that accompany speech do not have a grammar, I would like to propose that sonic analogues are *basic* to musical grammar. From this perspective, then, the notion of a musical gesture is not a metaphorical one but a reflection of the essential materials of musical expression.

I would like to use this chapter explore some of these topics in a bit more detail. In the first section I shall sketch a cognitively based approach to musical structure, using as my example Jerome Kern and Dorothy Fields's 'The Way You Look Tonight', a tune written for the 1935 Fred Astaire and Ginger Rogers' vehicle *Swing Time*. In the second section, I shall review recent work by the psycholinguist David McNeill and others on the spontaneous gestures that accompany speech, with particular attention to how the thought processes associated with such gestures correlate with the thought processes revealed through speech. McNeill's analysis of the structure of gestures can help us understand some of the features of 'The Way You Look Tonight', a connection I explore in the third section, in which I shall also elaborate further my approach to musical grammar. In the fourth section, I want to take a closer look at the gestures Fred Astaire makes as he performs the song in the course of the movie, gestures that suggest a very close relationship between the basic materials of music and the physical gestures that accompany language, and that can help us better understand some of the properties of musical grammar.

The Musical Materials of 'The Way You Look Tonight'

Let me begin, then, with an analysis of some of the musical materials Kern made use of in crafting 'The Way You Look Tonight' (Example 4.1 provides a lead sheet for the song). As do many of the songs of this period, 'The Way You Look Tonight' has an AABA' form; in what follows my principal focus will be on the melody of the first A section. One way to both describe and hear this melody is in terms of a number of smaller units. There is, for instance, the falling fifth of bars 1 and 2, which is answered by the arch-like rise and fall through a third that occupies bars 3 and 4. The latter motion is replicated (a step higher) in bars 5 and 6, and again in bars 7 and 8. This last arch turns out to be a bit more complicated, for as soon as it has returned to its starting G it ascends once more, this time continuing up to the D of bar 9. After the continuous crotchets of bars 7 and 8 there is a leisurely fall from the D of bar 9 to the D of bar 10, a descent through an octave that both echoes and expands the descent through a fifth of bars 1 and 2. (The connection between these two moments in the melody is all the stronger in that they both stand at the beginning of an eight-bar sub-phrase, and both conclude on D.) The octave descent of bars 9 and 10 is followed by a figure that ascends and descends, much as did the figures of bars 3 and 4, and 5 and 6, but with important differences: the arch is not as smooth; the durations of the notes become longer (in successive stages); and the entire figure ends on D, a whole step below where it started.

The small units that I have described – the opening falling fifth, or the arch-like melody of bars 3 and 4 – are often called musical motives; in that these units combine pitch and rhythmic materials, they are also similar to Arnold Schoenberg's *Grundgestalten*. As part of my efforts to approach such basic materials in a way that conforms with recent research in cognitive science, I have suggested that such units could be thought of as categories of musical events (Zbikowski 2002: Chapter 1). Bars 1 and 2, and 9 and 10, for instance, could be put into one category – let's call it Category X – and bars 3 and 4, and 5 and 6, could be put into another – Category Y. Note that all of the members of a category need not be identical to one another. For instance, bars 7 and 8 could well be included in Category Y, but with the understanding that they are less typical of the category than are bars 3 and 4, or 5 and 6. In general, the categories basic to musical understanding demonstrate what are called typicality effects: membership in the category is graded, and some members are more typical of the category than are others.

Although it may seem somewhat cumbersome to think of the constituent pitch sequences of 'The Way You Look Tonight' as members of a cognitive category rather than musical motives or instances of a Grundgestalt, this approach comes

Example 4.1   Lead sheet for 'The Way You Look Tonight' by Jerome Kern and
              Dorothy Fields

with two advantages. First, by drawing on the explanatory framework provided by empirical research on typicality effects in categories it becomes possible to describe in a principled and consistent way relationships between non-identical but similar sequences of musical materials. Although I shall not pursue such a description here (having already done so for works by Mozart and Beethoven in Zbikowski 1999 and 2002), this methodology offers an important resource to those who would seek to understand relationships between musical materials – and not just those conventionally described as 'motives' – over the course of a work of music. Second, and more significant for the perspective I wish to develop in this chapter, thinking of the basic materials of 'The Way You Look Tonight' in terms of cognitive categories connects these materials with other sorts of categories through which we structure our understanding of the world. This connection can help us to come to terms with the part music plays in our cognitive lives, both as an object of understanding and as a means of structuring knowledge.

With these thoughts in mind, I would like to propose that categorization – understood as an active cognitive process, one used by humans to structure their understanding of the world – offers a way to explain how musical communication comes about. On the one hand, listeners actively organize sound phenomena into musical categories to make sense of what they hear. On the other hand, composers and improvisers structure sequences of musical events so that listeners have easy access to elements out of which musical categories can be built. The overarching idea behind this perspective is that human cognitive capacities shape the production and reception of music. In the approach to musical structure that I have developed over the past few years, I have been interested in how cognitive capacities associated with categorization, as well as those associated with analogy and the use of conceptual models, are manifested in our understanding of music, taking the approach that these capacities inform both the organization and the meaning of music. As I view it, both the organization and meaning of music are central to its grammar, a notion I shall return to toward the end of this chapter.

Gesture and Thought

An interest in the cognitive resources behind communication of the sort that has informed my research on musical structure can also be seen in research on gesture and language. Over the past 25 years David McNeill and his colleagues have developed compelling evidence that the gesture that accompanies language introduces new information into discourse structures. Put another way, the gestures that accompany our speech reflect a mode of thought that is independent from but coordinated with language. Understanding why some parts of our thought are captured by gesture and why others are captured by language gives crucial insight into both the goals of human communication and the way these goals are accomplished.

One way McNeill studied the relationship between gesture and language was to show subjects a short, action-packed, but wordless clip from a cartoon and then ask them to describe what they saw. In a typical example, a 40-second long clip showed a scene in which Sylvester the cat attempts to get to Tweety Bird, who is apparently safe and sound in an apartment many stories above the street, by climbing up the inside of a drainpipe. Tweety manages to thwart this effort by retrieving a bowling ball and dropping it down the drainpipe. The viewer sees the progress of the bowling ball down the drainpipe as well as the moment when it comes into forcible contact with Sylvester, rendered as an almighty crash and noticeable increase in the bulge of the drainpipe. The bowling ball then continues its descent, accompanied by Sylvester, and when both emerge from the end of the drainpipe we see that Sylvester has in fact swallowed the bowling ball. The bowling ball, now inside Sylvester, begins to roll down the street, gradually gathering speed until, at the bottom of the street, it enters a bowling alley, with Sylvester helplessly pulled along the whole way. A moment later we hear the crash of the bowling ball hitting the bowling pins, the force and volume of which suggests that Sylvester has achieved a strike.

In his discussion of these experiments McNeill provided a relatively full transcript of the responses of one subject identified as Viv., which is provided in Table 4.1. In the videotape from which the transcript was drawn (which runs about 20 seconds), Viv. sits in a chair, addressing an off-camera interviewer. As she speaks, she makes a series of small, relatively contained gestures with her hands. McNeill divides Viv.'s description up in accordance with the gestures she makes, yielding the nine lines indicated in the leftmost column of the table; square brackets are used to indicate the initiation and conclusion of each gesture stroke. (The gesture stroke in line 2, for instance, does not begin until Viv. has begun to say 'ball'.)

Table 4.1   McNeill's analysis of gestural catchments in Viv's description of the Sylvester and Tweety Bird scene (adapted from McNeill 2005: 118)

Line	Utterance	Gesture feature	Catchment
1	He tries going [up the inside of the drainpipe and]	1-hand (right)	C1
2	Tweety Bird runs and gets a bowling ba[ll and drops it down the drainpipe]	2-similar hands	C2
3	[and as he's coming up]	2-different hands	C3
4	[and the bowling ball is coming d]	2-different hands	C3
5	[own he swallows it]	2-different hands	C3
6	[and he comes out the bottom of the drai]	1-hand (left)	C1, C3
7	[npipe and he's got this big bowling ball inside h]im	2-similar hands	C2
8	[and he rolls on down into a bowling all]	2-similar hands	C2
9	[ey and then you hear a stri]ke	2-similar hands	C2

In his analysis, McNeill focuses on a small number of gestural features that recur over the course of the description; McNeill calls these structures *catchments*. In general usage, a catchment is something that temporarily catches water – the successive basins of a waterfall are a helpful image. The catchments with which McNeill is concerned are imagistic rather than hydraulic – in his words, 'A catchment is a kind of thread of visuospatial imagery that runs through a discourse to reveal the larger discourse units that encompass the otherwise separate parts' (2005: 116–117). More formally, we might describe a catchment as a distinctive sequence of physical movements that can be combined with similar sequences to create an analogue for a series of events relevant to discourse. McNeill identifies three catchments in this section of Viv.'s discourse. Catchment 1 is concerned with a single moving entity; its recurring gestural feature makes use of just one hand. Catchment 2 is concerned with the bowling ball; its recurring feature is a rounded shape using two similarly shaped hands. Catchment 3 concerns the relative position of the bowling ball and Sylvester in the drainpipe; its recurring feature involves two hands that, through their different functions, represent the appropriate spatial configuration.

What is remarkable about the gestures and language of Viv.'s description is the insight they give into her view of Tweety Bird's role in the scene. Were one to read only the first two lines of the transcript it would be easy to accord Tweety Bird a fairly significant role – after all, he is the agent that drops the bowling ball and sends Sylvester on his way to a strike. Viv.'s gestures, however, tell a different story: her gesture in line 2 begins not with the mention of Tweety Bird but with the description of the bowling ball dropping. As the description continues, the focus is on the bowling ball as an antagonistic force, one that shapes the rest of the scene. The gesture of line 2 thus marks the beginning of a process through which gesture and language, working together, structure thought. McNeill calls the whole of this process a *growth point*. As he puts it, 'Growth points are inferred from the totality of communicative events, with special focus on speech–gesture synchrony and co-expressivity. Semiotically a combination of opposites, image [provided by gesture] and form [provided by language], the growth point creates a benign instability that fuels thought and speech' (McNeill 2005: 105). In the present case, the relevant instability is one that shifts focus onto the bowling ball, and turns *it*, rather than Tweety Bird, into the main antagonistic force of the scene that is then described.

McNeill's research demonstrates two important things about gesture and its relationship to language. First, gesture offers a dynamic, imagistic resource for conveying thoughts that would be cumbersome to express through language. Second, gesture informs and shapes our use of language. As McNeill, Adam Kendon (2004), Susan Goldin-Meadow (2003a, 2003b), and a number of other writers have argued (Duncan et al. 2007), to express our thought we need both the dynamic, imagistic resources of gesture and the firm, stable constructs of language.

Musical Gesture, Physical Gesture, and Musical Grammar

The musical categories I described in my analysis of 'The Way You Look Tonight' might well seem like the firm, stable constructs we typically associate with language, but this is really just an artefact of my analysis. In truth, I think of such categories as highly dynamic structures, analogous in many respects to the catchments described by McNeill. As do gestural catchments, musical catchments contribute to the development of something analogous to a growth point. To explore these ideas, let's return to Kern's tune, this time turning our attention to Dorothy Fields's lyrics. I shall again concentrate on the first verse, with only a few comments on the second and third verse.

The first verse of Dorothy Fields's lyrics is framed with respect to a future state of affairs, which is invoked by the opening 'Someday'. At this future point the speaker, beset with rather dire circumstances – depression and an uncaring world – will be comforted by the remembrance of the object of his affections and, more specifically, by the way she looks on this particular night. As is hinted at by the transformative effect of the appearance of the beloved, and confirmed by the second verse, what is involved here is not simply a kind of passive looking, with one person gazing on another, but an intimacy of association that has both power and depth. The trajectory of the first verse is not simply into a future that looks back to the present as a golden past, but one that establishes 'the way you look tonight' as central to a highly charged romantic relationship.

The trajectories described by the verse have their correlate in the organization of the melody of the tune. Bars 1 and 2, and 9 and 10 – that is, the members of Category X – serve to anchor the tonal frame. These bars are correlated with the words that establish the temporal context that frames the lyrics (the 'Someday' of bars 1–2), and that introduce the beloved (the presumed referent for the 'of you' in bars 9–10). Bars 3 to 8, populated by members of Category Y, explore and expand this tonal frame, in part through destabilizing it. Note, for instance, that the D major harmony implied by bar 5 (and confirmed by the chord symbol) does not act as a stable tonic, but as a way station along an ascending sequential path. It is also in these bars that the lyrics fill out the scene ('When I'm awf'ly low / and the world is cold') and set up the motivation for the contemplation of the beloved ('I will feel a glow just thinking [of you]'). Bars 11 to 14 are occupied with a cadential figure that brings the melody to a close, both through a deceleration of the rhythmic activity and a scalewise descent from A to D. These bars, of course, set the lyrics central to the conceptual frame of the verse: 'the way you look tonight'.

Again, I view these categories as analogous to gestural catchments. As do gestural catchments, these musical catchments interact with and shape the story that is told through language. As one example, in the lyrics set in bars 3–6, which focus on things with a negative valence, the music proceeds with materials typically associated with a positive valence – that is, an orderly, sequential major-mode melody that ascends. This strategy redirects the focus of the line away from the immediate thoughts presented in the lyrics for bars 3–6 and toward the ideas presented in bars 7–10. It is these ideas that draw everything together into a coherent whole with a particularity aimed at the beloved: 'I will feel a glow just thinking of you'. The effect is analogous to that of a growth point: ideas presented by the music and by the lyrics come together in a dynamic process that yields a single unified thought. Similar growth points can be seen in the second and third verses. In the second verse, it is the compelling, even bewitching attractiveness of the beloved that emerges: 'There is nothing for me but to love you'. In the third verse, what emerges is the speaker's desire for reciprocity – the beloved is asked to acknowledge the speaker's love by never changing: 'Won't you please arrange it, 'cause I love you'.

In my review of McNeill's approach to the analysis of gestures I suggested that we could think of a gestural catchment as a distinctive sequence of physical movements that can be combined with similar sequences to create an analogue for a series of events relevant to discourse. As I conceive of it, a musical catchment is a distinctive sequence of sound events that can be combined with similar sequences to create an analogue for a dynamic process. In the case of 'The Way You Look Tonight', the sonic analogues of music – and the dynamic processes with which they are concerned – occur on two levels, one local and quite specific, the other more global and rather less specific. Together, these various sonic analogues not only provide an analogue for gestural catchments, but also the basis for the musical grammar of the passage.

The local level of sonic analogues is occupied with the musical materials of Category X, Category Y and the cadential figure. We need not anchor these categories to specific dynamic processes, but can instead simply note how the kinds of movement they summon contrast with one another: Category X as expansive and leisurely, for instance, and Category Y as more compact, with more of a sense of directed movement. On a more global level, these sonic analogues are organized by syntactic processes. The first such process sets out, in bars 1–4, the materials for musical discourse: Category X and Category Y. These materials are then explored and ramified in bars 5–14. The expansion of the tonal frame enacted in bars 5–8 exploits the open-ended nature of the presentation of Categories X and Y (concluding, as it does, with the melody on scale step 2 in bar 4, harmonized with a dominant seventh chord), and makes use of modified repetitions of Category Y to explore the materials and tonal context established in bars 1–4. When a member of Category X returns, in bars 9–10, it serves both to complete this development of material (as an almost inevitable consequence of the ascending scale of bar 8), to arrest it (by replacing the steady crotchets of the preceding two bars with minims) and to break the regular sequence of two-bar sub-phrases in place from the beginning of the tune. This is, in turn, followed by the cadential figure of bars 11–14, which, as mentioned above, brings the melody to a definitive close. The syntactic processes that organize the musical materials of Category X, Category Y and the cadential figure – the first presenting the topics for musical discourse, the second developing those topics and the third closing off the process of development – are themselves analogues for dynamic processes, but made up not of individual sequences of sounds but of *categories* of such sequences.

I will readily acknowledge that this is a rather novel approach to musical grammar, but it is one that conforms, in its broad outlines, with similar approaches developed by cognitive linguists over the past 20 years. One of the basic assumptions shared by these approaches is that form and function – syntax and semantics, if you like – are deeply linked in the grammar of any mode of communication. With this in mind, I would like to suggest that one of the reasons humans have kept both language and music around is because they have different functions. The most primary and basic function of language within human culture is to direct the attention of another person to objects or concepts within a shared referential frame (Tomasello 1999: Chapter 5). The most primary and basic function of music is to provide sonic analogues for various dynamic processes that are central to human experience, processes that include the movements of our body through space (Zbikowski 2008a), and the physiological transformations associated with emotions. In the grammar of a mode of communication, these functions are linked with forms; this is the basis of what linguists call construction grammar. In the case of language, constructions are 'stored pairings of form and function, including morphemes, words, idioms, partially lexically filled and fully general linguistic patterns' (Goldberg 2003: 219). In the case of music, constructions are sequences of musical materials – such as the members of Category X and Category Y, or the cadential figure that closes off each of the verses – that serve as sonic analogues for dynamic processes. These basic constructions are organized into larger structures through syntactic processes such as those that shaped the melody for the first verse of 'The Way You Look Tonight'; in keeping with the construction grammar approach, in which *all* grammatical elements are pairings of form and function, syntactic processes are themselves sonic analogues for dynamic processes.

It has often been the case that when music theorists have tried to formalize musical grammar they have drawn on their knowledge of linguistic grammar, relying on the sort of metaphorical mapping that has also informed thinking about musical gesture. Thus Heinrich Christoph Koch, writing in 1787, drew comparisons between the organization of language and the organization of music, and suggested that a complete sentence in speech, with subject and predicate, could serve as a model for a complete phrase in music (Koch 1983[1787]: 4). Although I have no doubt that some similarities between music and language obtain, inasmuch as both are the products of human cultures, the different functions each serve within human culture suggests that their grammars will also be different – indeed, it is grammar that makes it possible for each form of communication to realize its function. What these grammars *do* have in common is a reliance on basic features of human cognitive processing, something also shared by the sonic analogues of music and the physical gestures that accompany speech.

Moving to Music

I have been careful, up to this point, to describe musical materials and musical processes as being *analogous* to things that happen in the world of physical gestures. This is not simply technical fastidiousness on my part: in the account of musical organization I seek to develop I want to keep music and gesture separate, if only because music involves sound and gesture typically does not. My assumption, however, is that the two are deeply linked in cognitive organization. Support for this sort of linkage is provided by a scene from the movie *Swing Time*, in which 'The Way You Look Tonight' made its first appearance. In the movie, Fred Astaire plays a dancer who has recently come to New York to earn some money. He encounters Ginger Rogers, who plays a dance instructor, and soon has designs on her, both as a dance partner and a possible romantic interest. In the relevant scene, Astaire is trying to win Rogers over – he has managed to get in to her hotel suite, and, even though she has repeatedly spurned him, gives it his best effort by singing 'The Way You Look Tonight'. Rogers, for her part, has locked herself in her room and started shampooing her hair, which provides the basis a dramatic situation that is both intimate and comedic.

Let me once more focus my comments on the first verse, but in this case because in the movie the performance of the verse is captured in one sustained take, which uses only one camera angle and which has as its sole object Astaire's performance; a still from the opening of the scene is given in Figure 4.1. For my discussion of the gestures Astaire makes in the course of his performance I will rely on line drawings created from still shots taken from the movie; although these drawings will necessarily leave out some very interesting details, they will allow us to focus on the principal features of Astaire's movements.

Figure 4.1   Still of Fred Astaire at the piano from *Swing Time*

On 'Someday', Astaire moves toward the right side of the frame, lifting his shoulders and chin slightly, and then concludes the movement by dipping his head toward the keyboard; the beginning and end of the gesture are shown in Figure 4.2. This gesture is typical of those he makes in his performance: constrained by the conceit that he is accompanying himself on the piano, his movements are restricted to those he can make with his head and his torso. The movements he makes with his arms are much less noticeable and, in that the camera angle takes a view of Astaire from over the top of the piano, are almost invisible.

As Astaire sings 'When I'm awf'ly low' he makes a slight circular motion with his shoulders, moving first to the left of the frame (a displacement not shown in Figure 4.3) and then back past the centre, holding this position for his arrival on the long note that sets 'low'. This same basic movement is repeated as he sings 'And the world is cold'. Astaire then uses a varied version of this movement for the fourth line of lyrics: as shown in the first image of Figure 4.4, he begins

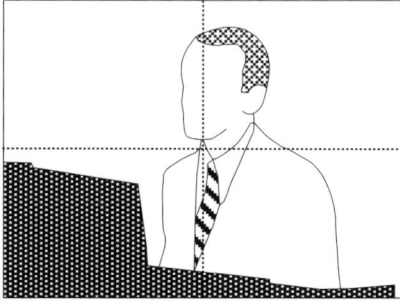
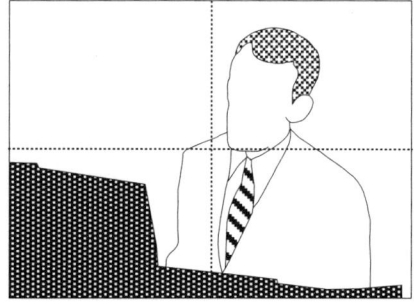

"Some-"   "day"

Figure 4.2   Astaire's gestures as he sings 'Someday'

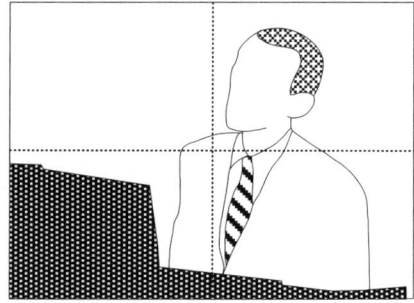

"When I'm"   "awf'ly low"

Figure 4.3   Astaire's gestures as he sings 'When I'm awf'ly low'

'I will feel' in the centre of the frame; as he sings 'a glow just thinking' he moves toward the right and top side of the frame, reaching and holding the extent of this motion on the note that sustains 'of' (shown in the second image of Figure 4.4). For the completion of the line Astaire then moves forward and dips his head, such that as he sings the word 'you' his chin reaches its lowest point in this sequence of gestures. It is worth noting that this is an expansion of the movement he made at the opening of the verse when he sang 'Someday', something that can be seen by comparing the images of Figure 4.2 with the first and last image of Figure 4.4.

For the last line of lyrics Astaire makes use of a new sort of gesture as well as returning to one he used previously. The beginning of the line ('And the') finds him dipping his head just a bit further down than it had been when he sang 'you' and moving toward the left of the frame (compare the last image of Figure 4.4 and the first of Figure 4.5). As he continues with 'way you look to-' he moves

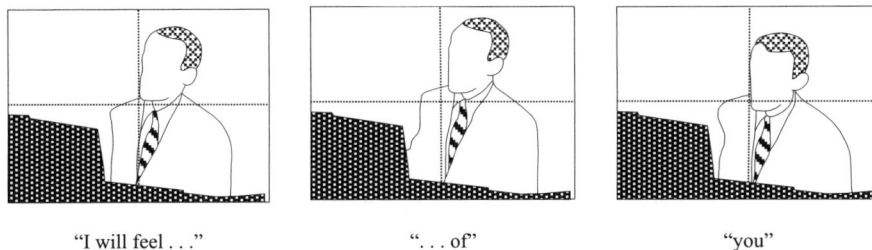

"I will feel . . ."   ". . . of"   "you"

Figure 4.4   Astaire's gestures as he sings 'I will feel [a glow just thinking] of you'

"And the"   "way you look to-"   "night"

Figure 4.5   Astaire's gestures as he sings 'And the way you look tonight'

straight back away from the keyboard, reaching and holding the furthest point of the entire sequence. The gesture and the verse conclude as he moves back toward the keyboard, lowering both head and torso, for 'night'.

Astaire's movements as he sings the first verse of 'The Way You Look Tonight' can be analysed in terms of three gestural catchments, the occurrence and features of which I have summarized in Table 4.2. The first catchment, whose identifying feature is a dip of the head, correlates with the music of Category X. The second, whose identifying feature is a circular movement to the left of the frame and then back to centre, correlates with the music for Category Y. The third, whose identifying feature is a move away from and then back towards the keyboard, correlates with the cadential figure. Although the majority of these catchments occur singly, note that the last catchment is extended by a brief recall of the first.

Astaire's movements, then, provide a set of visuospatial images coordinated with both the music and the words of the song. They are different from the gestures studied by McNeill, however, in one important way: Astaire's movements are not part of a process through which thought is shaped, but instead *reflect* the shaping of thought accomplished through musical materials. The manifold connections between music and gesture manifested in these relationships not only speak to their connection in cognitive structure, but also point to linkages between the way a communicative medium is organized and the meaning it comes to have.

Table 4.2   An analysis of gestural catchments in Astaire's performance of 'The Way You Look Tonight'

Line	Lyrics	Gesture feature	Catchment
1	Someday,	Dip of head	C1
2	When I'm awfully low	Circular movement	C2
3	And the world is cold	Circular movement	C2
4	I will feel a glow just thinking of	Circular movement	C2
5	You	Dip of head	C1
6	And the way you look tonight	Movement away from and back towards keyboard, dip of head	C3, C1

Researchers on physical gesture generally agree that the spontaneous gesture that accompanies speech does not adhere to any sort of grammar (McNeill 2005: Chapter 2). So why would the sonic analogues of music have a grammar while the gestures that accompany speech do not? One reason is that the sonic analogues of music operate within contextual frames provided by musical rhythm and musical pitch. Rhythm – especially *metered* rhythm – offers a temporal anchor for the dynamic processes of music. For instance, each of the musical categories basic to 'The Way You Look Tonight' begins on a strong beat on an odd-numbered measure and each, save the cadential figure, ends on a strong beat on an even-numbered measure. Musical pitches – and especially *relationships* among musical pitches – provide a framework for gauging the similarity of and difference between musical events. Thus the importance of D for the melodic structure of 'The Way You Look Tonight', a pitch that earns its place as a tonal focus by its placement at key points within the tune.

The world of gesture does not typically have anything like these sorts of contextual anchors, although on occasion they do crop up. A striking example is provided by Astaire's movements as he sings 'The Way You Look Tonight'. Note the position of Astaire's chin in the second image of Figure 4.2 ('day'), the last image of Figure 4.4 ('you'), and the last image of Figure 4.5 ('night'). In Figure 4.2 and Figure 4.5 his chin ends up in almost exactly the same place; in Figure 4.4 his chin is somewhat lower, but is in approximately the same place with respect to the midline of the frame. Of course, each of these images captures an arrival point – that is, the end of a gesture. In general, there is no requirement for gestures to terminate at close to the same point in space, but this is just what happens with all three of these gestures. In the case of the tonal 'space' set up by the melody, however, these gestures conclude in *exactly* the same place: the melodic pitch D. What gesture does only rarely and approximately, then, music does frequently and with a high degree of precision, a capacity that provides a reliable contextual framework for the sonic analogues of musical grammar.

Conclusion

As I suggested in my opening comments, in many cases our characterizations of musical gesture have a metaphorical basis. On the analysis I offered there, such characterizations involve mapping structure between two domains – that is, from the source domain *physical gestures* onto the target domain *sequences of musical materials*. Astaire's gestures as he sings 'The Way You Look Tonight' suggest that this mapping can also be reversed: the sequence of musical materials set out by Kern shape the pattern and structure of Astaire's movements. From a broader perspective, my analysis of the relationship between the music and lyrics of the tune showed how musical materials, in a rather detailed way, can shape our understanding of words. The basic materials of Kern's tune – which I described in terms of cognitive categories, and which provide sonic analogues for dynamic processes – can be seen as analogous to gestural catchments, and to participate in the sort of process McNeill calls a growth point.

As research on the spontaneous gestures that accompany language has shown, gesture gives access to a dynamic, imagistic mode of thought that is inaccessible to language. In this chapter, I have endeavoured to argue that music involves a similar mode of thought, and suggested that both music and gesture draw on a common pool of cognitive resources to create analogical representations of dynamic processes. Where the analogical representations of gesture have not typically been organized into a grammar, those of music have, in part through exploiting the contextual frames provided by rhythm and pitch.

I want to emphasize that the descriptions of the relationship between music and gesture that I have offered and the outline of musical grammar that I have sketched are at a very basic level. There is much work to be done before we can understand how the dynamic processes of music give rise to the subtle and remarkable range of expression we see in the musical compositions that continue to hold our fascination. I am convinced, however, that this understanding can be based on an account of the cognitive resources humans employ in making music, resources that are closely bound to those that are also used for the gestures that accompany our speech.

References

Duncan, S. D., Cassell, J. & Levy, E., eds. (2007). *Gesture and the Dynamic Dimension of Language: Essays in Honor of David McNeill*. Gesture Studies, Vol. 1. Philadelphia: John Benjamins Publishing Company.

Goldberg, A. E. (2003). Constructions: A New Theoretical Approach to Language. *Trends in Cognitive Science* 7/5: 219–24.

Goldin-Meadow, S. (2003a). *Hearing Gesture: How our Hands Help Us to Think*. Cambridge, MA: Harvard University Press.

— (2003b). *The Resilience of Language: What Gesture Creation in Deaf Children can tell us about how all Children Learn Language*. Essays in Developmental Psychology. New York: Psychology Press.

Grady, J. E. (2007). Metaphor. In D. Geeraerts & H. Cuyckens (eds.), *The Oxford Handbook of Cognitive Linguistics* (pp. 188–213). Oxford: Oxford University Press.

Iverson, J. M., & Goldin-Meadow, S. (1997). What's Communication Got to Do With It? Gesture in Children Blind from Birth. *Developmental Psychology* 33/3: 453–67.

Kendon, A. (2004). *Gesture: Visible Action as Utterance*. Cambridge: Cambridge University Press.

Koch, H. C. (1983[1787]). *Introductory Essay on Composition: The Mechanical Rules of Melody, Sections 3 and 4* (from *Versuch einer Anleitung zur Composition*, 1782–1793) (trans. N. K. Baker). Music Theory Translation Series. New Haven: Yale University Press.

Lakoff, G. (1993). The Contemporary Theory of Metaphor. In A. Ortony (ed.), *Metaphor and Thought* (pp. 202–51). Cambridge: Cambridge University Press.

McNeill, D. (2005). *Gesture and Thought*. Chicago: University of Chicago Press.

Tomasello, M. (1999). *The Cultural Origins of Human Cognition*. Cambridge, MA: Harvard University Press.

Zbikowski, L. M. (1999). Musical Coherence, Motive, and Categorization. *Music Perception* 17/1: 5–42.

— (2002). *Conceptualizing Music: Cognitive Structure, Theory, and Analysis*. New York: Oxford University Press.

— (2008a). Dance Topoi, Sonic Analogues, and Musical Grammar: Communicating with Music in the Eighteenth Century. In V. K. Agawu & D. Mirka (eds.), *Communication in Eighteenth Century Music* (pp. 283–309). New York: Cambridge University Press.

— (2008b). Metaphor and Music. In R. Gibbs, Jr (ed.), *The Cambridge Handbook of Metaphor and Thought* (pp. 502–24). Cambridge: Cambridge University Press.

Chapter 5
Distraction in Polyphonic Gesture

Anthony Gritten

> Once set out a word takes wing beyond recall.
> (Horace, *Epistles*)

If music drifts relatively mindless of the pressure put on it by interpretative intervention, then how might listeners engage with it? What type of aural intentionality might be appropriate if it is true that in the contemporary era 'Music escapes from musicians' (Attali 1985: 115)? How might listeners respond to the cavalier attitude of music to its own future?

Concerned with such issues around perception, intentionality and responsibility, this chapter complicates an attractive and commonsensical thesis that has been circulating for as long as people have talked about music. In the last quarter century or so, the thesis has afforded a welcome and emphatic paradigm shift in the humanities (back) towards humanity and its citizens, and in the case of music towards the ecologically grounded concerns that motivate the judgements that real listeners make and debate as part of their engagement with music. This thesis has been phrased in various ways, of which the following statement is representative: 'people can and do enjoy music without being able to make what are, in terms of musicological representation, the most elementary and basic perceptual judgements' (Cook 1990: 218; cf. Cook 1987, 1994). Acknowledging this statement's kernel of truth, I note, as Nicholas Cook did and still does, that the situation is somewhat more complex.

This chapter unpacks one issue that makes it so, working in the wake of the dialogical turn in the humanities that readings of Mikhail Bakhtin have inspired, and in the shadow of Walter Benjamin's lifelong concern to understand the 'decay of experience' that has characterized Modernity. My intention is to suggest one way of accounting for the invigorating experience of listening to musical gestures and to begin to loosen the stranglehold of an uncritical and partial appropriation of Bakhtin that has worked its way into many disciplines, musicology included. What might it mean to suggest that 'dialogic' and 'distraction' are words we live by, and what might the consequences be for understanding musical gestures?

I

In the third movement of Stravinsky's Violin Concerto (1931), *Aria II*, one of the solo violin's gestures in the first section exhibits a multi-dimensionality, opening its constituent voices outwards towards gestures that can be heard in Bach's Double Concerto, Brahms's Violin Concerto and Tchaikovsky's Violin Concerto (Examples 5.1–5.4). The presence of such multi-dimensionality within the aesthetic fabric of this and other works has generated an industry of scholarship devoted to searching for the right terminology for such gestures, from the vulgar Freudianism of quote-spotting through to aesthetically sophisticated interpretations of the music's relationships to its others: allusion, re-modelling, pastiche, parody, intertextuality, reference, sideshadowing, re-composition, quotation, wrong-note harmony, multi-voicedness, and so on.

Example 5.1   Stravinsky, Concerto for Violin, III, bars 77–8 with relevant gesture boxed in the extract

Example 5.2   Bach, Concerto for Two Violins in D Minor, BWV 1043, II, bars 16–19 with relevant gesture boxed in the extract

Example 5.3 Brahms, Violin Concerto in D Major, Op. 77, I, bars 445–51 with relevant gesture boxed in the extract

Example 5.4 Tchaikovsky, Violin Concerto in D Major, Op. 35, II, bars 39–51 with relevant gesture boxed in the extract

A brief context for the multi-dimensionality of this gesture is useful here. It hardly needs pointing out that Stravinsky's music is dominated by *agon*. From the shock tactics of *The Rite of Spring* to the ritual juxtapositions of *Symphonies of Wind Instruments* to the conflict of styles in *Apollo* to the tonal parody of the Symphony in C to the hieratic panels of *Threni*, it is an infamous Stravinskyian signature, both the technique and the result. Many have written about the extraordinary influence of *agon*, using or coining terms such as concerto principle (Asaf'yev 1982), stratification and interlock (Cone 1962), concertante idea (Walsh 1993), discontinuity (Hasty 1986; Kielian-Gilbert 1991), *drobnost'* (Taruskin 1996), explosive disintegration (White 1930), anti-organicism (Rehding 1998), moment form (Kramer 1978, 1988) and block juxtaposition (Cross 1998; Van den Toorn 1983), to cite only a few. The particular *agon* within this gesture in *Aria II* is, like the writing in *Apollo* a few years earlier, softer in tone than in some Stravinsky, and contributes to a strain of expressive *tendresse* in Stravinsky that is yet to receive proper critical attention.

Some preliminary observations can be made about the *agon* of voices in this single Stravinskyian gesture. The three 'other' gestures embody varying degrees of similarity to the gesture in *Aria II*, and thus their voices can be heard differently within it. The Bachian voice is initially embodied as a result of Stravinsky reading the notes off the stave and ignoring Bach's key signature, and bears the closest material resemblance to the Bach. The Brahmsian voice is used most frequently at the same transposition levels as its two occurrences in the Brahms (bars 206 and 445): E♯–F♯ and G♯–A appoggiaturas. The Tchaikovskyian voice is furthest removed in syntax, but seems through its generic affiliations and stylistic attributes to contribute to the overall tone of the Stravinskyian gesture; many other musical moments could have been invoked in order to illustrate such generic links outwards from *Aria II*. More generally, as *Aria II* unfolds, the appoggiatura gesture takes with it some of these other overtones, and it comes to play a quasi-structural role in the movement. In George Balanchine's 1972 choreography of the concerto, *Aria II* was created as a *Pas de Deux* and the appoggiatura gesture was taken up directly and centrally in the dance (Jordan 2007: 184–8).

This violinistic gesture in *Aria II* has an individuality, autonomy, and self-managing quality that is not co-extensive with the musical work as a whole, and a multiplicity of meaning and function that exceeds the boundaries of its syntax. It is found and constructed at the middle levels of perception, and is thus implicated as anthropomorphic because it fits via metaphorical transfer into its virtual world like listeners do into theirs: it has parts (appoggiatura, leap down to longer note, overall descent in lower part), is found in groups (there are three here, and various groups later in *Aria II*) and is subject to wider imperatives (the movement's A major/F♯ minor tonality, the physical constraints of violin bowing, the stylized expressive topos of grief). For all these reasons and more, this gesture in *Aria II* can be described in Bakhtinian terms as a matter of polyphony.

II

What does Bakhtin mean by polyphony? In *Problems of Dostoevsky's Poetics* (1984) Bakhtin develops a philosophy of consciousness, rethinking the essentially Hegelian question of how part and whole relate to each other. Unlike his earlier writings, in which the discourse was a mixture of philosophical aesthetics and phenomenology, his nominal subject here is literary theory and the novel, and thus 'part' and 'whole', 'object' and 'subject', 'other' and 'self' become 'character' and 'novel'. In a nutshell, there are three issues at stake for Bakhtin: the nature of the novel as an open whole, the manner in which the characters are combined, and (most important) the self-governing autonomy of the individual character. This is a matter of finding a way to accommodate the singularity of the individual character, the simultaneity of the individual characters, and the plurality of the overarching novel.

For Bakhtin, polyphony is the solution to this ethical and aesthetic problem, for it is based on the premise that within every utterance there can be heard an 'irrevocable *multi-voicedness* and *vari-voicedness*' (Bakhtin 1984: 279). Inside every utterance 'dialogic relationships' exist within and between constituent voices, each of these voices belonging to a separate character and contributing its own tone or intonation to the material. This means that, from a moral perspective, 'The truth about a man in the mouths of others, not directed to him dialogically and therefore a secondhand truth, becomes a lie degrading him and deadening him, if it touches upon his "holy of holies," that is, "the man in man"' (Bakhtin 1984: 59). For this reason, Bakhtin attempts to theorize an aesthetic object in which the most important element is the character's self-consciousness, in which any words taken as (provisionally) final are those that come out of the character's mouth, not those that come out of the author's mouth. If this configuration is possible, as Bakhtin claims (differently from his earlier writings), there are radical implications for the relationship between author and character. For if the author truly 'affirms the independence, internal freedom, unfinalisability, and indeterminacy of the hero' (Bakhtin 1984: 63), rather than treating the character as merely one of his creations, that is, if the author treats the character as a real subject complete with tone of voice and decision-making capabilities, then many of the traditional activities of the textual function going by the name of 'author' need to be rethought.

While, relying on the groundwork of his earlier essays in which authorship is more than a narrowly literary affair, Bakhtin is clear about the ethical moments of polyphony and the character's perspective (their right to reply), he is less clear about how the apparent aesthetic paradox concerning the author might be resolved (how to write without putting words into the character's mouth). For the purposes of this chapter, however, this potential problem can be bracketed. Returning from talk of characters to talk of gestures, Bakhtin's claims about the autonomy of the individual characters can be worked through in order to make use of perceptual analogies between the terms author and listener and between character and gesture.

III

I have drawn attention to a few relationships between voices in a gesture in *Aria II* that embodies the spirit of Stravinsky's mature Neoclassicism, and outlined the conditions of possibility for polyphony, as Bakhtin defines it. My concern is with how and with what listeners are afforded perceptions of the gentle polyphonic *agon* of this multi-dimensional gesture.

I will now follow a theme of distraction taken from Benjamin in order to explore the phenomenology of the agonistic Bakhtinian polyphony in *Aria II*:

less the diverse dialogic relationships that can be teased apart amongst its voices (there are obviously more than just the three voices selected here to get the ear rolling) and transcribed with respect to their syntax and style, more the nature of the perceptual process affording the analytical and hermeneutic moments of such musical listening. What is it like to listen to the dialogic relationships between and within its appoggiaturas? I first unpack a little genealogy of distraction, before exploring how it provides a useful grounding for polyphony.

Distraction has long histories in a variety of domains and various meanings. Theologians have despaired of it for millennia, anxious that human failings not delay the advent of the Divine; think of the narratives of texts such as Saint Augustine's *Confessions*, in which books 1 to 8 tell of Augustine's life prior to and leading up to confession in the Milan garden, dominated as it was more by secular curiosity than by a proper sense of awe and pleasure (Saint Augustine 1991); or the idea in Corinthians 13 that partial knowledge shall become, through love, full understanding and being understood; or the 'wandering spirit' of the Psalms (Psalm 77: 39); and so on. Pascal wrote about distraction centuries ago in terms of its sociological and existential functions, acting respectively as entertainment and as a way of tempering or putting off profound thoughts (cf. Bauman 2007: 107). The Cartesian *cogito* was constructed upon an essential assumption of its absence. Closer to the needs of this chapter, Siegfried Kracauer discussed the term in the 1920s with reference to film (Kracauer 1987), and Benjamin revisited the term a few years later in the now classic 'The Work of Art in the Age of its Mechanical Reproduction' (Benjamin 1968), wherein he developed an account of how technologies that allow artworks to be recorded and copied have transformed their reception and interpretation. Rather than focussing on Adorno's critique of atomistic listening, the important thing here is Benjamin's attention to overcoming distance, to highlighting and valuing positively the intimacy and closeness of objects in a post-auratic era (Benjamin 1986; Benjamin 2005; Gasché 1994).

In the wider world of late Modernity, understanding and controlling distraction has become important in numerous domains. The distraction of sound has been developed, tested and implemented, from the role of distraction in urban life (Latham 1999) to its impact on potentially dangerous activities such as driving (Brodsky 2002; Dibben & Williamson 2007; Wiesenthal et al. 2000), from its medical use to help reduce pain and anxiety (Gaberson 1995; McCaffrey & Good 2000; Wang et al. 2002), to its reduction in the ubiquitous human–computer interaction that demands a large proportion of attention (Horvitz et al. 2003). In such contexts, distraction across all of the senses is usually referred to in terms of interference, the point being that in most cases the intention is to reduce distraction and improve performative efficiency and productivity within the social totality (Furnham & Allass 1999; Furnham & Bradley 1997; Furnham & Stephenson 2007; Furnham & Strbac 2002; James 1997; Lesiuk 2005; Nelson et al. 1985).

In the musical world, the reduction of distraction is important in the training of performers, whether relating to, for example, performance anxiety (a pathological type of distraction; Sloboda et al. 2003), the inner 'audiation' of musical percepts

(Brodsky et al. 2008), the development of sight-reading abilities (Wöllner et al. 2003), or teaching them to shift attention between structural levels (Williamon et al. 2002). In the domain of listening that is the focus of this chapter, much work has been done by music theorists, cultural and media theorists, historians and philosophers, of which the following are representative highlights. Listening to popular music differs from classical music both because of the music and because of the dynamics of its media and discursive set up (Goodwin 1992; Rutsky 2002; Waters 2003), though pop music can obviously be listened to attentively as well (Smith 1995: 40 in Clarke 2005: 150). In contemporary 'concatenationist' culture musical attention has become more fragmentary and moment-to-moment (Cook 2006; Levinson 1998). In the historical shift from late nineteenth to early and mid-twentieth century worldviews, 'sustained attentiveness, rather than fixing or securing the world, led to perceptual disintegration and loss of presence', to a certain 'unbinding of perception' (Crary 1989, 1994, 1999). Navigating a path between concert music and ambient music, a theory of 'ubiquitous listening' is needed that, being based upon a more flexible notion of attention, is adequate to the contemporary networked world (Kassabian 2001). Within everyday life there is plenty of distraction (often under other names) already within the popular discourse on music appreciation, understanding music being predicated upon the ability to 'follow it', which means the ability to respond appropriately to each musical event as it comes into hearing.

These genealogies of distraction could be expanded with examples from inside and outside musical discourse, but I simply note that there are two complementary approaches to distraction: to reduce it or use it. This chapter attempts the latter. My focus on distraction is not historical, and avoids the rich implications of Benjamin's social and cultural theses, an important one being the idea that distraction is 'part of a constellation of terms, including *attention, curiosity, distraction, fascination, indifference* and *reverie* or *day-dreaming*, that point towards a phenomenology of modernity as utopian longing' (Osborne 2006: 38). I do not ask whether, beyond the spectacular distractions organized by the Culture Industry and the attention-hungry media, distractions can be planned, constructed and delivered to the public at a set time so that they might pass the time between events and purchases. Benjamin did not develop the concept of distraction far into the acoustic domain (Eiland 2003; Koepnick 2003), and I am not concerned with whether the phenomenology of distraction is appropriate to musics other than Stravinsky's modernism. My focus is on a phenomenologically grounded aesthetic notion of distraction, with a view to its role in the judgements that listeners might make about the Bakhtinian polyphony of gestures in *Aria II*.

IV

There are many signposts pointing from polyphony back towards distraction. Rich possibilities can be extrapolated, for example, from Eric Clarke's *Ways of Listening*

(2005) and Peter Szendy's *Listen* (2008), both of which make various appearances below, and both of which take distraction (not always their term) or its cognates to be a necessary and pragmatic constituent of any cognitively and culturally appropriate theory of listening. However, my opening gambit comes from Rose Subotnik's essay, 'Toward a Deconstruction of Structural Listening' (1996), and a recent volume of essays on it, *Beyond Structural Listening?* (Dell'Antonio 2004). This is for the reason that, tackling the matter head-on, these essays highlight the ways in which the concept of polyphony (not their term) needs to be grounded in distraction in order to afford a more phenomenologically adequate sense of the listeners' engagement with *Aria II*.

Structural listening arose alongside the consolidation of the work concept (Szendy 2008: 110). As Dell'Antonio summarizes, it 'seeks to transcend the potential sloppiness and impreciseness inherent in the physical manifestations of sound; the written score is seen (!) as having more integrity than any sonic realization of the musical work, and as more indicative of the creative process of the composer, which manifests itself through the structural necessity and organic completeness of the musical ideas that unfold from the beginning to the end of a musical work' (Dell'Antonio 2004: 3). Just as the focus of work around structural listening has tended to drift towards a complementary focus on the structuring of listening, from structure towards affect, epistemology towards phenomenology, so the polyphony of the appoggiatura gesture in *Aria II* needs to be grounded – reverse engineered – in a similar way. Since structural listening as Subotnik expands Schoenberg's, Adorno's and Stravinsky's conceptions of it is a subset of Bakhtinian polyphony, examining the discourse of structural listening will provide us with a sense of how to listen to polyphony. Recall what is at stake with polyphony:

Polyphony provides a theory of distributed networks (not Bakhtin's term) inside and outside the musical work, comprised of multiple dialogic relationships between voices. It presupposes a listening set-up focused on:

> what goes on when someone, whether or not a musical trained someone, listens to music seriously, attentively, the way a serious composer intends and hopes. *That* person is attending to musical sound events not with a mind completely blank and bereft of thought, nor a mind occupied with thoughts and problems for which the music may serve as a soothing background, but a mind occupied *with the music*. (Kivy 2002: 81; see also Kivy 2002: 70, 75, 76, 105–7, 250; Godlovitch 1998: 44, 46)

It is a matter, as Szendy says, of 'a *great listening* corresponding to *great music*, with whose form and details it is supposed to agree perfectly' (Szendy 2008: 99). Listening polyphonically means apprehending, segmenting, categorizing and cognizing a gesture as a gesture, and this may be describable in terms of, *inter alia*, metaphorical transfer, mirror neurons, schemata building, Schenkerian reduction, mapping semiotic squares, and so on – ultimately, some form of (value) judgement as to the aesthetic singularity and significance of the gesture. If listeners hear a gesture (tone rather than just sound) then they are hearing polyphonically; conversely, if they are not listening polyphonically then they do not hear the dynamic life of the gestures in the music.

Polyphony, then, is biased towards the musical work, towards its structure and towards modes of listening focussing on structure (however widely conceived) at the expense of other things. Even if the concept of structure is broadened to include everything within the orbit of the musical object, it is still biased towards interrupted musical attention *per se*, and assumes that this is how listeners listen (cf. Crowther 1993: 84–93). It is unclear, despite Bakhtin's invocations of 'sideways glances' and other nominally process-oriented relations between voices (Bakhtin 1984: 31–2, 201, 232; Benson 2006: 76–7), to what degree polyphony is static and spatial in conception. If polyphony does not spontaneously come into being *ex nihilo*, its emergence and temporality need refiguring, especially since Bakhtin's goal is the 'dialogism' of free indirect discourse rather than the mere call-and-response of 'dialogue'. In part, polyphony needs to be imbricated with a theory of perception and understanding as 'over-hearing', where 'the *over* is used in four discrete but related senses: it is at once the complex *over* of overdetermination; the temporal, historical *over* of something repeated, done over again; the incomplete, falling short *over* of overlooking; and the combination of fortuitousness and intention that informs the *over* of the more usual sense of over-hearing' (Aczel 1998: 597, 2001).

Thus, consider how Subotnik's interlocutors describe the type of engagement often advocated by structural listening's closest ally in the music business, music analysis. Listening begins with awe, with wonder 'at the different kinds of conceptualization that the same phenomena can sustain' (Dell'Antonio 2004: 174). The heard musical work 'is a *clue* to the range of its possible appearances within the hearer, which can be further teased forth by processes such as memory, association, and reflection' (Dell'Antonio 2004: 247). Music can stimulate various desires, one of which is a desire to engage analytically with structure (Dell'Antonio 2004: 184–6). What music has tended to afford in Western Modernist music such as Stravinsky is a particular set of activities and grammar of conceptualization, in which the grammar of attending to music has followed certain patterns, particularly inside scholarly discourse. It is, for example, often maintained that it is the listeners' business to attend to music and fulfil an obligation to a life of rigour and discipline justified with reference to the legitimacy and pertinence of the contract between composer and listener, the characteristics of which are 'silence, attention, greatness' (Szendy 2008: 119). This aids the upkeep of a type of utterance that Bakhtin calls 'direct and unmediated object-oriented discourse' (Bakhtin 1984: 186). At bottom, as one philosopher puts it, according to this standard analytical set-up grounding structural listening, 'what it means to understand music is to enjoy and to appreciate it for the right, relevant reasons: that is to say, to enjoy and appreciate in it those aspects of it that the composer intended you to enjoy and appreciate, and to enjoy and appreciate them in the way or ways intended' (Kivy 2007b: 217).

This is a robust and rigorous methodology, as is appropriate for musicological inquiry. Nevertheless, it is worth asking if it is always appropriate or possible, given the following: 'the capacity of the listener to bring visual or other associative experience to bear upon the act of listening, *while* listening' (Dell'Antonio 2004: 251 n. 2); 'the vagaries and interplays of memory and attention' (Dell'Antonio 2004: 248); the 'listeners or readers, who may or may not have been, at the time, thinking of something else entirely' (Godlovitch 1998: 127); and 'musicians' testimony that for them expressive, communicative, and other performative aspects are equally vital to the listening experience' (Marshman 2007, 2008). After all, a dose of pragmatism affords the acknowledgement that 'Even the ideal listener, trained to maintain constant attention, is sometimes flooded by a host of associations. If he manages to keep them aside, in the margins of his mind, they will lose consistency, shed their contents, melt into listening. But their silent presence still enriches the music with an invisible trail of feelings' (David 1996: 89):

Now that you have seen and perhaps imagined the sounds of the music examples above, I could ask you to try to forget these voices while I play you a recording of *Aria II*. Even without recourse to such shortcuts, it is easy to hear such acknowledgements of pragmatism (related to what Bakhtin calls 'loopholes') itching to get out from *Aria II* and drive themselves into your mind. To wit: did you think back to that concert in the Royal Festival Hall when you heard Hilary Hahn play the concerto, when you were sat in that unfortunate acoustic position right at the very back? Did you hear an interesting orchestral balance in the opening motto chord of *Aria II* that you didn't remember hearing on any of the recordings you had studied? Did you get something communicative out of the soloist's facial expressions and the way her body language worked through the four-square metre of the movement with a steady swaying that only interrupted itself at the 1/8 bar in the second section? Did the interpretation of *Aria II* play out the helpful programme notes? (Did you go on to reflect, given that this was Stravinsky, whether it was an 'interpretation' at all?) Wasn't it rather like 'Erbarme dich' from the St Matthew Passion? Did you notice that the third and fourth utterances of the motto chord are respectively metrically and motivically disembowelled, yet still make the Da Capo form clear – was their re-voicing here even noticeable? Didn't that listener's watch alarm down in front on the left seem to annoy those sitting near it – even though others, too, surely noticed that it chimed in time with the pulsing quavers in the orchestra? And the coughing?

The list of such distractions during and after listening (call them 'thoughts' to dignify them) goes on. Stepping back, what is interesting to follow through slowly is the basic principle at work here: what several of the writers in *Beyond Structural Listening?* describe as 'a distracted sort of listening' (Dell'Antonio 2004: 218, 157, 162, 239, 298 n. 23, 299 n. 26). In the broadest sense this might be 'a distraction from form' (Dell'Antonio 2004: 112; Lyotard 2006: 277; Smith 1998), a certain 'wavering' at the heart of listening (Szendy 2008: 122). As one writer puts it, 'The thing being turned over in memory is not exactly the single measure, of course: the pitch pattern *extends* the figures into pairs of measures, and, even more significantly, *complicates* them, by making composites' (Dell'Antonio 2004: 186). Following the general idea that 'a free listening is essentially a listening which circulates, which permutates, which disaggregates, by its mobility, the fixed network of the roles of speech' (Barthes 1985: 259), it is (to use Lawrence Kramer's rhetoric) an opportunity rather than an obstacle, for 'the experience is like nothing so much as my novice attempts at meditation, in which my attention wanders, again and again and again, from its object' (Dell'Antonio 2004: 239–40), while 'synopsis perpetually unravels into process' (Dell'Antonio 2004: 240; Foucault & Blanchot 1990: 22), and 'what ends up getting interpreted may not be what one set out to prove' (Dell'Antonio 2004: 241). In this respect, the musical object is an enigmatic rebus (cf. Eagleton 1990: 329). If, as Catherine David analogizes, 'It is meaning itself that is leaking through these unravelling gestures, like a drop of water from a leaky tap' (David 1996: 145), or, in Szendy's poetic words, 'the inscribable flow of a musicality that, like wine or blood, pours out in waves' (Szendy 2008: 109), then it is up to listeners to catch, or at least watch, these drops moving in time with gravity (to continue the metaphor).

Such an opening of thought is in line with the tendency for description to end up far from its starting point and from its object of attention, and the oft-repeated notion that 'a text's unity lies not in its origin but in its destination' (Barthes 1977a: 148). It is the general idea that aesthetic activity:

> cannot ... be reduced to an absorbed attention to the surface qualities of the object ... . Rather the object is also the centre of, and is the occasion of, many possible lines of reflection or movements of the mind, transformations of perception, attitudes and feelings that may affect a person's life and modify the quality of his experience long after he has ceased to contemplate the particular object itself. (Hepburn 1984: 1)

Indeed, 'In order to do justice to the qualitative moments of the thing, thought must thicken its own texture, grow gnarled and close-grained; but in doing so it becomes a kind of object in its own right, sheering off from the phenomenon it hoped to encircle' (Eagleton 1990: 341). This is not a cause for regret: after all, as Kramer asks in all seriousness:

> Am I failing to experience the music when I vary my attention level or simply let it fluctuate, when I interrupt a sound recording to replay a movement or a passage, when I find myself enthralled by a fragment of a piece that I hear on my car radio without losing concentration on the road, when I intermittently accompany my listening by singing under by breath or silently verbalising commentary on what I hear, when I perform some part of a piece in my mind's ear, perhaps vocalising along, and perhaps not? (Kramer 1995: 65)

Most potently, one might be led to reflect on the radical human potential afforded by a certain distraction:

> How seldom it was that you fully inhabited your surroundings, engaging not only your senses but your awareness. On the occasions that you did so, time had a way of slowing, or appearing even to stop. So did we hurry on with other thoughts because we were preoccupied, so well adjusted to the world that it was scarcely worth our attention? Or would committing ourselves to it more fully involve experiences of time or doubt or fear that we did not really wish to have? Had the ability to escape into abstraction, to live outside our surroundings, been favoured by natural selection? (Faulkes 2005: 316)

V

With these suggestions that distraction might yet be recognized as a key cognitive skill concerning cross-modal redescription and adaptation (cf. Clarke 2005: 5, 43, 122, 123, 132, 154; Crowther 1993: 7), I am beginning to drift from analysis and memory (and their handmaiden, recording) as the regulatory mechanism of structural listening (Clarke 2005: 9), and from structural listening as the regulatory mechanism of the polyphony in *Aria II*, towards analysis as creative distraction. Indeed, distraction seems to be coeval with the analytical enterprise, for it is not only directed at a general transformation of consciousness: it aids the recognition of specific thoughts and feelings that (note the tense) we may have been having but were not aware of (Dell'Antonio 2004: 60, 176, 187; Rosen 1994: 72–126) and encourages listeners to become 'much more aware of their *perspective* on the objects of perception' (Clarke 2005: 124, 52). However, there is a corollary to acknowledge: unpacking this single gesture in *Aria II* necessarily opens up listening and analysis to further listening and analysis; it is like translation (Szendy 2008: 47–56). According to one analyst, analysis 'always changes the way things look, and sound, and feel ... the story changes, and keeps changing as one analysis enters into the endlessly proliferating stream of other possible interpretations' (Perrey 2007). There is a displacement of the musical thought and attention is 'directed elsewhere, inflected or bent from its path to focus on something else' (Evens 2005: 27), 'not as a chronological displacement but as a multi-dimensional reconfiguration' of the gestural relationships in *Aria II* (Dell'Antonio 2004: 11; see also Benson 2006: 80).

What are the implications of this for polyphony? It is clear from the concept of distraction emerging from within the constellation of writings around structural listening and its cognates that in order for listeners to listen to the polyphony of voices in this appoggiatura gesture in *Aria II*, there needs to be a certain 'loosening' (rather than tightening) of attention. This is in line with a wide range of developments across the humanities (Barthes 1975: 64; Barthes 1977b: 159; Bruns 1999: 27, 31, 45, 62, 67, 92, 116–7, 127; Butt 2002: xii, 16, 41, 54, 68, 74, 84;

Derrida 2002: 36; Eagleton 1990: 341, 345; Kivy 2007a: 130; Negus & Velázquez 2002: 135). This loosening goes hand in hand with a need for a 'measure of calm quiet attentiveness – of "evenly hovering" attention' (Barthes 1985: 253) that can satisfy (and, more importantly, exceed) structural listening. The point is that:

> whereas the speaking subject moves consecutively along syntactical lines, the listening subject is ... nonlinear, open to distraction, indeed in a constant state of interruption, because a world organized according to listening is a world of simultaneous events that, unless one is ready to exclude most of what happens, one is bound to sort out into lists rather than into narratives and propositions. (Bruns 1999: 152)

This makes sense, given that thinking about music tends to require a move away from the object, followed by an oblique return: it requires turning it over in the mind, or perhaps being turned over by it – to adapt the classic Freudian schema, 'bending' the ear to music's affordances. The extent to which listening can bend before the virtual elastic anchoring listeners to the music breaks, often causes theoretical anxiety, as, for example, when the nominal distinction between conscious and self-conscious listening is considered: what might happen when listeners 'start thinking about what I am perceiving as I am perceiving it' (Kivy 2007b: 230), about the fact that 'sensation points out the direction the technical search much take; in return, each technical progress brings forth new sensations' (David 1996: 43). This anxiety is not surprising, given that, although listening to music is said to involve an open-ended and pleasurable passage of emergence and 'the experience of going from our world, with all of its trials, tribulations, and ambiguities, to *another* world, a world of pure sonic structure' (Kivy 2002: 260), still this is often countered by an underlying drive to suppress any distractions that this very passage might entail, lest it is unproductive (in what should now be clear is a crude sense of 'productivity').

In the standard Western Classical set-up distractions are usually conceived in terms of 'non-musical noise which is inessential and even a distraction', such noise being a matter of '"real-world" distractions' and a potential 'distraction or barrier to understanding' (Hamilton 2007: 41, 43, 57). The ideological basis for these exclusions can be bracketed in the search for a more inclusive understanding of listening somewhere between this conventional boundary and the non-boundary set up by Cage in *4'33"*, in which distractions are simply classed as music. Some distractions come from outside the music and the mind, others within (Currie 2007: 122). Some happen on an imperceptible timescale, while others are triggered suddenly (Kassabian 2001). 'Sometimes the thoughts associated with a strain of music ... have no relation to the gesture being made [... they are] the babble of the banal' (David 1996: 121). Some nominally non-musical distractions are contextually obvious and transient (the police car screeching past the concert hall, the screeching of fans as Herbie Hancock strolls onto the Barbican stage). Internal musical distractions are usually more subtle, encompassing events such as another segment of the same work, a different musical parameter (distracted by the grain of the voice, the implications of the libretto, the diminished harmony, the motivic return, her arm gestures or breathing), sound perceived as tone, and so on. They are, perhaps paradoxically, 'structural distractions' (Hatten 2008), taking place 'at the intersection between part and whole in the material realm, and between instant and process in the temporal realm' (Hoeckner 2002: 4) and complete with multiple formal and hermeneutic affordances. In addition, if one classifies extraneous mental associations (such as the few selected just above, or those personalized earlier) as a common form of secondary distraction, then it is necessary to note methodologically that 'just as associations are many, varied, and highly personal … they are vague, blurry around the edges, and fade into one another. Furthermore, they are constantly changing, not static, innate, set pieces' (Kivy 2002: 171).

Distractions, however, are not just or always multiple, as they happen to be in the case of the dialogic relationships between the voices in the polyphony around Stravinsky's appoggiatura. They are equally singular: every gesture in itself is distracting, both seductive and dangerous (Currie 2007: 125–7) by virtue of its resolute physicality. Indeed, because distraction is a matter of cognitive and hermeneutic attention, there is an infinite regress: listening is itself a matter of distraction (the boundary between 'primary' and 'secondary' distractions noted above is not rigid). This means, fundamentally, that it is not that distraction is opposed to the concentrated structural listening advocated by Adorno, Schoenberg, Stravinsky and others, and that the latter is pure and uncontaminated by the sound and noise of music and its performers. Rather, distraction is built into structural listening as an integral moment of its Modernism (Hirschkop 2008); it is part of a constellation of terms 'fracturing any simple binary dialectical relations' (Osborne 2006: 42–3). Thus, rather than continuing to oppose distraction to structural listening, as in the standard ideology (cf. Evens 2005: 8), rather than opposing 'analytical' to 'holistic' listening or 'test conditions' to 'normal listening' (Cook 1994: 88, 71; Sloboda 2009), and rather than opposing virtuosity to a transparent performing in which instrument and body are un-distracting (O'Dea 2000: 49, 53, 58, 60), what is needed is a graded typology of forms and modes of distraction (cf. Derrida 1988: 18). Roland Barthes had it right when he wrote that 'structurally, there is no difference between "cultured" reading and casual reading on trains' (Barthes 1977b: 162); in Bakhtinian terms, pleading claims to pure structural reading or listening are, because monologic, false and not to be trusted. As Joseph Dubiel notes, 'the relevant sort of contrast is between different kinds of perceptibility, different terms of conceptualization for what is sensed' (in Dell'Antonio 2004: 173–4).

Consider the 'continuity' criteria governing work, performance time and personnel (Godlovitch 1998: 34–41). These keep ritual disruption and other large-scale forms of distraction outside the boundaries of what constitutes a true and proper performance of a work, although it is difficult to prove or disprove 'interpretive continuity' from the acoustic evidence alone of a performing event.

Stan Godlovitch goes a step further, noting that 'success conditions apply to listening too' and seeking to marry up the concerns of the performer and listeners, whereby the former produces a state of 'active concentrated attention' in the latter, and the latter responds in like terms to the former's efforts (Godlovitch 1998: 44–9). Beyond the analytic rigour of these definitions, however, 'there will always be a [synthetic] gap in our knowledge, hence a gap where the performer's own decisions will prevail – decisions dictated by her own taste, judgement, and artistry' (Kivy 2002: 244), and it is here that distraction has the potential to reconfigure intentional decision making, for it happens despite the listeners' decisions before or during performance. Indeed, who is to say that even when listeners think that the change in their focus of attention was the result of their choice or intention, that it was not equally the effect of a distraction that they have unconsciously appropriated and to which they have given a name? Extrapolations of Benjamin that talk of the post-auratic era of distraction as 'the time of hypersurveillance, in which the past, digitized and stored, is available all of the time and the future ... is omnisciently and algorithmically and more or less probabilistically predictable' (Lash 1998: 155) are overly technocratic and utopian, old-fashioned – if not paranoid – in their belief that the human listener can summon up, synthesize, and use such resources without break, lapse, relief, or pause, let alone without fault, history, or distraction – '*without any difficulties*' (Szendy 2008: 137). Although empirical research naturally refers to the subject's 'selective auditory attention' (Jones 1999), it is worth pausing to ponder the necessary assumption that all attention is 'selective', in the sense of it being a matter of choice (at whatever level of reflective awareness). It could be that musical attention results from distraction. After all, as Benjamin noted, experience 'is less the product of facts firmly anchored in memory than of a convergence in memory of accumulated and frequently unconscious data' (Benjamin 1973: 110–11). The faultlines in listening – its inability to hold itself together attentively for long – are the evidence of its happening.

When defined narrowly, then, distraction is a removal of attention away from (rather than towards) the polyphony of voices in the Stravinskyian gesture: initially listeners are able to attend fully to the music, but is subsequently distracted. And this is true if distractions are taken to be a barrier to proper structural listening, which 'is silent, stationary, uninterrupted, ears glued to the musical structure and eyes closed. [However, as Clarke notes,] It hardly needs pointing out how uncharacteristic this actually is of most people's listening habits. ... . Overwhelmingly, people listen to music in a far more pragmatic and "instrumental" manner' (Clarke 2005: 136 and 144), as with the personalized interjections above; could it have been that listening to Hahn play *Aria II* had been a temporary distraction from the latest budget crisis in the Higher Education sector? Indeed, Benjamin's insight that 'Truth is the death of intention' (Benjamin 1977: 36) can be turned round into the suggestion that distraction is the birth of intention, that moment from and within which listening proceeds. In the manner of Proust's infamous *madeleine*, distraction draws involuntary memory towards the riotous, over-populated present of listening.

To extend distraction in this direction (so that it encompasses not just listening to muzak but to Modernist music, full-circle) requires short-circuiting a tradition that includes, *inter alia*, Brahms, Schoenberg, Hindemith and Ives, which has sometimes argued that sound gets in the way of music and that thinking that moves anywhere outside of the music at hand is 'ceasing to think about the music altogether' (Kivy 2007b: 231). The idea is to acknowledge the inherent elasticity of attention and to allow the emergence of distraction as itself a form of musical thinking (Levinson 2003), as, like dance, a Nietzschean metaphor for thought itself (Badiou 2005): gestures like the appoggiatura in *Aria II*, like certain words in context, seem to attract listeners' attention by '*glistening*' and '*shimmering*' (Barthes 1975: 42, 1985: 259). The idea is that '*distraction, lacunary* listening, might also be a means, an attitude, to make *sense of the work*; that a *certain* inattention, a certain *wavering* of listening, might also be a valid and fertile connection in *auditory interpretation at work*' (Szendy 2008: 103, 119, 122, 128, 134). This idea embraces the position that 'Music must be allowed to linger, – but not to listen to itself' (Adorno 2006: 104, 232) alongside its flipside; listeners may linger as long as the music (broadly conceived) retains their attention in one way or another – as long as it distracts them. 'Thought', as Terry Eagleton notes, 'must deploy a whole cluster of stubbornly specific concepts which in Cubist style refract the object in myriad directions or penetrate it from a range of diffuse angles' (Eagleton 1990: 328).

The idea, then, is that distraction works alongside familiar and still useful Enlightenment values of clarity, teleology, singularity and communication, producing ambiguity, circularity, multiplicity (sideshadows), timbre and tone. No longer repressed as an annoying way of preventing time-saving efficient data communication, distraction becomes the surreal, simple and pleasurable (decadent but not excessive) experience of time itself as played out in the dialogic relationships between the voices in the gesture in *Aria II*. Such a concept of distraction has important ethical and political elements with respect to the constellations within which distraction emerges, the 'idiosyncratic free-wheeling of the imagination which recalls the devious opportunism of the allegorist' (Eagleton 1990: 332); indeed, for Benjamin himself (after Baudelaire), ethics and politics came together historically in the figure of the *flâneur*. Since listeners cannot get (back) to what they were listening to prior to the distraction in the same manner as before (rather like the duck–rabbit phenomenon), and may not always even have been aware of the distractions impinging upon their listening, they are forced back upon their own resources and must react in an appropriate manner to the distractions that they do hear, and cope with the movements that they set in motion: they must decide 'what is to be done' – a matter of reflective judgement. In this sense, distraction is not quite an opening to carnival, and in a post-auratic era it remains the case that 'Schoenberg's *construction* and Stravinsky's *masks* both register the liquidation of the subject' (Roberts 1991: 99) only if 'liquidation' is read (at a poetic tangent) to refer to the 'becoming liquid' characterizing the current stage of Modernity (Bauman 2000, 2005, 2007), in which listeners are forced to develop ways of 'encountering and coping' with distraction (Bruns 1999: 80) and to cultivate a virtue ethics of listening alongside the older quandary ethics presupposed by structural listening and polyphony (in its narrowly un-distracted Bakhtinian form).

There are implications, too, for the commodification of music and its industries, now that the nature of the historical 'work' that functions as the site for exchange has changed: 'We certainly do now hear music as a *fragmented* and *unstable* object ... as we have taken power over music on records ... so the musical work has ceased to command respectful, structural, attention' (Frith 1996: 242; Szendy 2008: 135). The appoggiatura gesture in *Aria II* should be engaged 'less as expressive media than as material ceremonies, scriptive fields of force to be negotiated, dense dispositions of signs less to be "read" than meditatively engaged, incanted and ritually re-made' (Eagleton 1981: 117).

VI

I have been led far from Stravinsky and the gesture in *Aria II*. In rethinking Bakhtin, I have appropriated a partial reading of Benjamin. If it is not already clear, the following remarks from Clarke's study of ecological approaches to the perception of musical meaning will illustrate the broad sweep of distraction that I have tried to convey: 'One of the remarkable characteristics of our perceptual systems, and of the adaptability of human consciousness, is the ability to change the focus, and what might be called the "scale of focus", of attention – from great breadth and diversity of awareness to the sense of being absorbed in a singularity.' (Clarke 2005: 188) Of particular importance is the transferrable value of such adaptability. Clarke continues with the observation that 'the transition between these different perceptual worlds, or the interruption of one by another, can be disturbing and disruptive (when the ticking of a neighbour's watch breaks into the environment of [a performance of Beethoven's String Quartet] Op. 132, for instance)' (2005: 188). Just as important, too, as this chapter has suggested, is the notion that it can be a positive musical experience.

There can be benefits and pleasures in being 'led to look up often, to listen to something else' (Barthes 1975: 24), for example, 'diverting our attention from sound to time' (Dunsby 1995: 75), or switching attention from one salient musical gesture or parameter to another, from Stravinsky to Tchaikovsky, from the sound of the E string to the compound melodic line (insofar as such voices can be teased apart) – 'with sudden, deceptively decisive turns, fervent and futile' (Barthes 1975: 31). Indeed, it works both ways: 'Just as concentrated listening ... can be diverted in unexpected directions, so too a listener can be unexpectedly and suddenly drawn *into* some music that until then had been paid more distracted and heteronomous attention – as, for instance, when telephone hold music actually engages your undivided attention rather than being just a sound to fill the waiting' (Clarke 2005: 136). All this playful agitation and oscillation, to use Kantian terms, is a self-strengthening and reproducing activity, a dark joy that is key to the emergence of aesthetic judgements. The point is that listeners should seek to retain a certain looseness and mobility in their engagement with *Aria II*, both as their own creative practice and as conceived by others within the disciplinary walls of Musicology, a looseness open to distraction and its creative possibilities rather than 'hardening and thereby tending to reduction' (Barthes 1981: 8) and lapsing back into the clanking chains of structural listening. This is because, if their listening to *Aria II* is to have any hope of ethical and social leverage (Adorno 2002; Leppert 2005: 121–4), as well as the easy pragmatism and realism noted at the outset of this chapter with reference to Cook (1990), then it needs to remain 'languid yet secretly vigilant' (Eagleton 1981: 25), open, and fleet of ear.

Gnawing away at the certainties of cognition, distraction works over polyphony and structural listening and loosens their useful and necessary assumptions and elective analytical discourse. It reminds listeners, less that they need to engage with the lapses from order to disorder within *Aria II*, and more that they need to engage with the creation of musical order, which is not given but created by and through its polyphony of gestures. Their task is to learn how to respond to the affordances of gestures like the appoggiatura within and around the polyphonic texture, and this includes gestures that are usually bracketed off as unwanted noise. Doing so, that is, listening with awe – structurally *and* atomistically, attentively *and* distractedly – is certainly difficult. Luckily, though, the polyphonic open-endedness of the gestures always affords further attempts, since (again, note the tense) the first attempt will never have been finished, since it kept getting pleasurably distracted.

If all of this high-pitched rhetoric seems like re-inventing the wheel with regard to listening, it probably is; with the caveat that a central desire in this chapter has been to withdraw the mastery from listening and listen to whatever might be left (assuming that 'listening' remains the process in question once some of its aggressive colonising has been short-circuited). What if, in the wake of Bakhtin and Benjamin, after the suggestive contributions of Subotnik, Dell'Antonio and his contributors, Clarke, Szendy and others, and alongside our standard theories of listening (we listen 'to' music), music can be felt withdrawing from us and therefore affording us the very experience we call listening? This would, not be to resort to a primitive or un-mediated irrationalism about sense perception, but to return to an open acknowledgement of the *wonder* of listening – what sets us to work in the first place.

The trick is to judge sensitively: how am I to listen to *this* appoggiatura gesture?

References

Aczel, R. (1998). Hearing Voices in Narrative Texts. *New Literary History* 29/3: 476–500.

— (2001). Understanding as Over-hearing: Towards a Dialogics of Voice. *New Literary History* 32: 597–617.

Adorno, T. (2002). Little Heresy (trans. Susan Gillespie). In T. Adorno, *Essays on Music: Selected, with Introduction, Commentary and Notes by R. Leppert"* (pp. 318–24). Berkeley: University of California Press.

— (2006). *Towards a Theory of Musical Reproduction: Notes, a Draft and Two Schemata* (trans. Wieland Hoban). Cambridge: Polity.

Asaf'yev, B. (1982). *A Book about Stravinsky* (trans. R. French). Ann Arbor: UMI Press.

Attali, J. (1985). *Noise: The Political Economy of Music* (trans. B. Massumi). Minneapolis: University of Minnesota Press.

Badiou, A. (2005). Dance as a Metaphor for Thought (trans. Alberto Toscano). In A. Badiou, *Handbook of Inaesthetics* (pp. 57–71). Stanford: Stanford University Press.

Bakhtin, M. (1984). *Problems of Dostoevsky's Poetics* (trans. C. Emerson). Minneapolis: University of Minnesota Press.

Barthes, R. (1975). *The Pleasure of the Text* (trans. R. Miller). New York: Farrar, Straus & Giroux.

— (1977a). The Death of the Author (trans. S. Heath). In R. Barthes, *Image Music Text* (pp. 142–8). London: Fontana.

— (1977b). From Work to Text (trans. S. Heath). In R. Barthes, *Image Music Text* (pp. 155–64). London: Fontana.

— (1981). *Camera Lucida: Reflections on Photography* (trans. R. Howard). New York: Hill & Wang.

— (1985). Listening. In R. Barthes, *The Responsibility of Forms: Critical Essays on Music, Art, and Representation* (trans. R. Howard) (pp. 245–60). Berkeley: University of California Press.

Bauman, Z. (2000). *Liquid Modernity*. Cambridge: Polity.

— (2005). *Liquid Life*. Cambridge: Polity.

— (2007). *Liquid Times: Living in an Age of Uncertainty*. Cambridge: Polity.

Benjamin, A. (1986). The Decline of Art: Benjamin's Aura. *Oxford Art Journal* 9/2: 30–35.

— (ed.) (2005). *Walter Benjamin and Art*. London: Continuum.

Benjamin, W. (1968). The Work of Art in the Age of Mechanical Reproduction (trans. Harry Zohn). In W. Benjamin, *Illuminations: Essays and Reflections* (pp. 217–52). New York: Schocken.

— (1973). *Charles Baudelaire: A Lyric Poet in the Era of High Capitalism* (trans. H. Zohn). London: New Left Books.

— (1977). *The Origin of German Tragic Drama* (trans. J. Osborne). London : New Left Books.

Benson, S. (2006). *Literary Music: Writing Music in Contemporary Fiction*. Aldershot: Ashgate.

Brodsky, W. (2002). The Effects of Music Tempo on Simulated Driving Performance and Vehicular Control. *Transportation Research, Part F: Traffic Psychology and Behaviour* 4: 219–41.

—, Kessler, Y., Rubenstein, B., Ginsborg, J. & Henik, A. (2008). The Mental Representation of Music Notation: Notational Audiation. *Journal of Experimental Psychology: Human Performance and Perception* 34/2: 427–45.

Bruns, G. (1999). *Tragic Thoughts at the End of Philosophy: Language, Literature, and Ethical Theory*. Evanston, IL: Northwestern University Press.

Butt, J. (2002). *Playing with History: The Historical Approach to Musical Performance*. Cambridge: Cambridge University Press

Clarke, E. (2005). *Ways of Listening: An Ecological Approach to the Perception of Musical Meaning*. Oxford: Oxford University Press.

Cone, E. (1962). Stravinsky: The Progress of a Method. *Perspectives of New Music* 1/1: 18–26.

Cook, N. (1987). Musical Form and the Listener. *Journal of Aesthetics and Art Criticism* 46/1: 23–9.

— (1990). *Music, Imagination, and Culture*. Oxford: Oxford University Press.

— (1994). Perception: A Perspective from Music Theory. In R. Aiello & J. Sloboda (eds.), *Musical Perceptions* (pp. 64–95). Oxford: Oxford University Press.

— (2006). Playing God: Creativity, Analysis, and Aesthetic Inclusion. In I. Deliège & G. Wiggins (eds.), *Musical Creativity: Multidisciplinary Research in Theory and Practice* (pp. 9–24). Hove: Psychology Press.

Crary, J. (1989). Spectacle, Attention, Counter-Memory. *October* 50: 96–107.

— (1994). Unbinding Vision. *October* 68: 21–44.

— (1999). *Suspensions of Perception: Attention, Spectacle, and Modern Culture*. Cambridge, MA: MIT Press.

Cross, J. (1998). *The Stravinsky Legacy*. Cambridge: Cambridge University Press.

Crowther, P. (1993). *Critical Aesthetics and Postmodernism*. Oxford: Clarendon Press.

Currie, J. (2007). Review of Matthew Riley, *Musical Listening in the German Enlightenment: Attention, Wonder, Astonishment* (Aldershot: Ashgate 2004): Impossible Reconciliations (Barely Heard). *Music and Letters* 88/1: 121–33.

David, C. (1996). *The Beauty of Gesture: The Invisible Keyboard of Piano and T'ai Chi*. Berkeley: North Atlantic Books.

Dell'Antonio, A. (ed.) (2004). *Beyond Structural Listening? Postmodern Modes of Hearing*. Berkeley: University of California Press.

Derrida, J. (1988). Signature Event Context (trans. S. Weber & J. Mehlman). In J. Derrida, *Limited Inc* (pp. 1–23). Evanston, IL: Northwestern University Press.

— (2002). *Positions* (trans. A. Bass). London: Continuum.

Dibben, N. & Williamson, V. (2007). An Exploratory Survey of In-vehicle Music Listening. *Psychology of Music* 35/4: 571–89.

Dunsby, J. (1995). *Performing Music: Shared Concerns*. Oxford: Oxford University Press.

Eagleton, T. (1981). *Walter Benjamin: Or, Towards a Revolutionary Criticism.* London: Verso.

— (1990). *The Ideology of the Aesthetic.* Oxford: Blackwell.

Eiland, H. (2003). Reception in Distraction. *Boundary 2* 30/1: 51–66.

Evens, A. (2005). *Sound Ideas: Music, Machines, and Experience.* Minneapolis: University of Minnesota Press.

Faulkes, S. (2005). *Human Traces.* London: Vintage.

Foucault, M. & Blanchot, M. (1990). *Maurice Blanchot: The Thought from Outside / Michel Foucault as I Imagine Him* (trans. B. Massumi & J. Mehlman). New York: Zone.

Frith, S. (1996). *Performing Rites: On the Value of Popular Music.* Cambridge, MA: Harvard University Press.

Furnham, A. & Allass, K. (1999). The Influence of Musical Distraction of Varying Complexity on the Cognitive Performance of Extroverts and Introverts. *European Journal of Personality* 13/1: 27–38.

— & Bradley, A. (1997). Music while you Work: The Differential Distraction of Background Music on the Cognitive Test Performance of Introverts and Extraverts. *Applied Cognitive Psychology* 11/5: 445–55.

— & Stephenson, R. (2007). Musical Distracters, Personality Type and Cognitive Performance in School Children. *Psychology of Music* 35/3: 403–20.

— & Strbac, L. (2002). Music is as Distracting as Noise: The Differential Distraction of Background Music and Noise on the Cognitive Test Performance of Introverts and Extraverts. *Ergonomics* 45/3: 202–17.

Gaberson, K. (1995). The Effect of Humorous and Musical Distraction on Preoperative Anxiety. *Journal of the Association of Operating Room Nurses* 62/5: 784–91.

Gasché, R. (1994). Objective Diversions: On some Kantian Themes in Benjamin's The Work of Art in the Age of Mechanical Reproduction. In A. Benjamin & P. Osborne (eds.), *Walter Benjamin's Philosophy: Destruction and Experience* (pp. 183–204). London: Routledge.

Godlovitch, S. (1998). *Musical Performance: A Philosophical Study.* Oxford: Oxford University Press.

Goodwin, A. (1992). *Dancing in the Distraction Factory: Music, Television and Popular Culture.* Minneapolis: University of Minnesota Press.

Hamilton, A. (2007). *Aesthetics and Music.* London: Continuum.

Hasty, C. (1986). On the Problem of Succession and Continuity in Twentieth-Century Music. *Music Theory Spectrum* 8: 58–74.

Hatten, R. (2008). Personal Communication, 5 September.

Hepburn, R. (1984). *'Wonder' and Other Essays: Eight Studies in Aesthetics and Neighbouring Fields.* Edinburgh: Edinburgh University Press.

Hirschkop, K. (2008). Personal Communication, 1 August.

Hoeckner, B. (2002). *Programming the Absolute: Nineteenth-Century German Music and the Hermeneutics of the Moment.* Princeton: Princeton University Press.

Horvitz, E., Kadie, C., Paek, T. & Hovel, D. (2003). Models of Attention in Computing and Communication: From Principles to Applications. *Communications of the ACM* 46/3: 52–9.

James, F. (1997). Distinguishability versus Distraction in Audio HTML Interfaces. Unpublished Paper. (ftp://reports.stanford.edu/pub/cstr/reports/cs/tn/98/69/CS-TN-98-69.pdf; accessed June 2009)

Jones, D. (1999). The Cognitive Psychology of Auditory Distraction: The 1997 BPS Broadbent Lecture. *British Journal of Psychology* 90/2: 167–87.

Jordan, S. (2007). *Stravinsky Dances: Re-Visions across a Century*. Alton: Dance Books.

Kassabian, A. (2001). Ubiquitous Listening and Networked Subjectivity. *Echo* 3/2 (http://www.echo.ucla.edu; accessed August 2006).

Kielian-Gilbert, M. (1991). Stravinsky's Contrasts: Contradiction and Discontinuity in his Neoclassic Music. *Journal of Musicology* 9/4: 448–80.

Kivy, P. (2002). *Introduction to a Philosophy of Music*. Oxford: Oxford University Press.

— (2007a). *Ars Perfecta*: Toward Perfection in Musical Performance. In P. Kivy, *Music, Language, and Cognition: And Other Essays in the Aesthetics of Music* (pp. 111–34). Oxford: Oxford University Press.

— (2007b). Music, Language, and Cognition: Which Doesn't Belong? In his *Music, Language, and Cognition: And Other Essays in the Aesthetics of Music* (pp: 214–32). Oxford: Clarendon Press.

Koepnick, L. (2003). Distracted by Sound: Walter Benjamin and the Acoustic. Paper presented at the CentreCATH conference on 'Warp: Woof Aurality, Musicality, Textuality', University of Leeds, UK, 10–12 July.

Kracauer, S. (1987). Cult of Distraction: On Berlin's Picture Palaces (trans. T. Levin). *New German Critique* 40: 91–6.

Kramer, J. (1978). Moment Form in Twentieth Century Music. *Musical Quarterly* 64: 177–94.

— (1988). *The Time of Music: New Meanings, New Temporalities, New Listening Strategies*. New York: Schirmer.

Kramer, L. (1995). *Classical Music and Postmodern Knowledge*. Berkeley: University of California Press.

Lash, S. (1998). Being After Time: Towards a Politics of Melancholy. In S. Lash, A. Quick & R. Roberts (eds.), *Time and Value* (pp. 147–61). Oxford: Blackwell.

Latham, A. (1999). The Power of Distraction: Distraction, Tactility, and Habit in the Work of Walter Benjamin. *Environment and Planning D: Society and Space* 17/4: 451–73.

Leppert, R. (2005). Music 'Pushed to the Edge of Existence' (Adorno, Listening, and the Question of Hope). *Cultural Critique* 60: 92–133.

Lesiuk, T. (2005). The Effect of Music Listening on Work Performance. *Psychology of Music* 33/2: 171–91.

Levinson, J. (1998). *Music in the Moment*. Ithaca: Cornell University Press.

— (2003). Musical Thinking. *Midwest Studies in Philosophy* 27: 59–68.

Lyotard, J.-F. (2006). Time Today (trans. G. Bennington & R. Bowlby). Repr. in K. Crome & J. Williams (eds.), *The Lyotard Reader and Guide* (pp. 265–80). Edinburgh: Edinburgh University Press.

Marshman, A. (2007). Permission to Speak? A Dialogic Approach to the Performer's Voice. Paper presented at the 'Performa' conference, University of Aveiro, Portugal, 10–12 May.

— (2008). Lend Me Your Ear: The Musician as Listener in a Postmodern Age. Paper presented at the conference on 'The Musician as Listener', Orpheus Institute, Ghent, Belgium, 22–23 May.

McCaffrey, R. & Good, M. (2000). The Lived Experience of Listening to Music While Recovering from Surgery. *Journal of Holistic Nursing* 18/4: 378–90.

Negus, K. & Velázquez, P. (2002). Belonging and Detachment: Musical Experience and the Limits of Identity. *Poetics* 30: 133–45.

Nelson, J., Duncan, C. & Frontczak, N. (1985). The Distraction Hypothesis and Radio Advertising. *Journal of Marketing* 49/1: 60–71.

O'Dea, J. (2000). *Virtue or Virtuosity? Explorations in the Ethics of Musical Performance*. Westport, CT: Greenwood.

Osborne, P. (2006). The Dreambird of Experience: Utopia, Possibility, Boredom. *Radical Philosophy* 137: 36–44.

Perrey, B. (2007). Music Analysis as Performance: Or, Glenn Gould as Performative Analyst. Paper presented at the Royal Northern College of Music, Manchester, UK, 7 December.

Rehding, A. (1998). Towards a 'Logic of Discontinuity' in Stravinsky's *Symphonies of Wind Instruments*: Hasty, Kramer and Straus Reconsidered. *Music Analysis* 17/1: 39–67.

Roberts, D. (1991). *Art and Enlightenment: Aesthetic Theory after Adorno*. Lincoln, NE: University of Nebraska Press.

Rosen, C. (1994). *The Frontiers of Meaning: Three Informal Lectures on Music*. New York: Kahn & Averill.

Rutsky, R. (2002). Pop-up Theory: Distraction and Consumption in the Age of Meta-Information. *Journal of Visual Culture* 1/3: 279–94.

Saint Augustine (1991). *Confessions* (trans. H. Chadwick). Oxford: Oxford University Press.

Sloboda, J. (2009). Music in Everyday Life: the Role of the Emotions. Paper presented at the Institute of Musical Research, London, UK, 7 May.

— Minassian, C. & Gayford, C. (2003). Assisting Advanced Musicians to Enhance their Expressivity: An Intervention Study. Paper presented at the Fifth Triennial Conference of the European Society for the Cognitive Sciences of Music (ESCOM), Hannover, Germany, 8–13 September.

Smith, G. (1995). *Lost in Music*. London: Picador.

Smith, R. (1998). Distraction. *Angelaki* 3/2: 133–46.

Subotnik, R. (1996). Toward a Deconstruction of Structural Listening: A Critique of Schoenberg, Adorno, and Stravinsky. In R. Subotnik, *Deconstructive*

Variations: Music and Reason in Western Society (pp. 148–76). Minneapolis: University of Minnesota Press.

Szendy, P. (2008). *Listen: A History of our Ears* (trans. C. Mandell). New York: Fordham University Press.

Taruskin, R. (1996). *Stravinsky and the Russian Traditions: A Biography of the Works through Mavra*. Oxford: Oxford University Press.

Van den Toorn, P. (1983). *The Music of Igor Stravinsky*. New Haven: Yale University Press.

Walsh, S. (1993). *The Music of Stravinsky*. Oxford: Oxford University Press.

Wang, S.-M., Kulkarni, L., Dolev, J. & Kain, Z. (2002). Music and Preoperative Anxiety: A Randomized, Controlled Study. *Anesthesia & Analgesia* 94: 1489–94.

Waters, L. (2003). Come Softly, Darling, Hear What I Say: Listening in a State of Distraction – A Tribute to the Work of Walter Benjamin, Elvis Presley, and Robert Christgau. *Boundary 2* 30/1: 199–212.

White, E. W. (1930). *Stravinsky's Sacrifice to Apollo*. London: Hogarth Press.

Wiesenthal, D., Hennessy, D. & Totten, B. (2000). The Influence of Music on Driver Stress. *Journal of Applied Social Psychology* 30/8: 1709–19.

Williamon, A., Valentine, E. & Valentine, J. (2002). Shifting the Focus of Attention between Levels of Musical Structure. *European Journal of Cognitive Psychology* 14/4: 493–520.

Wöllner, C., Halfpenny, E., Ho, S. & Kurosawa, K. (2003). The Effects of Distracted Inner Hearing on Sight-Reading. *Psychology of Music* 31/4: 377–89.

Chapter 6
The Semiotic Gesture

Ole Kühl

Musical meaning is fluid. The same piece of music can mean different things to different people, and the same person can experience a piece of music differently in different contexts. This does not mean, however, that the relationship between music as perceived structure and music as experienced content is absolutely arbitrary. We can share a musical experience, we can identify with specific musical styles and, most importantly, we seem − in all cultures and at all times − to use music as an indispensable part of our most meaningful moments, as a device for sharing and bonding. So, although musical meaning cannot be pinpointed in any specified manner, like the meaning of language, there is still an amount of stable substance in musical communication, which can be defined. The most important, stable element in a musical semantics is the primary signification from musical phrase to gesture and from musical gesture to emotional content and social belongingness.

The musical gesture epitomizes human expressivity. It represents an implied level of communication, in which a musical phrase signifies a gesture. In this way, gesture becomes the key to the understanding of musical meaning. To borrow an elegant formulation from Colwyn Trevarthen, 'music is audible gesture' (Trevarthen 2000: 172). Our perception seems to extract certain shapes and patterns from the surface of the musical stream, which are subsequently represented in the mind as internalized gesture. This is no surprise for those of us who happen to experience music in this way and there is further confirmation from neuroscience that somatosensory centres in the brain are active when we are engaged in musical activities. It is, perhaps, a little more surprising that one of the primary voices against the idea of extramusical meaning − that of Eduard Hanslick − also could be interpreted in support of this idea. What else should Hanslick mean by his famous statement that music is 'Tönend bewegte Formen', which has been variously translated as 'dynamic sound patterns' by Susanne Langer (Langer 1942: 225); as 'tonally sounding form' by Robert Hatten (Hatten 2004: 224); and as 'sonically moving forms' by Thomas Grey (Grey 2006)?

In what follows, I shall discuss the psychological and cognitive perspectives of this strange phenomenon of metaphoric mapping from the sound domain to the body domain. I shall then plead for a reorientation of musical semiotics, where I will be arguing that the gesture represents a denotational level in music. Finally, I shall propose that the musical gesture, as a sign, represents the link between music as sound, on the one hand, and an intersubjectively founded social and emotional content on the other.

Gesture as Expressive Sharing

The view of musical gesture that I am advocating here is inspired by the work of developmental psychologists such as Colwyn Trevarthen and Daniel Stern (Trevarthen 2000; Stern 1998). According to their account of the development of social and cognitive skills, our unique human ability to have a language and a culture begins with the primordial experience of the intersubjective sharing of emotion and sensation between infant and carer. It seems that our earliest, dyadic communication combines gestures with vocalizations and touch, thus unfolding in several modalities simultaneously: visually, somatically and aurally.

There is ample clinical evidence that perception at the earliest stages of consciousness is not modality specific (Stern 1998: 57 ff. Trevarthen 1994; Trevarthen 2000). A perceived gestalt in the mind of a baby is thought not to be tied to the visual, the auditive or the sensorymotoric modality, but rather to be represented amodally. When an infant is engaged in the exchange of gestures, vocalizations and facial expressions with a carer, there is no distinction for the infant between the different modes of communication (somatic, auditive and visual). They are, according to this theory, represented in the mind of the infant as a unified, amodal gestalt. Stern describes the properties of such a gestalt in the following terms: 'The experiments on crossmodal capacities suggest that some properties of people and things, such as shape, intensity level, motion, number, and rhythm, are experienced directly as global, amodal perceptual qualities' (Stern 1998: 53).

The primordial perception can be characterized as integrated, amodal, pre-verbal and generic, and only at a later point does it become stratified into different modalities, in fact much of the learning process in kindergartens and preschools is concerned with the establishment of a modality-specific perception in which the child becomes adept at distinguishing the functioning of the ears, the eyes, and so on. At a later age many of us lose the ability to consciously access the level of amodal perception, but it is believed that much artistic expression originates from layers of pre-verbal consciousness, thus being partly dependent on functions of crossmodality.

Considering the development of human cognition in this light, we find that cognitive functions are active at all levels of consciousness. At the deeper, or earlier, levels they form the foundation of a mature and sophisticated cognition, emerging at a later age. It is important to understand that the earliest levels of what Stern calls 'senses of self' are not simply replaced, the way a snake sheds its hide, but stay with us as more abstract levels of thought. And, just like the next stage of consciousness does not replace the earlier form, but depends on it like the learning of arithmetic depends on the ability to count, the development of more sophisticated cognitive functions does not mean that simpler forms are excluded. In other words, even though we may not be aware of it, this early state of intersubjective sharing of amodal gestalts remains with us as fundamental for our social and communicative skills. Such is the origin of the musical gesture.

Musical Element and Cognitive Response

But how are we to understand this phenomenon we call a musical gesture? Can music make gestures? Or is music merely 'auditory cheesecake', something that pleases the senses like a stream of hot water in the shower? Cognitive science teaches us that neither is true. Music is sound structured in a human fashion. The structure makes it feasible for humans to respond in certain ways when perceiving the sound. These responses are biologically constrained, while being shared by many people in a culture, and the creators of the music – musicians and composers – shape the music they produce based on their knowledge of our cognitive responses.

The musical gesture is a cognitive phenomenon, emerging in the mind in response to musical priming. When we listen to music, what we actually hear is an auditory stream, which is subsequently being processed by auditory perception. In order to economically and effectually process the sonic stream of information, our cognitive apparatus stands in need of organizing input in 'chunks' of a certain size. These chunks are represented amodally in the mind as gestalts, and variously described as 'moving forms' (Hanslick), 'vitality affects' (Stern) and 'energetic shaping' (Hatten). Musical gesture stems from the generic level of perception, where it is tied to gestalt perception, motor movement and mental imagery. Gestures, accordingly, are rich gestalts that combine auditory information (hearing the movement) with implied visual information (imagining the movement), somatosensory information (feeling the movement) and emotional information (interpreting the movement). At a higher level of cognition, gestures are organized in groups and sequences, leading to musical form and narrative, but that will not be considered here.

The Musical Sign

The pairing of musical element with cognitive response, the metaphoric mapping from music domain to motor domain, is semiotic by nature. It pertains to the way human beings make sense of the world. In other words, I am suggesting that the musical gesture – as a cognitive response to musical priming – is a way of making sense of music, through the transformation of the auditory stream to interpretable chunks. The gesture becomes a way of understanding music as a semiotic system, which is comparable to other semiotic systems. Such a view could help to bring music out of its isolated status as a highly specialized phenomenon and into the broader social and aesthetic field of human activity, expression and communication.

In order to understand this, we have to perform a careful analysis of the sign function. Interestingly, the analysis of the sign as a cognitive function brings us right back to Saussure. In his original definition of the sign function, Saussure declares that 'the two elements involved in the linguistic sign are both psychological and are connected in the brain by an associative link' (Saussure 1983: 66). In the sign, Saussure sees the linking of a sound pattern with a concept, where the former is to be understood as 'a hearer's psychological impression of a sound' (Saussure, 1983: 66) and not as the physical sound itself (see Figure 6.1).

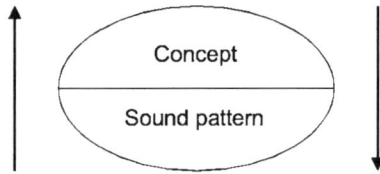

Figure 6.1   The Saussurean sign function

For Saussure, the sign is a mental entity, and the sign function is purely phenomenological. We can contrast this with the sign according to Peirce, for whom a sign stands for something to someone (Peirce 1992). He tries to combine the best of both worlds, holding the sign to be something that links the phenophysical (mental world) with the genophysical (real world), thus leaving the status of the sign ontologically adrift. Whether signs are physical, psychological, both or neither is never quite clear with Peirce, and his development of sign typologies and levels of signification has not made this crucial question any clearer. This is the crux of the controversy between American semiotics and European semiology, with the American branch leaning ever stronger to the physical side, and the European branch to the phenomenological.

It concerns the present discussion, because musical semiotics to date mainly has been based on Peircean theories. The two best known and most influential theories, those of Philip Tagg and Eero Tarasti (Tagg 1992; Tarasti 1994), have, their many qualities notwithstanding, developed intricate, music-specific sign typologies based on Peirce. This means that they analyse musical phenomena through a coding system in which a specific musical element is said to belong to a specific class of signs. In order to understand this code, you have to understand the sign system, and this understanding fails at a certain point, because of an insufficient analysis of the sign function. Taking a system that is already unclear at the outset, and applying it to something as enigmatic as music, does not bring greater clarity to the field. At the same time, such a procedure adds to the division between music and the rest of the human sphere, because it is based on the assumption that musical cognition is separate from general cognition. Nothing could be more wrong!

The Sign Function

All human activities can be subject to specialization, and humans can develop great skills in any field they set their mind to, including music. But, at the outset, an activity such as musical expression and reception is ubiquitously human, and therefore must proceed from general human cognition first, before being specialized. Therefore, an understanding of highly developed musical cognition cannot be valid if it does not proceed from an account of 'natural', generic musical cognition. And this account must be based on a theory of general cognition first, before a musical specialization of theories is attempted. A theory of musical cognition can only be useful and valid – for musicology as well as for general cognitive science – when the following is clear: what is the limitation of the general theory that forces us to look for a specialized theory? And, how does the specialized theory relate to and improve the general theory?

An analysis of the sign function must be based on cognitive theory and neuroscientific data to be plausible. Using the musical gesture as a paradigm example, we have seen that the auditory system extracts patterns, such as musical phrases, from the auditory stream. In a Saussurean sign function these will function as signifiers or *signifiants*. Then a cognitive response is evoked in the form of a musical gesture, which will serve as the signified or *signifié*. The sign is a unified whole with an expression plane (signifier) and a content plane (signified). This makes the musical phrase be experienced semiotically as a sound pattern signifying a gesture. Movement is embedded in sound (see Figure 6.2).

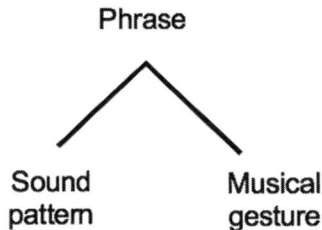

Phrase

Sound pattern   **Musical gesture**

Figure 6.2   The musical sign function

This is the basic musical sign function, and it represents the denotational level of musical signification. The cognitive function – musical element to evoked response – is basically a sign function with an expression level and a content level, as Hjelmslev demands of a bi-planar or true semiotics (Hjelmslev 1961). One can find many other music response pairs like this, but the sound-to-gesture sign is generic because it instantiates the embodied level of musical experience.

Just like the musical gesture is the key to musical meaning, the phrase-to-gesture sign invokes a new, semiotic approach to musical analysis.

The Meaning of Gesture

When we compare a sign such as the musical phrase with a sign such as a sentence, we see, of course, that the musical sign has a low level of specification, while the linguistic sign has a high level of specification. The musical sign is more vague, more general, while the linguistic sign is more precisely defined. This difference does not make the musical phrase any less a sign. Instead, it should be seen as a qualitative distinction between two semiotic systems, telling us something about what it means to be human. The apparent vagueness of the musical sign does not make it completely empty, a non-sign as Umberto Eco would have it (Eco 1976). The specification is at a lower level, indicating a general direction rather than a specific object. A gesture communicates, in fact it represents a more basic or generic level of communication than words. It is a natural form of communication, the first one learned, and the last resort when language fails. It has become internalized through a so-called Vygotskyan turn, and now it can be activated by music as a mentally represented gesture, as indicated by activity in the Supplementary Motor Area (SMA).

The gesture is a physical expression of feeling and sensation. The intersubjective sharing of facial expressions and communicative gestures means the sharing of inner states of being. These kinds of somatic signs are directly conveying information of a subject's emotional state and intention. Such information is embedded in the gesture-as-sign, and evoked by the implied gesture of a musical phrase. The signified becomes a new sign with a signifier (movement) and a signified (emotional state), yielding a so-called sign cascade (see Figure 6.3).

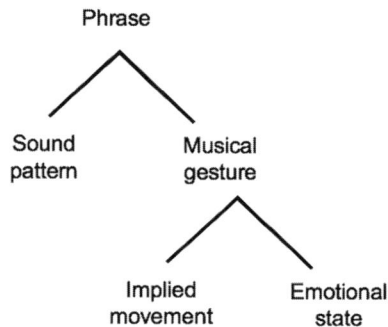

Figure 6.3   The gesture as sign

As part of our cultural programming, the re-performance of specific manners of gesticulation and signification – as in classical concerts and other musical rites – represents a level of learning and reinforcement of cultural values and of stylized levels of communication. Music can be seen as a whole semiosphere of signs and sign functions, of signs yielding signs, of learned evoked responses to certain types of input. Gestures transmit meaning, not only in the present, but through history as well. Consider the gallant style of Mozart, which transmits gestures from the royal courts of eighteenth-century Central Europe to the present; or the vocal articulations of joy in gospel music that has saturated so much of twentieth-century popular music. As embodied meaning, gestures are an important part of our national and cultural identities. And in music, the sharing of gestures is further intensified through the pulse, which brings about a synchronization of implied movements. This is the power of music.

We can share a musical experience, we can identify with specific musical styles, and, most importantly, we seem – in all cultures and at all times – to use music as an indispensable part of our most meaningful moments, as a device for sharing and bonding. So, although musical meaning cannot be pinpointed in any specified manner, like the meaning of language, there is still an amount of stable substance in musical communication, which can be defined. The most important, stable element in a musical semantics is the primary signification from musical phrase to gesture and from musical gesture to emotional content and social belongingness.

References

Eco, U. (1976). *A Theory of Semiotics*. Chicago: Indiana University Press.

Grey, T. (2006). Eduard Hanslick. In L. Macy (ed.), *Grove Music Online*. (http://www.grovemusic.com; accessed May 2006).

Hatten, R. S. (2004). *Interpreting Musical Gestures, Topics and Tropes*. Bloomington: Indiana University Press.

Hjelmslev, L. (1961). *Prolegomena to a Theory of Language*. Madison: University of Wisconsin Press.

Langer, S. K. (1942). *Philosophy in a New Key*. Cambridge, MA: Harvard University Press.

Peirce, C. S. (1992). *The Essential Peirce: Selected Philosophical Writings: 1867–93*. Volume 1. Chicago: Indiana University Press.

Saussure, F. de (1983). *Course in General Linguistics*. London: Duckworth.

Stern, D. (1998). *The Interpersonal World of the Infant*. London: Karnac.

Tagg, P. (1992). Towards a Sign Typology of Music. In R. Dalmonte & M. Baroni (eds), *Secondo Convegno Europeo di Analisi Musicale* (pp. 369–78). Trento: Università Degli Studi di Trento.

Tarasti, E. (1994). *A Theory of Musical Semiotics*. Bloomington: Indiana University Press.

Trevarthen, C. (1994). Infant Semiosis. In W. Nöth (ed.), *Origins of Semiosis: Sign Evolution in Nature and Culture* (pp. 219–52). Berlin: Mouton de Gruyter.

— (1999). Musicality and the Intrinsic Motor Pulse. *Musicae Scientiae, Special Issue*: 155–215.

Chapter 7

Gestural Economies in Conducting

Phillip Murray Dineen

This chapter was born in part of an unlikely interdisciplinary research study, a comparison of ice hockey coaches and orchestral conductors.[1] The study took mental preparedness in expert performance – the process and results of preparation for competition and concert – as its object. The author worked in collaboration with human kinetics experts whose scholarly interests lay in competitive sport – in particular mental focus under competitive duress.[2] The study had its successes, notably the transfer of qualitative aesthetic modes of assessment from music to sport and the adaptation of quantitative social science models to the study of musical performance. But it foundered on one principal problem – the lack of clear-cut outcomes in orchestral performance like those in competitive sport. Winning and losing in competition are consistent measures against which all aspects of performance, including gesture, can be measured both quantitatively and qualitatively. No such consistency of outcomes is to be observed in orchestral performance (at least not to the same degree or in a manner as clear cut), and this made the comparison of music and sport difficult.[3]

---

[1]   A Social Sciences and Humanities Research Council of Canada Fellowship for a study entitled 'Career Markers and Personal Performance Strategy Development of Expert and Novice Symphony Orchestra Conductors and Professional Ice Hockey Coaches' by Dr John Salmela (University of Ottawa), principal investigator, and Dr Murray Dineen (University of Ottawa) and Dr John Partington (Carleton University), co-investigators. While the two endeavours – coaching and conducting – seem incompatible, they are at least comparable, certainly in terms of what Malhotra calls the role of 'focus coordinator', who draws the players' attention to key elements in performance (1981: 108).

[2]   Reference will be made principally to the observations I drew in the study (by use of the first person singular); since I was the music expert, most of the conclusions drawn on conducting were mine. Without the close collaboration of my colleagues in human kinetics, however, few of these conclusions would have been drawn. At the commencement of research, one co-investigator, John Partington, had undertaken a study of performance and orchestral musicians (1995). The principal investigator, John Salmela, had no research expertise in music, but his work in competitive sport, conducted largely along the qualitative lines of the social sciences, is well regarded in the discipline of human kinetics (see, for example, Côté & Salmela 1994; Côté et al. 1993a, 1993b; Côté et al. 1995a, 1995b).

[3]   This is not to say that complex performance variables do not exist in hockey coaching, as they do in conducting, but they are often subject to one outcome and thus one proof – victory or defeat.

Our study was by no means a failure, however. Like most interdisciplinary projects, it had unanticipated positive results. I observed in both sport and music a number of what I shall call *artistic economies* holding sway over performance. By *artistic economy*, I mean a relationship between expenditure and outcome in the creation of some artistic thing. In the economies of competitive sport, expenditures such as mental preparation, practice, and the development of strength and stamina all have a bearing upon winning. Much the same expenditures characterize the acts of conducting and of playing in an orchestra in general.[4] As noted above, however, the outcomes in an artistic economy can seldom be seen from one encompassing perspective. Accordingly, when applying the model of economies to artistic endeavours, I have linked expenditures to several outcomes.

In music, many of these economies are transacted through the medium of gesture. I shall call these *gestural economies*, the subject matter of this essay. In this chapter, I shall examine these gestural economies in light of five theoretical frameworks: semiotics, politics, style, aesthetics and the psychological nature of expert performance, in particular the evidence of expert practice and of pathology. The general rubric under which this chapter operates is the burgeoning field of performance theory, a field in which our human kinetics colleagues have anticipated in many regards (but on the same hand have much to learn from us).[5]

In the economies addressed here, gesture serves as a vehicle linking expenditure and outcome. The usage of *economy* will be revised accordingly to mean *expenditures required by gestures so as to produce given outcomes*. In this study, I shall concentrate primarily upon the gesture of the conductor's right hand (the baton hand) on the downbeat that marks the first note of the performance.[6] This downbeat gesture links an expenditure of effort (both kinetic and cognitive) to a simple outcome, an acoustical result – the beginning of the performance. The conductor's downbeat gesture is, of course, one of many made during rehearsal or performance.[7] But where it is the first note of the piece, the downbeat has a special significance for the task of leading an orchestra, a significance out of keeping with its apparent simplicity.[8]

---

[4]   See Faulkner (1973a: 152): 'The physical and mental effort of paying attention, or concentrating, of listening, of constantly adjusting.'

[5]   Rink (1995) is a well recognized landmark (indeed a watershed moment) in music performance scholarship.

[6]   See Strauss's famous verdict on the left hand (Bamberger 1965: 120). And see Schuller (1997: 59–60) on the respective duties of the two hands.

[7]   The importance of eye contact (not a gesture proper) is not to be underestimated. It is a kind of gesture, since the content conveyed by the eyes – cues, character, remonstrance, for example – could be expressed by the hands and the body, albeit with greater expenditure of energy (see Holden 2003: 12).

[8]   The importance of the downbeat relative to the up or preparatory beat is a matter of some disagreement. Compare Otto Klemperer (In Holden 2003: 5): 'It's the upbeat and not the downbeat that makes an audience attentive.'

An analogy with sport will serve as an example of a simple economy. In the competitive track and field sport called the *shot put*, the gesture of putting the shot clearly joins expenditure to outcome. By means of the gesture of elevating the shot into the air at an incline, the athlete links a considerable expenditure of energy with a clear outcome, the distance travelled by the shot.

Mechanical and Abstract Economies

In terms of economy, the outcomes of the downbeat gesture must at a very minimum include results that are mechanical, for example simply marking a moment in time. In its simplest mechanical terms, then, the initial downbeat indicates one moment in time as a point of beginning. Giving an initial downbeat elicits mechanically the start of musical sound and nothing more.

Pierre Boulez speaks of 'yield' in this regard: a particular outcome is yielded by an appropriate gesture; anything above and beyond that gesture is extravagant, and thus largely irrelevant to the yield.[9] This is the very essence of *economy* in the mechanical sense used here. At its simplest, a gesture can be evaluated in direct causal relationship with immediate sound as its only output or yield.

Since the gesture of the downbeat in and of itself produces no musical sound, however, it is in large part abstract and thus not simply mechanical. For example, the concrete moment in time it marks makes implicit reference to preceding and subsequent moments – to time both within and outside (during and before or after) the musical work.[10] It also refers to the nature of the music (for example, its tempo or its character) and to the conductor's expressive state of mind (sombre, playful). In this abstract regard, the economy of the initial downbeat expands temporally to the moments around it (thus enlarging a mechanical economy centred on one and only one moment) and grows in complexity so as to encompass more than just marking time.

Consider, for example, the velocity and shape of the preceding and following gestures, which are determined by the downbeat gesture. Of necessity, the preparatory upbeat is linked physically to the downbeat. In terms of kinetics, the upbeat brings the arm to the starting elevation required by the downbeat. Qualitatively, the shaping of the preparatory upbeat gesture must accord with the downbeat in terms of *affect* (the quality, part emotional part associative, of a musical moment), so that the orchestra does not misinterpret the affect required of the subsequent downbeat: 'The conductor's preliminary beat acts as a kind of code for the musicians and singers

---

[9]   'It's a question of yield, yes. I think useless gestures are superfluous' (Boulez 1996: 68).
[10]   For example, it indicates the end of the preparatory concert process that begins with the entrance of the musicians on stage and includes on-stage warm up and tuning (see Malhotra 1981: 121).

being led, and the direction and speed adopted are related directly to the rhythmic disposition of the bar performed' (Holden 2003: 6).

So too the downbeat is linked to the second and subsequent beats. If, for example, a firm tempo is to be established, the subsequent beats must accord with the initial downbeat, must follow the firmness established by the downbeat. While this seems the epitome of common sense, the inability of a conductor to link these gestures is a major irritant for orchestral players:

> A very common conductorial problem is giving an upbeat in one tempo and the succeeding downbeat and further beats in another tempo. This drives orchestras crazy; and the conductor in question will have totally lost the respect of the musicians after two or three such inept moves. (Schuller 1997: 19)[11]

Wilhelm Furtwängler linked the nature of the preparation with the sound produced. In conducting, one cannot shape the sound as it sounds; sound can be shaped only at the moment of its preparation, or as he put it, by a preceding 'optical preparation':

> The gesture which corresponds to the rhythm, to the point, is by nature itself rhythmical, itself like a point, and given with the utmost precision. But, and this is the practical problem of all conducting, this point, this precision, cannot be attained with an orchestra when one makes such a point in the air, because what induces a group of people to come in at the same moment needs a certain optical preparation. It is not the moment of the down-beat itself, nor the accuracy and the sharpness with which this down-beat is given, which determines the precision achieved by the orchestra, but the preparation which the conductor gives to this down-beat. That the down-beat itself is short and accurate has at most an effect on the succeeding down-beats, since it marks the pulse of the rhythmical entity. But it is meaningless for the first note, for which this down-beat is after all intended. (In Bamberger 1965: 211)

Thus the downbeat is linked inextricably to the beat that precedes it, and it links in turn as a kind of preparation to the beats that follow.

Speaking in general terms and not merely about the downbeat, every gesture is part of an expressive pattern designed to capture the work as a whole. Gestures should support, not contradict one another; the total sum of all gestures should express a unified conception and elicit a unified outcome. The importance of coordinated gestures becomes obvious where a conductor lacks such a conception or is equivocal about certain of its aspects. Equivocation is a failure of technique

---

[11]   And see Strauss: 'What is decisive is that the upbeat which contains the whole of the tempo which follows should be rhythmically exact and that the downbeat should be extremely precise. The second half of the bar is immaterial. I frequently conduct it like an *alla breve*' (In Bamberger 1965: 120).

as expressed in gesture, a failure to decide firmly the meaning of a gesture and its relationship to other gestures. As Faulkner puts it:

> Performers' depictions of the meanings of a conductor's actions stress the negative consequences of equivocation. They see behind a series of expressive signs an underlying pattern in which the conductor cannot decide what he wants. This is different from the maestro who either does not know what he wants from the orchestra or is incapable of communicating it to its members. (Faulkner 1973: 150)

The gestural establishment of a given character at the initial downbeat, then, has an impact upon the remainder of the piece, up to and including its last beat, for if the piece starts with a confusion of metre or affect, the character of its continuation will be compromised.

Furtwängler linked as well the quality of the gesture to the effect produced. The mechanical gesture – a sharply pointed downbeat, for example – will achieve a mechanical result:

> There is no doubt that the sharp down-beat has its disadvantages. It means fixing the gesture at the one point, and results in a reduction of the expressive possibility that the living flow of the music demands. A point always remains a point; it is obvious that an orchestra which is conducted with points will also play with points, that is, everything rhythmical will be rendered with the required precision. But everything melodic, everything that lies between the individual beats (and that is sometimes quite a lot: one only has to remember the abundance of signs of expression, crescendo, and decrescendo which are so important in the works of some composers) will not be influenced. It is characteristic of such an interpretation ... that the rhythm, the meter come into their own, but not the music. (in Bamberger 1965: 211–12)

Beyond its mechanical import, then, the downbeat has an abstract content to which the beats before and after refer. The expenditures required by a mechanical economy are largely kinetic in nature: move the arm at this time. The outcome elicited is equally kinetic: the orchestral player's body moves so as to make music at the appropriate moment. With an abstract economy, however, decisions about the nature of the sound must be made and translated into gestures well before the actual sound and at considerable cost of mental effort. And then these decisions must be evaluated in light of the sounds produced. In other words, the gestural signal must be compared with the sound produced, and that comparison – signal with sound – falls classically under the rubric of semiotics.

Semiotic Economies

Under the rubric *semiotic economy* as applied to conducting, I shall concentrate not on *what* the downbeat gesture means but rather on *how* the gesture signifies a desired outcome. Initially the conductor decides upon an outcome, the sound image to be projected to the orchestra. To attain this image, the conductor must negotiate the semiotics of the gesture – again not simply what the gesture means, but how it will convey or produce that meaning. In doing so, the conductor negotiates with the orchestral players, who, bringing different experiences and capacities to the task of reading a conductor, will require adjustments to the gestures.

Let us say, for example, that a given orchestral player has a broad stock of experiences with conductors to which they refer when confronted with a new conductor. Conductor X's downbeat was simply mechanical (shoulders back, head straight ahead, the baton simply drops); since the affect of the opening bars was agreed upon in rehearsal, there was no need to conjure it again in performance. Conductor X's gestures, then, were to be understood for the most part as simple mechanical indications. For Conductor Y, on the other hand, affect took on a new and fresh intensity in performance; thus the evocation of a new and intense affect was one of the duties of their gestures (shoulders hunched, head inclined downward and to one side, the baton slicing expressively through the air). Faced with a new conductor, Z, the orchestral player enters into negotiation: 'Just how are your gestures going to mean? Will they indicate or eschew affect?' Above all, the players usually ask themselves if the conductor's downbeats are going to be consistent and always clear, or if they will play a cat-and-mouse game with the orchestra, withholding clarity so as to keep them 'on their toes' and thus fresh and focused (and invariably irritated and frustrated).

The mechanical downbeat can itself carry a complex semiotic content. Does it mean, for example, that the conductor is content simply to mark time and give cues, or does it mean the conductor is angry with the orchestra and is pouting: 'Since you can't play the work well anyway, I'm not going to expend any energy on expressive effect with you.' Implicit in the latter case is a distinction between the surface meaning of the gesture – 'Go!' – and a hidden or subverted content: 'I'm angry with you.'

Overriding all these considerations is the semiotic question of competence. Is the conductor capable of expressing and negotiating outcomes through their gestures? Semiotic incompetence, the inability to convey the meaning of the gesture clearly, is something quite different from kinetic incompetence (the physiological inability to make the gesture or to make it correspond to one's intent) or aesthetic incompetence (the conceptual inability to convey the aesthetic features of the work through gesture). The semiotic incompetent cannot express the meaning of the gesture to the orchestra. The gestures may be correct in the textbook sense, but misunderstood by the orchestra. Or the demeanour of the conductor on the podium may be so indecisive that the orchestra decides not to trust them, and thereby negotiations are curtailed. Not uncommonly, a conductor from one part of the world finds themselves in another part where orchestral demeanour is markedly different. The technique might be assured, the interpretation faultless, the politics peaceful, but if the conductor cannot work with the orchestra to determine the meaning of the gesture, then they are incompetent and their performance on the podium unacceptable.[12]

As the economy of the gesture expands, then, beyond the downbeat in its simplest mechanical form, the gesture takes on a semiotic complexity. When the downbeat, in other words, is merely the mechanical equivalent of the instruction 'Go!', its semiotic import is usually simple, *iconic* in precision: dropped baton means start at beat 1 and continue to the end.[13] The abstract content of the downbeat, however, necessitates an expanded semiotic, an *indexical* counterpart: 'Follow me!' The conductor's gestures invoke a definite relationship, a social structure, in ways similar to the descent of the gavel at the commencement of a court of law: they acknowledge an authority and a set of conventions to be observed. At the very least, the wielding of the baton points in indexical fashion to a distinction between the social functions fulfilled by the conductor (principally that of leader) and those fulfilled by members of the orchestra (as followers). The mechanical, iconic content of the gesture cannot draw this distinction, for it merely acknowledges the start of the work.[14]

This distinction between leader and follower is also fully *symbolic*. (Especially since the very notion of leadership that the downbeat gesture expresses is often contested in an orchestral setting, as we shall see shortly.[15]) The conductor's downbeat refers tacitly to a highly conventional social structure, one that requires the agreement of all parties involved, the meaning of which is constantly under negotiation.

The philosopher and aesthetician of dance Francis Sparshott addresses the symbolic content by calling the conductor a 'mediator', a third party who interprets and thus validates the actions of the musicians to the audience. In the dance and in opera, the people on stage represent themselves to the audience, and thus no intermediary is necessary. The members of the orchestra, however, are usually too busy producing sounds to engage the audience directly, person to person. That role is given to the conductor, who says by means of gesture, in effect: 'Dear Audience,

---

[12]   The converse being true as well: bad technique, questionable interpretation, wrathful politics, but clarity of gesture may succeed, this in the Chomskian sense of performance, that the ungrammatical might still be acceptable in the performance of an utterance (see Chomsky 1965: 10–11).

[13]   In the strict semiotic sense the downbeat gesture is a true and direct action situated in the field of producing sound, although it may not itself produce an actual individual sound.

[14]   See Pfitzner in Bamberger (1965: 136–7): 'If the silent gestures at the performance are to be more than mere mechanical time-beating or giving of cues, then the motions made by the man with the little baton must serve as reminders of his previous preparation. They must represent the renewed transfer of his will by means of mute signals.'

[15]   See Hindemith on the conductor as despot in Bamberger (1965: 237–8).

at my behest some musicians are about to produce sounds for you to listen to.' As Sparshott puts it:

> Theatre dance has no non-dancing mediator; the trainer of the dancers does not purport to guide them in the course of the dance or show the audience how to react, and may not even appear at the end to share the applause ... no more is it in opera ... . Why this difference [with conducting]? Presumably because dancers and singers are active as humans and their behaviour is as perspicuous to humans as anything could be, so that a mediator could be effective only by misleading; whereas in [the performance of] an instrumental work, the performers are active not as humans but as expert manipulators of information or of noisemakers. (Sparshott 1995: 190)

Conductors do not allow themselves to be moved as audience members do (Sparshott calls the conductor the 'unmoved mover'). Nor do they produce sounds as musicians do, but merely solicit the orchestra's collaboration. Conductors do not 'cause' sound, only musicians do, but orchestral musicians produce sound in public only 'because' a conductor has countenanced the performance. For Sparshott, then, conductors 'symbolize the unmoved mover generating the music of the musicians, who play in the way they do *because of* the conducting although it does not *cause* them to play ...' (Sparshott 1995: 189). In this symbolic sense, the conductor's gestures point not merely beyond themselves to a given agreement but also to the contrived and conventional nature of orchestra conducting itself.[16]

Some of the functions fulfilled by the conductor (marking time, shaping the sound, coordinating the ensemble, expressing a particular interpretation) could be assumed by other participants in the ensemble (as in the chamber orchestra without conductor, or in the case of the click track in a recording studio).[17] Thus the function of the conductor is to a certain degree arbitrary.[18] The semiotics of the downbeat gesture reflect this: why after all is the spatial attribute 'down' and its corresponding downward gesture assigned to the beginning of a temporal phenomenon, the bar? It is only a matter of convention. The very choice of the baton is arbitrary too: while by its finely pointed shape it lends a precision to orchestral direction, alternatives are possible and indeed common – principally the

---

[16]   Sparshott calls the conductor a mediator who transforms the situation by controlling 'the menacing mass of musicians': 'The mediating individual effects a transformation of the occasion, reducing the menacing mass of musicians to human scale' (1995: 189).

[17]   At least in certain repertoires. 'A good orchestra, fully trained, will be able to play most symphonic works of the classical period without any conductor at all. It might not have the stamp or the personality of an enlightened musician on it, but the performance would not come to an actual halt' (Mackerras 2003: 65).

[18]   'There are kinds of gesture which nobody can imitate – those that indicate phrasing for example. There you have as many types of gesture as you have conductors' (Boulez 1996: 65).

fingers of the outstretched hand, or a violin bow, but on occasion a pencil or even a cigarette.[19]

The use of the baton is motivated by a division between the kinds of labour involved in making orchestral music. The baton reifies the distinction between the gestures that produce actual sound and those that elicit sound's production, as the distinction between the work of management and the work of actual sound producers.[20] The baton is the boss's tool, to put it bluntly. With an irony that verges on the uncanny, the baton is the flimsiest – least substantial – apparatus for making music in the orchestra; its physical weight and shape is the converse of its actual power. And thus it wields its power arbitrarily and conventionally (in a way that exemplifies the Saussurian ideal of the semiological process).

The semiotic distinction accomplished by the baton between the conductor and the orchestra is of course an expression of a real division between the two forces. Given that the conductor's side of the division is weighted unevenly, politics emerges out of semiotics. The economics of politics in conducting are grounded largely (but not exclusively) in the control of gestural meaning and its making.

Political Economies

The rubric *political economy* covers in part the social division between the conductor and the orchestra, in particular the power to make decisions about the meaning of the conductor's gestures. In effect, those who wield this power will determine how the expenditures made by the conductor – the energies expended in creating meaningful gestures – will bear fruit as outcomes. When it comes to conducting, this power is never settled ultimately, but is instead the constant subject of negotiation. As Faulkner puts it, power (in the guise of respect and deference) is created, in effect constructed:

> A conductor must create respect for himself. He is not accorded a fixed distribution of deference because of the position he occupies ... Performers respond to the man and his cues, they develop interpretations into situational definitions, and project lines of concerted action on the basis of these constructions. (Faulkner 1973: 149)

Given that negotiations sometimes turn wayward, the moments leading up to the initial downbeat gesture and those following immediately on its heels are fraught with political significance and treated with apprehension on everyone's part.

---

[19] See Holden (2003: 4–5) and Bowen (2003: 102, fig. 8.2), where Weber conducts with what appears to be either a roll of paper or a hollow log.

[20] Pfitzner drew the distinction between '"indirect" artists' and '"direct" artists, the singers and players of all kinds' (Bamberger 1965: 134).

In our study of orchestral conductors, we observed that the nature of the relationship between an orchestra and its conductor is sometimes established irrevocably in the first few moments of their engagement, an observation I call *the first ten seconds paradigm*. As Robert Ripley (2003: 80) puts it: 'They will size up a new conductor immediately; from the moment you walk in.'[21] In fairness, first impressions, while significant, are seldom final, always subject to change depending on variables as diverse as the repertoire performed or the length of the conductor's tenure with a given orchestra.

The distinction between a simple mechanical economy and a more complex political economy was put into stark relief in our research by two largely social aspects of orchestral conducting: the presence of what I shall call the *shadow ensemble* within the orchestra, and the palpable delay or lag in some orchestras between the conductor's gestures and the orchestra's response. I define the *shadow ensemble* as a small group of key players, often highly visible to the other members of the orchestra, who assume some of the leadership roles normally assigned exclusively to the conductor. In recognized practice, the concertmaster plays a limited leadership role of this sort, certainly with regard to setting bowing and in leading the strings by means of gestures made with the bow, head, and torso.[22] The leadership role of the shadow is akin to but extends beyond that customarily given to the concertmaster.

In one Canadian orchestra, this group of key players encompassed the concertmaster, principal flute, principal double bass, principal trumpet and the timpanist. In concert and rehearsal, eye contact between these players was constant and often regular, supplemented by facial or upper torso gestures.[23] The remaining members of the orchestra took constant note of this group, and on occasion (certainly when the conductor was either unclear or became momentarily confused) this shadow organization assumed temporary direction of the ensemble through a set of small gestures (including indicating downbeats by nodding the head).

---

[21]   Schuller (1997: 19) gives a generous 'five to ten minutes of a first rehearsal'. Casals (in Bamberger 1965: 158) held it to 'one look sometimes'. Faulkner (1973: 149), citing Schonberg 1967, gives a generous 'about ten or fifteen minutes', but later (1973: 153) 'just a few minutes'. Atik (1994: 24–5) refers to this as the 'testing phase'. The converse is true as well: the conductor will make an estimation of the orchestra's abilities in rapid course, 'fifteen or twenty minutes', according to Boulez (1996: 102).

[22]   See Barber (2003: 21), who recommends that conductors seek out the advice of the concertmaster and section heads, a strategy that might alleviate tensions arising between conductor and shadow.

[23]   Visual communication is ubiquitous in musical performance (see McPherson and Schubert 2004: 68–9 and bibliographic references therein to Davison, Williamon and Davidson, Clayton, and especially Yarborough).

Ostensibly the shadow ensemble existed to remedy the conductor's errors and to assure a continuity in ensemble direction.[24] (On one occasion, when a visiting conductor took the stage in a visibly drunken state, this shadow group took full direction of the orchestra.) Sometimes unbeknownst to the conductor, however, the group filtered the signals sent via the baton in creative ways not designed merely to remedy a conductor's inadequacies. Indeed, the group could alter the production of sound in a rich and complex manner. The shadow ensemble did so through its own set of gestures, these presumably worked out *ad hoc* and thus in ways proper to one and only one orchestra.

In these and other instances, the shadow ensemble gained a semiotic power over the meaning of the conductor's gestures. The conductor's own gestures became first-order gestures, conveying the conductor's explicit intentions. Supplemented with the shadow ensemble's interpretations, they attained a kind of second-order status, a second and more authoritative meaning. Ultimately, the work of the shadow ensemble became a commentary upon the efficacy of the conductor's work – that it required a supplement to be effective, and thus implicitly was defective. In the semiotic process of negotiating how a conductor's gestures are to be interpreted, the shadow ensemble clearly won a notable victory.

On this line of thought, the gestures of conducting fulfil not merely mechanical and interpretive functions, but also involve a political negotiation at the ground level of semiotics – not merely 'What do these gestures mean?', but also: 'How will these gestures take on meaning?' Will the conductor's gestures be understood as authoritative and definitive: 'Follow my baton exactly, no matter what.' Or will they be subject to negotiation between participants: 'My baton gives a mere sketch; let us work the rest out collectively'; or: 'Do with them what you will.' As an outcome in this political economy, the notion of winning or losing takes on a tangible form in orchestral conducting: who wins out in determining the final realization of the score, the conductor or the orchestra?

Not surprisingly, the process of negotiation with the shadow orchestra and with the orchestra as a whole turns antagonistic from time to time, especially where the musical result differs from that anticipated by the conductor.[25] For a conductor to fully acknowledge the presence and authority of the shadow group would be to

---

[24]   Schuller (1997: 19) assigns this function to orchestral musicians in general.

[25]   Malhotra (1981: 112) postulates that musicians project a 'self' in their playing, presumably a close personal identification with the sounds they produce. Consequently, corrections by the conductor can be taken as affronts to the self. Kaplan (1955: 354) describes how this process of identification solidifies as the concert approaches, and outlines the conductor's role in this process. Antagonism can be avoided if a basic groundwork like that proposed by Leon Botstein (2003: 289) is established: 'Players in the orchestra help a conductor and engage in rehearsal if they sense a distinct contribution they themselves cannot make; they will give what they can in exchange for what a conductor uniquely provides.' And see Botstein (2003: 289–90) on the optimal relationship of orchestra to conductor and its problems.

cede authority and to create a two-tiered hierarchy within the orchestra itself. And yet from the research undertaken in our study, I believe that, although the strength of this shadow ensemble in the orchestra in question was quite remarkable and in that sense unusual, shadow ensembles of various kinds and strengths exist in most orchestras, often without the comprehension of the conductor.

The most palpable symptom of the division of authority between the conductor and orchestra lies in an evident delay or lag in some orchestras, a brief moment between the conductor's gesture and the sound it elicits. Whereas some orchestras play right 'on top' of the conductor's beat, in other ensembles the delay can stretch disconcertingly, as Robert Ripley describes it:

> You give a good hefty downbeat and … nothing happens! In a split second, you say to yourself, 'What's wrong?!' Then you hear it; the chord is late. But why? You start the next chord and the same thing happens … . Almost inadvertently, the orchestra is sending you two messages: (1) We want to be led; (2) Not one of us will play until we are sure that everyone else is playing. (Ripley 2003: 79)

Ostensibly the function of the lag is to create a buffer zone of a few milliseconds during which the orchestra deciphers and interprets the conductor's gestures (and remedies errors), and then, through a kind of sixth sense, plays 'all at the same time', as Ripley puts it. Latent here, however, is an antagonism between conductor and ensemble. The downbeat gesture is transformed from the mechanical moment at which sound is to start to a symbolic moment at which the orchestra decides to start, declaring thus both its independence and resistance to the conductor.

A conductor's style, no doubt, is a vehicle for distinguishing their own interpretation from those of other conductors. But gestural style is also a vehicle for asserting a conductor's role and place in the orchestra. Given the kind of power an orchestra is capable of mustering in taking interpretive control over a conductor's gestures, conductors are constrained to impress their identity upon their work in a fashion that cannot be usurped. This identity takes the form principally of a conductor's gestural style. While many of the functions filled normally by a conductor's gestures can be taken over by other members of the orchestra or by the shadow ensemble, no orchestra member can fulfil those functions with a gestural style to the degree a conductor does. Nor can they necessarily assume all the functions met by the style of the conductor – the expressive adjusting of the volume and balance during the performance (which a player seated in the orchestra proper might not be able to determine), or giving clear cues (while looking the cued player directly in the eye) in such a manner as to build confidence. In the political economies that hover around the downbeat gesture, style, then, affords the conductor a vehicle for maintaining control over their identity. Style itself, however, presupposes its own economies.

Stylistic Economies

In order to address economies of style in the gestures of conducting, we must consider two kinds of expenditure – conceptual and kinetic – and two kinds of outcome – functional and a non-functional, primarily visual aspect of gestural style. The expenditures in the stylistic economies of gesture are in part conceptual in nature: the conductor must consciously determine how to express a unique identity while meeting the basic mechanical needs of the score (a process that requires considerable preparation of the score). But expenditures can also be kinetic: a gestural style takes form in bodily movement, which requires expenditure of energy and effort. The two political outcomes just touched upon – distinguishing one's conducting style from that of another conductor, and stylistically solidifying one's role in the orchestral workplace – require a conductor to impress a functional style upon their work: their style functions to secure identity and role. But one of the principal outcomes of a well-wrought conducting style is to lend a visual component to the primarily aural phenomenon of music, a stylistic visual component that is largely superfluous to functional style.

The arbitrary nature of the gesture (in the semiotic sense touched on above) is enriched by this variability of style. In kinetic terms, some conductors are highly economic, preferring compressed beats, for example, while others are extravagant, giving grand indications.[26] These differences are reflected in the interpretation of the musical work, although not necessarily in a fixed correspondence. (That is to say compressed beats do not necessarily result in compressed volume, and extravagant gestures do not necessarily produce luxurious sounds.)

Gestures in hockey coaching are not so highly stylized as in conducting (nor necessarily the object of the audience's sustained attention), but differ only slightly from everyday gesticulations, this largely in intensity. Coaches sometimes do rely, consciously or otherwise, on a set of fixed gestures during competition, but these are nowhere so subtle as in conducting, since the hockey player's eyes are seldom fixed in the proximity of the coach, unlike the eyes of an orchestral player, who normally has a ready visual access to the conductor. In general, gestures in hockey coaching are a semiotic supplement to transactions usually conveyed by words.[27]

Conductors, on the other hand, told us that words in rehearsal (and certainly in performance) are inefficient, and in fact excessive reliance upon words may reflect a bad rehearsal situation, where the conductor is pressed to exert their authority.[28] As

---

[26]   The conductor Igor Markevich is reported to have said, 'Use only the amount of energy necessary for the desired results' (Markevich in conversation with Otto Werner-Mueller, in George 2003: 60; see 307 n. 22; also see Schuller 1997: 9 n. 5).

[27]   This is not the case in all team sports; take, for example, the transactions conducted by gestures between pitcher and catcher in baseball.

[28]   See Faulkner (1973: 152). Compare, however, Weeks's (1996: 262) distinction between 'VES' (verbal expressions) and 'IES' (imitative expressions – sung or mimed) as the conductor uses them in rehearsal.

one conductor is reported to have said of rehearsal with the Vienna Philharmonic: 'Around here, every word you speak is another nail in your coffin.'[29] Words take too much time to establish an interpretation that might instead be established by gesture in a millisecond.[30] Gestural style in conducting can be described by means of a tripartite scheme: functional fixed basic gestural codes (such as generic beat patterns), modifications of these codes (the way in which, for example, a ritardando is expressed by the apparent drag of the hand that distorts the generic pattern), and entirely individual gestures of the conductor's own contrivance, which can be both functional or merely decorative. Basic gestural codes, such as the generic beat patterns, are almost universal. They operate on a largely mechanical level, in the workaday world of getting things going and keeping them on track. Basic codes allow little leeway for the expression of an individual style, and yet it is precisely the security and consistency of the gesture at this level that endears a conductor to an orchestra. In this regard, gestural style is expressed in the negative: the conductor does not allow the gestural expression of an individuality to detract from the basic stability of their gestural style. Meeting the fundamental need for clarity and consistency, however, does not preclude modifying the basic and generic gestural codes, as long as clarity is preserved. Even the most basic beat patterns can take on a modest stylistic imprint.

The principal vehicle for expressing identity is a largely non-functional set of gestures unique to a given conductor, which often accomplish little or nothing mechanical in and of themselves, but instead either work to elicit a particular and specialized affect from the players or serve merely as interesting bodily motions for the aesthetic satisfaction of the audience. In regard to the latter, when style exceeds utility, it takes on an aesthetic function, to which we turn shortly. It is important, however, to note here a residue of politics in style. The stylistically basic generic gestures can be called *local*, since their mastery does nothing to distinguish a conductor, to make their work special beyond merely getting an orchestra going. The *Kappelmeister* functions at this level, doing a job that is of strictly local importance. On the other hand, highly individual gestures unique to a given conductor can be called *travelling*, since it is often this high level of stylization that gives a conductor a reputation and a consequent travelling career. Leonard Bernstein was a master of stylization, and for this reason (among others) his career was international in scope. The travelling conductor does not necessarily surrender basic generic gestures, such as the beat patterns. But in extreme cases the generic recedes behind a facade of idiosyncratic gestures, thus style leaves behind function, and the gesture becomes an artistic thing in its own right, an object of aesthetics.

---

[29]   In Barber (2003: 24). Compare Robert Ripley's description of Erich Leinsdorf in Ripley (2003: 82).

[30]   Malhotra (1981: 105) describes an intense interpersonal immediacy (called 'we relationship') dependent almost exclusively on gesture. And see Kaplan (1955: 354–5).

Aesthetic Economies

The aesthetic economy of the gesture involves at least two kinds of beauty: the beauty resident in the style of the gesture in and of itself, and the beauty that accrues to the style of a gesture by virtue of its association with the music performed.[31] We call the former *resident*: a conductor is doing their job, and in doing so they move the body gratuitously in an aesthetically interesting manner. Let us call the latter *sympathetic*: if the conductor's gestures match visually some aural aspect of the music (quite apart from any mechanical function being fulfilled), this may engender an aesthetic experience on the part of the audience. The author recalls watching Pierre Boulez conducting Stravinsky's *Rite of Spring* with the New York Philharmonic. While one would have been hard pressed to call the gestures beautiful, they carried with them a certain *resident* aesthetic interest in their crisp clarity and the evident security with which they were executed. The author recalls as well Raphael Kubelick conducting the New York Philharmonic in a Bruckner symphony. His gestures seemed to have little to do with the customary mechanical needs of the orchestra, but instead seemed designed to trace a *sympathetic* path reflecting the intensity – the volume, the length of the line, the nature of the articulation – of the work at any given moment. This kind of aesthetic engagement resembles that of choreographed dance.[32] The resident aesthetics of gestural style can be seen in light of the familiar action studies of the pioneer photographer Eadweard Muybridge (1830–1904), in which a moving figure was photographed repeatedly at intervals of a second or less (resembling the effect of a present-day stroboscopic light). The photographic sequences were intended simply as kinetic studies of human motion-studies of what I call here the *mechanical* aspect of gesture. Fortuitously, however, they reveal the aesthetic beauty of the human body (and of other bodies, notably the horse (Winger 2007)). In the movement studies of Rudolph Laban, the graphs of which are aesthetically pleasing in their own regard, much the same kind of fortuitous aesthetic interest is elicited, quite apart from their utility as score-like transcriptions of dance. Aesthetics resides, in these instances and in the instance of the conductor's movements, in the requirements of the task at hand.

As a simple experiment, we can attain a similar aesthetic focus on the kinetic activity of the conductor with a digital video disc recording by simply turning off

---

[31] Pfitzner (in Bamberger 1965: 135) said 'whatever the conductor himself does at the performance is something which is only seen; what is heard is produced by other living beings'.

[32] Which unfortunately is a largely underdeveloped field of scholarly research. See Francis Sparshott (1995: 189): conductors 'perform an interpretive gesture-play for the audience, in which the overall expressive meaning (but not the structure) of the music is symbolized. The conductor makes the dynamics of the sound visible'. See Barber (2003: 19–20) on the necessary relationship between choreography and tempo.

the sound.[33] In the resultant silence, the conductor seems to move to their own choreography, as if miming. The basic generic motions are choreographed by the needs of the score-cues, beat patterns, variations in tempi, the adjustment of balance. To this the conductor adds their own, seemingly spontaneous improvisations in motion. In this regard, the conductor becomes like a dancer freely dancing to the music, rather than an actual producer of musical sound. (This contradicts the mediator role assigned the conductor by Sparshott, as noted above.) I hold these to be the proper grounds for an aesthetic of gesture in conducting – considering the bodily motion in light of the customary tasks of the conductor, but appreciating it as bodily motion in and of itself.[34]

Confusion arises in an audience's mind where the resident aesthetic qualities of the gesture are confounded with the sympathetic aesthetics of the work performed or with a spurious metaphysics of conducting.[35] In the former case, a cause and effect correspondence is drawn between the quality of a conductor's gestures and the quality of a musical composition, as if the gestures somehow composed the music spontaneously. Gestures will aid no doubt in realizing the score. But gestures will never (at least in the standard symphonic repertoire) substitute for the score; they do not elicit musical sounds but merely facilitate their production.

Something of the superstar aura that clings to a conductor with a thriving career stems from this confusion, as it leads to a state of mind that verges on metaphysics. Yielding apparently omnipotent power, the conductor's gestures seem to harness the minds and energies of the orchestra with a truly remarkable facility calibrated in microseconds. To the unwitting audience eye, the conductor wields a force completely out of keeping with normal human capacity (comparable only to great leaders in the very throws of precarious fate).

In any given concert situation, however, there is a functional equality between the work of the orchestral player and the conductor: both are necessary to the very basic mechanical economy and to the supplementary abstract economies described above. To slip briefly into Marxist terms, there is a *use value* to the work accomplished by both parties – in the here and now, dedicated to finite, concrete and local ends.

---

[33]   See the stylistic experiments designed to reduce 'overconducting' as described in George (2003: 60): 'scale your choreography for an imaginary group [of 100, 50, 24, or 12 musicians]; use a mirror, conduct a pianist, or videotape yourself'. Pfitzner (in Bamberger 1965: 137) said: 'What can one say of a conductor by merely listening to the performance? Almost nothing'.

[34]   In comparison, my wife is a dancer with no knowledge of the rules and procedures of ice hockey. When attending a game, she concentrates largely upon the kinetics of the skaters, as if a mysterious choreographic force were set loose on the ice, with a rich aesthetic result.

[35]   'The result of some magical, unfathomable, inexplicable God-given gifts' (Schuller 1997: 3 and passim).

A superstar or a conductor intent on a travelling career will add to that equalizing use value a mystical aesthetic supplement (if this is not demanded of them by the audience or by management). They will cultivate a basic inequality: the conductor is possessed of mythic insight (as expressed in gestures that connote a psychic state of deep awareness), which they must of necessity convey to an orchestra as if driven by mythic force (it being understood that orchestras lack such insight, at least in mythic proportions). In this manner, the conductor distinguishes themselves (or is so distinguished by their audience and fans) from their co-workers. Thus the work of the orchestra is abstracted in the sense of an *exchange value*, which the conductor can then manipulate. But the forces that would seem to grant the gestures of the superstar conductor a role well above that of the orchestra are merely fictive and become mythological when put to exploiting orchestral labour.[36]

This constitutes a basic division of labour within the orchestra. Since it has no basis in fact – the actual sound – but is produced visually by means of decorum and gesture, the distinction is entirely artificial. An entirely visual phenomenon, such as the mythic quality of conducting, is an aesthetic thing quite devoid of relationship to the proper stylistic functions of the gesture. Its use or end is largely superfluous to the task of creating music.

A more useful aesthetic dimension can be discerned in the gesture with the help of the philosopher J. L. Austin (by recasting the title of Austin's famous monograph *How to do Things with Words* (1975) as 'How to Do Things with a Baton'). The conductor's gestures are contractual: when the baton falls, all participants are obligated to participate in good faith (bearing in mind the precise terms of the contract are subject to negotiation by groups such as the shadow ensemble). By way of illustration, the downbeat gesture signals that all participants will observe the strictures of musical time: for example, musical time does not allow for interruptions or uncalled-for repetitions.[37] In musical time, the oboist cannot reach for their cell phone: 'Excuse me for a second. I've got a call coming in.' In essence, once the downbeat falls, the conductor elicits an agreement like that produced by Austin's 'I thee wed' (Austin 1975: 5): start now, play to the end, don't interrupt the flow.[38] The gesture carries with it a host of codicils, some stipulated verbally (in musicians' contracts), most observed tacitly – don't talk or blow your nose, don't get up and move around unless called upon to do so, pay attention, don't read a book. The gesture does something, then, well beyond its semiotic accomplishments as described above: it binds legally and in doing so

---

[36]   See Schuller (1997: 21) on marketing and conductor's whimsy. And see Lebrecht (1991 and 2007: Part 1, 'Maestros').

[37]   The distinction between clock time and musical time in the context of an orchestra is discussed in Malhotra (1981: 109–12).

[38]   Malhotra (1981: 119) describes the conductor as the only participant who can break legitimately the world of musical time so as to invoke the real world of clock time during a rehearsal. Individual players will do so if a misunderstanding arises grave enough to prejudice their continued participation; a union steward will do so for contractual reasons.

confirms the validity of a legal framework and the beauty of a group of individuals working as one. In essence, the conductor elicits a contractual obligation with the initial drop of the baton at the downbeat much like the curtain rising on a theatrical spectacle.

Herein lies an essential aesthetic property of the gesture. The beauty of the gesture in conducting lies in the contractual agreement among the parties involved: the agreement achieved through gesture as well as the gesture that elicits the agreement are objects of aesthetic contemplation. Where the agreement is harmonious, a certain satisfaction arises among all participants, including the audience. In its own right (quite apart from the music produced thereby), this is an object of aesthetic pleasure.

This aesthetic quality is counterfeited regularly in the recording studio. The practice of splicing many recorded takes undoes the contractual obligation to begin at the beginning and stop only at the end, and the auxiliary constraints that follow. As Michael Haas puts it:

> The conductor in the studio ... can be compared with a train driver on a journey from A to Z, but traveling R to Z first, and A to B last, with all of the bits in between jumbled together, sometimes twice or three times over, to allow for passengers who missed the train the first time. (Haas 2003: 28)

In rehearsal, the performance of a work can be interrupted, players can be asked to get up and can be moved around the studio, and they can read and sometimes even converse quietly (and even take a call on their cell phone, if necessary).

The result of this counterfeit is a diminishing authority. Breaking the contractual observation of musical time falls from being a major crime to a mere felony. The infraction (having one's cell phone go off in a recording session, for example) can be undone rapidly by rerecording and splicing. This gives rise to a certain ambivalence on the part of orchestra and conductor alike. Knowing that errors can be amended (albeit at the not insubstantial cost of studio time), the participants lose something of the edge that live performance stimulates. The downbeat gesture is no longer absolutely contractual. The authority of the conductor's gesture – which at heart has an urgency about it: 'Attention please!' – is thereby weakened.

In recording sessions, then, the conductor's gestures can be transformed from one kind of contract to another. The simple performative gesture is a matter of direct agreement among participants in one location and at one point in time. The gesture that marks the onset of a recording, however, may retain little of that local urgency, and mark instead the ownership of a commodity, the proprietary rights to which belong to the conductor and the recording company (the orchestral musicians, the actual producers of sound, having signed away their rights contractually for a cash settlement at the initial moment of production). The performative, in this instance, is complex and abstract: the conductor is performing not merely their role as initiator of local action ('Start now!') but also their role as producer and ultimately purchaser of labour. The downbeat gesture comes to mean: 'Every sound from this moment onward is contractually subject to my decision, subject to my control as its producer.'[39] The inequality in the commodified economy of orchestral making in both live and recorded instances was made clear by the advent of the superstar conductor, whose allegiances belong to several orchestras and whose identity thus eclipses partnership with any one orchestra. Adorno discerned elements of the fetish in the aesthetics that arise from this development. In lieu of an authentic performance worked out by equal musical forces, the conductor produces an *ersatz* substitute focused upon an aesthetics of gesture that has little or nothing to do with music-making.

> The consumer is really worshiping the money that he himself has paid for ticket to the Toscanini concert. He has literally 'made' the success which he reifies and accepts as an objective criterion, without recognizing himself in it. But he has not 'made' it by liking the concert, but rather by buying the ticket ... . The specific fetish character of music lies in this quid pro quo. The feelings which go to the exchange-value create the appearance of immediacy at the same time as the absence of a relation to the object belies it. (Adorno 2002: 296)

To paraphrase Adorno, it is as if in paying exorbitantly for a ticket to hear Toscanini, we are rendered deaf to the actual sounds produced and concentrate instead upon the conductor's exaggerated gestures and grimaces, so as to justify the purchase of the ticket. We might have paid less for a performance of calibre by a lesser-known but capable conductor. To justify the difference in ticket price, we turn the conductor's gestures into a fetish, the object of our desires. This fetish object eclipses an authentic musical engagement between conductor, orchestra and audience.[40]

To sustain this fetish, audiences build a kind of theology of musical art, with the conductor as its principal ritual celebrant. A conductor's gestures become a conduit to the world their vision opens upon.[41] Thus the conductor becomes a seer, casting spells with arcane movements of the hand, gifted with second sight.

I draw a line here between an authentic and a spurious aesthetics of gesture. Authentic gestures are resident – bound up with immediate and local circumstances, where the conductor plays a role unique but equal in worth to the other members of the orchestra. This is an aesthetic of *disinterested contemplation*, according to which no one participant benefits unequally. Spurious mysticism obscures this

---

[39]   Which violates the spirit of Bramwell Tovey's motto *primus inter pares* (2003: 210), first among equals, which he got presumably from either Max Rudolf or Paul Hindemith (see Bamberger 1965: 287 and 236 respectively).

[40]   See Bensman (1967: 55–6) on the reflexive relationships of prestige that characterize musicians and audiences and on the system of exchange that supports these relationships (1967: 59).

[41]   The conductor has been 'anointed in the public imagination as the overriding source of a great performance' (Botstein 2003: 287).

equality and replaces it with an abstract division between the conductor and all other participants. This is an aesthetics of *interested contemplation* in the sense that it serves the interests of certain participants – notably the conductor themselves – at the expense of other participants.

Psychological Economies

Belief in this mystical insight as embodied in the conductor's gestures is sustained in conductors themselves by what I shall call *belief complexes*, groups of beliefs that create a state of mind ready to expend the energies required by artistic economies. In other words, the expenditures required by gestures so as to produce an artistic outcome can be psychological in nature, a bundling of ideas not necessarily related logically. Conducting, on this account, requires not only kinetic resources (strength and coordination) but also psychological energies, especially those energies that argue for validity and authenticity. Foremost among these is a state of mental preparedness in which belief complexes are put to work, a state easily corroded by normal and everyday stresses. When the pressures upon mental preparedness are abnormal and extraordinary, the mind becomes incapable of mustering the energies required to meet outcomes, in particular becomes incapable of explaining to itself why and how to do so. The economies of conducting then lapse into error, and eventually, without correction or remediation, they become dysfunctional.

Perhaps on account of the fragility of this mental state, some conductors are given to mystical contemplation, to belief in a sense of a calling, of being exceptionally or at least specially suited to the task, and of a connection to supra sensible things.[42] This is sometimes expressed in the terms of the spiritual, as in Scherchen:

> Let it be repeated that the conductor's activities are exclusively spiritual; that the spirit is the mightiest human power; and that we have to define the conductor as the most spiritual form of the manifestation of reproductive art. No man is adequate to so lofty a calling unless the spiritual really lives within him, and encompassing knowledge is associated with sensitiveness and creative organization. (Scherchen 1989: 19)

To address this mystical state of mind fully is a task far exceeding the scope of our study, but we did come across a curious mind state linked to the kinetics of gesture in several conductors, one that might be accounted for as part of a mystical complex. We called this a 'flow' state attained during performance (after Csikszentmihalyi 1990), where the act of musical creation – in particular the conductor's gestures – appears to take place of its own accord, with minimal

---

[42]   A belief that the audience participates in (see Liébert 1990: 85).

conscious direction.[43] Some of the conductors surveyed in the study described the state as being beyond volition, a kind of automatic state, where gestures were made without the conductor's immediate control. It was the belief of some conductors that, in economical terms, conscious input was a hindrance and could jeopardize creative output. This flow state was in their eyes the optimal state, highly desirable. I believe the actual flow state is *bona fide* (although requiring more investigation), but the mystical beliefs sometimes associated with it are not.[44] This discrepancy between actual and mystical itself can produce dysfunction, and in extreme cases take on the trappings of a pathology.

By way of illustrating the optimal flow state, one of our conductors described a performance of the *Adagietto* movement to Mahler's Fifth Symphony. He recalled an impression something like hovering above his body (in the sense of a simile, *like* hovering above the body). From that vantage point, he could observe himself dispassionately, evaluating both his bodily gestures and the effect they produced upon the orchestra. The control he exerted upon his body was indirect. Where a problem arose, this hovering awareness would slide almost instantly back to join the body, thus resuming direct kinetic control over the gestures. In the absence of problems severe enough to compromise this state of conscious separation, the flow state could last for several minutes. Although it was somewhat disconcerting, the strength and persistence of the state was a measure of the confidence he felt both in himself and in the ensemble, and he tried to cultivate it.

We called this flow state 'going through the window' because it seemed to involve a process of separation, as if observing one's body from the other side of a pane of glass. I shall call this the *flow economy*: it requires a definite expenditure of relaxation built on trust, its medium is the automatic gesture to which the conscious mind seems removed by a step, and its outcome is a sense of relaxed control, spontaneous, fresh, and vital, which can be communicated to the orchestra. While the experience was not universal, and certainly not universal in either kind or frequency (one conductor describing it as a once-in-a-lifetime experience), I did note its presence in the testimony of several respondents, an agreement that leads me to recommend its further study.[45] Eugen Jochum described something like the division between mind states in the preparation of a score:

> I take care first of all to have, so to speak, a passive attitude toward the work; that is to establish a lack of bias, a receptiveness that will allow the work of art to best develop its own reality ... the piece becomes so self-evident that it begins to live its own life, still practically completely withdrawn from my conscious will

---

[43]   Compare that which Scherchen (1989: 17) calls 'unpremeditated': 'coming into existence, without any appearance of deliberation, without effort'.

[44]   See Atik's (1994: 26–7) description of 'transformational leadership'.

[45]   See Schuller (1997: 57–8), who describes the activity of the mind when conducting a performance: 'the human brain can only deal with one mental activity at a time'. The flow state presumes otherwise. And see Ormandy (in Bamberger 1965: 254).

and shaping impulses. The condition described as passivity now reveals itself as having many layers; only the intellectual layers of consciousness are actually passive. The possessive, forming will is only excluded by the thinking mind. On the other hand, the deeper layers of consciousness are vibrantly awake, straining toward the work, so that an emotional field of tension is formed in which 'the spark leaps over.' This is the decisive point. When it is reached, conscious work of the greatest precision can and must begin.[46] (Bamberger 1965: 260)

Presumably a conductor working directly with an orchestra in a relationship of mutual trust would be inclined to this kind of experience. There is nothing to forbid, however, a conductor in other circumstances attaining much the same state; it requires merely the impression of a secure relationship with the orchestra (even if the truth may be otherwise). This kind of mind state connotes an altered consciousness, which might tend toward the mystical and thus support the theology of conducting, as described above.

We sometimes encountered the opposite of the flow state, a blockage that produced a paralysis – physical or psychological – in conductors.[47] I call this *pathological* in the sense of a disease, since it departs from a normal, healthy state – the conductor working at capacity, realizing their physical and psychological capabilities to the full. In this pathological state, gestures are modified, sometimes even stopped, by a problematic cause or motivation. Following Aaron Williamon (2004: 10–11), the symptoms of this pathology can be described as 'physiological' and classified thereunder as behavioural (manifest in overt physical behaviours – shaking or stiffness, for example) or cognitive (manifest in less overt mental behaviour – anxieties and low self-esteem). The pathological states we discerned were largely cognitive, an excess of conscious interference in the act of conducting, this motivated, for example, by a state of mistrust within the conductor – doubt of the abilities of the orchestra or of their own ability. I note that in a recent survey where orchestral musicians were asked to list the top ten stressors in their professional lives, the top two concerned conductors: 'a conductor who saps confidence, an incompetent conductor'.[48] No doubt the stressors involved are mutual in relation, and incompetent or aggressive musicians produce their fair share of dysfunction in conductors. Pathology did not figure large in our study. Either our respondents were reluctant to acknowledge its presence, or in instances

---

[46] And see Ormandy (in Bamberger 1965: 254): A conductor 'must, while identifying himself with the music, keep a constant watch upon the progress of the work, allowing a portion of his analytic mind to constantly evaluate the sound and pace of the performance'.

[47] In the rush to account for excellence in performance, the field of performance studies has not explored these blockages at length, especially their psychological components, and thus the following observations are tentative.

[48] See James (2000), in Parry (2004: 56). And see Westby (1960: 228–9).

of great severity, conductors simply quit the profession and thus were unavailable to us.[49]

In one of our respondents, however, traces of a pathology were evident albeit under control at the time of our investigation. Over time their psychological economy as a conductor had become dysfunctional. The case was so severe that a change of career was necessary. Leaving conducting entirely, the respondent reverted to a position in the orchestra. This pathology appeared as cognitive in origin but ultimately behavioural in expression. Gestures became difficult; from a cognitive perspective, the body came to feel like lead in motion.[50] Soon any cognitive and ultimately kinetic association between the body and the music was rendered problematic (in particular the association of lightness and rapidity as required by fast passages). The range of gestures available to this conductor became sharply attenuated; they could neither move nor conceive of moving the hands with the facility required. In other words, in this pathological state, our conductor became incapable of meeting the basic gestural requirements of conducting, incapable of expressing the beat patterns, let alone of supporting musical associations through gesture. Their psychological economy was completely disrupted, and they quit the podium.

No doubt in behavioural terms the mechanical economy of the gesture can be affected by physiology – a stroke, for example. In the cognitive terms of this particular respondent, the symbolic economy of the gesture was affected by less tangible causes, diminishing the ability to function within the symbolic realm, to associate the gesture with a symbolic content.

The psychological economy of the gesture occupies a regulatory position in relationship to the other economies. The mechanical economy will be affected by physiology – trembling produced by fear will disrupt the downbeat. The semiotic economy will be affected by cognition – depression, for example, will disrupt the association of a gesture with an affect. In the instance just cited, the conductor seemed psychologically incapable of associating a gesture with a symbolic content. I venture that this might have been produced by depression (accurate diagnosis being well beyond our scope and capacities). The normally free association between music and gesture was severely constricted: the conductor simply could not produce gestures that matched the affect of their work, or more likely the conductor themselves ceased to believe in the adequacy of their gestures to produce the desired artistic outcomes. Their gestures were thus deprived of what I shall call *motivation*.

By *motivation*, I mean a symbolic account that supports the act of conducting and its gestures. In a conductor, no doubt, there are the customary social structures

---

[49]   Additionally, we observed from time to time a level of distress that, having no clinical experience, we were incapable of addressing. Ethics forbade pursuing an investigation of pathology beyond very limited queries.

[50]   Their account calls to mind the burnout syndrome described in the literature of sport psychology (see Cresswell & Eklund (2007) for a concise survey of the literature).

that enliven their sense of worth and in doing so motivate their day-to-day life – esteem within their community, appreciation by the musicians they direct. But alongside this lies a belief in the worth of the musical work and in the conductor's ability to bring this worthy aspect to life, an *intrinsic* belief.[51] In other words, something entirely musical seems to motivate a conductor, the nature of which is highly symbolic in its relation to score and performance. Under the rubric of motivation, I call this *commitment*, while recognizing the informality of the term as used in musical practices compared with its usage in sport scholarship.[52]

Committing oneself to performance in this intrinsic sense is customarily a private, highly symbolic affair, seldom observed authentically in overt, public gesture. It is sometimes highly coded and ritualistic – eating a particular meal or having a short nap prior to performance. Often a commitment to musical performance is dogmatic and sometimes prejudiced irrationally: a conductor believes, let us say, in Mahler as a symbolic value against which to measure declining standards in culture: 'Mahler stands in the face of all this noise coming through our radios.' In an instance like this, commitment acquires a symbolic complexity, a cognitive structure both extenuated and fragile.[53] Our conductor might confound Mahler as a personal symbol (as a deeply held symbol of resistance to decay) with Mahler as an actual bulwark (as a vehicle by which to halt decay):

> For me, personally, Mahler is a yardstick, a measure of our decline, and the more civilization declines, the more solace I find in Mahler. Given this sensitivity, my responsibility is not merely to conduct but to observe and indicate through Mahler the decline of Western Civilization. Accordingly, the more society declines, the more it will be revealed to me how important it is that I conduct Mahler.

Along these albeit circular lines of reasoning, the gesture of conducting can be construed as an act of resistance, even if its aim is not particularly clear or concrete. The commitment is dogmatic: its circularity allows of no counter-opinion. Ingrained in a particular kind of gesture – a specifically Mahlerian downbeat freighted with psychosocial import – the commitment rigidifies and will brook no modification, certainly no moderation.

The particulars of the thought process detailed above are entirely fictional. But they encapsulate a complex motivational thinking lying behind the gesture. Given the inevitable decline of physiological abilities produced by aging (the gesture losing kinetic subtlety) or the alteration of society in unanticipated ways (the supposed decline proves an illusion or yields to a fresh revival), something in

---

[51]   Extrinsic motivation being, for example, a conductor's salary.

[52]   Raedeke (1997) contains a concise review of the literature on commitment in sport. In terms of orchestral players, see Westby (1960: 228–9).

[53]   In ways that resemble pathologies catalogued by the psychologist R. D. Laing.

this thought process is bound to go awry, and thereby a psychological pathology is born. The gesture falls out of sync with reality.

In this regard, and by way of a conclusion, I return to the complexity of outcomes mentioned at the beginning of this chapter. For the athlete, where standards are tied customarily to winning, a mismatch of expenditure and outcome usually produces immediate results, often the termination of a career. This is not the case in making music, since without clear-cut outcomes, one can continue in the profession well beyond a normal state of proficiency, let alone optimal or expert proficiency. The impact of a lack of motivation upon the musician, the conductor in particular, is sorely felt, in gestures in particular. As shown in this chapter, the gesture lies at the heart of various economies, connecting expenditures with outcomes. If an optimal state or a pathological state applies itself in this economy, it will do so in the gesture. For this reason, above all others, the study of gesture recommends itself to students of conducting.

References

Adorno, T. (2002). *Essays on Music: Selected, with Introduction, Commentary and Notes by R. Leppert* (trans S.Gillespie). California: University of California Press.

Atik, Y. (1994). The Conductor and the Orchestra: Interactive Aspects of the Leadership Process. *Leadership & Organization Development Journal* 15: 22–8.

Austin, J. L. (1975). *How to Do Things with Words*. Cambridge, MA: Harvard University Press.

Bamberger, C. (ed.) (1965). *The Conductor's Art*. New York: Columbia University Press.

Barber, C. F. (2003). Conductors in Rehearsal. In J. A. Bowen (ed.), *The Cambridge Companion to Conducting* (pp. 17–27). Cambridge: Cambridge University Press.

Bensman, J. (1967). Classical Music and the Status Game. *Transaction* 4: 54–9.

Botstein, L. (2003). The Future of Conducting. In J. A. Bowen (ed.), *The Cambridge Companion to Conducting* (pp. 286–304). Cambridge: Cambridge University Press.

Boulez, P. (1996). *Conversations with Boulez: Thoughts on Conducting*, with Jean Vermeil. (trans. C. Nash). Portland, OR: Amadeus Press.

Bowen, J. A. (2003). The Rise of Conducting. In J. A. Bowen (ed.), *The Cambridge Companion to Conducting* (pp. 93–113). Cambridge: Cambridge University Press.

Chomsky, N. (1965). *Aspects of the Theory of Syntax*. Cambridge, MA: M.I.T. Press.

Côté, J. & Salmela, J. H. (1994). A Decision-Making Heuristic for the Analysis of Unstructured Qualitative Data. *Perceptual and Motor Skills* 78: 465–6.

— , Salmela, J. H., Baria, A., & Russell, S. J. (1993a). Organizing and Interpreting Unstructured Qualitative Data. *The Sport Psychologist* 7: 127–37.

—, Trudel, P. & Salmela, J. H. (1993b). A Conceptual Model of Coaching. In S. Serpa, J. Alves, V. Ferreira & A. Paula-Brito (eds), *Sport Psychology: An Integrated Approach* (pp. 201–4). Lisbon: Eighth World Congress of Sport Psychology.

— , Salmela, J. H. & Russell, S. J. (1995a). The Knowledge of High-performance Gymnastic Coaches: Methodological Framework. *The Sport Psychologist* 9: 65–75.

—, Salmela, J. H., Trudel, P., Baria, A. & Russell, S. J. (1995b). The Coaching Model: A Grounded Assessment of Expert Gymnastic Coaches' Knowledge. *Journal of Sport and Exercise Psychology* 17: 1–17.

Cresswell, S. L. & R. C. Eklund (2007). Athlete Burnout: A Longitudinal Qualitative Study. *The Sport Psychologist* 21: 1–20.

Csikszentmihalyi, M. (1990). *Flow: The Psychology of Optimal Experience*. New York: Harper Collins.

Faulkner, R. R. (1973). Orchestra Interaction: Some Features of Communication and Authority in Artistic Organization. *The Sociological Quarterly* 14: 147–57.

George, V. (2003). Choral Conducting. In J. A. Bowen (ed.), *The Cambridge Companion to Conducting* (pp. 45–64). Cambridge: Cambridge University Press.

Haas, M. (2003). Studio Conducting. In J. A. Bowen (ed.), *The Cambridge Companion to Conducting* (pp. 28–39). Cambridge: Cambridge University Press.

Holden, R. (2003). The Technique of Conducting. In J. A. Bowen (ed.), *The Cambridge Companion to Conducting* (pp. 3–16). Cambridge: Cambridge University Press.

James, I. M. (2000) 'Survey of orchestras'. In R. Tubiana and P. C. Amadio (eds.), *Medical Problems of the Instrumentalist Musician* (pp. 329–42). London: Martin Dunitz.

Kaplan, M. (1955). Telopractice: A Symphony Orchestra as it Prepares for a Concert. *Social Forces* 33: 352–5.

Lebrecht, N. (1991). *The Maestro Myth*. London: Simon and Schuster.

Lebrecht, N. (2007). *The Life and Death of Classical Music*. New York: Anchor.

Liébert, G. (1990). *Ni Empereur ni Roi, Chef d'Orchestre*. Paris: Gallimard.

Mackerras, C. (2003). Opera Conducting. In J. A. Bowen (ed.), *The Cambridge Companion to Conducting* (pp. 65–78). Cambridge: Cambridge University Press.

McPherson, G. E. & Schubert E. (2004). Measuring Performance Enhancement in Music. In A. Williamon (ed.), *Musical Excellence: Strategies and Techniques to Enhance Performance* (pp. 61–83). Oxford: Oxford University Press.

Malhotra, V. A. (1981). The Social Accomplishment of Music in a Symphony Orchestra: A Phenomenological Analysis. *Qualitative Sociology* 4: 102–25.

Parry, C. B. W. (2004). Managing the Physical Demands of Musical Performance. In A. Williamon (ed.), *Musical Excellence: Strategies and Techniques to Enhance Performance* (pp. 41–60). Oxford: Oxford University Press.

Partington, J. T. (1995). *Making Music*. Ottawa: Carleton University Press.

Raedeke, T. D. (1997). Is Athlete Burnout More Than Just Stress? A Sport Commitment Perspective. *Journal of Sport and Exercise Psychology* 19: 396–417.

Rink, J. (ed.) (1995). *The Practice of Performance: Studies in Musical Interpretation*. Cambridge: Cambridge University Press.

Ripley, R. L. (2003). The Orchestra Speaks. In J. A. Bowen (ed.), *The Cambridge Companion to Conducting* (pp. 79–90). Cambridge: Cambridge University Press.

Scherchen, H. (1989). *Handbook of Conducting* (trans. M. D. Calvocoressi). Oxford: Oxford University Press.

Schonberg, H. (1967). *The Great Conductors*. New York: Simon and Schuster.

Schuller, G. (1997). *The Compleat Conductor*. New York: Oxford.

Sparshott, F. (1995). *A Measured Pace: Toward A Philosophical Understanding of the Arts of Dance*. Toronto: University of Toronto Press.

Tovey, B. (2003). The Conductor as Artistic Director. In J. A. Bowen (ed.), *The Cambridge Companion to Conducting* (pp. 205–19). Cambridge: Cambridge University Press.

Weeks, P. (1996). A Rehearsal of a Beethoven Passage: An Analysis of Correction Talk. *Research on Language and Social Interaction* 29: 247–90.

Westby, D. L. (1960). The Career Experience of the Symphony Musician. *Social Forces* 38: 223–30.

Williamon, A. (2004). A Guide to Enhancing Musical Performance. In A. Williamon (ed.), *Musical Excellence: Strategies and Techniques to Enhance Performance* (pp. 3–18). Oxford: Oxford University Press.

Winger, R. (2007). *Muybridge's Horse*. Gibson's Landing, British Columbia: Nightwood.

Chapter 8
Computational Analysis of Conductors' Temporal Gestures

Geoff Luck

Musicians playing in a conducted ensemble can utilize both auditory and visual cues in order to synchronize their performances with each other. Auditory cues are provided solely by the other musicians, while visual cues are primarily provided by the conductor. The musicians, too, may provide some visual synchronization cues to each other, even in a conducted ensemble, but it is the conductor who is the sole visual-only cue-provider. Musicians' ability to pick up and make use of these auditory and visual synchronization cues is, therefore, a necessary skill for a polished ensemble performance (Keller 2001).

The conductors' role has changed over the centuries, from a simple time-beater to an interpreter and communicator of the emotional content of the music being played, but the modern conductor is still expected to provide temporal information to the ensemble, combining this with expressive information regarding their interpretation of the music. A typical temporal, as opposed to expressive,[1] conducting gesture denotes the tempo or speed at which the music should be played, and may be best described as a periodic sequence of beats. These periodic sequences are combined into various patterns, dependent upon the time-signature (number of beats in the bar) of the music being played.

Research has shown that most people, even those with little or no previous experience with conductors' gestures, are able to tap in-time with such sequences of beats (Luck 2000), suggesting that the detection of these temporal events appeals to rather basic human perceptual processes. What is less clear is what physical features of a movement trajectory induce the perception of a beat.

The analysis of conductors' gestures may be approached in a number of different ways. Conducting manuals, such as those by Prausnitz (1983) and Rudolf (1995) (and many others), for example, offer intuitive descriptions of conductors' gestures based upon the authors' training and experience as professional conductors. More theory-driven accounts are provided by Ashley's (2000) application of the philosopher

---

[1] Note that a gesture can be both temporal and expressive, with basic temporal gestures often being embellished so as to indicate expressive intentions of the conductor. What we refer to here, however, are the simplest beat-patterns denoted in conducting texts, the basic tools of time-keeping employed by conductors.

H. Paul Grice's theories to the pragmatics of gestures, and Venn's (2003) model of the semiotics of gestures based on Prausnitz's (1983) intuitive descriptions.

All of the above approaches have their merits. However, they tend to lack the objectivity and generalizability that an experimental and computationally driven approach can offer. This chapter will examine how empirical methods of music psychology can be combined with sophisticated statistical, signal-processing and motion-capture techniques, to investigate how the beat is communicated by a conductor. Three main areas of research will be discussed: computational feature extraction techniques, the kinematics of conductors' gestures and musician–conductor synchronization.

Computational Feature Extraction

When examining the movement of an individual, be it in music, dance, sport or whatever, there are two basic ways in which the movements in question may be recorded: with a video camera or with a motion-capture system. The main advantages of using a video camera are relatively low cost, ease of set-up and use, and the fact that you get the 'bigger picture'; that is, the recording shows the context in which the movements were made. In contrast, most motion-capture systems are expensive, complicated to set up and operate, and record only the specific movements specified by the researcher, providing no information about the context in which the movements were made. However, the main advantages of motion-capture over video are the higher temporal and spatial resolution, and the three-dimensional (3D) nature of the recording. It is these factors that make motion-capture recordings particularly amenable to computational analysis. The present author has used a combination of motion-capture and computational feature-extraction to examine conductors' gestures in a number of studies (Luck & Nte 2008; Luck & Sloboda 2007, 2008, 2009; Luck & Toiviainen 2006).

In one such study (Luck & Nte 2008), a conductor had reflective markers attached to his right arm, and the spatial position of these markers was recorded while he produced simple, single-beat gestures. The aim was to examine how accurately observers (both musically trained and untrained) could tap in time with conductors' gestures. Thus, the recorded gestures were presented in life-size displays and the timing of observers' finger taps recorded. The main finding was that individuals who themselves had some conducting experience synchronized more consistently than did any other group of participants. This finding will be discussed in more detail later on in this chapter, but for now what we are interested in is the computational extraction of movement features from motion-capture data.

Part of study involved the development of a suite of software enabling the presentation of stimuli to participants, and the automatic extraction of gestural features for subsequent analysis. This software was designed to collate participants' tapping responses, and display information regarding the characteristics of the gestures presented to participants, as well as characteristics of participants' responses to these gestures. As regards the physical characteristics of the gestures, it calculated four spatio-temporal features for each recorded point along a gesture's trajectory: instantaneous speed [v], radius of curvature [r], acceleration along the trajectory [a], and rate of change of radius of curvature [r']. The software allowed any given gesture to be plotted in a two-dimensional (2D) static form, either with or without indicating v (r was apparent in the 2D trace of a gesture, and a and r' could be inferred from the full display). In addition, information relating to v could be displayed either along the actual trajectory of a gesture, or along a timeline underneath a gesture.

As regards participants' responses, the software calculated each participant's mean response point for each gesture, and its associated standard deviation. In cases where more than one response per gesture was required (such as in multi-beat gestures), responses were classified according to the beat of the bar they were in response to, and a mean response and standard deviation was generated for each beat. Individual responses by a participant, or the mean of these responses, could be superimposed onto the 2D trace of a given gesture. In addition, a participant's individual and/or mean response points could be indicated along the v timeline underneath a gesture. Thus, any gesture could be plotted in a 2D static form, with or without information relating to v at all points throughout its duration, and with or without information regarding a participant's responses to it.

The same suite of software was also used in the studies by Luck and Sloboda (2007, 2008, in press), the first of which investigated musicians' synchronization with more complex temporal gestures, while the latter two examined the spatio-temporal properties of conductors' temporal gestures. Both of these studies, as well as Luck and Nte (2008), were carried out under experimental conditions since the aim was to see how people responded in an optimal environment. A more ecologically valid study by Luck and Toiviainen (2006) is described later in this chapter.

The movement feature extraction approach described above parallels recently developed automatic musical feature extraction methods (e.g. Downie 2003; Leman 2002). These methods are based on principles of signal processing, music processing, machine learning, cognitive modelling and visualization. Typical application areas are, for instance, computational music analysis (e.g. Cambouropoulos 2006; Lartillot 2004, 2005), automatic classification (e.g. Pampalk et al. 2005; Toiviainen & Eerola 2006), organization (e.g. Rauber et al. 2003) and transcription (e.g. Klapuri 2004) of music, as well as content-based retrieval (Lesaffre et al. 2003).

The present author has used such methods in the investigation of emotional responses to musical features in music therapy improvisations (Luck et al. 2008), and in diagnosing level of mental retardation from music therapy improvisations (Luck et al. 2006). In these two studies, various types of features (relating to temporal surface, register, dynamics, tonality, dissonance and pulse of the music) were extracted in Matlab using the MIDI Toolbox (Eerola & Toiviainen 2004). However, the ability to extract features from audio material, such as the performance of an ensemble, is of much more use when examining musicians' synchronization with conductors.

The movement- and audio-based feature extraction approaches have been combined in a study by Camurri et al. (2005; see also Camurri et al. 2003), who used computational methods to analyse expressiveness in audio and movement data. Starting from a video input, they quantified a collection of expressive parameters such as the quantity of motion, the orientation of body parts and the contraction index. This study was not the first systematic analysis of music and movement (see, for example, Krumhansl & Schenk 1997), but did demonstrate the potential of an automated, computational feature extraction approach to the analysis of both music and movement data.

This combined music and movement approach raises the possibility of moving out of the laboratory and into the real world when investigating conductor–musician synchronization. As mentioned above, a more ecologically valid investigation of conductors' gestures, and musicians' synchronization with them, was carried out by Luck and Toiviainen (2006). In this study, the gestures of a conductor directing an ensemble were recorded, and the conductor–musician interaction examined. For this purpose, two types of features were extracted: movement features of the conductor's gestures and musical features of the ensemble's performance.

The aim of the study was to examine the features of conductors' gestures with which ensemble musicians synchronized their performance. An optical motion-capture system was used to record the gestures of an expert conductor directing an ensemble of expert musicians over a 20-minute period. A simultaneous audio recording of the performance of the ensemble was also made, and synchronized with the motion-capture data. Four short excerpts were selected for analysis, two in which the conductor communicated the beat with high clarity, and two in which the beat was communicated with low clarity.

In this study, 12 movement features relating to x, y and z positions, their velocity and acceleration components, speed, magnitude of acceleration, and magnitude of acceleration along the trajectory, and a single musical feature, spectral flux, were extracted from the conductor's gestures and the ensemble's performance using Matlab. The movement features were extracted using a set of algorithms that were subsequently developed into the recently released Motion Capture (MoCap) Toolbox (Toiviainen, 2009), while the musical feature was extracted using an early version of the Music Information Retrieval (MIR) Toolbox (Lartillot & Toiviainen, 2007). This latter toolbox permits the automatic extraction of a large number of musical features, similar in scope to the features available in the MIDI Toolbox (Eerola & Toiviainen 2004). The findings of this study will be reported in the next section.

The research reviewed here has shown that a large number of movement- and music-related features can be computationally extracted from motion-capture and audio data. Adopting a computational approach to movement and musical feature extraction increases the speed and precision of the process, and makes it possible to analyse a large dataset with relative ease. In the next section, we will see how a combination of computational feature extraction and statistical modelling can be used to investigate the spatio-temporal properties of conductors' gestures.

Kinematics of Conductors' Gestures

When attempting to synchronize their performances with each other, musicians can utilize auditory cues from other ensemble members, and, when a conductor is present, the visual cues provided by the conductor's gestures. Whilst both auditory and visual cues can aid synchronization, there may be times at which one or other modality comes to the fore. Previous work suggests that auditory cues tend to be favoured over visual cues most of the time, but that visual cues are more important during rhythmically complex passages, or when no auditory cues are available, such as at the beginning of a piece. Given that it is the aim of a conductor to optimize coordination between ensemble musicians (notwithstanding their desire to convey expressive elements of the music) using visual cues alone, there must be a mutual understanding between the conductor and the musicians as to exactly which features of a gesture indicate a beat, and which features fulfil other functions. By increasing this level of understanding, higher quality ensemble performances could be achieved.

In an investigation of the spatio-temporal properties of gestures that induce the percept of a beat, Luck and Sloboda (2008) carried out three experiments, in each of which participants synchronized a single tapping response with the beat communicated in point-light representations of simple, single-beat gestures. A tapping response is the most basic proxy for the performance of a musical sound (for example, by a key press on a musical instrument), and a single beat the most basic form of temporal gesture. Point-light representations (see Johansson 1973) remove all ancillary information from a visual display by reducing bodily movement to one or more small points of light, representing joints or other bodily locations, moving against a dark background.

In Experiment 1, participants synchronized a tapping response with gestures varying in curvature and produced by an experienced conductor. In Experiment 2, the curvature component of the gestures was held constant, resulting in stimuli that moved in a straight line, but with the average speed profile of the original gestures. In Experiment 3, the speed component was held constant, producing stimuli that followed the paths of the original gestures, but at constant speed.

In each experiment, perception of the location of a visual beat was investigated by correlating participants' synchronization responses with four spatio-temporal features of the stimulus motions: instantaneous speed [v], acceleration along the trajectory [a], radius of curvature [r], and rate of change of radius of curvature [r']. A series of regression analyses were used to identify which (combinations) of these features best predicted participants' indication of the location of a visual beat. A key assumption of this method was that each response made by a participant reflected the perception of a visual beat.

Experiment 1, in which participants synchronized with the original gestures, indicated that beat induction was related to periods of negative acceleration (deceleration) and periods of high speed. Specifically, there was a positive linear relationship between v and the number of synchronization responses, and a curvilinear relationship between a and the number of responses, such that synchronizations were positively associated with periods of high acceleration and deceleration, and negatively associated with periods of low acceleration/deceleration. Neither r nor r' appeared to be related to visual beat induction. The relative contribution of these four spatio-temporal variables to beat induction was further investigated in Experiment 2, in which participants synchronized with the constant curvature stimuli, and Experiment 3, in which participants synchronized with the constant speed stimuli. Experiment 2 revealed that beat induction was similarly curvilinearly associated with periods of acceleration and deceleration, but even more strongly associated with particularly high levels of v. Experiment 3, meanwhile, confirmed that neither r nor r' alone were related to visual beat induction. To summarize, visual beat induction was mediated by (changes in) speed along the trajectory of a gesture. Changes in direction of movement, and/or rate of change of direction, were not responsible for the induction of a visual beat.

The finding that a was associated with visual beat induction in both Experiments 1 and 2 supported the overarching hypothesis of the study, that visual beat induction is related to variables that reflect change in a parameter. Thus, it was proposed that the curvilinear relationship observed between a and participants' responses was evidence for a causal relationship between a and visual beat induction.

The fact that, in Experiment 1, v was found to be associated to visual beat induction was surprising, and ran contrary to the initial hypothesis about this variable. However, it was suggested that the apparent beat-inducing effect of this variable was an artefact arising from a combination of the linear relationship between v and participants' responses, and the overlap of speed values and number of synchronizations throughout the duration of the gestures. Thus, it was argued that v was merely associated with visual beat induction, and not causally related. Based on the findings of Experiment 1, it was predicted that v would again be associated with beat induction in Experiment 2. The results of Experiment 2 supported this prediction, although they revealed an even stronger association than in Experiment 1. It was again argued that this association was not evidence of a causal relationship, but was the result of the unexpected 'two-beat' properties of the constant curvature stimuli.

The lack of an association between r and participants' responses demonstrated in Experiments 1 and 3 supported the notion that visual beat induction is not related to variables that reflect a constant value of a parameter. Meanwhile, the lack of an association between r' and participants' responses shown in these two experiments suggested that changes in the direction of a movement are not in themselves enough to reliably communicate the beat. Thus, not *all* variables that reflect change in a parameter are necessarily related to visual beat induction.

This overall pattern of results, then, suggests that a visual beat is communicated by periods of acceleration or deceleration, and, as such, supports the theory that the percept of a visual beat is created by a variable that reflects a change in the value of one of the parameters that defines a movement's trajectory.

The gestures used in this study are shown in Figure 8.1. Changes in instantaneous speed are represented by both the size and shade of the marker at each point along a gesture's path – larger, brighter markers indicate greater speeds, while smaller, darker markers indicate lower speeds. In addition, the instantaneous speed profile of each gesture is also plotted. Each profile plots instantaneous speed (y-axis) against time (x-axis), and changes in shading are similarly associated with changes in speed.

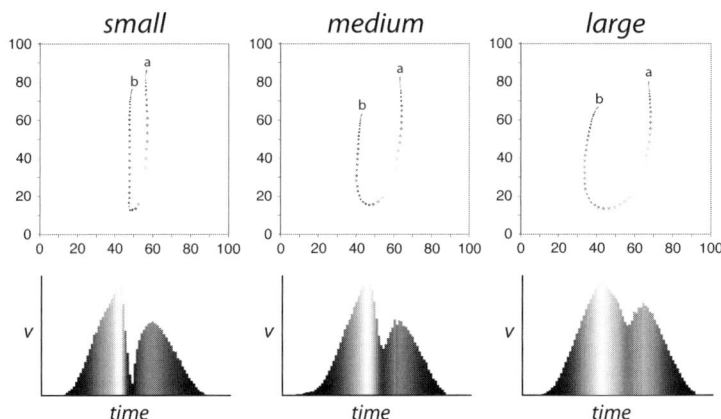

Figure 8.1   Plots of the three single-beat gestures, at the three radii of curvature, showing changes in instantaneous speed along the trajectories. In the upper portion, the gestures are plotted as seen by participants (that is, the conductor is 'facing' the reader), and move right to left, from point a to point b. The instantaneous speed of each gesture is indicated by the brightness and size of each recorded point along the trajectory, with brighter, larger points indicating higher instantaneous speed. Beneath each gesture, instantaneous speed is plotted against time. The values of instantaneous speed are not normalized across gestures. All measurements are in centimetres

It can be seen from Figure 8.1 that in each gesture the conductor's hand accelerates downwards, slows down through the curve at the bottom, then accelerates again as it ascends. This deceleration is particularly clear in the speed profiles – it can be seen that speed reaches a peak, then drops in the middle of the gesture (that is, through the curve at the bottom), then increases again following this point, before slowing down again at the end of the gesture. It can also be seen that the smaller the radius of curvature at the bottom, the clearer this pattern is.

Thus, in all three gestures, instantaneous speed and radius of curvature are clearly positively related. This finding, then, supports the body of literature on the structure of human movement that proposes an inverse relationship between velocity and curvature in human movement (e.g., Lacquaniti et al. 1983). The commonly held view that velocity is greatest at the lowest point of the trajectory is shown to be erroneous.

A follow-up study developed this research by presenting extended sequences of beats to participants (Luck & Sloboda in press). The results of this study supported the earlier one, with absolute acceleration along the movement trajectory emerging as the main cue used by participants to synchronize with the conductors' gestures. Moreover, factors such as the clarity of the beat, and the tempo at which the gestures were produced, impacted upon the accuracy with which statistical models identified cues for synchronization: the clearer the beat, and the faster the tempo, the better the cues for synchronization were identified.

The studies described above were deliberately carried out 'in the laboratory' in order to examine how people would synchronize with biological motion, in this case conductors' gestures, under optimal conditions. A more ecologically valid study was reported by Luck and Toiviainen (2006).

In this study, the 3D position of a marker attached to the tip of the baton was captured at a frequency of 120 Hz, from which a number of movement variables were derived. First, the velocity and acceleration components along each of the three dimensions were derived by applying numerical differentiation to the position data. The time derivative at each point of time was estimated by fitting a second-order polynomial to 13 subsequent data points centred at the point in question, and computing the derivative of the thus obtained polynomial at the centre point. In addition, the total instantaneous speed and acceleration of the marker was derived as the length of the vector consisting of the velocity and acceleration components, respectively. Finally, the instantaneous acceleration along the movement trajectory was derived by calculating the projection of the acceleration vector on the direction determined by the velocity vector.

To summarize, the following 12 variables were used: x, y, z (position; in this case x = left–right, y = up–down, and z = forward–backward); v_x, v_y, v_z (velocity components); a_x, a_y, a_z (acceleration components); v (speed); a (magnitude of acceleration); and a_t (magnitude of acceleration along the movement trajectory).

The location of beats in the audio track was estimated by calculating the spectral flux of the signal, a reliable feature for beat estimation from audio (e.g. Jensen & Andersen 2003). In this study, the spectral flux was determined by calculating the Euclidean distance between amplitude spectra determined from two 2048-point windows with 1024-point overlap, the overlapping section being centred at the particular time point. Hamming windowing was used.

The 12 movement variables were subsequently cross-correlated with the pulse of the ensemble's performance. Results of the analysis indicated that the ensemble's performance tended to be most highly synchronized with periods of maximal deceleration along the trajectory, followed by periods of high vertical velocity (a higher correlation than a_t, but a longer delay).

The results of this study also support the idea (for which there is much anecdotal evidence) that the ensemble tends to lag behind the conductor somewhat. The fact that the ensemble's pulse was strongly positively correlated with vertical velocity suggests that the conductor's hand was moving in a fast upward direction, and away from the generally regarded location of 'the beat', when the ensemble played. This is further evidenced by the relatively large lag between the maximum correlation between vertical velocity and the ensemble's performance.

These results may be contrasted with the findings from the previously mentioned laboratory-based studies, which have found that musicians tend to be synchronized with features such as high, and frequently negative, acceleration, and low position in the vertical axis (Luck & Sloboda 2008, in press). The reason for the lag in the real-world setting is not clear, but one explanation might be the inertia created by the ensemble – musicians in the laboratory-based studies synchronized in isolation, while those in the present study obviously did not. Moreover, the musicians in the present study were given no specific instructions to be as accurate as they could with regards to the conductor's gestures, while those in the laboratory-based studies were.

These studies have revealed relationships between certain features of conductors' temporal gestures and observers' perception of the beat. For example, both acceleration along the trajectory and instantaneous speed have been found to correlate with beat location in laboratory-based synchronization studies. Another study by the present author (Luck 2007) employed a temporal adjustment task designed to eliminate temporal lag inherent in the synchronization process.

Participants were presented with point-light representations of single-beat gestures produced by an experienced conductor. Each gesture was presented repeatedly and was accompanied by a short auditory tone with the same periodicity as the visual beat. For each gesture, participants adjusted the temporal location of the auditory tone until it matched the perceived temporal location of the visual beat. Four spatio-temporal variables – instantaneous speed, radius of curvature, absolute acceleration along the trajectory, and absolute change of radius of curvature – were then extracted from the gestures, and their relationship to participants' indicated beat locations examined using multiple linear regression.

Each gesture was analysed separately, and significant models emerged from all analyses, each accounting for 79 to 88 per cent of the variance in participants' responses. Absolute acceleration along the trajectory was the only significant variable in all models. This study therefore demonstrated that, when temporal lag associated with synchronization tasks is removed, beat location in conductors' gestures is related solely to acceleration along the trajectory.

Taken together, then, the research described above suggests that the induction of a visual beat is related only to changes in speed of movement, and not to overall speed of movement, direction of motion or change in direction of motion.

Synchronizing with Conductors' Gestures

In terms of people's synchronization with conductors' temporal gestures, there is a dearth of relevant literature. The content of conducting manuals tends to focus more on conveying emotional expression rather than temporal information (for good examples of such manuals, see Prausnitz 1983 and Rudolf 1995), and most research on conductors' gestures has focused on expressive aspects of conducting. For example, classification of expressive gestures has been carried out by Maruyama and Furuyama (2002), while Braem and Braem (2000) undertook a preliminary investigation of the effectiveness of typical expressive gestures to convey the desired emotional message. More general work on the expressive gestures used by conductors includes studies by Holt (1992), who has applied the movement techniques of Rudolf von Laban to the construction of conductors' gestures, and Benge (1996) and Miller (1988), who have used these same techniques to analyse conductors' gestures, and enhance the expressiveness of them respectively.

Serrano (1994), however, carried out an interesting study in which observers synchronized with point-light computer-generated simulations of conducting gestures. Results indicated that both musicians and non-musicians responded with a high degree of uniformity when the stimuli resembled the kind of motion produced by gravitational forces. Other types of motion, however, received less consistent responses. A study by the present author examined musicians' synchronization, using pre-recorded, video-taped, gestures with which participants had to synchronize a tapping response (Luck 2000). Synchronization accuracy was found to be negatively related to previous synchronization experience, with the most experienced musicians tending to lag behind the beat more than less experienced musicians. Precise recording of the level of conductor–musician synchronization was not, however, possible due to the low frame rate of the recordings. Temporal issues were also examined by Fredrickson (1994), who found evidence to suggest that the visual cues provided by a conductor were in some cases as important as auditory cues provided by other players in achieving a synchronized ensemble performance. This was despite the fact that, in traditional synchronization tasks, the auditory modality tends to be favoured over visually presented stimuli (Repp & Penel 2004).

There is also a growing body of work on computer-based interactive conducting systems, such as those described by Ilmonen and Takala (1999) and Lee et al. (2005), as well batons and jackets that can be used to control music, and direct virtual ensembles, such as the *radio baton* and *conductor's jacket* by Nakra (see Nakra 2001 for an overview), and the 'virtual orchestra' project at Helsinki University of Technology (see Helsinki University of Technology, n.d.). The main shortcoming of such systems is that they tend to presuppose that the beat is conveyed by the change in direction from downward to upward motion (as was indeed assumed by Luck 2000), and do not allow for the fact that other features, such as acceleration, are related to beat induction, thus complicating the investigation of conductor–musician synchronization.

The present author has carried out two investigations of musicians' synchronization with conductors' gestures, the aims of which were to quantify synchronization with real conducting gestures through the systematic manipulation of relevant variables. In one such study (Luck & Nte 2008), participants were presented with single instances of point-light representations of simple, single-beat, conducting gestures, and had to tap in synchrony with the beat in each case. Three factors were manipulated: the experience level of the conductor who produced the gesture, the 'clarity' of the gesture[2] and participants' previous experience. Of these three factors, only participants' previous experience affected the consistency with which they were able to synchronize with the gestures. Specifically, those with both previous synchronization *and* conducting experience (conductors) synchronized more accurately than both those with synchronization experience only (musicians), and those with neither types of experience (non-musicians).

Luck and Nte (2008) suggested that the participants with conducting experience themselves were able to make better use of the kinematic information contained in the gestures presented to them, compared to participants who had no such previous experience. Consequently, they had a deeper understanding of how the beat was communicated, and, as a result, were able to synchronize more consistently with these gestures. Such performance-facilitating effects of domain-specific experience have been found in other movement-synchronizing activities, such as in relation to tennis players' ability to return a serve (e.g. Goulet et al. 1989), and in squash players' anticipation of ball trajectory and required court position (e.g. Abernethy 1990; Abernethy et al. 2001).

The other study (Luck & Sloboda 2007) examined synchronization with more complex conducting gestures, namely traditional beat patterns. As in the previous study, several pertinent variables were manipulated. Participants were divided into three groups – conductors, musicians and non-musicians – depending upon the type of previous experience they had, and the gestures were produced by two different conductors with different levels of experience. The use of extended beat patterns allowed the investigation of two further factors, namely the tempo at which the sequence of beats was conducted and changes in synchronization consistency related to beat position in the overall sequence.

It was found that synchronization consistency was again positively related to participants' previous experience, with participants who had previous conducting experience being the most consistent overall. Meanwhile, synchronization consistency was negatively related to the conductor's level of experience, with the novice conductor eliciting slightly more consistent synchronizations overall. Furthermore, beat patterns conducted at faster tempi were responded to more consistently than those conducted at slower tempi, and the first beat of each bar received more consistent responses than the second and third beats.

---

[2] This was accomplished by varying the radius of curvature with which the beat was defined.

The finding that participants who were conductors achieved the highest level of synchronization, followed by musicians, while the non-musicians achieved the lowest level of synchronization, is in line with a previously described study (Luck & Nte 2008). Again, the conductors' superior performances may be explained by their better understanding of what exactly characterized a visual beat, and an increased sensitivity to the kinematic information contained in the gestures of other conductors. Thus, it can be seen that when attempting to synchronize with both single-beat gestures and traditional beat patterns, it is previous conducting experience that allows participants to achieve the highest level of consistency.

The implication here is that a higher level of conductor–musician synchronization could be achieved if all ensemble musicians received (at the very least) basic conducting tuition. This tuition would lead to a greater understanding of how the beat is communicated, and result in higher-quality ensemble playing when a conductor is present. With regard to the surprising finding that the novice conductor elicited more consistent synchronizations than the experienced conductor, there are at least two plausible explanations. First, the inconsistency with which the novice conductor produced the gestures may have resulted in participants having to concentrate on synchronizing with every individual beat, as they could not be sure exactly where and when the next beat would be communicated. This increased attention may have resulted in more consistent synchronizations over repeated presentations.

A second possible explanation is that the experienced conductor deliberately (and perhaps unconsciously) introduced some sort of structure into their beat patterns, emphasizing the downbeats, and relegating the second and third beats to a subordinate status in terms of the accuracy of their production. Participants may thus have responded in a similar manner, maintaining good consistency to the downbeats, but being less concerned with the other two beats, the effect of which was to lower overall consistency. Indeed, results of a statistical analysis supported this theory. More specifically, the experienced conductor elicited the most consistent synchronizations on the first beat, but the least consistent synchronizations on the second and third beats.

The fact that participants tended to synchronize most consistently with the first beat of each bar provides experimental evidence to support the widely accepted view that conductors and musicians tend to 'come together' on the downbeat. Moreover, downbeats naturally have greater clarity compared to all other beats because of the effect of gravity on their production. Gravity causes higher downward acceleration, necessitating a more marked deceleration as the gesture rounds the corner, due to the negative speed–curvature relationship characteristic of human movement (see Lacquaniti et al. 1983; and Luck & Nte 2008 for an application to conductors' gestures). This results in spatio-temporal changes of greater magnitude, and thus greater clarity, for the first beat of each bar compared to all other beats.

As regards the positive relationship between tempo and synchronization consistency, this is in line with Rasch's (1988) finding that faster tempi tend to be associated with higher levels of synchronization between performers, while slower tempi tend to be associated with less accurate synchronizations. Moreover, it suggests that a similarly positive relationship between speed of presentation and accuracy exists for both auditorily and visually presented stimuli. Taken together, these findings suggest how one might go about improving the level of synchronization musicians are able to achieve with conductors' gestures. In other words, the transfer of domain-specific corporeal skill in this context highlights the benefit of offering conducting tuition to ensemble musicians in order to improve their synchronization with the conductor.

Conclusion

This chapter has examined the computational analysis of conductors' temporal gestures in the context of three interrelated areas of research, namely the computational extraction of music- and movement-related features from audio and motion-capture recordings, the kinematics of conductors' temporal gestures and musicians' ability to synchronize with conductors' gestures. We have seen that a large number of features can be extracted from both the gestures of a conductor and the performance of an ensemble. Moreover, these features can be calculated quickly and accurately using algorithms specifically written for this purpose. These features can then be used in empirical investigations and more natural observations of the conductor–musician interaction to investigate the characteristics of conductors' gestures and musicians' synchronization with conductors. In terms of the kinematics of conductors' gestures, research has shown that communication of the beat is related to acceleration along the trajectory rather than a change in direction. In terms of musicians' synchronization with a conductor, research indicates that the synchronizer's previous experience is the most important factor, with previous conducting experience aiding subsequent synchronization the most.

Finally, it should be noted that the computationally driven approach espoused in this chapter is not proposed as a replacement for other analysis techniques. Instead, it should be considered as complementary to other approaches, and best suited to situations in which objectivity and generalizability are considered important.

References

Abernethy, B. (1990). Expertise, Visual Search and Information Pick-up in Squash. *Perception* 19/1: 63–77.

— , Gill, D. P., Parks, S. L. & Packer, S. T. (2001). Expertise and the Perception of Kinematic and Situational Probability Information. *Perception* 30/2: 233–52.

Ashley, R. (2000). The Pragmatics of Conducting: Analysing and Interpreting Conductor's Expressive Gestures. In C. Woods, G. Luck, R. Brochard, F. Seddon

& J. A. Sloboda (eds.), *Proceedings of the Sixth International Conference on Music Perception and Cognition*. Keele: Keele University.

Benge, T. J. (1996). Movements Utilised by Conductors in the Stimulation and Expression of Musicianship. *Dissertation Abstracts International* A54/03: 0018.

Braem, B. & Braem, P. (2000). A Pilot Study of the Expressive Gestures used by Classical Orchestra Conductors. In K. Emmorey & H. Lane (eds.), *The Signs of Language Revisited: An Anthology to Honour Ursula Bellugi and Edward Klima* (pp. 143–67). Mahwah, NJ; Erlbaum.

Cambouropoulos, E. (2006). Musical Parallelism and Melodic Segmentation: A Computational Approach. *Music Perception* 23/2: 249–68.

Camurri, A., Lagerlöf, I. & Volpe, G. (2003). Recognizing Emotion from Dance Movement: Comparison of Spectator Recognition and Automated Techniques. *International Journal of Human-Computer Studies* 59/1–2: 213–25.

—, De Poli, G., Friberg, A., Leman, M. & Volpe, G. (2005). The MEGA Project: Analysis and Synthesis of Multisensory Expressive Gesture in Performing Art Applications. *Journal of New Music Research* 34/1: 5–21.

Downie, J. S. (2003). Music Information Retrieval. In B. Cronin (ed.), *Annual Review of Information Science and Technology*, Vol. 37 (pp. 295–340). Medford, NJ: Information Today.

Eerola, T. & Toiviainen, P. (2004). *MIDI Toolbox: MATLAB Tools for Music Research*. University of Jyväskylä: Kopijyvä, Jyväskylä, Finland (http://www. jyu.fi/musica/miditoolbox/; accessed October 2007).

Fredrickson, W. E. (1994). Band Musicians' Performance and Eye Contact as Influenced by Loss of a Visual and/or Aural Stimulus. *Journal of Research in Music Education* 42/4: 306–17.

Goulet, C., Bard, C. & Fleury, M. (1989). Expertise Differences in Preparing to Return a Tennis Serve: A Visual Information Processing Approach. *Journal of Sport and Exercise Psychology* 11/4: 382–98.

Helsinki University of Technology. (n.d.). The EVE: A Virtual Environment at HUT (http://eve.hut.fi/; accessed 30 November 2010).

Holt, M. M. (1992). The Application of Conducting and Choral Rehearsal Pedagogy of Laban Effort-Shape and its Comparative Effect upon Style in Choral Performance. *Dissertation Abstracts International* 53/02: 437A.

Ilmonen, T. & Takala, T. (1999). Conductor Following with Artificial Neural Networks. In *Proceedings of the 1999 International Computer Music Conference* (pp. 367–70). San Francisco: CA: International Computer Music Association.

Jensen, K. & Andersen, T. H. (2003). Beat Estimation on the Beat. In *Proceedings of the IEEE Workshop on Applications of Signal Processing to Audio and Acoustics* (pp. 87–90). New York: New Paltz.

Johansson, G. (1973). Visual Perception of Biological Motion and a Model for Its Analysis. *Perception & Psychophysics* 14: 201–11.

Keller, P. E. (2001). Attentional Resource Allocation in Musical Ensemble Performance. *Psychology of Music* 29/1: 20–38.

Klapuri, A. (2004). Automatic Music Transcription As We Know It Today. *Journal of New Music Research* 33/3: 269–82.

Krumhansl, C. L. & Schenk, D. L. (1997). Can Dance Reflect the Structural and Expressive Qualities of Music? *Musicae Scientiae* 1: 63–83.

Lacquaniti, F., Terzuolo, C. A. & Viviani, P. (1983). The Relating Kinematic and Figural Aspects of Drawing Movements. *Acta Psychologica* 54: 115–30.

Lartillot, O. (2004). A Musical Pattern Discovery System Founded on a Modelling of Listening Strategies. *Computer Music Journal* 28/3: 53–67.

— (2005). Multi-Dimensional Motivic Pattern Extraction Founded on Adaptive Redundancy Filtering. *Journal of New Music Research* 34/4: 375–93.

— & Toiviainen, P. (2007). A Matlab Toolbox for Musical Feature Extraction from Audio. In *Proceedings of the Tenth International Conference on Digital Audio Effects* (pp. 237–44). Bordeaux: University of Bordeaux.

Lee, E., M. Wolf & Borchers, J. (2005). Improving Orchestral Conducting Systems in Public Spaces: Examining the Temporal Characteristics and Conceptual Models of Conducting Gestures. In *Proceedings of the Conference on Human Factors in Computing Systems* (pp. 731–40). New York: ACM.

Leman, M. (2002). Musical Audio Mining. In J. Meij (ed.), *Dealing with the Data Flood: Mining Data, Text and Multimedia* (pp. 440–56). Rotterdam: STT Netherlands Study Centre for Technology Trends.

Lesaffre, M. Tanghe, K., Martens, G., Moelants, D., Leman, M., De Baets, B., De Meyer, H. & Martens, J.-P. (2003). The MAMI Query-By-Voice Experiment: Collecting and Annotating Vocal Queries for Music Information Retrieval. In *Proceedings of the Fourth International Conference on Music Information Retrieval* (pp. 65–71). Baltimore: John Hopkins University.

Luck, G. (2000). Synchronizing a Motor Response with a Visual Event: The Perception of Temporal Information in a Conductor's Gestures. In C. Woods, G. Luck, R. Brochard, F. Seddon and J. A. Sloboda (eds.), *Proceedings of the Sixth International Conference on Music Perception and Cognition*. Keele: Keele University.

— (2007). Identifying Beat Location in Conducting Gestures: A Temporal Adjustment Study. Paper presented at the International Society for Gesture Studies Conference: Integrating Gestures, Northwestern University, Chicago, 18–21 June.

— & Nte, S. (2008). An Investigation of Conductors' Gestures and Conductor–musician Synchronization, and a First Experiment. *Psychology of Music* 36/1: 81–99.

— & Sloboda, J. (2007). Synchronizing with Complex Biological Motion: An Investigation of Musicians' Synchronization with Traditional Conducting Beat Patterns. *Music Performance Research* 1/1: 26–46.

— & Sloboda, J. (2008). Exploring the Spatio-Temporal Properties of the Beat in Simple Conducting Gestures Using a Synchronization Task. *Music Perception* 25/3: 225–39.

— & Sloboda, J. (2009). Spatio-temporal Cues for Visually-mediated Synchronization. *Music Perception* 26/5: 465–73.

— & Toiviainen, P. (2006). Ensemble Musicians' Synchronization with Conductors' Gestures: An Automated Feature-extraction Analysis. *Music Perception* 24/2: 189–200.

—, Toiviainen, P., Erkkilä, J., Lartillot, O., Riikkilä, K., Mäkelä, A., Pyhäluoto, K., Raine, H., Varkila, L. & Värri, J. (2008). Modelling the Relationships Between Emotional Responses To, and Musical Content of, Music Therapy Improvisations. *Music Perception* 36/1: 25–46.

—, Riikkilä, K., Lartillot, O., Erkkilä, J., Toiviainen, P., Mäkelä, A., Pyhäluoto, K., Raine, H., Varkila, L. & Värri, J. (2006). Exploring Relationships between Level of Mental Retardation and Features of Music Therapy Improvisations: A Computational Approach. *Nordic Journal of Music Therapy* 15/1: 30-48.

Maruyama, S. & Furuyama, N. (2002). Functional Variations and Organisation of Gestures by a Classical Orchestral Conductor. Paper presented at the First Congress of the International Society for Gesture Studies, University of Texas, Austin, 5–8 June.

Miller, S. (1988). The Effect of Laban Movement Theory on the Ability of Student Conductors to Communicate Musical Interpretation through Gesture. *Dissertation Abstracts International* 49/05: 1087A.

Nakra, T. M. (2001). Translating Conductors' Gestures to Sound. Paper presented at the International Workshop on Human Supervision and Control in Engineering and Music, University of Kassel, Kassel, 22–25 September.

Pampalk, E., Flexer, A. & Widmer, G. (2005). Improvements of Audio-Based Music Similarity and Genre Classification. In *Proceedings of the Sixth International Conference on Music Information Retrieval* (pp. 11–15). London: University of London.

Prausnitz, F. (1983). *Score and Podium: A Complete Guide to Conducting*. London: Norton.

Rasch, R. A. (1988). Timing and Synchronization in Ensemble Performance. In J. Sloboda (ed.), *Generative Processes in Music: The Psychology of Performance, Composition and Improvisation* (pp. 70–90). Oxford: Oxford University Press.

Rauber, A., Pampalk, E. & Merkl, D. (2003). The SOM-enhanced JukeBox: Organization and Visualization of Music Collections based on Perceptual Models. *Journal of New Music Research* 32/2: 193–210.

Repp, B. H. & Penel, A. (2004). Rhythmic Movement is Attracted more Strongly to Auditory than to Visual Rhythms. *Psychological Research* 68/4: 252–70.

Rudolf, M. (1995). *The Grammar of Conducting: A Comprehensive Guide to Baton Technique and Interpretation*, 3rd edition. New York: Schirmer Books.

Serrano, J. G. (1994). Visual Perception of Simulated Conducting Motion. *Dissertation Abstracts International Section A: Humanities and Social Sciences* 55/4-A: 797.

Toiviainen, P. (2009). MoCap Toolbox: A MATLAB Toolbox for the Analysis of Motion Capture Data (http://www.jyu.fi/music/coe/materials/mocaptoolbox; accessed June 2008).

— & Eerola, T. (2006). Autocorrelation in Meter Induction: The Role of Accent Structure. *Journal of the Acoustical Society of America* 119/2: 1164–70.

Venn, E. (2003). Towards a Semiotics of Conducting. Paper presented at the First International Conference on Music and Gesture, University of East Anglia, UK, 28–31 August.

Chapter 9

Gestures and Glances:
Interactions in Ensemble Rehearsal

Elaine King and Jane Ginsborg

Performers use physical gestures in numerous ways. They can be used to communicate musical expression, generate sound production, facilitate technical movements while playing or singing, regulate temporal aspects of performance, and provide musical and social cues to co-performers and others, including audiences. Sometimes these gestures are produced deliberately, following careful choreography and rehearsal; sometimes they are produced spontaneously during performance, whether consciously or unconsciously, in response to the way the performer feels the music at that moment, wishes to 'shape' it or perceives the audience's reception of the performance. In the study of Western art and popular music performance, there is increasing emphasis upon the need to understand performers' bodily actions and physical gestures in the generation, execution and reception of music (see Davidson 2005). Various approaches to analysing and interpreting physical gestures have emerged from different perspectives, focusing, for example, on their types, functions, sources and effects.

Many studies have already been made of gestures produced during live and recorded performances by solo musicians, including renowned classical, jazz and popular artists, such as Glenn Gould (Delalande 1988), Keith Jarrett (Elsdon 2006), Annie Lennox (Davidson 2001) and Robbie Williams (Davidson 2006), and other soloists, notably pianists (e.g. Clarke & Davidson 1998; Davidson 1993, 1994; King 2006; Windsor et al. 2003), violinists (e.g. Davidson 1993, 1994), clarinettists (e.g. Wanderley & Vines 2006) and singers (e.g. Davidson 2005; Ginsborg 2009). There is a growing body of research on gestures made by ensemble musicians, including classical piano duos (e.g. Keller 2008; Williamon & Davidson 2002), flamenco (Maduell & Wing 2007), jazz and popular groups (Davidson 2005). In this chapter we build on research on physical gestures in classical ensembles by looking at singer-pianist duos, specifically to investigate the ways in which student and professional singers and pianists use gestures and eye contact ('glances') in rehearsal. Furthermore, we looked at the kinds of gestures used by performers as they rehearsed with familiar and new partners of similar and different levels of expertise (student/professional) so as to ascertain the extent to which gestures and eye contact vary with the performers' experience of performing and the length of time they have worked with a particular duo partner. The idea was to extend the study of physical gesture by looking beyond the 'single performance' scenario that has dominated so much research hitherto, and consider other factors that might influence the nature of gestures in ensemble practice.

We begin by outlining the ways in which physical gestures have been examined in previous research, reflecting trends in analysis and interpretation, and establishing a theoretical basis for the present study. We go on to consider relevant empirical research on expertise and familiarity in ensemble rehearsal, which were the variables of particular interest to us, prior to reporting the results and discussing the findings of our study.

Understanding Physical Gestures

In order to study performers' physical gestures, researchers have observed video recordings of rehearsals, improvisations and/or performances (most commonly live performances) through systematic and repeated viewings and, in so doing, analysed the material in one or more of the following ways: described and/or measured the *types* of physical gestures (e.g. body sways, head nods, hand lifts) and, by extension, other non-verbal behaviour, such as eye contact and facial expressions; interpreted the *function* of the gestures (e.g. expressive, technical); considered the *source* of the gestures (e.g. the music, co-performers, audience members); and examined their *effect* (e.g. musical, social). Some studies provide frequency analyses of the types of observed gestures in relation to music-structural or other parameters of a score (e.g. King 2006; Williamon & Davidson 2002), while others use sophisticated equipment and tracking devices to enable precise measurement of performers' physical movements, such as their amplitude, in laboratory-style settings (e.g. Clarke & Davidson 1998; Wanderley & Vines 2006). Key issues relating to the types, functions, sources and effects of gestures are discussed below.

Types and Functions

The process of coding performers' gestures into types can be enabled through the adoption of categories used in previous and related studies, of which there are many. For example, Davidson's extensive research in this area (1993, 1994, 2001, 2005, 2006) makes widespread reference to the five classifications of body movement that have communication functions defined by Ekman and Friesen (1969): *emblems* (those with direct verbal translations, such as thumbs up for 'yes'), *illustrators* (those used to describe or reinforce points), *adaptors* (those that satisfy personal needs, such as twiddling the fingers), *affect displays* (those revealing our affective or emotional state) and *regulators* (those that regulate interaction).

Davidson (2005) also draws parallels between non-verbal gestures used in music and in speech (after Kendon 1980; McNeill 1992), notably referring to Cassell's (1998) speech-accompanying gestures: *propositional* (to denote meaning, such as the height of a pianist's finger lift in relation to the dynamic of a staccato attack), *iconic* (describing an action, such as the way in which a singer might plead with her hands together as if begging for forgiveness from a lover), *metaphoric* (illustrating metaphor, such as the use of pianist's finger tremolo to reflect vibrato), *deictic* (indicative or pointing gestures, such as a hand signal between co-performers to cue an entry) and *beat* (repetitive motor gestures, such as pulsing with the hand or arm to regulate tempo). There are potential overlaps between the latter set of categories and those put forward by Ekman and Friesen: illustrators could be described as iconic, emblems and adaptors propositional, regulators deictic or beat.

Alternatively, physical gestures might be described according to the postures and movements enacted by the performer in relation to the musical score. Wanderley and Vines (2006), for example, draw upon the categories of expressive gesture delineated by Delalande (1988), who identified gestures in Glenn Gould's piano playing defined as meditative (*recueilli*), vibrant (*vibrant*), fluid (*fluant*), delicate (*délicat*) and vigorous (*vigoureux*). All of these gestures might be regarded as types of 'illustrators'. In the present study, reference will be made to some of the types of gestures discussed here, although new kinds will be defined in line with Delalande's specific descriptions according to the postures and movements made by the singers and pianists in their ensemble rehearsals.

In general, gestures have two functions. The first function is that of enabling the performer actually to produce sound, technically realizing the notes contained in a musical score. This often combines with the second function, that of achieving and conveying an expressive effect. Although much of the research literature distinguishes between performers' gestures that are described as technical (or biomechanical; see Davidson 2005) and those that are described as expressive, the viewer may or may not be aware of this distinction or even recognize the gestures as such. Moreover, the way he or she interprets the physical gestures made by the performer will depend on a range of factors, including the perceiver's musical, cultural and social knowledge, beliefs and mood at the time of the performance, the environment in which it takes place and, indeed, his or her auditory – as well as visual – perception of the music. Thus the function of every gesture will be different for every viewer and subject to change in repeated performances. For the purpose of this discussion, we will refer to *technical*, *expressive* and *communicative* gestures in describing the function of the performers' gestures where appropriate (cf. Delalande 1988). The latter might arise between co-performers as well as performers and audiences, both of which could be technical and/or expressive in orientation.

Sources and Effects

The sources of physical gestures, like their functions, vary from one performer to another and are understood differently by different viewers. Nevertheless, they coexist and overlap with each other, and play a part in the reciprocal relationship between performer and audience. There are two main sources: first, the music (e.g. as the performer imagines it, produces it, feels it, expresses it, shapes it and responds to it); and second, the social ritual of performing itself (e.g. as the performer interacts with him-/herself in the performance, with co-performers and with audiences). In both cases, the performer's physical involvement with the music and social situation will entail simultaneous and sometimes overlapping processes of anticipation, production and reflection. As the performer's physical gestures determine the way the music is produced and the social interaction between musician(s) and audience, so the latter's physical gestures influence the performer's music-making (see Davidson 2005; Elsdon 2006; Maduell & Wing 2007) in a continuous cycle of reciprocation.

Performers' physical gestures are personal as well as musical and social – that is, they convey information about the performer, such as his/her character, emotions and feelings as well as messages about the music. This mirrors the effects of gestures in everyday human behaviour, whereby they carry information (personal and otherwise) from one person to another, whether that information is received correctly or not. Indeed, Davidson (2005) maintains that performers' physical gestures are part of a (mental) representational system of non-verbal behaviour in the same way that humans develop thoughts as part of a representational system of verbal communication. In the light of the findings of her research on classical, jazz and popular singers, she argues that vocal performers rely upon non-verbal codes of the same type as those used in speech for coordination purposes, and the expression of narrative ideas about songs (2005: 233).

It has been suggested in previous research that music performers might develop a repertoire of physical movements, or a 'gestural rhetoric' (Clarke & Davidson 1998), as particular actions, postures and movements are consistently bound to the realization of technical and expressive aspects of the musical sound, thereby providing some kind of specific meaning to the performer, co-performers and audiences. In the present study, we tried to interpret the uses and effects of individual singers' and pianists' gestures in relation to their type, function and source, as well as considering the possibility of a combined rhetoric emerging as the performers worked towards achieving their goal of giving a unified performance through ensemble rehearsal. In terms of cognitive and information-processing theories, such a combined gestural rhetoric might be understood as being part of a shared internal (mental) representation of the music (see Shaffer 1984; Sloboda 1985). Such representations are generated through the anticipation of auditory and motor images in rehearsal and performance (Keller 2008). What is interesting, of course, is the extent to which the same and different gestures were used in rehearsals when the performers in this study worked with unfamiliar as well as familiar partners at the same and different levels of expertise.

Expertise and Familiarity

There are numerous reports of research on chamber ensemble rehearsal that provide insight into the ways in which student and professional musicians work together (see Blank & Davidson 2007; Butterworth 1990; Davidson & Good 2002; Davidson & King 2004; Ginsborg et al., 2006; Goodman 2002; King 2006; Murnighan & Conlon 1991; Young & Colman 1979). Some research focuses on ensembles that have been together for many years, such as Blum's (1986) story of the Guarneri String Quartet, while others concentrate on newly established groups, including Williamon and Davidson's (2002) exploratory study of a piano duo formed by two local professional pianists. There are, however, few detailed cross-comparison studies that specifically address the effects of short- or long-term partnership on ensemble rehearsal. Similarly, while some empirical studies exploit the differences between practice habits of student and professional musicians (e.g. Gruson 1988; Williamon 1999), little research has been undertaken to assess the effects of expertise on outcomes for musicians with different levels of expertise, such as students and professionals, working together. Nevertheless, there is some evidence relating to the possible impact of expertise and familiarity on co-performers in ensemble rehearsal, raising three key issues.

First, when practising a piece of music, performers use their perception of the structure of the piece to guide their practice. The evidence suggests that the more experienced the performer, the more effective the use of musical structure: 'identification and continued use of meaningful structure in practice ... seems to be an ability that develops with musical competence and one that can be shared between performers' (Williamon & Davidson 2002: 63). Earlier research (Gruson 1988) indicated that novice pianists would tend to run through a piece over and over again in order to iron out mistakes, while more experienced pianists would segment, or 'chunk', the music into meaningful segments in order to practise tricky bits. While the student participants in the present study were very advanced, so differences between them and the professional musicians might not be as pronounced as in Gruson's research, for example, it was nevertheless possible to explore two informal hypotheses: first, the professional musicians might use the musical structure more consciously and therefore perhaps more effectively than the student musicians, in the interests of rehearsal efficiency; second, the duos comprising unfamiliar partners ('virgin' ensembles) might prefer to run through the music, rather than break it down into shorter segments, in order to get to know each other's styles of performing. These two approaches would necessarily impact upon the ways in which physical gestures might be used in rehearsal: during repeated run-throughs, for example, the musicians might establish gestures to be used in performance at certain locations in the piece; during rehearsal of practice segments, the musicians might use gestures to assist in the clarification of technical details, such as rhythms, pitch and diction, or expressive details, such as the 'shaping' of musical material such as melody and harmonic progressions.

Second, there is evidence relating to the comparative amounts of time spent talking and playing during rehearsals. In a study of newly established student and professional cello–piano duos, Goodman (2000) observed more talking than playing in rehearsals. By contrast, Williamon and Davidson (2002) noted that their professional piano duo spent more than 90 per cent of their rehearsal time actually playing. The amount of talk probably depends upon several factors, including the familiarity of the players with each other, their expertise (student musicians might prefer to talk more than professionals), the context of the rehearsal (especially its proximity to a performance), the personalities of the players (notably if there are any talkative members of the group) and individual practice habits. Performers in newly formed ensembles might spend more time playing than talking in order to get to know each other's styles of playing, including movements and gestures; alternatively, they might talk more than they play so as to get to know each other on a socio-emotional level. In the present study, which involved a short rehearsal followed by a performance, the limited timeframe influenced the relative amounts of talking and singing/playing: typically, numerous run-throughs were interspersed with short episodes of talking and brief spells of focused activity on particular sections of the music.

Third, research suggests that non-verbal communication between co-performers increases as they familiarize themselves with the music being rehearsed. According to Williamon and Davidson (2002), physical gestures – specifically hand lifts and swaying – and eye contact increase across rehearsals at important locations in the music (e.g. those points identified by the players used for coordinating performance and communicating ideas, including structural boundaries and rehearsal letters). In their study the performers' movements effectively became more synchronized across the rehearsal process. Members of well-established ensembles, of course, are likely to have developed a sense of each other's movement styles, albeit unconsciously, so that the synchronicity of their physical gestures should be evident from the outset of the rehearsal period even when a new piece is being prepared for performance. Furthermore, professional performers might possess a broader repertoire of physical gestures than student performers; it should therefore be possible to observe different degrees of flexibility in the development of non-verbal communication between student, professional and mixed duos.

To summarize, then: the findings of existing studies indicate that familiarity and expertise might impact upon various aspects of ensemble rehearsal, notably in the structure of rehearsal (run-throughs versus segmented practice), the amount of verbal communication across rehearsals (talk versus sing/play), and the amount of non-verbal communication across rehearsals (physical gestures and eye contact between co-performers). The latter issue is of particular concern in the current study. It should also be noted that familiarity effects work at two levels: familiarity with the music (i.e. as performers get to know a piece); and familiarity with the ensemble (i.e. as performers get to know each other). In this study, all the ensembles rehearsed songs that were new to them so that they were all observed at an equivalent stage of practice.

Empirical Study

The study we report in this chapter is part of a larger research project investigating potential differences in approaches to preparation for performance, in the short term, by singers and pianists of different levels of expertise and familiarity as duo partners. As performance involves interaction between performer(s) and audience, so rehearsal involves interactions between performers. We have reported an investigation of verbal interactions during rehearsal elsewhere (Ginsborg & King 2007a, 2007b, 2008); in the present study we asked how performers' physical gestures and use of eye contact compare when they collaborate in ensemble rehearsal with (1) performers of different levels of expertise, and (2) their regular (i.e. familiar) and new (i.e. unfamiliar) duo partners. An observational case study was carried out using four established singer–pianist duos, each comprising a female soprano and a male pianist (see Table 9.1).[1] The students were based at the Royal Northern College of Music in Manchester, UK, and the professional musicians were from the Hull, UK, region.

Table 9.1   Participants by age, experience and expertise

Name (singer & pianist)	Mean age	Experience together (years)	Level of expertise
Amanda & Colin	68	10	Professional
Isobel & George	57	15	Professional
Betty & Robert	25.5	2	Student
Sophie & Guy	21.5	2	Student

The four duos were asked to prepare a short song individually prior to rehearsing and performing it in two conditions: (1) with their regular duo partner (established/same-expertise); (2) with a new duo partner of the same level of expertise (new/same-expertise). The songs used were by Ivor Gurney (1890–1937): the professional duos rehearsed and performed 'An Epitaph' in Session 1 and 'On the Downs' in Session 2 while the student duos rehearsed and performed 'On the Downs' in Session 1 and 'An Epitaph' in Session 2. Two duos, one professional and one student, were also asked to prepare a third song, 'I Shall Be Ever Maiden', in a subsequent session (Session 3) with a partner from the other duo (new/different expertise). These songs (discussed below) were chosen because they were of a similar length and level of difficulty, and they were unknown to the participants, although they had performed other works by the same composer. As noted above, the participants' lack of familiarity with the selected pieces meant that they were all at equivalent stages of practice when the observation of their rehearsals took place. Each session undertaken by the participants took place on a separate occasion and

---

[1]   All participants' names are pseudonyms.

lasted around 90 minutes. It included individual practice (20 minutes) followed by an ensemble rehearsal (40 minutes), a performance of the selected song (4 minutes) and a post-performance discussion. Each session was video-recorded and stored on a DVD.

In this chapter, we focus on the performers who completed all three sessions (Isobel, George, Betty and Guy) so that we could observe and analyse their physical gestures and glances, and, as it were, interrogate their rehearsals. It should be noted that the singers were provided with a music stand so that their hands were not restricted to holding the score in rehearsal and performance, and they were not required to perform the music from memory at the end of the rehearsal, since time was so short. Before we go on to discuss our findings, we provide a brief overview of the three songs.

The Three Songs

Ivor Gurney was a renowned British war poet and song composer. These songs were chosen to represent different aspects of his output. 'An Epitaph', composed in 1920, sets a text by Walter de la Mare. The two verses are reflective. The music begins and ends with relative stillness through soft, calm chords in the piano, exposing seventh harmonies (see Example 9.1). Gurney's harmonic language gives rise to some unusual progressions, such as a shift from D to C major at the end of the first verse, and to G♭ major in the second verse, all of which provoke a sense of yearning and curiosity towards 'that lady'.

Example 9.1 Gurney, 'An Epitaph', bars 1–7

'On the Downs' is a lively, but sinister song that depicts gruesome tribal rites. Composed in 1919, the song is based on a poem by John Masefield. The piano part depicts the dark scene through persistent off-beat quavers over a rolling bass line that is rooted in the tonic key of G minor (see Example 9.2). The central verse is fierce: it moves into the tritonal region of C♯ minor and contains a sweeping

Example 9.2   Gurney, 'On the Downs', bars 3–6

descent followed by a climactic ascent in the vocal line. The original temper is restored in the final verse as the opening musical material returns.

The third song, 'I Shall Be Ever Maiden', was composed in 1919 upon Gurney's discovery of William Bliss Carman's *Sappho* poems. He portrays this love poem with a lightly flowing accompaniment in G major (see Example 9.3). The vocal line is expansive and, after 'fragile' tonal excursions into D♭/C♯ minor in the central verse, soars to a climax on 'gladness' before closing softly, albeit without resolve.

Example 9.3   Gurney, 'I Shall Be Ever Maiden', bars 5–8

Physical Gestures in Rehearsal

The professional software program *The Observer XT* (Noldus) was used to carry out quantitative analysis of the video-recorded rehearsals; qualitative analyses were made in the course of repeated viewings of the DVDs. The gestures under scrutiny were those made during practice segments involving singing and/or playing, and partial or complete run-throughs only (i.e. not during episodes of talk). First, the types of non-verbal communication occurring most frequently were noted and categorized as either *states* (actions with a duration: e.g. pulsing with the hand across several bars of the music; gazing at the co-performer during a bar/phrase) or *points* (actions with no specified duration; e.g. a quick glance at the co-performer; a physical gesture that coincided with a downbeat) in line with categories used in previous research (see Table 9.2). The last category in Table 9.2, 'gestures', included all kinds of meaningful physical actions that were not otherwise regarded as types of pulsing, shaping, conducting, gazing or glancing. There were many kinds of gestures produced by the performers across the rehearsals and these will be described in the ensuing discussion.

Table 9.2   Types of actions/gestures coded in the ensemble rehearsals (column 1) with example (column 2) and corresponding function based on existing categories by Ekman & Friesen (EKFR: column 3) and Cassell (CASS: column 4)

Category / Type	Example from data	Function (EKFR)	Function (CASS)
States			
Pulsing with hand	Little beats with hand	Regulator	Beat
Pulsing with head	Nods or shakes head	Regulator	Beat
Shaping with hand	Sideways hand sweep	Illustrator	Metaphoric
Conducting	Beating time to co-performer	Regulator	Deictic
Gazing at each other	Look at co-performer	Adaptor	Deictic
Gazing elsewhere	Look out to 'audience'	Affect	Propositional
Points			
Glance at each other	Quick look at partner	Regulator	Deictic
Glance elsewhere	Quick look at audience	Affect	Propositional
Gestures	Hands plead (singer)	Illustrator	Iconic

An 'event log' was compiled using the software that recorded *when* each action/gesture occurred during rehearsal with the music, *who* produced the action/gesture (singer or pianist), and *how long for* (the duration). For state categories, the duration of actions was recorded in seconds and subsequently calculated as a proportion (%) of the overall rehearsal time; for point categories, the frequency of glances/gestures was reflected in the rate of occurrences per minute of rehearsal time. These figures enabled direct comparison of the proportions of time spent gesturing in different rehearsals by each performer.[2]

---

[2]   In the event log, there were two default categories, 'still' and 'look at music': if no specific types of actions/gestures were observed by the performers, they were coded accordingly.

Isobel

Isobel's first session was with George, her regular partner. Throughout their rehearsal of 'An Epitaph', Isobel tended to pulse with her right hand as if to help her 'feel' the tempo of the music. There were various attempted run-throughs of the piece, of which five were complete; the first occurred after 15 minutes when they had already worked through the piece several times with stops and starts. As she rehearsed with George, Isobel continually pulsed to the music, switching hands on occasions. Interestingly, the size of the pulsing seemed to reflect how comfortable she was with the music and her growing sense of familiarity with the piece: to begin with, the gestures were relatively large and pronounced, and they were clearly visible to George. There was a sense of mutual need for these pulsings as they both worked together to settle upon a tempo (indeed, they also pulsed together whilst reciting the words in tempo). Later on, as the rehearsal progressed, Isobel's pulsing became smaller and more self-regulatory (see Figure 9.1).

Figure 9.1   Isobel's beating gesture (in rehearsal with George)

During the first run-through, there were also a few little hand gestures of emphasis on certain words – as distinct from the pulsing – notably on 'light', 'most [beautiful lady]' and, in the second verse, 'lady'. Midway through the rehearsal, these same gestures occurred on 'rare (it be)' during consecutive run-throughs. There was no obvious pattern to Isobel's use of these little emphatic hand gestures in repeated run-throughs, although when they appeared, they seemed to articulate her shaping of the line (for instance, see emphasis on 'most' in Example 9.4).

In her second session, Isobel rehearsed 'On the Downs' with Colin, a pianist with whom she had never worked before, although they were of a similar level of expertise. There were numerous attempted run-throughs, with three complete ones, and, as in her first session, Isobel tended to pulse with her hand (see Figure 9.2). Here, however, she mainly used the left hand (the hand furthest away from the pianist) and the pulsing was relatively small and self-contained. There were a

Example 9.4   Gurney, 'An Epitaph', bars 11–13, vocal line

I   think she was - the   most beau-   ti-ful   la-dy

Figure 9.2   Isobel's beating gesture (in rehearsal with Colin)

couple of moments when she produced larger beats, notably when she seemed insecure with pitching. When indicating to Colin at the end of the third run-through the need to enunciate 'blood and air' in the final verse, she produced little upward gestures of emphasis with her left hand on 'blood' and 'air'. Also, to convey the need for a short hiatus in the music before placing the last word 'bare', she gave a little flick of the left hand. In later runs of the piece, Isobel tended to glance or gaze outwards, as if communicating the song to an imaginary audience.

In her final session, Isobel worked on 'I Shall Be Ever Maiden' with Guy, a new partner of a different level of expertise. They made two complete run-throughs of the piece towards the end of the rehearsal, although they covered lengthy chunks throughout as well as working on small sections and phrases. Once again, Isobel pulsed with her left and right hands, although these gestures seemed to be mainly self-guiding and self-reassuring rather than being directed towards Guy. Sometimes the nature of her pulsing mirrored the character of the music; for example she seemed to be dancing sideways during the opening few bars in a light, youthful manner. No other distinctive gestures were apparent in our repeated viewings.

Given Isobel's predilection for pulsing in all three rehearsals, it is worth comparing the relative proportions of rehearsal time in which this gesture was used. The data indicate pulsing for approximately one third of each rehearsal: 34.7 per cent of Session 1 (with George); 33.2 per cent of Session 2 (with Colin);

and 29.3 per cent of Session 3 (with Guy). Regardless of partner, therefore, Isobel was relatively consistent in using this gesture across rehearsals. How she used the gesture, though, seemed to vary depending on her familiarity with her partner and with the song:

- With her regular partner, pulsing was overt, often directed at the pianist, used to share ideas of tempi and secure the 'feel' of the piece.
- With new partners, pulsing was self-guiding and self-reassuring, sometimes reflecting the character of the music, but rarely as a means of interacting with the pianist.
- Pulsing was larger (in terms of the height of up–down motions) when securing pitching and rhythmic details in the music (often when rehearsing short phrases or segments of the piece).
- Pulsing was smaller when she felt comfortable with the music (often during run-throughs in the later stages of rehearsal).
- Pulsing sometimes occurred in circular or sideways sweeps which reflected her perception of the character of the music.

George

George's first session was with Isobel, his regular partner. As indicated above, when he and Isobel worked through 'An Epitaph', George provided numerous regulatory gestures, including pulsing with the hand and conducting. The accompaniment includes a number of sustained chords; during these passages George lifted his hands from the keys and used them for expressive purposes. Thus, for example, he pulsed with his hands during pauses, and provided little beats under Isobel's solo lines. He gave cues to Isobel by indicating entries with quick 'pointing' gestures, glances or nods, and articulated rhythms by nodding (e.g. 'will [remember]'). George conveyed messages about the musical content in four ways: first, by flicking his hand to emphasize particular words, such as 'who'; second, by leaning forwards into the keys towards certain notes/words in phrases ('passes', 'vanishes'); third, by creating a spiral shape with his hand after releasing chords as if helping the sound to resonate (see Figure 9.3); and fourth, by lifting his hands visibly from the keys in time with the music at the end of phrases.

By using these gestures George supported Isobel in various ways in order to help her feel at ease as she sang the vocal line, especially by providing musical cues and confirming tempo and rhythm. Moreover, he contributed to their shared musical interpretation by indicating the phrasing of the song through gesture, by emphasizing the articulation of particular words and above all shaping the sound of the piano accompaniment with lifts and spiralling movements of the hands. Clearly, fewer gestures were observed overall as he played, since his hands were in use at the piano for the bulk of the time spent playing during the session; nevertheless pulsing of the hand predominated (4.97%) followed by shaping of the hand (0.92%), conducting (0.22%) and gazing at Isobel (0.18%). Other gestures,

Figure 9.3   George's hand loop (in rehearsal with Isobel)

including hand lifts, hand spirals, hand flicks, head nods and leaning forward were made at the rate of 1.15 per minute and glances towards Isobel were made at the rate of 0.11 per minute.

In his second session, George worked with Amanda, a new partner of the same level of expertise. The relatively dense piano part for 'On the Downs' meant that his hands were busy with passagework. Nevertheless, at the outset of the rehearsal when they discussed the tempo of the song, George pulsed with his hands underneath the vocal line. The rehearsal included five run-throughs as well as work on small and large chunks of the piece. As the rehearsal progressed, George displayed consistent gestures across the piece: while his body sway was relatively contained, he nevertheless leaned forward at certain points, notably to punctuate the start of the second verse ('Once the tribe'), and to emphasize the words 'blood' and 'air'. He started to nod his head on 'gods' when beginning the arpeggio flourish beneath the climax ('And the gods came'), and, later in the rehearsal, combined this nod with leaning forward as if to highlight his entry even more definitively (see Example 9.5). He also nodded frequently on key verbs, such as 'choke', and adjectives, such as 'bare'. He shook his head when playing through the third verse on 'the hawkes, the

Example 9.5   Gurney, 'On the Downs', bars 20–21 (the arrow indicates location of pianist's nod/bodily lean)

grasses', as if responding to the chill on the downs. Furthermore, he always gazed at Amanda prior to her entry of the second verse.

Overall, the proportion of gestures produced throughout this rehearsal was much less than in his rehearsal with Isobel: pulsing of the hand (0.08%); shaping of the hand (0.084%); gazing at Amanda (0.13%); gestures (at the rate of 0.6 per minute); glancing at Amanda (at the rate of 0.05 per minute).

In his third session, George worked with Betty on the song 'I Shall Be Ever Maiden'. Betty was a new partner of a different level of expertise. They completed one run-through of the song at the start of the rehearsal, then worked through short and long segments of the piece before making two further run-throughs towards the end of the rehearsal. As in the previous song, much of the piano part contains detailed passagework, so George was fairly limited in what he could do with his hands while he was actually playing. Nevertheless, he produced several (discreet) hand lifts off chords, notably beneath the phrase 'Henceforth and forever', and under the word 'holy' at the end of the second verse. A distinctive little loop of the left hand, like the spiral gesture observed in his rehearsal with Isobel, appeared as if to round off the phrase after the word 'incense' (end of the second verse; see Figure 9.4). He also provided some cues to the singer with head nods, for example at the singer's entry on 'Calm' at the end of the song. George's gestures, however, were relatively limited and were made at the rate of 0.7 per minute.

Figure 9.4   George's hand lift (in rehearsal with Betty)

Overall, George produced two main kinds of physical gesture in his rehearsals: hand lifts (or spirals/loops) and head nods. The former appeared to function primarily as expressive gestures at the ends of phrases or rising from sustained chords as a way of releasing the sound or denoting continued resonance. These 'resonating' lifts could be regarded as illustrators, or metaphoric gestures. The latter seemed also to function as regulatory gestures to indicate either an entry to the singer or to achieve coordination with the singer in placing a chord beneath a particular word. In his first session, George also tended to lean forwards to indicate emphasis towards certain parts of a phrase or particular words. This kind of expressive bodily gesture, though, was less apparent in the other rehearsals. One explanation for this is the relative simplicity of the writing for piano in 'Epitaph'; another is George's familiarity with the singer, which may have resulted in more 'flexibility' in his playing. Interestingly, while George seemed to be relatively consistent in his use of particular gestures, he produced far fewer gestures with his new partners than he did with his regular partner. There was a real sense of shared involvement and combined development of ideas in the rehearsal with his regular partner; the video-recorded data suggest a sense of mutual understanding of each other and the need to master the technical and musical demands of the song together. In sum, the following points can be made about George's physical gestures in rehearsals:

- With his regular partner, he produced more physical gestures than with his new partners.
- With the singer of a different level of expertise, he produced fewer gestures.
- In all of the rehearsals, he produced a small repertoire of expressive gestures, notably 'resonating' hand lifts and regulatory head nods.
- In rehearsals with singers of the same level of expertise, he produced a similar range of gestures, including pulsing, shaping and some bodily movements, including leaning forward.

Betty

In her first session, Betty rehearsed 'On the Downs' with her regular partner, Robert. During the first run-through, she pulsed constantly with her left hand and, later, nodded with her head in time with the music. This pulsing and nodding continued for much of the first half of the rehearsal. On later runs, she started to reflect the music by shaping with her hands, for example producing little scoops on 'the hawkes' and 'the grasses' with her left hand. Certain gestures reappeared in repeated runs, including nods of the head with the pianist on 'air', pointing gestures on 'bare', and the use of the left hand to signal the downbeat of 'gods' at the climax ('And the gods came'). Overall, Betty's most frequent gestures were pulsing with the hand (17.2%) and pulsing with the head (11.4%). Other 'illustrative' gestures include shaping with the hand (2.98%) and in distinctive scoops or points (at the rate of 1.66 per minute). There was no perceptible gazing or glancing in this rehearsal, either towards the pianist or elsewhere.

In her second session, Betty worked with Guy, a new partner of the same level of expertise, on the song 'An Epitaph'. Interestingly, on their first run-through at the outset of the rehearsal, Betty remained quite still with the exception of some gentle head nods on occasional words ('passes' and 'remember'). As the rehearsal progressed, Betty started to produce more obvious gestures. Initially, this involved pulsing with the right hand and pulsing with the head, then, as the tempo settled, shaping with the hands too. Betty frequently moved one hand inwards and outwards with the palm turned upwards, as if 'smoothing out' the music. This 'smoothing' gesture normally accompanied held notes (such as 'was' in the second phrase), as if reflecting sustained sound, or moving lines ('And when I die'), as if giving direction through a phrase. In addition, she developed regular eye contact at certain locations in the piece, notably through the phrase 'who will remember'. The overall amount of 'gazing' at her co-performer was relatively high (4.74%) compared with other physical gestures: pulsing of the hand (1.83%), pulsing of the head (0.21%) and shaping of the hand (0.7%). The occurrence of gestures, made at the rate of 1.3 per minute, and glances, made at the rate of 0.12 per minute, was relatively high.

In her third session, Betty worked with George on the song 'I Shall Be Ever Maiden'. George was a new partner of a different level of expertise. In this rehearsal, she produced a range of gestures used for either technical or expressive purposes. When working on particular technical aspects of the vocal line, such as pitching and rhythm, she used hand signals to assist with internalizing the notes (e.g. pointing down with the hand next to the ear to denote a descent in pitch or to flatten the note) and learning the rhythm (e.g. beating to establish the triplet rhythm of the opening phrase). More strikingly, she used both hands in a number of expressive gestures to mark the ends of phrases or highpoints of phrases: for example, at the end of the first verse on the closure of the word 'forever', she produced a cradle-like gesture (both hands swept inwardly in a circle before resting in a cupped position; see Figure 9.5) on one run-through, then a 'rounding off' gesture at the same point on a different run-through (both hands making an inward circle with the fingers touching together; see Figure 9.6); on the last run-through, she made a passionate 'swoop' with her left hand when reaching the climactic top G in the final verse ('gladness') – here, she bent her knees, swooped upwards with her left hand and leaned against the piano with her right hand for extra support. In this rehearsal Betty was most likely to shape (10.36%) or pulse with her hand (3.59%); she made gestures such as the cradle-like, rounding-off and scooping movements at the rate of 0.8 per minute.

Figure 9.5   Betty's cupped hands after her cradle-like gesture (in rehearsal with George)

Overall, Betty tended to move from pulsing gestures towards shaping gestures in each rehearsal. Even though she produced fewer gestures in the sessions with her new partners, there were commonalities in the way she moved during rehearsals:

- With all of her partners, she produced pulsing and shaping gestures.
- Shaping gestures appeared to be expressive in function – such as to reflect a sustained note ('smoothing out'), the direction of a line ('scooping'), a highpoint ('swooping') or phrase end ('rounding off').
- With her new, same-expertise partner, there was a high proportion of 'gazing' – this might be explained by the nature of the piece ('An Epitaph' is reflective in tone) or the need to establish coordination with an unfamiliar partner.
- With her new partner of a different level of expertise, her shaping gestures were often directed inwardly, including 'cradle-like' and 'rounding off' actions, which might have given a sense of self-assurance.

Figure 9.6   Betty's 'rounding off' gesture (in rehearsal with George)

Guy

In his first session, Guy rehearsed 'On the Downs' with his regular partner, Sophie. In all of his run-throughs, he produced extensive body sway along with movements of the head to highlight the shaping of phrases. When playing shorter sections, he helped Sophie to establish the tempo by pulsing with his hands (0.08%) or conducting with his right hand (0.08%). At certain locations in the piece, he consistently produced hand lifts, for example at the end of the arpeggio flourish at 'And the gods' and in the quick rest before the final utterance, 'bare'. These helped express the drama of the music. Guy occasionally glanced (at the rate of 0.16 per minute) or gazed (0.65%) at his co-performer.

In his second session, Guy worked with a new same-expertise partner, Betty, on the song 'An Epitaph'. As before, Guy's playing was underpinned by continuous body sway; here, however, his swaying was broader and slower than in the previous session, which helped to express the calmer mood of this song. As in that session, he often nodded his head to mark the starts of phrases and produced hand lifts at the ends of phrases. He gazed at Betty during the phrase 'will remember' (3.29% of his rehearsal was spent gazing) and glanced at her on a few other occasions. As the rehearsal progressed, he was more likely to drop his head on 'beau-ti-ful', 'was' and 're-mem-ber'. In his third session, Guy rehearsed 'I Shall Be Ever Maiden' with Isobel, a new partner of a different level of expertise. Once again, Guy's body sway was distinctive, along with his hand lifts (see Figure 9.7) and head nods. There were, however, fewer gestures produced here than noted in his other sessions. Similarly, the amount of time spent gazing and glancing at his co-performer was significantly less than in previous rehearsals (0.19% gazing; glancing at the rate of 0.02 per minute).

Figure 9.7   Guy's hand lift (in rehearsal with Isobel)

Overall, Guy produced very similar *types* of physical gestures in his three sessions, which we can characterize as body sway, head nods and hand lifts with occasional gazing or glancing at the singer; these, however, varied in length of time and rate per minute from one rehearsal to the next. In addition, we noted that:

- With his regular partner, Guy produced what we can infer as his 'normal' repertoire of gestures, as well as additional ones for technical purposes, including pulsing and conducting.
- With his new same-expertise partner, Guy produced a relatively high proportion of 'gazing', which seemed to express both the nature of the song and to assist in coordination of entries with the singer.
- With his new different-expertise partner, Guy produced fewer gestures overall.

Discussion

We suggested earlier that the professional musicians who took part in the study might use the musical structure of the songs they were preparing for performance more consciously and therefore perhaps more effectively than the student musicians, in the interests of rehearsal efficiency; furthermore, the duos comprising unfamiliar partners might prefer to run through the music, rather than break it down into shorter segments, in order to get to know each other's styles of performing. Neither hypothesis was supported. Rehearsal styles, in terms of preference for run-throughs as opposed to short segments, were similar in all rehearsals, with the following caveat: the faster the singers were able to learn the songs, under the pressure of a 20-minute individual practice session followed immediately by a 40-minute ensemble rehearsal, the more run-throughs there were. Betty made the most run-throughs, with each of her partners (familiar and unfamiliar), since she preferred to carry on when an error occurred, and go back later to correct it rather than halting the run-through there and then. In contrast, the fewest run-throughs were made by Isobel and George (both familiar partnerships), since Isobel struggled to a greater extent with 'An Epitaph' than either of the other two songs. Thus the crucial factor was neither expertise nor familiarity, but the singer's speed of acquisition for a particular song.

Our main research question asked how performers' physical gestures and glances compare when they collaborate in ensemble rehearsal with (1) performers of different levels of expertise, and (2) their usual (familiar) and new (unfamiliar) duo partners. The results of the quantitative and qualitative analyses showed that the performers used physical gestures to a *greater extent* when rehearsing with familiar and same-expertise partners than new or different-expertise partners. Furthermore, a *wider range* of gestures was produced in familiar partnerships. The study also highlighted the common functions fulfilled by the physical gestures of singers and pianists (individually and combined), whether in new or mixed-expertise partnerships:

- to consolidate technical details via 'emblems' and 'illustrators' used to establish rhythms and secure pitching, and 'beats' used in conducting;
- to establish tempo or pulse – 'beat' or 'deictic' gestures were particularly important to singers feeling the pulse;
- to convey musical information via 'metaphoric' gestures and 'illustrators' used to share ideas about conveying the narrative of the song by shaping phrases and striving to achieve simultaneous climaxes;
- to coordinate entries via 'regulators', such as nods of the head and leaning forward with the whole body, which provided cues for vocal entries and coordination at structural boundaries.

A range of gestures were used by the singers and pianists for technical, expressive and/or communicative ends:

- Both singers appeared to use gesture for self-assurance or self-guidance, for example pulsing throughout the song to feel the tempo, pointing down to indicate awareness that the pitch needed to be flattened and moving the hand upwards to help the support of high notes.
- Both singers clearly used gesture to indicate understanding or convey the expression of the text, for example making little hand motions or flicks to emphasize key words, producing 'cradle-like' or 'rounding off' movements to mark the ends of verses, using the hands for 'smoothing out' to sustain sound and 'scooping' upwards to mirror the direction from which high notes were approached.
- Both pianists tended to use hand lifts and head nods at 'structural' points such as the beginnings and endings of verses, and coordination points such as vocal entries.
- Both pianists swayed with their bodies in the tempo of the song, and tended to lean forward into climaxes or the high points of phrases, and the frequency of these gestures increased as each rehearsal progressed.

The singers engaged, occasionally, with an imaginary audience through glancing or gazing outwards, although there was surprisingly little direct eye contact between the co-performers, other than in Betty's rehearsal with Guy. Indeed, the extent to which the singers and pianists were aware of each other's gestures during the rehearsals was hard to gauge, although they must have been conscious of some of each other's physical actions via peripheral if not central vision. In the case of the established professional duo, Isobel and George, there appeared to be more explicit sharing of gestures in their rehearsal than evidenced in the other rehearsals we observed, suggesting a closer working relationship.

Conclusion

During the rehearsals, the performers produced some consistent gestural patterns in their physical realization of the songs, thus indicating the development of internal (mental) representations. The pianists, for example, made specific gestures, such as nodding their heads, lifting their hands and leaning forward with their bodies, at particular locations in each song, notably at phrase boundaries or vocal entries; similar results were found in Williamon and Davidson's (2002) study of a piano duo. The gestures of the pianists in the present study seemed to be primarily expressive and communicative. The singers, on the other hand, used gestures to reflect or indeed support the technical production of the sound, especially pitching, as well as conveying information relating to the meaning of the lyrics or the expressive content of the songs. Different gestures were used by the singers and pianists, however, who did not necessarily mirror each other. This combination of performers, of course, although typical, is less obviously 'blended' than an ensemble in which the musicians play the same instrument or instruments within the same 'family', such as a piano duo or string quartet, and are therefore capable of synchronizing with each other much more closely. The findings of the present study thus support Keller's claim that, for musicians in mixed ensembles, 'movement-related information may be limited to relatively general, instrument-independent forms of body motion (e.g., swaying, rocking, and expressive gesturing)' because they cannot readily synchronize with one another (2008: 209).

Nevertheless, the familiar co-performers in the present study gestured more frequently and for longer periods of time than did the unfamiliar co-performers, whether at the same or a different level of expertise, and seemed better able to communicate non-verbally. This suggests that familiarity and expertise do influence the use of physical gestures in ensemble practice. In the case of Betty and Guy, the new, same-expertise duo, the two performers' head movements became increasingly coordinated in the later stages of their rehearsal, which suggests that the synchronization of body movements can develop relatively quickly in new partnerships. The established professional duo revealed closer harmonization of gestures in the establishment of the tempo and 'feel' of the song through joint pulsing than did the established student duo, as well as the individual production of gestures. They reflected something of a 'combined rhetoric' of gestures insofar as their non-verbal communication was integral to their rehearsal style.

Complex cognitive processes are at work as ensemble performers become familiar with a song and each other's physical realization of it, notably through anticipating, attending and adapting to their own and each other's playing (Keller 2008). In effect, co-performers gradually learn to predict, read and respond to each other's auditory and motor imagery. It is likely that co-performers in familiar partnerships produced more frequent and varied gestures in their rehearsals because they had more efficient and effective (i.e. superior) cognitive processing abilities: they were more adept at anticipating, attending and adapting to each other's auditory and motor imagery, including physical gestures. While familiarity and expertise do impact upon cognitive processing as well as general musical and social interaction skills, further research is necessary to explore this idea.

One limitation of this study concerns the choice of songs. While an independent singer and pianist rated the three songs – selected on the grounds of their unfamiliarity and length – as being of comparable difficulty, it transpired during the post-rehearsal debriefing that all of the duos found 'An Epitaph' the easiest, liked 'On the Downs' the most and found 'I Shall Be Ever Maiden' the most challenging. The nature of the piano accompaniment in each song could well have influenced the gestures that were made by the pianists (for example, the sustained chords and rests in 'An Epitaph' meant that they were able to use their hands more freely than in the other songs, which included busy passagework), as indeed the nature of the vocal lines and meanings of the lyrics influenced those made by the singers. Researchers seeking to replicate this study might consider sacrificing ecological validity (and perhaps the enjoyment that the participants here reported as they learned new songs) by using material specially composed to ensure greater similarity.

Finally, further research should seek to test the points arising from this case study by observing a greater number of singer–pianist duos, and indeed to explore the use of gestures and glances further in a wider range of instrumental ensembles and repertoires, including classical, jazz, folk and popular music groups.

References

Blank, M. & Davidson, J. W. (2007). An Exploration of the Effects of Musical and Social Factors in Piano Duo Collaborations. *Psychology of Music* 35/2: 231–48.

Blum, D. (1986). *The Art of Quartet Playing: The Guarneri Quartet in Conversation with David Blum*. New York: Cornell University Press.

Butterworth, T. (1990). Detroit String Quartet. In J. R. Hackman (ed.), *Groups That Work (and Those that Don't)* (pp. 207–24). San Francisco, CA: Jossey-Bass.

Cassell, J. (1998). A Framework for Gesture Generation and Interpretation. In R. Cipolla (ed.), *Computer Vision in Human-Machine Interaction* (pp. 248–65). Cambridge: Cambridge University Press.

Clarke, E. F. & Davidson, J. W. (1998). The Body in Performance. In W. Thomas (ed.), *Composition, Performance, Reception: Studies in the Creative Process in Music* (pp. 74–92). Aldershot: Ashgate.

Davidson, J. W. (1993). Visual Perception of Performance Manner in the Movements of Solo Musicians. *Psychology of Music* 21/2: 103–13.

— (1994). What Type of Information is conveyed in the Body Movements of Solo Musician Performers? *Journal of Human Movement Studies* 6: 279–301.

— (2001). The Role of the Body in the Production and Perception of Solo Vocal Performance: A Case Study of Annie Lennox. *Musicae Scientiae* 5/2: 235–56.

— (2005). Bodily Communication in Musical Performance. In D. Miell, R. A. R. MacDonald & D. J. Hargreaves (eds.), *Musical Communication* (pp. 215–38). Oxford: Oxford University Press.

— (2006). 'She's The One': Multiple Functions of Body Movement in a Stage Performance by Robbie Williams. In A. Gritten & E. King (eds.), *Music and Gesture* (pp. 208–25). Aldershot: Ashgate.

— & Good, J. (2002). Social and Musical Co-Ordination between Members of a String Quartet: An Exploratory Study. *Psychology of Music* 30/2: 186–201.

— & King, E. C. (2004). Strategies for Ensemble Practice. In A. Williamon (ed.), *Musical Excellence: Strategies and Techniques to Enhance Performance* (pp. 105–22). Oxford: Oxford University Press.

Delalande, F. (1988). La Gestique de Gould: Élements pour une Sémiologie du Geste Musical. In G. Guertin (ed.), *Glenn Gould Pluriel* (pp. 85–111). Québec: Louise Courteau.

Ekman, P. & Friesen, W. (1969). The Repertoire of Non-Verbal Behavior: Categories, Origins, Sage, and Coding. *Semiotica* 1: 49–98.

Elsdon, P. (2006). Listening in the Gaze: The Body in Keith Jarrett's Solo Piano Improvisations. In A. Gritten & E. King (eds.), *Music and Gesture* (pp. 192–207). Aldershot: Ashgate.

Ginsborg, J. (2009). Beating Time: The Role of Kinaesthetic Learning in the Development of Mental Representations for Music. In A. Mornell (ed.), *Art in Motion* (pp. 121–42). Vienna: Peter Lang.

— & King, E. (2007a). The Roles of Expertise and Partnership in Collaborative Rehearsal. In A. Williamon & D. Coimbra (eds), *Proceedings of the International Symposium on Performance Science* (pp. 61–66). Porto, Italy: Association of European Conservatoires.

— & King, E. (2007b). Collaborative Rehearsal: Social Interaction and Musical Dimensions in Professional and Student Singer–Piano Duos. In E. Schubert, K. Buckley, R. Eliott, B. Koboroff, J. Chen & C. Stevens (eds) *Proceedings of the Inaugural International Conference on Music Communication Sciences* (pp. 51–5). Sydney: ARC Research Network in Human Communication Science (HSNet).

— & King, E. (2008). Rehearsal Talk: Collaboration Between Student and Professional Singers and Pianists. Paper presented at the Conference on Behavioural Research in Chamber Music, Royal Northern College of Music, Manchester, UK, 8 January.

—, Chaffin, R. & Nicholson, G. (2006). Shared Performance Cues in Singing and Conducting: A Content Analysis of Talk during Practice. *Psychology of Music* 34: 167–94.

Goodman E. C. (2000). *Analysing the Ensemble in Music Rehearsal and Performance: The Nature and Effects of Interaction in Cello–Piano Duos.* PhD dissertation, University of London.

— (2002). Ensemble Performance. In J. Rink (ed.), *Musical Performance: A Guide to Understanding* (pp. 153–67). Cambridge: Cambridge University Press.

Gruson, L. (1988). Rehearsal Skill and Musical Competence: Does Practice make Perfect? In J. Sloboda (ed.), *Generative Processes in Music: The Psychology of Performance, Improvisation and Composition* (pp. 91–112). Oxford: Clarendon Press.

Keller, P. (2008). Joint Action in Music Performance. In F. Morganti, A. Carassa & G. Riva (eds.), *Enacting Intersubjectivity: A Cognitive and Social Perspective on the Study of Interactions* (pp. 205–21). Amsterdam: IOS Press.

Kendon, A. (1980). Gesticulation and Speech: Two Aspects of the Process of Utterance. In M. R. Key (ed.), *The Relationship between Verbal and Nonverbal Communication* (pp. 207–27). The Hague: Mouton & Co.

King, E. C. (2006). The Roles of Student Musicians in Quartet Rehearsals. *Psychology of Music* 34/2: 262–82.

McNeill, D. (1992). *Hand and Mind: What Gestures Reveal about Thought.* Chicago, IL: Chicago University Press.

Maduell, M. & Wing, A. M. (2007). The Dynamics of Ensemble: The Case for Flamenco. *Psychology of Music* 35/4: 591–627.

Murnighan, J. K. & Conlon, D. E. (1991). The Dynamics of Intense Work Groups: A Study of British String Quartets. *Administrative Science Quarterly* 36: 165–86.

Shaffer, L. H. (1984). Timing in Solo and Duet Performances. *Quarterly Journal of Experimental Psychology* 36A: 577–95.

Sloboda, J. (1985). *The Musical Mind: The Cognitive Psychology of Music.* Oxford: Oxford University Press.

Wanderley, M. M. & Vines, B. W. (2006). Origins and Functions of Clarinettists' Ancillary Gestures. In A. Gritten & E. King (eds.), *Music and Gesture* (pp. 165–191). Aldershot: Ashgate.

Williamon, A. (1999*). Preparing for Performance: An Examination of Musical Practice as a Function of Expertise.* PhD Dissertation, University of London.

— & Davidson, J. W. (2002). Exploring Co-Performer Communication. *Musicae Scientiae* 6/1: 53–72.

Windsor, W. L., Davidson, J. W. & Ng, K. (2003). Investigating Musicians' Natural Upper Body Movements. Paper presented at the First International Conference on Music and Gesture, University of East Anglia, UK, 28–31 August.

Young, V. M. & Colman, A. M. (1979). Some Psychological Processes in String Quartets. *Psychology of Music* 7: 12–16.

Chapter 10

Imagery, Melody and Gesture in Cross-cultural Perspective

Gina A. Fatone, Martin Clayton, Laura Leante and Matt Rahaim

Musical action is also physical action. This is obvious in cases such as moving the arm to direct a bow across a cello string, turning the hand to control the vibrations of a drumhead or inclining the cartilages of the larynx to raise the pitch of a sung note. In addition to producing sound, however, physical motion can also serve as a means of conceiving and conveying music: motion is linked in turn to visual imagery and other aspects of the conceptualization of music. Auditory, motor, visual and conceptual counterparts may be integrated, generating a unified meaningful action. In this chapter we present some examples of such cross-modal phenomena[1] in the context of music and gesture: we discuss, for instance, ways in which visual information in the form of gestures contributes to the way musical performance is experienced, and how mental images of spaces, actions and object motion – co-presented in physical gestures – can influence the way music is performed and play an important role in teaching. The chapter, therefore, locates physical gesture within a complex of cross-modal actions associated with musical performance and transmission. We present four fieldwork studies – indeed four approaches – to analysing relationships between musical sound and gesture in the performances and teaching of individual musicians. Three of these studies are drawn from the world of North Indian vocal music, but the fourth comes from halfway around the globe: the world of bagpipe music in Atlantic Canada. The inter-references of our research acknowledge the possibility of shared elements of musical-gestural co-expression between cultures, and also point to the broader applicability of music and gesture research to both cognitive science and musicology.

We begin with a discussion of the multiple ways gesture may function in a single performance, based on an analysis of the *khyal* singer Vijay Koparkar.[2] This

---

[1] Our use of the term 'cross-modal' here is not restricted to interaction between lower-order sensory modes. For example, motor actions, vocalization, and imagination, would be considered 'modalities' in this usage of the term.

[2] Analysis developed and written principally by Martin Clayton. This performance was organized by Veena and Hari Sahasrabuddhe and recorded in Mumbai on 20 May 2005 by Martin Clayton, Laura Leante and Jaime Jones. This research was funded by Arts and Humanities Research Council grant number 19110. Clayton has written a more detailed

section is followed by an investigation of how imagery and gesture are implicated in the process of musical meaning construction, grounded in the teaching of three female vocalists from Maharashtra and West Bengal.[3] A third perspective approaches physical gesture and sound as parallel channels, with gesture conceived as motion in space, and includes an analysis of a *raga* performance by singer Girja Devi.[4] Finally, the manual gestures of two Scottish classical bagpipe teachers in Prince Edward Island, Canada, are interpreted as indexical to 'meta-images' or 'meta-gestures' manifested in multiple images of similar 'energetic shape'[5] co-occurring in the teachers' imagination.[6]

The Functions of Gesture in a *Khyal* Performance

Much has been written about the performance of *raga*s, but until recently little attention has been given to its cross-modal nature.[7] Gestures can be seen to complement several different aspects of the musical sound, and auditory cues also elicit movements of reaction and participation from co-performers and listeners. Many performers testify to the important role visual imagery plays in their *raga* presentation, and listeners attest to a similar importance in their listening experiences. For both performers and listeners this visual imaginary seems to be linked to patterns of motor movement (Clayton 2005), as detailed illustrations of singers' gestures presented in the following section strongly suggest. Physical gesture is thus implicated in a complex set of cross-modal interactions, and can provide information about different aspects of performance including sound production, communication between participants and issues of signification.

An account of these interactions might include study of the sounds produced, of the behaviour of participants in a performance (including physical gesture),

---

analysis of parts of this performance (2007), on which this description is based. *Khyal* is the predominant form of classical singing in the North Indian, or Hindustani, tradition, and is referred to in three of the four studies presented in this chapter.

[3]   Analysis developed and written principally by Laura Leante. Research conducted in the UK and in Pune, India by Laura Leante, funded by the UK Open University and the Arts and Humanities Research Council (grant numbers 19110 and 19244).

[4]   Analysis developed and principally written by Matt Rahaim. Based on research conducted in Pune, India by Matt Rahaim, funded by a 2006–07 Qayum Family Fellowship, and an American Institute of Indian Studies Junior Research Fellowship in 2007–08.

[5]   The term 'energetic shape' is borrowed from music theorist Robert Hatten's characterization of gestures of all types (see Hatten 2004: 93).

[6]   Analysis developed and principally written by Gina Fatone. Fieldwork conducted by Gina Fatone in Summerside, Prince Edward Island, Canada, in September 2001, funded by a Canadian Studies Graduate Student Fellowship Program grant.

[7]   *Raga* performance can be focused on either vocal or instrumental soloists or duets, although all of the examples in this chapter are based on vocal performance by a single soloist.

and of the ways in which a performance is imagined. The first two of these areas can be addressed with recourse to audio-visual recordings: where practical, multi-camera video recordings are a useful aid in that they allow the study of the behaviour of several individuals simultaneously and therefore facilitate study of non-verbal communication and interaction. The following observations of a *khyal* performance of *Raga Multānī* by the singer Vijay Koparkar are based on this approach. The description below focuses on two particular aspects of the performance: the relationship between singing and gesture and the interaction between participants in the performance situation. In his performance of *Raga Multānī* the singer uses three main types of gesture (in other words, he uses gesture in three different ways).[8] These three functions of gesture are as follows (terms in square brackets are from Rimé & Schiaratura 1991):

- Markers [nondepictive gestures] – gestures indicate aspects of musical structure such as a regular pulse or cadence.
- Illustrators [depictive gestures] – movements are linked to the movement or flow of the melody.
- Emblems [symbolic gestures] – gestures have verbal equivalents such as 'well done' or 'take a solo'.

Vijay Koparkar does not deploy these different types of gesture randomly: rather, the switching between different approaches seems to indicate changes in the focus of his attention. Thus, at important transitions such as that between the *ālāp* (unmetred introduction) and his first composition – the point at which his *tablā* accompanist Viswanath Shirodkar joins in – his gesture to the latter (a nod to confirm that the composition is about to start) indicates that his attention is on the need for the two musicians to start the composition together. Immediately after this his beat-marking gestures become prominent, presumably for the same reason, whereas in the *ālāp* phase his gestures seem to be tied much more closely to the melodic flow; for instance, hand movements upward and outward away from his body often accompany upward pitch movement.

The most important point about the deployment of gesture in performance is, therefore, that gesture can relate to the music in different ways, and the way in which it does so gives an indication of the focus of the musician's attention at any particular moment (in this case, shifting between the melodic phrases, the rhythmic structure and inter-performer coordination). More detailed analysis of this particular performance reveals three further points that are pertinent in this instance (we should take care with generalization, since different singers certainly have distinctive gestural styles, although there is a considerable degree of overlap between individuals):

---

[8] For more on these categories, see Clayton (2005) and Clayton (2008). For more on gesture classification in general, see McNeill (1992: 75ff.) and Kendon (2004: 84ff.).

1. When illustrative gestures accompany the melody they also frequently complement or modify the aural information in some way. Two effects can be observed. First, gesture units – the sequences of movement between returns to a low-energy 'rest' position (see Kendon 2004: 111) – are long (often over 30 seconds). More significantly, perhaps, gesture phrases comprising a 'stroke' usually occurring at the point of maximum effort – with its accompanying preparation movement and sometimes a subsequent holding of the final body position (see Kendon 2004: 112) – seem to incorporate more than one vocal phrase (if these are determined on the basis of the singer's pausing for breath). In this event the gesture phrase seems to indicate a level of intended organization of the melody that cannot be realized vocally because of physical limitations. Second, gestural movements often precede the audible melodic movements that they accompany. For instance, Vijay Koparkar holds his hand steady while sustaining the pitch *tivra* Ma (raised scale degree 4) then moves his hand upwards fractionally before his voice slides upwards to the Pa (scale degree 5).

2. Vijay Koparkar's gesture tends to display a bilateral asymmetry, with illustrative gestures being led by the left hand and beat markers by the right. This may relate to Trevarthen's observation on gesture in babies that 'assertive or demonstrative activity concentrates in the left side of the brain, moving the right arm and hand, often at the same time as apprehensive self-regulatory withdrawal is more active on the right side of the brain, moving the left limb' (1996: 575). Along similar lines, when discussing gesture in adult subjects with damage to the right brain hemisphere, McNeill and Pedelty suggest that the left brain alone, working with the right hand, 'produces a type of narrative in which there is linear form, but form deficient in imagistic content' (1995: 83), an observation that is also consistent with Vijay Koparkar's left hand taking the leading role in his Illustrators and his right hand predominating in his Marker gestures. It is interesting to note that the bilateral asymmetry in gesture displayed by Vijay Koparkar is also a common practice in Western orchestral conducting.

Analysis of video recordings can also be used as an approach to the study of interaction between participants in performance. In this case, analysis of Vijay Koparkar's performance of *Raga Multānī* suggests the following:

3. Interaction between performers cannot be reduced to the transmission and reception of cues. Observation of the different individuals' movements, orientation and facial expressions reveal a more dynamic process of interaction in which cueing gestures (such as the nod from singer to *tablā* player described above) are often, strictly speaking, redundant: they confirm something that all performers already know is about to happen but nonetheless form part of the ongoing performance management. (Some

performers argue that cues and instructions should not be visible to the audience, or even that they are not necessary at all: thus when gestures of instruction are frequent and obvious to the audience, it is likely to be taken by some observers as an indication of a lack of understanding between performers.)

4. The contribution of the audience to the performance can be divided into two kinds, which can be termed 'reaction' and 'participation'. In the former case, audience members respond to an especially beautiful phrase or impressive technical feat, and their gestures and vocal exclamations begin after it has been completed. In the case of participation, audience members show that they are following the music closely by tapping the beat, and particularly by marking the *sam* (beat one) in a manner essentially the same as that employed by the singer himself (this kind of gesture is initiated in advance of the *sam*, and cannot properly be described as a reaction).

It is clear from this analysis of Vijay Koparkar's performance of *Raga Multānī* that gesture can take on a number of different functions within a single vocal performance: although in one sense this complicates analysis, the alternation between different functions also provides a unique level of information in that it indicates the singer's focus of attention. Close examination of the relationship between sound and gesture can significantly enhance our understanding of the way the music is conceptualized by the performer, while study of audience members' gestural behaviour – in a musical tradition where such gesturing is not inhibited – can enable us to better understand the performance dynamics. The following two case studies, which also concern the performance of *khyal*, address in more detail some different gestures that can be described as 'illustrators' and their significance.

Imagery and Gesture in North Indian Vocal Music

North Indian classical musicians often make use of gesture and imagery together in the transmission and performance of their repertories; they do this both to describe the characteristics of the music, and to support techniques of sound production. Images can be conveyed through movement, and gesture thus becomes a way to embody and project qualities inherent in the meaning of music performance.

Taking into account both movement and the imagery associated with it can help shed light on how musicians conceive, construct and develop their music. For example, during an interview recorded in 2006, *khyal* singer Veena Sahasrabuddhe makes an upward movement of her arm while singing a note and describes how the gesture indicates how she was feeling that note in her mind: she explains that while performing *Dha* (the sixth degree of the scale) 'inside' she was also 'singing' *Sa* (the first scale degree) and the arm movement related to her intention of approaching that *Dha* as if it were coming from the lower *Sa*, as in the act of 'picking something [up]'.[9] In other words, the gesture reveals information about the performance that otherwise would not be available (that is, that there is more than the note we hear in the artist's mind). The image accompanying the gesture ('picking something up') clarifies why the singer makes the movement and how she intends to attack the note. Therefore, the performance of the *Dha* takes on a more specific and more complex meaning if analysed from the perspective of the musician, who was using imagery in order to reach the note in the way she intended (see Figure 10.1).

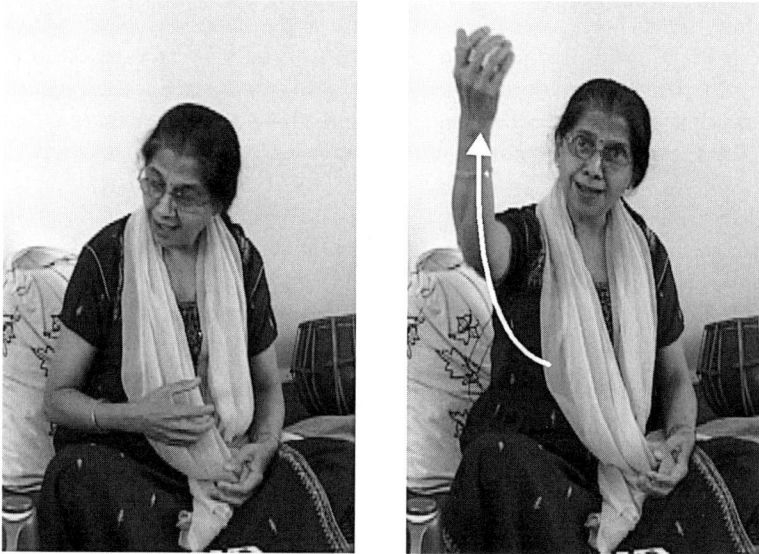

Figure 10.1   Veena Sahasrabuddhe: use of imagery in performance

Different musicians and traditions might value the aesthetic and communicative role of hand movement in performance differently. Nevertheless, gesture and imagery can play a key role in the transmission of music and are often part of a conscious didactic process. Providing an additional example, singer Sudokshina Chatterjee explains how she was encouraged to employ gesture and how her *gharana* (stylistic school) cherishes a vocal timbre that she describes with the aid of a symbolic hand movement, by drawing a parallel between 'open hand' and 'open sound':

---

[9]   Interview with Veena Sahasrabuddhe conducted and recorded in Pune, India by Martin Clayton and Laura Leante, 16 December 2006.

> Ustad Bade Ghulam Ali Khan Sahab used to say you have an open sound if you have an open hand. My teacher also says [that] you should open you hand – then you will have an open sound. (Sudokshina Chatterjee, 20 April 2004)[10]

When taking lessons from her nonagenarian guru Pt. Madhusudan S. Kanetkar (now deceased), singer Manjiri Asanare Kelkar used to rely heavily on visual information and gesture in order to understand instruction that her teacher would have not been able to demonstrate vocally. Their long and close relationship, she claims, allowed her to know what kind of sound quality or music passages would be represented in his gestures:

> Sometimes I guess what he is trying to do. So, now, as he is 90 or so it is easier for him … and for me. Sometimes he just gives the action [and] I understand what he means. (Manjiri Asanare Kelkar, 11 December 2006)[11]

Manjiri herself frequently has recourse to hand movement with her own students. For example, during a teaching session recorded in Pune in December 2006, she performed a gesture structured in a downward curve, followed by smaller arches. Afterwards, when asked about it, she repeated the gesture accompanying a short descending line in *Raga Jaunpuri* (see Figure 10.2), and she used the image of a bouncing ball to explain it (C is the tonal centre throughout):

> When you drop a ball … it just drops like that – it comes slowly, slowly, slowly – it … doesn't stop abruptly, it just doesn't stop where it is. (Manjiri Asanare Kelkar, 11 December 2006)

Strong emphasis is placed on the 'naturalness' of sound by many singers, and imagery is provided as a support for the artist to understand better how the stress and punctuation of musical phrases should be articulated throughout the performance, and Manjiri's bouncing ball is just one of many examples which could be mentioned. Another recurring one is the image of an elastic body being stretched:

> my guruji always uses this action, this thing [gestures] just like a rubber [band]: you stretch it and leave it. With that force it comes down. (Manjiri Asanare-Kelkar, 11 December 2006)

> just like any ball … I am just throwing it and then it comes automatically … it is just like elasticity. (Veena Sahasrabuddhe, 16 December 2006)

---

[10]   Interview conducted in the UK by Martin Clayton, Laura Leante and Nikki Moran.

[11]   Interview conducted and recorded in Pune, India by Martin Clayton and Laura Leante.

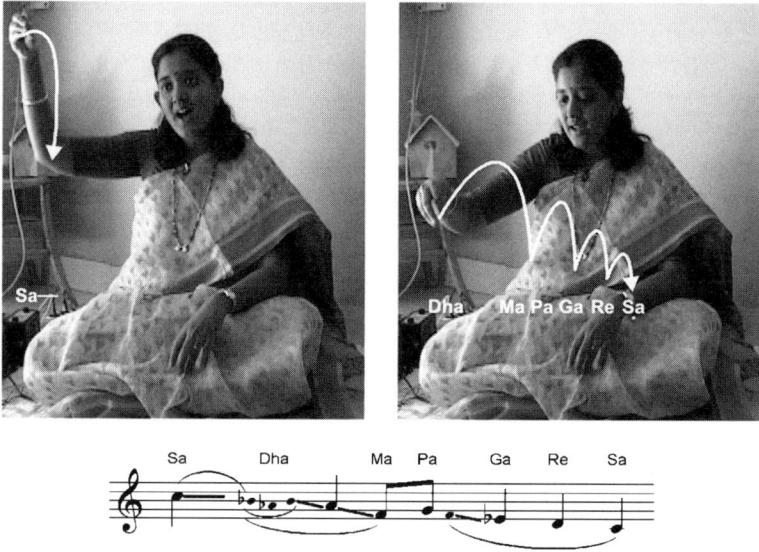

Figure 10.2   Manjiri Asanare Kelkar

All the examples above stress the co-expressiveness between gesture and sound. Nevertheless, in the last two cases (that of the pantomimic 'stretching' gesture and that of the iconic 'bouncing' one) the sound depicts an extra-musical experience. (The reader will no doubt find striking a parallel use of the 'elastic' reference by a bagpipe instructor in Atlantic Canada, presented later in this chapter.) Such sonic rendition is what semiotician Philip Tagg would define as an 'anaphone', a neologism he derived from 'analogy', so that 'if analogy means another way of saying the same thing, anaphone just means using an existing model outside music to produce musical sounds resembling that model' (Tagg 1999: 24). In Tagg's method of music analysis, anaphones account for iconic units of meaning present in a given music and can be of different kinds. The gestures illustrated here are 'kinetic anaphones': representations by means of sound of a pattern of movement. The gesture accompanying the performance of these anaphones is a way to embody, and at the same time to project, the meaning and the image the musician associates with it.

Instances of anaphones and pantomimic gestures abound in the performance and teaching of vocal music. Another case is presented by Veena Sahasrabuddhe, who explains how she uses the image of 'tying knots' to emphasize certain moments of the performance, for example when she sings an embellishment called *khatka*. In this ornament, a degree of the scale (the note on which the knot is 'tied') is highlighted by a quick movement (the 'knot' itself) that precedes the note and that is set out within a small range[12] (see Figure 10.3).

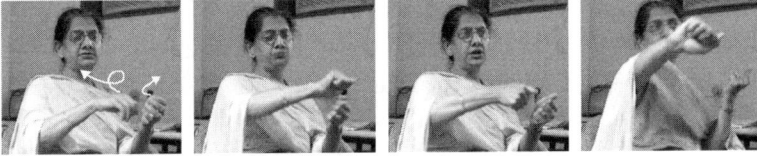

Figure 10.3   Veena Sahasrabuddhe: the 'knot' gesture

Veena used this 'knot' gesture during both interview and teaching sessions, and applied it in different *ragas*.[13] On one occasion she performed it repeatedly in order to show a student how to sing a *khatka* and she 'tied knots' higher or lower in the air according to different degrees of the scale on which she was performing the ornament. This practice seems to hint at a tendency to accompany singing with movements that correlate with the relative height of the pitch. Nevertheless, it should be noticed that most of the times she performed the knot, she 'tied it' just above her lap, and therefore the correspondence between pitch and space is not intrinsic to the performance of this gesture. In other words, the value of the 'knot gesture' lies mostly in its function of supporting the anaphone associated with it. During a concert, the knot would be less marked and the distinction from a more generic stretching movement could be less evident. In fact, anaphones should be considered within the wider context in which they are performed: as Veena herself once suggested, the performance of the knot gesture should also be considered together with the image of the elastic body discussed above, and interpreted within the wider aesthetics emphasizing the 'flow' of musical phrases.

> [the] knot comes whenever I am singing one swara [*note*] [and] I want to make
> that swara a little longer … and very firm at the same time. So, it comes like …
> elasticity. (Veena Sahasrabuddhe, 16 December 2006)

The examples analysed above show how different kinds of gestures are implicated in the performance and teaching of music. These gestures represent a way to embody and express qualities that the musician attributes to the sound and articulates through the use of images. Analysing movement and imagery together is therefore important in understanding how artists relate to their music and construct meaning in performance. Later in this chapter we will see how the combined domains of gesture and imagery function similarly in the transmission of an instrumental tradition from another part of the world.

---

[12]   'Gesture goes with the *swaras* [notes]. Suppose, if there is a little bit of *khatka* … in my mind it's going to be like just putting a knot there'(Veena Sahasrabuddhe, 18 May 2005).

[13]   Recordings carried out by Martin Clayton and Laura Leante in Mumbai (21 May 2005) and Pune (16 December 2006), India.

Gesture in *Raga* Space

The melodies and gestures of North Indian vocalists can also be seen as navigations through the space of a *raga*. A *raga*, in the music-theoretic approach that has been dominant for the last hundred years, is usually described in terms of a kind of melodic grammar: a set of rules. These rules dictate how notes should be arranged sequentially to generate acceptable melodies. For example, ascending to the third scale degree is accomplished quite differently in *Raga Bihag* and *Raga Yaman* (see Example 10.1). To sing the first melodic sentence in the middle of a performance of *Raga Yaman*, or the second melodic sentence in *Raga Bihag* is often described as a kind of 'grammatical' error.

Example 10.1   Ways of ascending to the third scale degree in *Raga Bihag* and
                Raga Yaman

Melodic action is not only described in terms of grammar, however. Informally, musicians sometimes also speak of *raga* as though it were a place or a space. It is common to say that one is 'in' a certain *raga* when one is performing it. Melodic action, likewise, is described as motion within the space of a *raga*. This metaphor is apparent both in English and in Hindi. For example, in *Bihag* [*Bihag mein*] one ascends [*arohan karna*] to the third scale degree by leaping over [*langhana*] the second. While in the space/place of a *raga*, one walks on certain paths, briefly touches certain points, stops to rest on others. Furthermore, musicians sometimes speak of various spaces/places ('*jagah*') within *raga*s – for example, the space between the first and third scale degrees described above.[14] A given *raga* may be further spatialized in visual imagery showing a dramatic scene, or representing a season or a time of day, as in *ragamala* paintings (see Ebeling 1973). A popular comic representation of the great singer Tansen, for example, shows jagged yellow and orange stripes emanating from his body into the space around him as he fills the air with the heat of *Raga Dipak* (Rizvi & Lien 1998[1975]: 29).

The depiction of a *raga* as a space may at first seem arcane, even deliberately mystifying. Equally mystifying to some, perhaps, are the gestures of North Indian vocalists. These gestures, caricatured by music critics as 'acrobatics', 'contortions' or 'spasmodic physical movements' (Nadkarni 2005: 178; Pingle 1962[1894]: 103–4 and 110; Chitra in Neuman 2004: 375), have generally been regarded as irrelevant to music. Gesture is widely considered a distracting sideshow to music, which, according to the dominant grammar-based model, is made of notes, as

---

[14]   For a detailed description of *jagah* in Hindustani music, see Neuman (2004: Chapter 4).

sentences are made of words. However, if we instead take seriously the sense in which melody is motion in space, the importance of gesture becomes clear. (This, after all, is no more of a metaphoric stretch than considering music to be like language.)

A close look at gesture in North Indian vocal performance suggests there is a way of knowing music that is spatial, kinesthetic and three-dimensional; one that is made physically present through gesture (see Rahaim 2008). The above illustrations of vocalists provide clear examples of common gestures that link melody with space and texture. Like speech gestures, these vary widely from singer to singer, and most singers have a wide repertoire of gestures at hand. Singers may, for example, gesturally model the phrase '1–6♭–4–5–3♭–2–1' (the example from *Raga Jaunpuri* performed by Manjiri Asanare Kelkar in Figure 10.2 above) as descending motion, or as motion from left-to-right, or right-to-left, or as a gradually shrinking space. There are numerous ways that a phrase with this pitch contour might unfold in space, depending on the singer and the context.

This interpretation brings us back to the widespread, if mostly implicit, conception of a *raga* as a space. The spaces of *raga*s serve as particularly important contexts for melodic motion. If a *raga* is a space, it is not an empty space, or a set of equal points. *Raga*s serve as flexible but stable topographies that singers explore through both melodic and gestural action. Singers navigate the space of a *raga* in the physical space around their body. Singers explore this space while elaborating on melodies, moving through particular regions via particular melodic paths, with particular textures and topographies.

An example of a special *raga* topology can be seen in a performance of the *Raga Ramkali*. Ramkali is closely related to one of the most well-known *raga*s in Hindustani music: *Bhairav*. Bhairav has a wide repertoire and many variants. *Ramkali* is almost universally considered a variant of *Bhairav*, rather than the other way round. Since the relationship between *Ramkali* and *Bhairav* are so important in the performance analysed below, it is helpful to begin with a basic grammatical sketch to highlight the similarities and differences. The scale of *Bhairav* is given below in Example 10.2.

Example 10.2   The scale of *Raga Bhairav*

The lowered-6 and the lowered-2 tend to be approached from scale degree 7 and scale degree 3, respectively. A few of *Bhairav's* characteristic phrases, or *calan* (literally, gait) are given in Example 10.3.

These phrases distinguish *Bhairav* from the several other *raga*s, such as *Gauri* and *Kalingda*, which have the same scale, but are not *Bhairav*. Unlike most variants of *Bhairav*, however, *Ramkali* also uses all of *Bhairav's* distinctive phrases. It is distinguished by an occasional use of a sharp fourth and flat seventh.

Example 10.3 *Bhairav calan*

These notes are used to elaborate on and emphasize the fifth scale degree to a greater degree than in *Bhairav* (which tends to emphasize the natural fourth as a resting tone). Here is an example of how these distinctive notes might be inserted into an otherwise *Bhairav*-ish sequence (see Example 10.4). *Ramkali* shifts are, in terms of notes, the primary feature that distinguishes *Ramkali* from *Bhairav*. The space of *Bhairav*-like melodic action in *Ramkali* is called 'quasi-*Bhairav*'.

Example 10.4 *Ramkali* shifts

So much for a grammatical sketch. Now we turn to the spatial enactment of *Ramkali*. We will take as an example Girja Devi's performance of *Raga Ramkalı* at the 1991 Savai Gandharva Music Festival in Pune, India.[15] Here, Girja Devi navigates the space of *Ramkalı* both by singing and by gesturing in the physical space around her. In particular, she broadly delineates two *sub-spaces*[16] (that is, consistent spaces within the *raga* space) one for the ordinary motion in quasi-*Bhairav* space, and one specially reserved for *Ramkali* shifts.

The quasi-*Bhairav* motion is generally one-handed (right), and takes place in a space roughly defined by her abdomen. The *Ramkali* shifts, in contrast, are two-handed, and are placed in a small sphere in front of her solar plexus. More striking is the distinctive internal contour of this space. Her hands curl around each other without touching, as though tracing a curvaceous three-dimensional figure. The movement in this space is rotational, just as the arc of the *Ramkalı* shift pivots around the fifth scale degree without any net motion. This stands in contrast to most of her other gestures, which are generally translational: they move from one

---

[15]   This concert took place at New English School in Pune on December 12, 1991. The recording is available on VCD from Fountain: FMRVCD-13.

[16]   Some readers may recognize the terms 'space' and 'sub-space' from the algebra of vector spaces. The loose analogy works to a certain extent: a *raga* space, like a vector space, is defined by relations between its elements rather than by pre-given boundaries. A *raga* space can furthermore be seen to be closed over certain melodic operations the way that a vector space is closed over certain arithmetic operations. However, like any analogy, it has limits: if *raga* spaces were actually vector spaces, a singer would be unable to stop singing one *raga* and start singing another!

point to another in space. Finally, the *Ramkali* shift is usually enacted with more shoulder tension than the rest of the performance (see Table 10.1).

Table 10.1   Quasi-*Bhairav* and *Ramkali* sub-spaces

	Quasi-*Bhairav* sub-space	*Ramkali* shift sub-space
Boundary	trunk	abdomen
Motion	translational	rotational
Number of hands	one	two
Relative tension	relaxed	tense

Note that the sub-spaces are defined only in part by their edges. They are defined also by the special contours along which gesture occurs in them. Although the gestural pattern above is very consistent in the particular performance of *Raga Ramkali* analysed here (of 34 *Ramkali* shifts, 30 are enacted via this gesture) we should not read this to mean that the space of *Ramkali* is the same no matter who is performing. Bhimsen Joshi's Savai Gandharva performance, for example, shows no trace of it. Unlike the grammar of *ragas*, which have gradually become more and more standard and precise, gesture remains idiosyncratic. Some patterns are particular to certain lineages, others are unique to individuals, some seem only to last as long as a single performance.

'Meta-gesture' in the Transmission of Scottish Classical Bagpiping

The studies so far described in this chapter posit relationships between melody and physical gesture among vocalists within one (broadly speaking) musical tradition. A study of gesture within an instrumental tradition provides a perspective on the roles of musicians' gestures within a different set of constraints. For example, how do we assess the importance of gestures when the hands are – in contrast to singers – occupied with producing musical sound?

Physical gestures can be an implicit component of one-on-one musical instruction (instrumental as well as vocal) – often a scenario in which one musician tries to communicate how to conceptualize and perform a given musical interpretation to another musician. This appears to be the case in the North Indian examples above referring to teaching situations. We have also seen that physical gestures made by teachers may be understood as indices to other kinds of images co-occurring in the teacher's imagination as she tries to communicate musical intent. These 'other kinds of images' are frequently metaphors of motion from non-aural domains; notably imagined object motion (such as Manjiri Asanare Kelkar's bouncing ball) as well as bodily motion (such as Veena Sahasrabuddhe's tying of knots). Each set of co-occurring images may be thought of as a unitary cognitive experience – a kind of 'meta-gesture' – with individual images from different modalities (aural, visual, motor, imagined) playing co-articulating roles. Viewed from this perspective, teacher gestures in the context of face-to-face musical transmission may be understood as one component of an inherently inter-modal experience we call 'musical'.

Analysis of several examples of teacher gestures in the context of classical Scottish bagpiping (called *piobaireachd*)[17] illustrates the idea of meta-gesture in the transmission of instrumental music. In video recorded *piobaireachd* lessons taught by pipe instructors Lynda Mackay[18] and Bruce Gandy[19] in Prince Edward Island, Canada in 2001,[20] it is possible to identify at least one 'energetic shaping' expressed repeatedly in various modalities within each teacher's demonstrated instruction. In the video-taped examples discussed here, the same *piobaireachd* tune ('Rout of Glenfruin') is taught by both teachers, using staff notation.

One meta-gesture in Mackay's teaching is the cycle or circle. She 'draws' circles of various sizes with her chanter while she's playing and with her hand while she's listening to students play. Mackay also verbally expresses the mental image of 'a circle going around', and the cycle of a wave as it repeatedly crashes on the shore and recedes. In each of Mackay's images of motion – the circle she draws 'going around' with her hand and with her chanter, and the crashing wave – there is a slight 'hitch' in the motion each time the figure comes around. In each case, the musical analogue is a repeated melodic figure that contains a point of elongation or marked stress somewhere along the way. Mackay's visual images convey finely nuanced patterns of lengthening and shortening of melody notes not discernible from the printed score (see Figure 10.4). This quality of nuance in timing, co-expressed in sound and manual gesture, is likewise achieved by Veena Sahasrabuddhe's combined repertoire of anaphones (following Tagg), taken together (as noted previously) to emphasize a broader aesthetic of musical flow.

A second set of images documents piper Bruce Gandy teaching privately in his home in Prince Edward Island in September 2001 (see Figure 10.5). Gandy's

---

[17]   Referred to as the classical solo repertoire for the Highland bagpipe, *piobaireachd* is a highly stylized, ground and variation form with roots reaching back as far as the sixteenth century.

[18]   Lynda McKay taught piping and drumming at The College of Piping and Celtic Performing Arts in Summerside, Prince Edward Island, from 2000 to 2005. She is currently Pipe Sergeant with the Peel Regional Police Pipe out of Brampton, Ontario, Canada.

[19]   Bruce Gandy was Piping Instructor and Pipe Major at The College of Piping and Celtic Performing Arts, Canada, from 1997 to 2002. An Inverness Gold and Oban medalist, he is currently Head Instructor at the Halifax Citadel Regimental Association in Nova Scotia.

[20]   These video recordings were made in September 2001 by Gina Fatone in Summerside, Prince Edward Island, Canada. This fieldwork was funded by a Canadian Studies Graduate Student Fellowship Program grant.

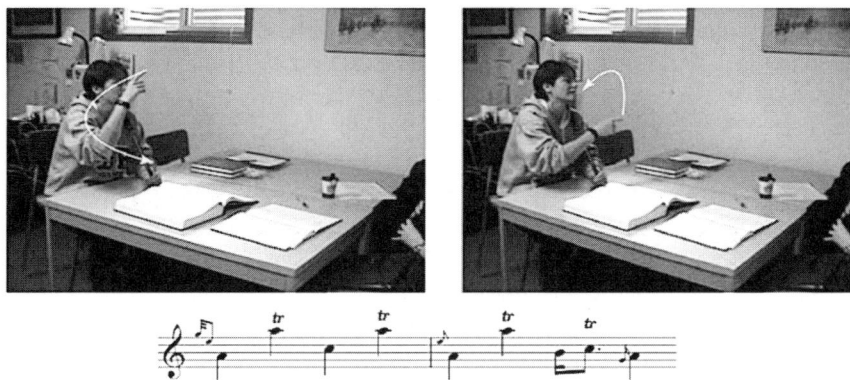

Figure 10.4   Lynda Mackay, The College of Piping, Prince Edward Island, Canada, September 2001. Rout of Glenfruin (Thumb Variation, opening bars)[21]

physical gestures are generally fluid, large and amorphous. The meta-image that comes up repeatedly in interviews and lessons with Gandy is 'elastic' – a striking parallel to the North Indian usage of the term described earlier. Gandy verbally refers to both the concrete object (an elastic band) and elasticity as a musical property directly; and also refers to the property indirectly, with language such as 'pull the tune at the edges', 'this tune has to bend' and 'tighten it up'.[22]

Figure 10.5   Bruce Gandy, Summerside, Prince Edward Island, Canada

In the teaching scenarios sampled above, the idea that the instrument itself is not the best way to 'get at the music' – even though the music is ultimately to be performed on the instrument – is implied repeatedly, and sometimes explicitly stated. In addition to instrumental demonstration, instructors use vocalization, conducting-like gestures with hands or chanter, or verbal presentation of metaphoric images of motion, to convey musical information. We take these multi-modal teacher

---

[21]   Notation excerpted from *The Kilberry Book of Ceol Mor* edited by Archibald Campbell, Sixth edition (1989[1948]: 91).

[22]   Bruce Gandy, 21 September 2001, Summerside, Prince Edward Island, Canada. Intercultural use of the same metaphor to communicate musical intent would seem to merit further attention.

behaviours for granted; they are implicitly understood as part of the teaching process. Yet, it is the implicitness itself that is intriguing. Several questions come immediately to mind: Why are such physical gestures made by these teachers in the first place? Why does cross-modal imagery (of which physical gesture is one type here) seem to be such an inherent part of the transmission process? Why does the teacher not just say, 'play it like this' and simply model the musical phrase for the student on the instrument? Is it not redundant to gesture and conjure metaphors?

As music theorist Robert Hatten (2004) notes in his recent theory of musical gesture, research in psychology and psycholinguistics propels one to consider more biologically fundamental reasons why gestures of all types occur. Psychological studies have determined that perception itself is cross-modal. Cross-modality is an empirically demonstrated, fundamental aspect of cognition. That is, our brains integrate input from the different senses to form a coherent interpretation of what is going on around us. Hatten's broad definition of gesture of all types, which is, 'significant energetic shapings through time' (2004:93) helps us grasp the concept of cross-modal images combining cognitively as a unitary experience. 'The basic shape of an expressive gesture', Hatten states, 'is isomorphic and intermodal across all systems of production and interpretation' (2004: 109). If this is the case, it may follow that 'multi-modalizing' musical content – or cross-modal occurrences in any aspect of musicking (whether one is performing, teaching, or listening) – is a spontaneous and automatic process.

Gesture analyst David McNeill maintains gestures co-occur with speaking, because as analog entities (as opposed to words, which are digital entities) gestures 'materialize' (his term) meaning that words cannot. Furthermore, McNeill states, 'Imagery is embodied in the gestures that universally and automatically occur with speech' (2005: 15). McNeill proposes language is inseparable from imagery. However, it seems that non-linguistic thought (in this case, music) is also inseparable from imagery, and the automaticity with which we access analogous images from other non-aural sensory modes, whether speaking about music, playing music or listening to music, is richly evident.

So, then, what may set gesture in teaching apart from gesture that co-occurs with other forms of musicking? In teaching, there tends to be a sophisticated elaboration of an idea. That is, there is often much repetition, and communication of the same concept in multiple ways, in hopes of finding something that will stick with the student. In performing, or in listening to a performance of music, on the other hand, there is one chance to convey meaning in any given musical micro-moment. Teaching is less of a 'one-shot deal'. In teaching, there are multiple opportunities to 'materialize' (to use McNeill's term) a musical moment. Perhaps, the struggle to *communicate how* to conceptualize and perform a given musical gesture (in other words the struggle to communicate about non-linguistic communication) makes the one-on-one transmission context especially rich in cross-modal imagery, including physical gesture.

Viewed from the perspective that musical experience is inherently synaesthetic (where higher-order perception and cognition is not excluded from the definition of the term), physical and non-physical gestures combine in the teacher's struggle to communicate musical intention. Teachers' visual 'materializations' of imagined images such as the crashing wave and the stretching of an elastic band; as well as physical hand and chanter gestures, help students refine their conceptualization of the musical gesture, which is greater than aurality alone.

Conclusion

The four case studies in this chapter, individually and collectively, locate physical gesture among a variety of cross-modal phenomena associated with musical performance and transmission. The first study examines the multiple functions of gesture within a single *khyal* performance, distinguishing illustrator gestures from markers and emblems, and placing their deployment within the wider performance context. The following two studies also describe *khyal* performances: one examines several illustrative gestures as observed in teaching and demonstration contexts, showing how they are linked to visual and kinesthetic imagery; the other considers how physical gesture relates to the idea of melodic space or place, with particular patterns of movement describing individual topographies. Moving away from India, our fourth fieldwork study demonstrates how many of the same features – broadly speaking – can also be observed in the transmission of bagpipe repertory in Atlantic Canada, and further develops the idea of 'meta-images' or 'meta-gestures' underpinning many individual instances of physical gesture and image deployed in musical performance and teaching.

Taken together, the work collectively presented in this chapter draws attention to physical gestures in musicking – of all types – as indices to mental representations of 'music as motion' as a possible feature of cross-cultural musical thought. The analyses of melody and physical gesture as parallel channels, or co-occurring realizations of the same meta-gesture, suggest that gesture is not limited to musical communication, but points to a fundamental constituent of musicking in general. Our discussion of relationships between imagery, melody and gesture has been restricted to two essentially monophonic musical traditions, however. A greater pool of research in music and gesture that takes a broad range of musical practices into account will undoubtedly challenge and expand our ideas of what music can be.

References

Campbell, A. (ed.) (1989[1948]). *The Kilberry Book of Ceol Mor*. Glasgow: The Piobaireachd Society.

Clayton, M. (2005). Communication in Indian Raga Performance. In D. Miell, R. MacDonald & D. Hargreaves (eds), *Musical Communication* (pp. 361–81). Oxford: Oxford University Press.

— (2007). Time, Gesture and Attention in a *Khyal* Performance. *Asian Music* 38/2: 71–96.

— (2008). Toward an Ethnomusicology of Sound Experience. In H. Stobart (ed.), *The New (Ethno)musicologies* (pp. 135–69). Lanham, MD: Scarecrow Press.

Ebeling, K. (1973). *Ragamala Painting*. Basel: Ravi Kumar.

Hatten, R. (2004). *Interpreting Musical Gestures, Topics, and Tropes: Mozart, Beethoven, Schubert*. Bloomington, IN: Indiana University Press.

Kendon, A. (2004). *Gesture: Visible Action As Utterance*. Cambridge: Cambridge University Press.

McNeill, D. (1992). *Hand and Mind: What Gestures Reveal About Thought*. Chicago: Chicago University Press.

— (2005). *Gesture and Thought*. Chicago: University of Chicago Press.

— & Pedelty, L. (1995). Right Brain and Gesture. In K. Emmorey & J. Reilly (eds.), *Language, Gesture and Space* (pp. 63–85). Hillsdale, NJ: Lawrence Erlbaum Associates.

Nadkarni, M. (2005). *The Great Masters: Profiles in Hindustani Classical Vocal Music*. New Delhi: Rupa.

Neuman, D. (2004). *A House of Music: The Hindustani Musician and the Crafting of Traditions*. PhD Dissertation, Columbia University.

Pingle, B. (1962[1894]). *History of Indian Music with Particular Reference to Theory and Practice*. Calcutta: Susil Gupta.

Rahaim, Matt. 2008. Gesture and Melody in Indian Vocal Music. *Gesture* 8(3): 325–47.

Rimé, B. & Schiaratura, L. (1991). Gesture and Speech. In R. S. Feldman & B. Rimé (eds.), *Fundamentals of Nonverbal Behavior* (pp. 239–81). Cambridge: Cambridge University Press.

Rizvi, D. & Lien, Y. (1998[1975]). *Tansen*. Amar Chitra Katha Series. Mumbai: India Book House Ltd.

Tagg, P. (1999). Introductory Notes to the Semiotics of Music (http://www.tagg. org; accessed June 2007).

Trevarthen, C. (1996). Lateral Assymetries in Infancy: Implications for the Development of the Hemispheres. *Neuroscience and Biobehavioral Reviews* 20/4: 571–86.

Vines, B., Krumhansl, C., Wanderley, M. & Levitin, D. (2006). Cross-modal Interactions in the Perception of Musical Performance. *Cognition* 101: 80–113.

Chapter 11
Whose Gestures? Chamber Music and the Construction of Permanent Agents

Roger Graybill

The string quartet genre of the late eighteenth and early nineteenth centuries is often characterized as a musical 'conversation' among equal partners.[1] To be sure, even in the quartets of Haydn, Mozart and Beethoven, one encounters many movements that do not exhibit anything approaching true equality between the parts; yet we commonly regard those movements that *do* exhibit such equality to be exemplars of the genre. It is as if we hold in our awareness an ideal picture of the quartet as a group of equals, despite the apparent advantage held by the first violin (and perhaps the cello), and that we derive special satisfaction when the composer allows each member to reach its true potential.

But the very notion of an idealized equal partnership among the four instrumental parts raises a problem. Who or what exactly are the 'partners' in this interaction? One might claim that it is the performers themselves; that is, all the performers contribute equally to the ensemble, simply because their parts are written that way. While certainly a valid interpretation, that cannot be the only possibility. We can also think of each instrumental part as a role that is adopted by the performer; according to that view, it is these roles, not the performers per se, that exhibit equal status. Such a distinction between the performers and their roles is validated to the extent that it supports some commonsense beliefs that we hold about performances; for instance, we intuitively assume that the expressive quality of a performer's musical gesture is not necessarily congruent with the emotional state or personal character of the performer rendering the gesture. While there are several ways one might make sense of such incongruity, this chapter will follow Fred Maus (1988) in assuming that the source of the expressive gesture in question is an imaginary musical *agent* that is distinguishable from the performer (as well as from the composer).[2] Maus explores how a musical idea or gesture can be understood to be an *action* by an imaginary musical agent, with 'action' denoting

---

[1] Parker (2002) distinguishes four types of quartet textures, of which 'conversation' is one type, in the last half of the eighteenth century. (The other three types are lecture, polite conversation and debate.)

[2] From a somewhat different perspective, Cox (2006: 53) also explores how a listener is able to distinguish the 'sound-producing actions of the performers' from an 'agency that cannot be identified directly with the actions of the performers'.

a behaviour that is explainable in some sense; that is, it can be described as arising from something within the agent – for instance, a belief, a desire, an emotion, or a character trait (1988: 66). To cite an example from the symphonic repertoire, the very opening of Mozart's Jupiter Symphony could be heard as the actions of two different agents, the first asserting itself emphatically, and the second countering with a lyrical gesture. We might imagine this second gesture as being motivated by some combination of beliefs and/or desires held by the agent: for instance, a belief that the certainty expressed by the first agent is unfounded, even delusional, and a desire to pull that first agent into an open-ended dialogue.[3]

Musical agency provides one possible framework for understanding the behaviour of individual instrumental lines within the string quartet: perhaps each instrumental part can be regarded as a series of actions (or an ongoing action) by an imaginary agent. Yet if by 'imaginary agent' we mean something roughly analogous to a real-life person or a dramatic character in a play, we quickly encounter difficulties. Consider a representative 'conversational' passage from the opening movement of Haydn's String Quartet in C Major, Op. 76 No. 3 (Example 11.1).[4] This passage contains two highly contrasting ideas: the opening five-note motive, and the ascending dotted-rhythm figure first heard in bar 5 in the second violin. Moreover, as is typical of a conversational texture, each instrumental part has the opportunity to play both ideas. But in the light of the resulting gestural contrast projected by each instrumental part, what does it mean to say that any one of them – say, the viola – is a coherent character? One possible answer is to say that the viola's behaviour is 'motivated' by some belief and/or desire to switch gestures as the passage progresses, and that such motivation might provide a key to its character. And in this passage the motivation seems clear enough: the viola desires to imitate (perhaps simply out of a playful impulse) ideas that have been already played by other instruments: in bar 5, it picks up the idea played by the first violin in bar 1, and in bars 6–7, it imitates the dotted-rhythm gesture just heard in the second and first violins. Yet, even if we do attribute to the viola a desire to imitate others, it is not clear how that in itself could help us to imagine it as a coherent character; indeed, its willingness to imitate strongly contrasting gestures could be regarded as a sign of *in*coherence. To add a further complication, even if we were somehow able to view the violist's propensity towards imitation as the manifestation of a stable ongoing agency, we seem to have no basis for regarding the viola as distinctive in any way from the other instruments, since they too evidently share the same impulse within bars 1–7. Thus, it is clear that the sharing of melodic material between parts within a conversational texture cannot in itself provide a toehold for the listener who is attempting to construe each instrumental part as a coherent and distinctive agent. This is not to deny that we intuitively

---

[3]   This example does not appear in Maus's article. However, Hatten (2006: 6) takes note of 'Mozart's dialectical oppositions in his opening themes, which suggest two competing agencies' – a description that applies very well to this opening.

[4]   Parker (2002: 238) cites this movement as an example of a 'conversation'.

Example 11.1   Haydn, String Quartet in C Major, Op. 76 No. 3 ('Emperor'), bars
1–9

might hear the passing back and forth of musical ideas between different parts as 'conversational' in some sense; the difficulty is in identifying reified stable agents – as opposed to ad hoc momentary agents – as the participants in that discussion.

How, then, can the listener hear a conversational texture as the interactions of four independent agents? This chapter will show that agency theory can, at least in certain movements from the string quartet repertoire, provide a basis for interpreting an individual instrumental line as a stable and coherent character – that is, as a single agent – even when its gestural language is extremely variable. Two general listening strategies facilitate such an interpretation. First, and perhaps most obviously, the listener needs to attend *closely* to the interactions between the instrument in question and the other instruments. For instance, if one instrument imitates another, does it do so exactly? If not, what character trait or motivation might explain the alteration? (In Example 11.1 the viola enters with its dotted rhythm two beats 'early'; is this a nascent sign of impetuousness?) Another example: when an instrument introduces a *new* motive (see the second violin in bar 5), what motivation or character trait could explain that?

A second listening strategy is equally essential: we can interpret an instrumental line as a stable agent only if we listen for an emerging *pattern* of motivations, desires, and so on as the movement progresses. If that pattern seems reasonably congruent with what we might observe in a real-life person, we can imagine the musical line to be the expression of a stable and coherent agent. For instance, in the Haydn movement, we see signs even within bars 1–7 that the viola is an assertive, even impulsive character. First, in the opening gesture it takes over the alto position in the texture from the second violin; second, it claims the opening theme in bar 5; and third, it jumps in two beats early with the dotted rhythm gesture, as mentioned earlier. In short, by tracing the behaviour of any particular instrumental line through a series of interactions, we may find that its disparate gestures actually make sense as the expression of a stable *permanent* agent (Cone 1974: 89), since different interactional contexts will quite naturally call forth different responses.[5]

Both listening strategies just outlined assume that a character profile can only be revealed through the interactions between the instrument in question and the other instruments. Such interactions can occur at two levels. First, the instrument interacts laterally with other individual instruments within the ensemble, as demonstrated by the Haydn excerpt.[6] As we shall see, it may even be possible for a *relationship* to form between permanent agents within the ensemble, provided that the successive interactions between them follow a coherent pattern. The analysis in the second part of this chapter will illustrate several such one-on-one relationships.

The second level of interaction is between the instrument and the quartet ensemble as a whole. Here I conceive of the ensemble as more than the sum of the four parts; rather, it is a reified entity unto itself. As such, it can *be acted upon* by the individual agent, and it can also *act upon* the agent. Moreover, this collective entity very often will follow its own narrative path that in principle is distinctive

---

[5]   Maus (1988: 68–9) argues that musical agency is in principle indeterminate; that is, it is impossible to assign agency in any one definitive way. Thus, to hear a quartet texture as four interacting 'permanent' agents is only one of a multiple possible hearings.

[6]   Such interactions would fall under Hatten's category of 'dialogical' interplay (2006: 6).

from – and yet intertwined with – the narrative paths of the individual agents.[7] Since a listener's attempt to interpret the behaviour of a permanent agent depends in part on the larger communal narrative, the latter will necessarily play a fairly prominent role in the forthcoming analysis; however, the primary analytical focus will be on interactions between the instruments.

Analysis of Brahms, String Quartet in C minor, Op. 51 No. 1, I, Exposition

To understand how a quartet texture might be heard as four interacting permanent agents along the lines just discussed, we now turn to the first movement of Brahms's C minor String Quartet. Example 11.2 shows the exposition, which will be the sole focus of this chapter; Figure 11.1 presents a formal overview of the exposition. As shown in that diagram, bar 32 initiates the second thematic area; accordingly, the forthcoming analysis falls into two sections, the first focusing on bars 1–32, and the second on bars 32–82.

first thematic area		transition	second thematic area		codetta
a	b	a'			
c: i → V (→IV?)	iv^6 → V (iii?)	i → e♭:V	e♭:V → (E♭: V$^{4/2}$)	→	I
bar 1	bar 11	bar 23	bar 32	bar 53	bar 75

Figure 11.1   Formal diagram of Brahms's String Quartet in C minor, Op. 51 No. 1, I, exposition

Bars 1–32 divide into three subsections, labeled *aba'* in Figure 11.1; *a'* also functions as the transition. Subsections *a* and *a'* share an aggressive forward-driving character, while the *b* section presents new motivic material as well as a relaxed lyrical character that strikingly contrasts with the two *a* sections.

If we were to interpret bars 1–32 through the lens of musical agency, where does that agency reside? At first, it may appear that individual agency plays a

---

[7]   Such reciprocal influences between the group and the individual agent touch upon a theoretical problem that has vexed sociologists throughout the twentieth century, namely how to define and coordinate the concepts of society and human agency. Sociologists have tended to fall into two camps on this issue, with the heart of the debate resting in part on the ontological status of 'society.' Is it a reified structured entity that constrains the actions of its members (the top-down view); or is it not really a *thing* at all, but rather a convenient term for designating the net result of interactions among individuals (the bottom-up view)? Some sociological theorists have sought to synthesize this apparent conflict, among the most notable being Anthony Giddens (1984).

Example 11.2   Brahms, String Quartet in C minor, Op. 51 No. 1, I, exposition *continued*

Example 11.2   *continued*

continued

Example 11.2 *concluded*

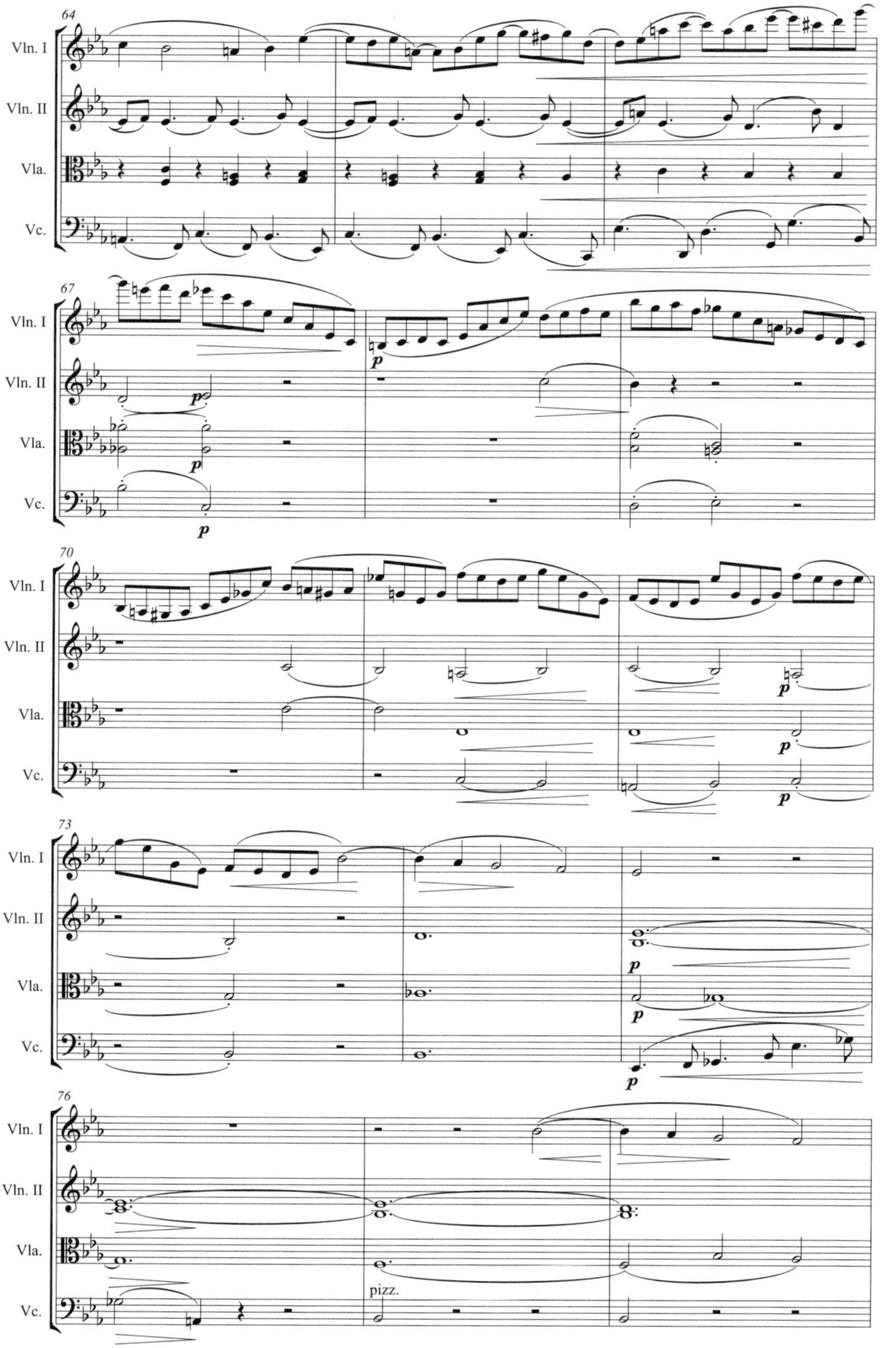

weak role at best. Indeed, the foregoing description of this passage as a clear *aba'* suggests the possibility of hearing the entire ensemble acting as a single agent, switching suddenly from an extremely aggressive gesture to a relaxed and expansive one, and then back again.[8] One might say that we have here the beginnings of a communal narrative consisting of three large gestures. But closer attention to this passage reveals that individual agency is also at work, especially at the juncture points between the three sections. The effect is highly dramatic in bars 7–8, where the viola tenaciously hangs on to the root of the dominant chord after the other instruments have dropped out. As if wanting to pull the reins on a forward momentum that has spun out of control, the viola's act immediately brings the musical flow to a virtual standstill. And the ploy works; the rest of the ensemble joins in with a transposition of bars 7–8 down a step (bars 8–9), in effect dissolving the dominant tension of bars 7–8, at least for the moment.

We also see individual agency at work at the juncture between the *b* and *a'* sections, though in a more subtle way. First we have to backtrack a bit: note that bars 11–19 lead to an arrival on the dominant chord in bar 19, as if to set up the return of section *a'*. But then the music takes a strange turn towards a tonicized B minor; the repeated F$\sharp$ is especially mysterious and disorienting. Only in bars 22–3 is the home key of C minor re-established. Individual agency contributes to the events of bars 19–23, though not through the dramatic act of a single agent, as in bar 7; here the listener is more aware of interactions *between* agents. The second violin's B–G–F$\sharp$ in bar 19 is immediately echoed by the viola; also, the viola's arrival on F$\sharp$ coincides with the cello's arrival on the same pitch, and the two instruments proceed together to bar 23.

Such instrumental pairing is actually a prominent feature of bars 1–32 as a whole, as can be seen especially clearly in the *a* and *a'* sections. The forthcoming analysis of bars 1–32 will focus on the behaviour of each instrumental line within the context of such pairings. While quartet textures contain six possible instrumental pairs (see Figure 11.2), my analysis will draw attention only to those pairings in which the two instrumental lines can be heard as being *in relationship*. As suggested earlier, two permanent agents can be said to be in relationship if (1) they behave with respect to each other such that the listener can explain the behaviour of each, and (2) they do so on an ongoing basis, and not merely in an ad hoc way.[9]

---

[8] Lewin (1983: 14) interprets the switch of character between the *a* and *b* sections as a composed-out juxtaposition of two opposing strands within the Viennese tradition from which Brahms drew inspiration: 'We observe here an abrupt shift of rhetorical mode, temporarily negating the peremptory demands of the Beethovenian sentence by indulging the lyric luxuriance of Mozartean dominant prolongation'. Lewin's reference to 'dominant prolongation' alludes to the fact that the lyrical passage leads linearly from the dominant that arrived in bar 7 to a second arrival of the dominant in bar 19.

[9] This formulation must be understood as a sort of convenient shorthand for what is actually a more complicated mechanism. The statement assumes permanent agency as a

first violin – second violin
first violin – viola
first violin – cello
second violin – viola
second violin – cello
viola – cello

Figure 11.2   Six possible instrumental pairings in a string quartet

Of the six possible pairings shown in Figure 11.2, I hear four as exhibiting such a relationship (see Figure 11.3). The forthcoming analysis will make four passes through bars 1–32 from the perspective of each pairing, following the ordering shown in Figure 11.3. Doing so will allow us to observe the behaviour of each instrument within two different pairings, from which will emerge a portrait of each instrumental part as a coherent agent.

first violin – second violin
first violin – cello
viola – cello
second violin – viola

Figure 11.3   Instrumental pairs that are in *relationship* in bars 1–32

- **First violin and second violin**: The first violin aggressively grabs the lead at the opening; its theme is a sentence (*Satz*) that motivically accelerates towards its climax in bar 7. The second violin at first hesitantly joins in, as if not sure of its role. But by bar 4 it is swept up by the forward momentum of the theme, joining it an octave lower. In bar 11, the first violin literally regains the lead over the second violin, but the second violin achieves some

given, with the listener simply attending to the mutual behaviours of two such agents for signs of a relationship between them. But strictly speaking, we cannot assume that permanent agency is at work in a quartet texture *unless* we observe it through the interactions between the instruments. In effect, we *construct* in our imaginations the very idea that a line is the expression of a coherent agent by observing its interactions with the other parts (or with the entire ensemble) as the music progresses.

independence by playing different motivic material. Moreover, the second violin's leaping contour in bars 11–14 seems to challenge the expressive prominence of the first violin. Starting in bar 15, the second violin goes a step further, taking over the first violin's material, and also invading its registral space with the leap to F in bar 16, and then a highly expressive leap to A (bar 18), which reaches *over* the first violin. But after the arrival of the dominant chord in bar 19, something odd happens. The first violin withdraws from the action altogether; now out on its own, the second violin leisurely transposes its minim motive from bar 17 such that its first two pitches, B and G, now fit within the dominant harmony. But upon reaching the third pitch, F♯, the second violin suddenly finds itself in the remote tonality of B minor (with the cello playing a contributing role). Confused and unsure how to proceed, it simply drops out. The next two bars of silence give the second violin time to ponder its future. After its sudden deflation in bar 19, will it resume its tentative subservience to the first violin as at the opening? Or will it take courage and claim equal (or at least near-equal) status? It takes the latter course, joining with the vigorous entry of the first violin in bar 22.

- **First violin and cello**: The cello initially supports the first violin, its pulsing quaver notes seeming to urge the first violin towards its climax in bar 7. In fact, beginning in bar 5 the cello emerges as an equal partner, forming an expanding wedge with the first violin that culminates with the extreme registral spacing on the downbeat of bar 7. In bars 9–10, both instruments move inward from that their extreme registral positions. But their paths diverge in bars 11–19 as they execute a textural exchange (Example 11.3). The net result is a decrease of activity in the first violin and an increase in the cello. The shift of leadership towards the cello is then confirmed upon the arrival of section *a'*, where the cello takes over the melody that had belonged to the first violin in bars 1–7. To be sure, in bar 22 the first violin returns to its opening aggressive stance (even superseding it, a point to be taken up later), but it remains subordinate to the cello until bar 29, where it joins the cello in leading the ensemble to the cadence in bar 32.

- **Viola and cello**: In bars 1–7, these two instruments join together with pulsing quavers, though the cello assumes more of a leadership role towards the end of the phrase with its powerful descent to a lower register. However, the viola boldly takes over in bars 7–11, not only with respect to the cello, but the group as a whole. In bars 11–14, the viola luxuriates in its new-found voice, more than compensating for the textural advantage of the cello. Is the viola challenging the cello for supremacy? Perhaps so: looking ahead, the viola's dotted-rhythm motive in bars 15–21 might be heard as a usurping of material that rightfully belongs only to the cello, on account of the textural exchange with the first violin discussed earlier (Example 11.3). But it makes more sense to regard these bars as a pleasurable interaction between friends. The viola is not really stealing anything from the cello,

Example 11.3   Textural exchange between first violin and cello, bars 11–19

(first violin takes over the cello material of bars 11-14)

(cello loosely inverts, and rhythmically alters, the first violin line of bars 11-14)   (etc. →)

since its material in bar 15 is an ongoing development of the preceding bars. And the cello chooses to playfully mimic the viola's dotted rhythm, even though it could just as well have borrowed the straight minim notes from the corresponding first violin part in bar 11. The sense of collegiality between the viola and cello takes a poignant turn as they converge on the problematic F♯, and they find their way out of the anxious moment together in bar 22. Like true collaborators, they each contribute something unique to this successful path in bar 22. The viola lends its minim motive of bar 20, now transposed, while the choice of G as its first pitch is the contribution of the cello; since bar 19, its ascending line seems to have been pointing to G all along. After bar 22, the two parts are inseparable, playing the opening theme in octaves; finally in bar 29, the cello goes its own way.

- **Second violin and viola**: For much of this passage, these two instruments seem not to pay much attention to each other, but they come into contact at two critical moments. Up to bar 7, the second violin is attending to the first violin, and the viola to the cello. However, this situation changes after the viola steps forth from the group in bars 7–10. As if given courage by that startling action, the second violin tentatively enters into dialogue with the viola in bars 11–14. Not surprisingly, the second violin is the follower here. However, its escape from the influence of the first violin, along with the salutary influence of the viola, emboldens it to mount a growing challenge to the first violin through bars 11–19, as noted earlier. As the second violin's challenge becomes more direct in bars 15–19, the viola shifts its attention back to the cello – that is, until bar 20, where it echoes the troublesome B–G–F♯ motive that got the second violin into such trouble. What motivates the viola here? Is it trying to reciprocate for its earlier exchange with the second violin by now becoming the follower, while being oblivious to the fact that doing so keeps the group in a state of tonal confusion? Or does it know exactly what it is doing? Perhaps its intent is to rescue the second violin (and the group as a whole) by taking over the troublesome motive, and then, with the cello's help, transposing it to get everyone safely back home to C minor. Indeed, this latter interpretation is more in keeping with the viola's earlier behaviour in bars 7–10.

From the preceding description of the instrumental interactions in bars 1–32, we can distinguish four unique dramatic paths taken by the four instruments. The first violin assumes the lead from the outset, charging towards an imperfect cadence in bar 7. However, the response by the viola in bars 7–8 has the effect of a corrective gesture, suggesting that the first violin has acted *too* impetuously. To be sure, the latter quickly regains its footing, leading with the new lyrical motive in bars 11–14. But its role is challenged by the second violin in these bars, and in bars 15–19, the first violin gradually loses energy, finally dropping out altogether for several bars. Is its yielding of the leadership role a gracious act, or is something else going on? Subsequent events suggest the latter. In bars 22–32, the first violin takes over what is essentially a secondary accompanimental role, but its jagged and repetitive leaps bespeak an extreme agitation, the meaning of which is unclear. It seems an expression of anxiety, or perhaps of a neurotic desire to draw attention to itself to compensate for its secondary role vis-à-vis the cello. Whatever the case, it gradually regains a leadership role in bar 29, leading (along with the cello) the ensemble to the imperfect cadence in bar 32, which explicitly recalls its big arrival in bar 7.

Within bars 1–32 overall, then, the first violin exhibits rather unstable behaviour; while it clearly aspires to a leadership role, its way of achieving it is tinged with neurotic agitation. And while the lyrical interlude of bars 7–21 suggests that the first violin has the ability to pull back its energy, the large picture suggests that it may be subject to mood swings that are not entirely of its own volition. (Its withdrawal in bars 15–19 might therefore be a sign of temporary loss of will rather than of graciousness.)

The second violin has a much less dominant personality than the first violin, though we witness it making a serious attempt to expand its expressive range during the lyrical interlude. Clearly subordinate to the first violin at the outset, it gains confidence as it joins that instrument in its drive towards the cadence in bar 7. The sudden emergence of the viola in bars 7–8 seems to inspire the second violin, and the two instruments play in dialogue for several bars. As if gaining courage from the viola, the second violin continues to expand its lyrical motive, to the point of overtaking the registral space of the first violin. It is not clear whether the second violin is simply flexing its expressive muscles out of sheer enjoyment, or actually attempting to usurp the role of the first violin; in any event, it quickly collapses into a state of confusion in bars 19–21. (Has it become overly self-conscious of its newly found power, and stumbled as a result?) After the aforementioned 'rescue' by the two lower instruments, the second violin seems to attain a more balanced relationship with the first violin in bars 22–32; in various ways it now cooperates with the first violin as an equal or near-equal partner. The fact that the instruments initiate this passage in unison suggests that a shift – however subtle – has occurred in their relationship.

The viola dramatically steps forth in bar 7 after assuming a subordinate role in bars 1–7, as if to halt the nearly-out-of-control momentum of the preceding bars.[10] It then participates in an elaborate give-and-take first with the second violin, then the cello – now as an equal partner with the latter, a natural consequence of its newly acquired confidence. Along with the cello, it rescues the second violin (as well as the ensemble as a whole) from confusion in bars 19–21 to bring the music back to C minor. In bars 22–32 it joins the cello as an equal partner until bar 29, at which point it recedes once again to a supporting role.

The cello projects an interesting tension at the outset between stasis (pedal point) and driving energy (pulsing quavers). It gradually acquires a clear profile as it approaches the cadence in bar 7, its descending arpeggiation mirroring the ascending arpeggiation in the first violin. Taking a cue from the viola's sustained pitches in bars 7–10, the cello moves into 'low gear' in bars 11–14 with its slow-moving line. In bars 15–21, it engages in dialogue with the viola; while it temporarily seems to go its own way in bar 19, its ascending line in 19–21 stops on the enigmatic unison F♯ with the viola. As noted above, it then joins with the viola to bring the ensemble back to C minor. At this point it takes over the opening theme, thus assuming a leadership role; around bar 29, the first violin joins the cello in leading the ensemble to the imperfect cadence in E♭ minor in bar 32.

The preceding account of these four individual paths and their interactions may make our original 'collective' interpretation of bars 1–32 – that is, aggressive–lyrical–aggressive – seem crude and overly simplistic. Yet, the overall contour of that collective narrative remains intact. Our detailed analysis does reveal, however, that this *aba'* expressive structure is not balanced and closed, but rather open and volatile; that is, the *a'* section (bars 22–32) intensifies the imbalanced trajectory of bars 1–7, and the fact that the opening gesture precipitated such an extreme shift of mood (bars 7ff.) now leads us to wonder what bars 1–32 as a section will call forth, both at the level of collective agency and from the individual agents. The ensuing analysis of bars 32–82 will focus on that question.

---

[10]   The viola's stepping forth could be viewed as the act of a good citizen; it sees the group in trouble (because of its out-of-control impulses), and puts on the brakes to rescue the group from the edge of chaos. According to that view, the viola is operating from *within* the group. But an intriguing alternative was suggested to the author during the question/answer session at the Second International Conference on Music and Gesture at the RNCM (July 2006): the viola's gesture sounds 'otherworldly', as if it is coming from *outside* the ensemble. Such a notion raises interesting questions: Does the viola express a transcendent agency as well as a more earthbound agency? How do those two agencies co-exist? Consideration of these questions lies beyond the scope of this chapter; I will be assuming that the viola is a full-fledged member of the community at all times – a view that I believe to be supportable, even if it is not the only possible interpretation.

As shown in Figure 11.1, the second thematic area prolongs a dominant-to-tonic motion in E♭ minor/major, with the tonic arriving in bar 75. The passage spanning bars 32–75 can be divided into three segments. Segment I (bars 32–41) begins on dominant harmony in E♭ minor, begins to modulate towards G♭ major (bars 37–40), and then at the last moment turns back to the dominant of E♭ in bar 41. The unstable tendencies of this first segment are then intensified in the second segment (bars 41–52). Beginning on a dominant in E♭ minor, then passing through the tonic chord (bar 42) to the subdominant (bar 44), the passage culminates with a remarkably unstable progression over a rising viola line (bars 45–48) that leads to a dominant 4/2 of D. After resolving to a D major triad, the harmony begins to swing back and forth between A major and D minor triads. The tonal context is so unstable that it is not clear whether D minor or A major is being tonicized; moreover, either possibility is very far removed from the tonality of E♭ major.[11] The tonal confusion is clarified by a startling dominant 4/2 in E♭ major in bar 53, which initiates the third segment. From here on, the music remains firmly in E♭ major (with some modal colouring), though the resolution to tonic is delayed until bar 75, as noted earlier.[12]

This overview suggests that the three segments in bars 32–75 may be interpreted within the framework of a larger two-part tonal plan. The first part, up to bar 52, is tonally unstable – increasingly so as the passage progresses, culminating in the frenetic stasis and tonal confusion of bars 50–52. The arrival in bar 53 of the dominant 4/2 brings us back to the home key – and in the 'correct' mode – in a single stroke, initiating the second part of this thematic area.[13]

Turning now to the role of individual agency in bars 32–75, we shall see that the four instrumental agents essentially remain 'in character', as established in bars 1–32. However, the one-on-one relationships that were so important in bars 1–32 recede into the background in bars 32ff; now the individual agents relate primarily with the group as a whole – that is, with the collective narrative as described above.

The viola initiates the second half of the exposition with an inversion of the agitated quaver motive of bars 24–28 (first violin). The viola's prominence as an agent unmistakably recalls bars 7–8; like at that earlier spot, the entire community

---

[11]   Frisch (1984) interprets the A major chord of bars 50–52 as a dominant of D minor. While this interpretation seems to be supported by the earlier A dominant seventh in bar 48 (with the seventh G appearing in the viola, the culmination of its rising chromatic line), I can just as easily hear that A dominant seventh chord as a V7/iv in A in retrospect.

[12]   As Frisch (1984) notes, 'even here our satisfaction at the sweet major chord is instantly snatched away by the ominous return of the main theme in the minor mode [bars 75–76]'. This unsettling codetta passage, along with the subsequent enharmonic return to the opening, would play a prominent role in a fuller analysis of this movement; for present purposes, however, our analysis will stop with the arrival of E♭ (tonic) in bar 75.

[13]   See Graybill (1988) for a more detailed discussion of the tonal dissolution within bars 32–52, as well as the dramatic 'watershed' moment in bar 53.

asserts two block chords, and the viola emerges from the cadential goal without a break. However, while the viola put a brake on the momentum in bar 7 with its drone on G, here it pushes forward. In doing so, it raises the stakes for the entire group. In bar 7, it checked the out-of-control impulses of the group, but here it seems to revive those very impulses, leading the other agents towards some unforeseen, perhaps cataclysmic goal.

In the ensuing bars, the other instruments respond to this challenge by forging ahead (albeit with apparent trepidation) into dangerous tonal territory. The two violins enter in bars 33–34 with a nervous offbeat figure over the dominant pedal, as if under the spell of the viola. The cello attempts to steer matters in another direction, entering with its falling-sixth figure from bars 29–30, but now with a highly charged lyricism. The two violins follow suit in bars 35–36, and especially 37–40, as they allow the cello to lead them towards presumed safety: a cadence in G♭ major. But the move towards G♭ fails at the last moment, and upon the return of the dominant of E♭ in bar 41, the anxiety-tinged material of bars 32–36 returns, now further destabilized. The jagged contour of the quaver figure lends it a more skittish character than before, and the harmony moves away from its steady dominant pedal. Even the cello has been infected by the collective anxiety, as expressed through its off-beat motive.

Bar 45 brings back the material of bar 35, including a slow-moving bass line, this time played by the viola. But unlike the cello in bars 35–40, the viola is not leading towards a reassuring G♭ major; rather, its ascending chromatic line (from C to G in bars 45–48) now leads the ensemble inexorably into increasingly alien tonal terrain, as explained earlier. The quaver motion in the other instruments is more constricted than in bars 41–44, culminating in a repetitive G♯–A figure in bars 48–52; kinetically, this figure conveys the paradoxical impression of paralysed hysteria, an effect that is amplified by the repetitive figures in the lower three instruments. The ensemble finally pushes through to a climax with the dominant 4/2 chord in bar 53, a moment of breakthrough and sudden clarity. Strikingly, this moment is truly a collective action; it is difficult to identify an individual agent that leads the group to this moment. The arrival of the dominant 4/2 brings about a release of enormous energy that requires an extensive cooling-down period that lasts through the rest of the exposition up to the cadence in bar 75. While the gradually relaxation of energy seems to hearken back to the lyricism of bars 11–21, this passage replaces the subtle inner tensions of the earlier passage with a more straightforward melody-versus-accompaniment texture. The rhapsodic passage played by the first violin sounds like a release of repressed tension, which seems appropriate in the light of its earlier tormented buzzing around G♯–A in bars 48–52. Finally it calms down and joins the other instruments for a cadence in bars 74–75.

With respect to instrumental agency, we can interpret bars 32–75 in the light of the earlier behaviour of the four instruments in bars 1–32. In those earlier bars, each instrumental part emerged as a distinctive character; the events of bars 32–75 flesh out these characters, with each instrument either continuing on a path already established in bars 1–32, or revealing more definitively certain traits that were tentatively exhibited in those bars. The following summarizes the profile of each instrument within the exposition as a whole.

The first violin aspires to be a leader from the outset, but its opening gesture is overly impetuous, leading to temporary failure; it subsequently tries to lead again in bars 11–14, but again it fails to sustain that role, and in fact never really achieves it again within the exposition. Even its luxuriously expansive passage in bars 63–75 seems more an expression of joy and relief upon the arrival of the dominant 4/2 in bar 53 than an act of leadership; that passage is a response to, not a stimulus for, that communal event. To the extent that such behaviour represents the integration of the first violin into the communal life of the group, this is undoubtedly a healthy sign. At the same time, the sheer extravagance of its line perhaps reflects at least a hint of narcissism, an interpretation that accords with its behaviour in bars 1–32. In short, throughout the exposition the first violin reveals itself to be appealingly extroverted, yet a bit neurotic; and despite its best efforts, it is not an especially effective leader.

The second violin goes through some difficult times at the opening of the movement. Bars 20–21 mark a decisive turning point, where it must decide how it will respond to its just-deflated ambitions. It emerges from that crisis by asserting its equality (or near-equality) with the first violin, and it remains tightly linked with that instrument through bar 40. After that its interactions with the ensemble become more fluid and changeable, as if it is now strong enough to venture out on its own.

The viola presents an interesting foil for the first violin. Content to be fairly unobtrusive much of the time, it nonetheless knows exactly when to step forth to lead or correct the community. It does so in dramatic fashion in bars 7 and 22–24. But its role in bars 32–52 is even more remarkable, if less overtly dramatic; indeed, here the tale of the viola seems more like a musical version of the hero's journey. The group finds itself in a disorienting tonal/formal landscape; if there is some path out, that path is not clear. (The cello tries vainly to lead the group to G♭ as a possible way out; but of course that would have been an illusory home in any case, given the C minor tonality of the movement as a whole.) Pushing through these uncertainties, the viola leads the group up to edge of an abyss with its rising chromatic line of bars 45–48; while the tonal path out of the resulting impasse proves to be a communal action (bar 53), that resolution would never have occurred without the leadership of the viola in the first place.

Finally, the cello seems to be a particularly stable, salt-of-the-earth character, assertive and proactive when necessary, but without being overly dramatic or neurotic. It takes on an effective leadership role within the *a'* section of bars 22–32, leading the group towards the imperfect cadence in the new key in bar 32. Within the second thematic area, it leads an exploratory foray towards the hoped-for haven of G♭, but turns back when it is clear that such a path is not the answer (bars 41–42).[14] While this could be viewed as a failure in one sense, it also demonstrates that the cello is at least willing to lead the group *somewhere* in the attempt to break away from the anxiety-ridden dominant pedal of bars 32ff. In any event, the cello later compensates for this aborted move with a strong – and again, slow-moving – bass support for the bars immediately following the arrival of the dominant 4/2 (bars 53–57).

Conclusion

In conclusion, this chapter shows that by attending to the interactions between the instrumental parts of a string quartet, a listener might be able to construct in his or her imagination each of those four parts as an individualized permanent agent. A few caveats are necessary here. First, it is not to be assumed that all string quartets, even those of the first Viennese school, can be heard in the way modelled in this chapter. In many cases such an interpretation would seemed forced – or even more likely, uninteresting. It may also happen that *part* of a movement, but not the entire movement, can be heard in such a way.[15] The objective of this chapter is not to offer a universally valid model for listening to string quartets, but to suggest a way of listening to *certain* works, or portions of works, that can make one's listening experience more vivid. Finally, there is one additional payoff to the kind of interpretation proposed here. By imagining an instrumental line as an agent within a dramatic narrative, one can bring an ethical sensibility to one's listening by *identifying* with the agents. If I were the second violin pondering my next step during bars 20 and 21, what would *I* decide? Would I have the courage to step forth like the viola in bar 7 or bars 32–52 if I saw that the community needed it – even in the face of a terrifyingly uncertain outcome?

References

Cone, E. T. (1974). *The Composer's Voice*. Berkeley: University of California Press.

Cox, A. (2006). Hearing, Feeling, Grasping Gestures. In A. Gritten & E. King (eds), *Music and Gesture* (pp. 45–60). Aldershot: Ashgate.

Frisch, W. (1984). *Brahms and the Principle of Developing Variation*. Berkeley: University of California Press.

Giddens, A. (1984). *The Constitution of Society: Outline of the Theory of Structuration*. Cambridge: Polity Press.

---

[14] While in one sense all the instruments – not just the cello – move towards G♭ and then turn back, the cello's slow-moving bass line plays the leading role, to my ears.

[15] This statement is of course exemplified by this account, which focuses only on the exposition of a sonata-form movement.

Graybill, R. (1988). Brahms's Integration of Traditional and Progressive Tendencies: A Look at Three Sonata Expositions. *Journal of Musicological Research* 8: 141–68.

Hatten, R. S. (2006). A Theory of Musical Gesture. In A. Gritten & E. King (eds), *Music and Gesture* (pp. 1–23). Aldershot: Ashgate.

Lewin, D. (1983). Brahms, his Past, and Modes of Music Theory. In G. Bozarth (ed.), *Brahms Studies: Analytical and Historical Perspectives: Papers Delivered at the International Brahms Conference, Washington, DC, 5–8 May 1983* (pp. 13–27). Oxford: Clarendon Press.

Maus, F. (1988). Music as Drama. *Music Theory Spectrum* 10: 56–73.

Parker, M. (2002). *The String Quartet, 1750–1797: Four Types of Musical Conversation.* Aldershot: Ashgate.

Chapter 12
In the Beginning was Gesture: Piano Touch and the Phenomenology of the Performing Body

Mine Doğantan-Dack

Whereas it is a commonplace that, for example, we have some idea what is involved in the act of walking (if only in general terms), we have no idea at all what happens during the split second when a person actually takes a step. We are familiar with the movement of picking up a cigarette lighter or a spoon, but know almost nothing of what really goes on between hand and metal, and still less how this varies with mood. (Benjamin 2002: 117)

The relationship between studying performance and doing performance is integral. (Schechner 2002: 1)

The Body in Performance Studies

The gradual emergence and establishment of performance studies as a 'musicological discipline in its own right' (Rink 2004: 37) over the last two decades has coincided with ground-breaking discoveries in contemporary neuroscience that challenged the long-standing Cartesian model of the relationship between the body, mind and the brain. For more than three centuries, the philosophy of Descartes, which radically separated the mind – and with it consciousness – from the body and the world, shaped much of Western sciences and humanities, and their epistemological foundations. Accordingly, the activities of *thinking* and *knowing* have been predominantly conceived as taking place in a disembodied mind,[1] and essentially through rational-discursive processes, which represented the presumed pinnacle of human essence. Because of their evident connection with the body, *affective* phenomena – including feelings, emotions, and moods – remained at the periphery of this epistemological landscape. Until recently, body

---

[1] During the late nineteenth and early twentieth centuries, when psychology was being established as a scientific discipline in close connection with the physiology of the day, motor theories of perception became fashionable. For an overview of some of these theories see Doğantan-Dack (2006).

and affect stood as antagonists to reason and cognition. Research carried out since the early 1990s by such neuroscientists as Antonio Damasio (1994, 1999, 2003), Joseph LeDoux (1996, 2002) and Alain Berthoz (1999, 2000) has shown that cognitive processes are fully embodied, depending on the input of not only the brain but of the whole body. It is through our bodies that we perceive, experience and come to know the world. Moving the body into central stage, recent scientific research has also prepared the grounds for the placement of affective phenomena on a par with cognition within the epistemological background of social sciences and humanities. We now know that feelings and emotions are necessary for the proper functioning of our cognitive faculties, which include reasoning, reflecting, deliberating and decision-making (Damasio 1994: xiii), and that affect is part of an information-processing system, a way of knowing the world. Each cognitive process has an affective counterpart, and both kinds of processes are neurologically intertwined with representations of bodily processes and states in the brain. These findings constitute the empirical pillars of much of the recent research in cognitive sciences where the separation of mind and body, of perception and action, and of consciousness and the world has given way to an embodied, enactive and ecological perspective on the nature of the human subject (Bermudez et al. 1995; Clark 1997).[2]

The implications for musicology of these recent advances in cognitive and neurosciences have been explored by several music theorists who have attempted to explain our experiences of the rhythmic and tonal structures in music by reference to so-called bodily image-schemas (Brower 2000; Cox 2001, 2006; Larson 1997; Saslaw 1996; Zbikowski 1997, 2002). Their main argument has been that listeners experience and make sense of musical phenomena by metaphorically mapping the concepts derived from their bodily experience of the physical world onto music.

Perhaps the most significant effect of the collapse of the Cartesian mind on musicology has been the growing scholarly interest in music performance, which represents quite literally the embodiment of the phenomenon we call 'music'. Throughout the larger part of the twentieth century, Western musical thought has regarded the essence of music to be the abstract relationships that exist between the sounds involved in its structural organization, which in turn has been defined primarily in terms of the variables of pitch and duration. Rooted in this assumption is the idea of a musical 'work' that exists independently of any of its realizations in sound; since its beginnings as an academic discipline, musicology conceptualized the musical 'work' essentially as a fixed text represented in the musical score (Cook 2003). Understanding and coming to know a piece of music has been regarded as the deciphering of such a text. In fact, the score has even been deemed sufficient to generate a musical experience independently of any musical performance. The philosophical perspective underlying these assumptions, which

---

[2]   In this connection, the influential work in cognitive linguistics by Lakoff and Johnson (1980) and Johnson (1987), showing the very fundamentality of metaphors of embodiment in our conceptual thinking, should also be mentioned.

has largely shaped musicology during the twentieth century, was encapsulated famously by Schoenberg:

> music need not be performed any more than books need to be read aloud, for its logic is perfectly represented on the printed page; and the performer, for all his intolerable arrogance, is totally unnecessary except as his interpretations make the music understandable to an audience unfortunate enough not to be able to read it in print. (Schoenberg in Newlin 1980: 164)

Based on this notion of music as text and abstract structure, which makes the embodiment of music in the performance event insignificant and encourages the musicologist 'to retreat from real music to the abstraction of the work' (Abbate 2004: 505), contemporary music theory and psychology conceptualized musical experiences almost exclusively in mental terms. The aim of most research has been the exploration of the cognitive dimension of our musical activities – of the mind behind music – but the input of the body proper to musical cognition has been neglected. Consequently, music psychology has privileged the listener such that the listening activity – modelled upon the behaviour of Western classical music concert audiences, who are largely silent and still, and attend to the music in semi-darkness – became the paradigm for all musical experiences.[3] For example, the work with which music psychology is regarded to have come of age (Sloboda 2005: 102), namely *A Generative Theory of Tonal Music* by Fred Lerdahl and Ray Jackendoff, is explicitly about the listening activity and sets out to provide 'a formal description of the musical intuitions of a listener who is experienced in a musical idiom' (Lerdahl & Jackendoff 1983: 1). Indeed, whenever I suggest to musicologist colleagues that there may be significant differences between the ways listeners and performers relate to music, the reply I receive almost invariably points out the obvious – and uninformative – fact that, after all, performers, too, are listeners; or that performing is in fact a species of composing, implying that what matters are the experiences of either the listener or of the composer.[4]

The recent performative turn in musicology (Cook 2001, 2003), therefore, signifies for many scholars a (welcome) ontological re-organization of musical

---

[3]   Clarke and Davidson hold the listener-oriented research responsible for fostering a disembodied approach and write that both 'listeners and performers are regarded as information-processing devices, with inputs and outputs coming to and going from a central "unit" which is located firmly in the head and which has little connection with anything as physical as an arm, a leg, a hand, – or even an ear' (Clarke & Davidson 1998: 74).

[4]   In the literature on analysis and performance, Fred Maus, who argues that analysing a piece through traditional analytical methods does not constitute a necessary condition for performing that piece well, concludes that this is because performance is a kind of compositional act and not an analytical one (Maus 1999). In this connection, Cook has observed that music theory 'is not committed to understanding performers in the way it is to understanding composers' (Cook 1999: 241).

phenomena manifested as a move away from an 'overriding preoccupation with the score, and towards an understanding of music as performance' (Cook & Clarke 2004: 10). Following 'a renewed emphasis on music as sound and event, an ontological status lost in the mid-nineteenth century, when music's notation gained the upper hand' (Rink 2004: 37), the foundation of musical scholarship, long relying on musical works, appears to be shifting to musical performances.

In principle – and quite logically – this newly acquired ontological primacy of musical performance would place the performer at the foreground of music scholarship, and thereby encourage and support the exploration of the bodily and affective dimensions of music-making. Musicological practice, however, has not pursued this logic. While it is certainly true that there has been an unprecedented interest in studying musical performance over the last two decades, it is questionable whether the deep-rooted ontological – and epistemological – primacy of the score and of abstract musical relationships in Western musical thought has indeed given way to a reconceptualization of music *as* performance. Musicological discourse is still dominated by the fundamental assumptions of a work-related philosophy, and the interest in studying performances, mostly as a reified thing rather than a process (Clarke 2004: 99), has not led to a similar interest in studying how performers actually make performance events happen. The hegemony of the analyst/theorist over the performer in the literature on analysis and performance, representing one of the main domains of contemporary performance studies, is well documented (Cook 1999; McClelland 2003). As for the research scene in psychology of performance, the findings are often 'all too remote from the reality of performance and perceptions of the performer, who is often treated more as a laboratory rat than a sentient being' (Rink 2004: 39). For instance, Eric Clarke states that musicologists have been interested in empirical performance studies 'as ways of documenting what goes on in performance' (Clarke 2004: 77), but does not address the epistemological implications of the fact that the documentation in question is done from the perspective of listener-researchers; nor does he explain the conspicuous absence of the professional performers' accounts of what happens in a performance situation.

The continuing dominance of the score is also evident in expressive performance studies, where the variations in tempo and dynamics observed in a performance are conceptualized to a large extent as functions of abstract musical structures, reinforcing a work-centred ideology and rendering the performer's role derivative of the score. Researchers thus conceptualize the decisions concerning dynamics and timing, which a performer needs to make, in terms of 'deviating from the metronomically-notated specifications of the score' (Cook 2001) while the phenomenological reality of performing presents the score as *always already* constituted with performance expression. Consequently, the artificial separation in research of notated parameters such as pitch and rhythm and of expressive parameters such as dynamics, timing and timbre, does not reflect the performer's approach to the musical score. As the written thing – the 'musical text' – still has priority over performance – consider the statement that 'the ultimate goal of research on expression in music performance is to understand what exactly the performer "adds" to a written piece of music' (Juslin 2003: 280) – the argument that the idea of *music-as-work* has given way to that of *music-as-performance* is currently difficult to sustain.

The absence in the majority of research discussions about the performing body is arguably the most important reason for – as well as the consequence of, some might argue – this state of affairs. In the large part of the published literature on the psychology of performance, for example, there is minimal, or more typically, no reference to the physicality of music-making and its contribution to musical meaning. There have been two kinds of exceptions in this connection: one of these concerns a small number of articles that explore the bodily bases of performance expression and propose body-based models of performance (Friberg & Sundberg 1999; Friberg et al. 2000; Kronman & Sundberg 1987; Shove & Repp 1995; Todd 1992, 1995). For example, in one model the timing of musical phrases in performance is explained by reference to the temporal shape of other rhythmic motor activities such as locomotion.

The second exception comes from the pioneering work carried out by Jane Davidson on actual physical movements and gestures involved in musical performance, and similar work inspired by her research. Since the early 1990s, Davidson has studied body movements of performers, notably of singers and pianists, with a view to understanding how gestural elements communicate performance intentions and contribute to the meanings audiences attribute to a musical performance (Davidson 1993, 1994, 1995, 2001, 2002, 2005, 2006, 2007; Davidson & Correia 2002). She discovered that performers use body movements to communicate information about both structural features of the music and their own expressive intentions to observers – and to co-performers in ensemble contexts; these movements can include head nods, head shakes, swaying of the torso and upper body wiggles. While constituting an important step towards an understanding of musical performance as a truly embodied event, it is important to note that Davidson's research has focused on the experiences of observers/ onlookers; her aim has been to explore 'what sort of movement characteristics might guide observer perception' (Davidson 2007: 384).

Consequently, within the literature that addresses the involvement of the body in musical performance, studies that explore performance movements and gestures from the performer's perspective are entirely absent. My interest lies in this neglected area of research, that is, in exploring the performer's experiences of bodily movements and gestures as a prolegomenon to a *phenomenology of the performing body*. To use a well-known distinction in phenomenology, my aim is to understand the contributions of the *lived and living body* of the performer, with its pulsating inner life and particular point of view, while existing research considers the *objective body* of performing musicians as something to be investigated with the methods of experimental sciences. Hence, the phenomenological project would involve exploring how a performer experiences bodily movement; how conscious they are of their bodily involvement in the performance event;

the kinds of movements and gestures that are musically relevant for the performer themselves; and how we can verbalize the embodied knowledge involved in executing performance gestures. Being a professional pianist, my investigation is confined to movements involved in playing the piano. Hence, the general term 'performer' will specifically refer to 'the pianist' unless otherwise indicated.

Timbre, Gesture and Phoronomy

If I have so far set up various dualisms – and fundamental oppositions – between a work-/score-based and a performance-based understanding of music, between the listener and the performer, and between abstract musical phenomena and concrete performance movements, I have done this in order to point out the preferences for – or favouritism towards – the first elements of the aforementioned dualisms in dominant musicological discourse, rather than to assert an essentialist position with regard to the second elements. The nature of musical phenomena in all its varying manifestations is complex, and no essentialist position would do justice to this rich variety. In the Western classical tradition, music needs to be understood as constituted both by abstract structures and performance movements, both by the score and by its performances; and musical meanings are emergent in the processes of listening, performing and composing, where the abstract and the concrete are in continual interaction. My interest, therefore, is in redressing the balance in performance studies by scrutinizing the performer's perspective on what it is like to physically perform music, rather than promoting a view of music that disregards the importance of the score, or of the listening activity.

A comparison of pitch and tone colour would illustrate the complexity of musical reality, and underline once again the need for vigilance in thinking about the relationship between the musical work and performance. Rink has argued that in empirical performance studies there has been 'a bias towards the study of tempo and dynamics, mainly because these lend themselves to more rigorous modelling than intractable parameters like colour and bodily gesture' (Rink 2004: 38). He believes that this 'obsession with tempo and dynamics is a latter-day counterpart to the obsession with pitch relations in traditional analysis' (Rink 2004: 49 n. 2). While it is true that scholarly research largely focuses on the abstract qualities of music related to pitch and duration, I would argue that such a focus is not musically unwarranted. The reason why tone colour or the bodily activity behind musical sounds can easily be neglected is not solely based on cultural and historical factors – or on the inability of the score to specify them precisely – but is related, at least in part, to the nature of sound perception itself.

Perceptually the *physical cause* of a sound is most directly revealed in its timbre rather than in its pitch or duration. The manner of physically initiating and sustaining a sound, that is, the *gestural* aspect in producing it, is one of the decisive factors for its timbral identity. The timbre of a sound and the human body behind it are thus intimately related, and form a single Gestalt in the psychological mechanism of sound perception (Smalley 1992: 523–5). In this sense, it is difficult, if not impossible, for a listener to abstract the timbral information from its physical source and cause (try to imagine a piano tone without imagining the piano – visually or otherwise – and any agent producing the tone!).

One of the most fascinating aspects of acoustical music is that the timbre of the sound-sources, that is, of musical instruments, are perceived as being constant or permanent even though research has revealed that 'the transient and steady-note frequency spectra change dramatically from note to note across an instrument's playing range' (Handel 1991: 170). The number and amplitude of the spectral components for low and high notes of a piano, for example, are very different. Yet, we experience the timbre of the piano as the same throughout all its registers, as being that of a 'piano'. We acquire our knowledge about the timbral identity of instruments culturally through long-term exposure to their timbral behaviour (Hajda et al. 1997). Precisely because sound-sources appear to have a constant timbre, non-timbral variables of musical structures take on a central role in the listening process; source-permanence causes us to take the existence of a material source for granted, so to speak, and pitch and durational features can be experienced as abstract structures.[5] In conjunction with timbre, the human gesture behind it is also taken for granted. In this connection, the French theoretician Pierre Schaeffer has insightfully written that:

> instrumental activity, the visible and first cause of every musical phenomenon, has the distinctive quality of tending first and foremost to cancel itself out as a material cause. (Schaeffer 1966: 43)

Hence, listeners remember a piece of music more easily through its rhythmic and pitch structure rather than through its timbral details. Furthermore, empirical evidence from music psychology suggests that while non-practising listeners of classical music are quite sensitive to the expressive details of a performance – including variations in timing, dynamics and tone colour – as long as the performer's expressive input is part of the ongoing experience of music, that is, *while the performance is still going on,* they hardly remember any of this detail in the long term. The listeners' 'memories of heard [expressive] nuances are rarely established to anything like the same degree as those of performers' (Snyder 2000: 92) who build up the skill to execute these nuances slowly over time, committing them to implicit long-term memory. It seems only natural, therefore, that the idea of a 'music', identified mainly through pitch and rhythm and existing independently of its performances, plays a significant role in the way people think about music.

---

[5]   One of the main issues in the aesthetics of electroacoustic music concerns the identification or recognition of the source and cause of a sound's timbre since the interactive relationship between a sound and a source or causal agent may not always be clearly established in this medium.

Another peculiarity of the phenomenon of timbre is that it is phenomenally the least mimetically available attribute of sound because we cannot faithfully reproduce in our own voice the timbres of natural events and musical instruments. This is not the case with pitch and duration, which can be imitated vocally and thereby abstracted from their original material context; paradoxically, such abstraction simultaneously involves an embodiment because the tune that was originally heard on, say, a violin, is transformed through an internal motor recoding process as its pitches and rhythms are stamped with the timbral quality of one's own voice. For listeners, the pitches and rhythms of a melody can be made one's own more readily than its original timbre.

The crucial point is that for the agent actually producing the musical sounds, that is, for the performer, the nature of timbre experience is somewhat different. Because the timbre of a sound and the human gesture initiating and sustaining this sound are indissolubly linked, timbre or tone colour is at the foreground of the performer's conscious experience of the music that they physically bring about. Being the owner of the gestures generating the tone colours, their attention is not focused mainly on pitch or rhythm as in the case of the listener, but more significantly on tone colour. Moreover, the timbral aspects of a melody the performer plays represent a true embodiment for them, because they 'own' these tone colours through the skilfully honed bodily gestures and kinaesthetic sensations that generate them. The timbre represents the unique interaction between their body and the instrument, the experiential result of the constant attunement between the force they supply to initiate and sustain the sounds and the counter-force exerted by the sounding instrument. In this connection, I would argue that the performer develops a memory for tone colour that is based on their kinaesthetic sensations.[6] Furthermore, part of a performer's subjectivity resides in their repertoire of tone colours, which are directly related to the movements and gestures of their performing body. When we recognize and speak of 'the sound of Rubinstein' we refer to his tone, among other expressive variables, rather than to his pitch production as such. In this connection, Naomi Cumming has observed:

> creating a 'beautiful tone', through a well-balanced physical adjustment to the instrument, is central to creating the impression of musical personality. The 'sonic self' is thus conceived. It is not a previously existing element of personality, but a creation that comes into being with sound … . A performer's self-knowledge is not a direct intuition of an observing 'I', but a sense of an integrated self as emerging from tangible signs: the self-as-gesturing and the self-as-articulating structure, among other things. (Cumming 2000: 23 and 32)

For the performer, the experiential continuity and unity between tone colour and gesture extends to the relationship between musical structure and performance

---

[6]   One area of research that has been neglected in music psychology concerns the ways that performers experience, represent and store timbre.

expression in general, which have been conceptualized as distinct phenomena in music theory and psychology. Musical structure, defined in terms of pitch and rhythm, is regarded in this literature as (capable of) existing independently of its expression in performance, which is conceived in terms of deviations from the nominal values in the score. From the performer's perspective delivering structural information independently of expressive intent is not meaningful because the two are conceived as unified functions of the way they want the piece to actually sound, and are indissolubly connected to their gestures. Consider, for instance, a melodic unit starting with an upbeat rhythmic structure: for the performer, information about the rhythmic structure of this unit (the fact that it starts with an anacrusis) is not represented separately from the expression it requires – and acquires – in its delivery by means of a certain forward impulse towards the downbeat, from the kinaesthetic feel of the particular gesture made to bring about this impulse and from the ensuing musical sounds, with their particular tone colours, timings and dynamics: the gesture employed, the acoustical profile of the resulting sound, and the upbeat structure are experienced as a single, unified Gestalt. I would indeed hypothesize that performers do not learn, represent and store rhythmic-melodic units without their accompanying gestural and expressive dimensions. As distinct from the listener's experience and knowledge of such local musical forms, the performer, in order to be able to unfold the dynamic shape of the musical unit from beginning to the end as in one single, unified impulse, needs a kind of continuous knowledge representation that is analogue and procedural rather than declarative (Reybrouck 2001: 126). This is the kind of knowledge that comes from *making* forms, which the idea of *phoronomy* would usefully illustrate. The phoronomic approach sets a contrast between the knowledge one acquires of a geometrical form – a curve, for example – by physically tracing it, and the knowledge that comes from looking at it as a static representation.[7] The phoronomic understanding of a shape comes from a continuous and indivisible movement experience. In a similar fashion, the performer does not come to know the rhythmic-melodic forms they express in sound separately from the physical gestures and movements required to bring them about. Any gesture made to deliver a unit of music will inevitably unify

---

[7]   Various philosophers (e.g. Merleau-Ponty 1968; Sartre 1978) have argued that there is an intimate connection and cooperation between vision and kinaesthetic sensations, the sense of touch. Sartre has written that a movement felt as a series of kinaesthetic sensations 'can function as analogue for the trajectory that the moving body describes or is assumed to describe, which means that a kinaesthetic series can function as analogical substitute of visual form' (1978: 115). The question whether kinaesthetic series in this sense can function as a substitute for aural forms has not been explored. Pedagogical methods that aim to teach the performer to better sense and execute musical rhythm (Dalcrozian eurhythmics, for instance) cannot translate the experience of producing musical rhythms on actual instruments to general bodily movements (see Doğantan 2002: Chapter 5). My intuition is that the relationship between aural forms and kinaesthetic forms would be of different kinds for non-musical and musical sounds. In the case of musical sounds, vocal and instrumental forms would also establish different relationships with kinaesthetic forms.

the structure and expression, as well the biomechanical and affective components, which theory keeps apart.

Davidson and Correia (2002) have suggested that performance movements and gestures can be classified according to identifiable functions such that they can be purely biomechanical, culturally learned, technically necessary or used for expressive purposes, while Davidson has noted that performance movements that are necessary for the biomechanical accomplishment of the task and those used for expressive effects 'coexist and occur in an integrated movement stream' (2005: 216). Indeed, in her recent work, Davidson concluded that 'the many potential contributing elements to the final body movement pattern may be difficult to assess, as there is no way each relative influence can be separated out' (2007: 383). This may be more than a methodological/empirical difficulty in that such categorization of performance gestures is built upon a misconceived dissociation of what is organically unified in the experience of the performing musician. As far as the performer is concerned categorical boundaries between performance gestures in terms of their functions, even if they exist, are at best fuzzy.

One difficulty that a phenomenology of the performing body needs to tackle has to do with the fact that 'with increasing skill mental representations for performance become successively more dissociated from the movements involved' (Gabrielsson 2003: 240); while performing, performers often do not focus on their bodily movements but on conceptual issues such as interpretation. There is, however, a kind of gesture that stands out within the gestural repertoire of a pianist, as it has a definable musical function and remains more or less at the foreground of the performer's conscious awareness of their physical movements, thus providing a useful starting point for a phenomenological inquiry into the performing body. I shall use the term 'initiatory' to refer to this type of gesture, as it is carried out before a musical unit actually starts sounding; as such, it prepares the moment of impact between the fingers and the instrument. Most significantly, an initiatory gesture has a profound effect on the tone quality of the ensuing musical sound, greatly contributing to the phenomenon of touch.[8]

Pianistic Touch

In a study titled 'A Microcosm of Musical Expression: Contributions of Expressive Timing and Dynamics to the Aesthetic Impression of the Initial Measures of

---

[8]   My investigation into initiatory gestures should be read in the context of modern piano technique. Over the last 300 years or so keyboard technique has changed dramatically in conjunction with the changes in the instrument. Hence, body movements related to keyboard performance have undergone profound changes. Modern piano technique is usually thought to have started with the teachings of Ludwig Deppe (1828–90), who emphasized the importance of upper arm and shoulder muscles, which were hardly mentioned in earlier finger-based methods. See Gerig (1990) for a thorough overview of changing keyboard techniques.

Chopin's Etude in E major' (1999), Bruno Repp found that the overall aesthetic quality of performances as assessed by judges selected specially for his research had little to do with timing and dynamics, which are the most scrutinized variables in empirical performance studies. Repp speculated that other variables – for instance, touch – might play a greater role than timing and dynamics in making aesthetic evaluations. Although it is one of the most valuable assets of a pianist, the precise physical basis and the psychological effects of touch are not well understood. There also is not sufficient research exploring the relationships between touch, timing, dynamics and phrasing in piano performance.

Touch occupies an important place in the historical literature on piano pedagogy.[9] The pianist Theodor Leschetizky stated that a knowledge 'of the many different qualities of touch … which give a never-ending variety to the tone must be learned before one can go very far [in piano playing]' (in Gerig 1990: 278). While it remains elusive in terms of empirical investigation, pianists often describe the different effects of different touches in vivid images that involve reference to affect, movement and gesture. For example, the American pianist William Mason, who was a pupil of Liszt, spoke of 'elastic touch' where the finger takes the key while 'on the wing':

> The tone produced by this touch has a buoyancy, lightness, and flexibility which is enlivening and exhilarating. The tones float and rebound, as it were, and are not dull, colorless or monotonous. (Mason 1897: 51)

The pianist Heinrich Neuhaus wrote:

> teachers inevitably and constantly use metaphor to define the various ways of producing tone on the piano. We speak of fingers fusing with the keyboard, of 'growing into the keyboard' (Rachmaninov's expression) as if the keyboard were resilient and one could 'sink' into it at will … (Neuhaus 1993: 62)

In the words of pianist György Sándor:

> touch and tone quality are most personal things, and they are clearly recognizable. Even if they are hard to define, the difference in tone qualities among certain artists undoubtedly exists and is not imagined. There can be no argument that the piano sounds different when Horowitz, Richter, Michelangeli, or Argerich play it. (Sándor 1995: 14)

---

[9]   Some of the important texts specifically on touch from the history of piano pedagogy are the following: William Mason's *Touch and Technic* (1897); Tobias Matthay's *The Act of Touch in all its Diversity* (1903); Otto Ortmann's *The Physical Basis of Piano Touch and Tone* (1925); Maria Levinskaya's *The Levinskaya System of Pianoforte Technique and Tone-Colour Through Mental and Muscular Control* (1930).

Since its beginnings, scientific research on the physics of the process of touch has put such remarks by pianists into doubt: whether a pianist can vary the timbre or tone colour of an individual tone by the manner in which they depress the key – independently of how fast they depress it – has been a matter of intense debate and controversy. The earliest experiments on the relationship of touch and piano tone were carried out during the 1920s and 1930s. Otto Ortmann, one of the pioneers in the science of piano playing who established a laboratory at the Peabody Conservatory, had experienced pianists play in a manner that they thought involved different kinds of touch – singing, dry, velvety, bell-like, pearly and so on. He discovered that each difference in quality corresponded to a difference in the speed of the key. Combining this finding with the earlier one he made, that increase in key speed is accompanied by increase in volume, he argued that 'all these supposedly qualitative differences as applied to the single tone are merely differences in intensity' (Ortmann 1925: 26).

In a well-known book titled *Science and Music* that was first published in 1937, physicist Sir James Jeans confirmed Ortmann's findings and argued that a pianist cannot influence the quality of sound by the way she depresses the key. He wrote:

> Many pianists are firmly convinced that they can put a vast amount of expression into the striking of a single note of the piano: some claim to be able to draw the whole gamut of emotion out of a single key. In reply, the untemperamental scientist points out that, in striking a single note, the pianist has only one variable at is disposal – the force with which he strikes the key; this determines the velocity with which the hammer hits the wires, and once this is settled, all the rest follows automatically ... all the shades of tone which a pianist can get out of one note form one linear sequence only, this corresponding to the different speeds with which the hammer can strike the wire. (Jeans 1968: 98)

Jeans also referred to research by American scientists who recorded the sound curves of single tones played by well-known virtuosi, and of the same note played by letting a weight fall on the keys. The curves recording the notes thus played showed no visible differences.

While the deep-rooted conviction of pianists that the way they *touch* the keys actually makes a qualitative difference in the sound produced has thus apparently been refuted by scientific evidence, most researchers in this area have been reluctant to regard what pianists experience in tone production as merely an illusion. To do so would also imply that composers such as Liszt, Debussy, Rachmaninov and Scriabin, among others, were merely encouraging the performer to dwell in illusions when they wrote on their piano scores such terms as *martellato, carezzando, con strepito, con delizio, con luminosita* and *étincelant*.[10] Ortmann,

---

[10]   It is noteworthy that Liszt occasionally wrote 'vibrato' on his piano scores. Although rocking the finger on a piano key does not alter the sound, Liszt, the theatrical performer, must have realized that the sight of a rocking finger might lead the listeners to believe that

for instance, acknowledged that the physiological and psychological mechanisms of listening may prompt one to hear 'more' than what the pianist actually achieves at the keyboard in terms of the physics of sound. More recently, Parncutt and Troup acknowledged that:

> Tone quality in piano performance is determined not only by the physics of individual keystrokes but also involves a complex and largely intuitive interaction among body movements, technical finesse, and musical interpretation. (Parncutt & Troup 2002: 290)

There is evidence indicating that pianists can in fact exercise some degree of control via touch over some components of a piano tone. Galembo et al. (1998), for example, argue that:

> there may still be two possibilities for the pianist to control the tonal properties of touch. One is related to the pianist's ability to control the noise components which accompany the acceleration of the key, and the second is connected with a bending of the hammer shank during acceleration. Both effects are directly connected with the forced history of the key motion, which in turn reflects how the pianist organizes the key acceleration from the moment the fingers contact the key to the stop at the bottom position of the key travel.[11]

More importantly, Galembo et al. (1998) note the role that kinaesthetic feedback from finger contact with the keys might play in the pianist's perception of timbre. They claim that:

> for the pianist the tone is the auditory feedback of his own activity. There are good reasons to assume that the pianist's opinions about the touch (the production) and the timbre (the perception) are intertwined. It is well known that in music, auditory perception interacts with perception of other modalities … . Pianists also include the kinaesthetic feedback when they evaluate timbre, making not only the tone but also the judgment of the tone touch-dependent.

Indeed, as far as a pianist is concerned, how *fast* a key on the piano is depressed is musically irrelevant, and the researcher needs to make sure that what a MIDI instrument can measure through the actions of the keys does not come to be regarded as a reflection of the performer's own experience of the performance variables. While the measuring device takes input from a linearly arranged keyboard, with

---

they were actually hearing a vibrato – confirming the importance of the visual information for the effect of a performance on listeners.

[11]   I am grateful to the authors for providing the full version of this unpublished conference presentation. Their findings have been confirmed in a later article (Goebl, Bresin & Galembo 2004).

equally distanced and weighted keys, the kinaesthetic sensations originating in the pianist's fingers, which cannot function independently as the keys of a piano can, provide information about speed and timing to the brain in an entirely different manner. Because of the specific anatomy of the human hand, and the way this is represented in the brain, information regarding speed that comes from different fingers is not registered in an objective one-to-one manner, by reference to a fixed unit. Furthermore, perception of the varying degrees of finger speed is relative, and depends on the condition of the muscles, such that a well-trained muscle will experience the same objective speed as slower compared to one that is 'out-of-practice'. Hence, a pianist's conceptualization of 'touch' does not involve reference to the absolute speed of the piano keys, but first and foremost to the pianist's own kinaesthetic sensations, and their relationship with the resulting sounds.

The 'Singing' Hand

At least since the Baroque period, the *singing voice* has been regarded as the ideal model for expressive performance. In the literature on piano pedagody, the ultimate criterion for a pianist's musicianship is thought to reside in their ability to make the piano 'sing'. Pianists have always been advised to take every opportunity to hear good singers (Doğantan 2002: Chapter 1).

In his *Performing Music: Shared Concerns,* Jonathan Dunsby argued that recent empirical research has finally shown how professionals make the piano sing; accordingly, this is achieved not by making a melodic line louder 'though this is also a factor, but most pertinently by its micro-aural anticipation of any notes that support it' (1995: 67). 'When I say the piano sings', Dunsby wrote, 'I am assuming this is what the players try to do; strictly, we need some kind of verification on the part of subjects judging [this kind of] playing' (1995: 72).

What is missing in Dunsby's account, and in the empirical research he refers to, is any reference to the physical aspect of singing and its relationship to piano performance. Is there a physical, kinaesthetic reason as to why pianists have been using the vocal analogy for ages? Research in voice production has established that 'the respiratory muscles, particularly those of the rib-cage, are subjected to a nervous control which is similar in both sensory and motor aspects to that of the limb muscles' (Sears 1977: 83). The rapidity of fluctuations of EMG (electromyography) activity registered during the singing of a phrase indicates that the intercostal muscles behave similarly to the small muscles of the hand. Research indicates that 'the muscle spindles of the rib-cage are admirably suited to the task of regulating sub-glottal pressure during speech and song' (Sears 1977: 92). In singing, this pressure is fixated at a certain level, and the phrase is delivered through a slow respiratory movement, a slow expiration, creating a smooth, flowing, uninterrupted effect. There is an unbroken, dynamically uniform level of force behind the tones thus produced.

Phenomenologically, the kind of initiatory gesture in piano playing that results in a singing touch is experienced by the pianist in precisely such kinaesthetic terms, and I would hypothesize that this is due to the similarities between the representations in the brain of the kind of muscular movements involved in singing and in piano playing, though there has not been any empirical research comparing the neurology of these two modes of music-making. The defining feature of the initiatory gesture that results in a 'singing touch' in piano playing is that the fingers and the hand assume a fixed position before striking the keys, and the rhythmic group thus delivered displays less micro-fluctuations in terms of its intensity. It is important to note that the singing touch does not affect a single note, but a group of notes, which become a *musical unit* through the initial unifying momentum the gesture provides. Figure 12.1 shows pianist Emil Gilels employing just such a hand gesture before striking the E♮ in the right hand in bar 441 of the first movement of Tchaikovsky's Piano Concerto No. 1 in B♭ minor (Example 12.1).

Figure 12.1   Emil Gilels's right-hand gesture before striking the E♮ at bar 441 in his performance of Tchaikovsky's Piano Concerto

Example 12.1 Tchaikovsky, Piano Concerto No. 1 in B♭ minor, Op. 23, first movement, bars 439–43

The most significant phenomenological feature of the 'singing hand' is that for the performer the musical event starts during the course of the gesture, before the initial contact with the keys. In a discussion of tone production in general, Galembo et al. (1998) have argued:

the pianist's judgment of tone includes some information, which is not available to the listener ... since the pianist controls the generation of the tone with the key, (s)he has much more exact expectations and thus better tracking of many small details of the event named 'tone'. For the pianist, the tone starts physically when the finger contacts the key (mentally much earlier) and includes all possible audible touch-dependent attack elements, as well as the mechanical feedback from the action via the key ... . Therefore, for the pianist, the time interval between the finger-key contact and hammer-string contact (between 25 and 80 ms approximately and controlled by touch) is a part of the perceived tone, while the listeners have only a vague idea about the activity during this part of the touch via the level of the attack noise.

I would argue, however, that particularly in the singing touch, the performer starts to experience the tone much earlier not only mentally, but also physically, at the beginning of the fixating gesture, before the hammer contacts the string and the tone actually starts sounding. The kinaesthetic sensations that accompany the gesture result from the adjustments in muscular tonus that the pianist makes to prepare the impact, and this adjustment in turn is guided by an aural image of the desired tone, the goal of the gestural movement. Pianists know – must know – what kind of tone will ensure that their touch is able to produce the intended tone at all.[12] There is experimental evidence suggesting that pianists implicitly anticipate the appropriate motor programme to execute a tone when they only see the score (Jäncke 2006). Over time, pianists build up a library of kinaesthetic images that correspond to different tone colours, which become part of their 'technical inventory'. The kinaesthetic sensations, the gesture and the resulting tone are, therefore, unified in a single percept for performers. Ortmann was already aware of this fact when he stated:

> The player imagines the key-resistance, and hence prepares the speed of muscular contraction, the necessary fixation of the joints, before the key is reached ... . This image can function very accurately, and upon its accuracy depends the question of whether or not the player will get the desired tonal result. (Ortmann 1929: 87)

The initiatory gesture is hence part of a rhythmic movement that starts with the aural image of the singing tone and its attendant muscular adjustments, and continues until the hand needs to 'breathe' again before the next musical unit that has to 'sing' is approached. Liszt, in this connection, is supposed to have told

---

[12]   In a section titled 'Piano Singing' in his *The Art of Performance,* Schenker has written that the thrust of the hand 'must be prepared from the outset, like bow strokes on strings and breathing in playing wind instruments; it must not be attempted during a passage while moving, from tone to tone as it were. The hand senses *in advance*, parallel to the composer's thinking ahead; it forms its gestures accordingly' (2000: 8).

pianist Anton Rubinstein: 'There is more rhythm between the notes than in the notes themselves' (in Gerig 1990: 274).

The unity of the initiatory gesture and the tone produced is also part of the listening experience, although the listener is not ahead of the music physically in the same way as the performer is. In empirical performance studies, the measurements of the expressive variables start with the onset of the sound, the attack; as far as the MIDI equipment is concerned, in the absence of physically sounding phenomena there is nothing to measure. The initiatory gestures, however, leave their imprint on the tone quality experienced by listeners. According to Shove and Repp, listeners do not just hear the onsets of sounds because 'attacks are nested events, constrained by, affected by, and thus lawfully specific to the performer's actions. To hear the attacks is to hear the performer move. The dynamic time course of these gestures is reflected in the resulting sound stream' (Shove & Repp 1995: 60). To be precise, it is not the attack that produces the sound, but the gesture bringing about the attack.

The initiatory gestures play a significant role in the listener's experience also through the way they affect the performer. In *Aspects of Cortot*, Thomas Manshardt wrote that '[i]n establishing the ability to share a feeling with one's hearers the first consideration of any pianistic movement or gesture must be its effect upon the player' (1994: 37). Surprisingly, this aspect of performance, that is, how the execution of various gestures actually makes the performer feel – both physically and affectively – has been entirely neglected in performance studies. Davidson and Correia do mention in passing the possibility that certain movements may serve an affective function for the performer, for instance 'to make him- or herself feel at ease in the social context of the performance and/or enjoy the musical sounds being made' (2002: 239–40).[13] I would argue, based on a well-known hypothesis in affective psychology, which states that making certain kinds of expressive movements actually causes a person to feel a certain way (James 1884) – and reverses the folk-psychological order of feeling-first-expression-later – listeners, through a certain motor empathy, can indeed perceive in the sounds they hear the affective quality of the performer's kinaesthetic experience.[14] In this sense, a complete understanding of the nature of the listening experience requires tackling the physicality of performing. If the experience of

---

[13]   In one of the few existing studies on the subjective experiences of the performers (Persson 2001), which aims to outline 'exploratory research into the *phenomenology of emotion in performance*' (: 275), the author includes a discussion of such issues as motivation, and meaning construction, but leaves out any consideration of the bodily basis of emotional involvement in performance.

[14]   An interesting research question à la James, who wrote in 1884, 'without the bodily states following on the perception, the latter would be purely cognitive in form, pale, colourless, destitute of emotional warmth' is: What would remain of the tone-percept for the performer, if we take away its affective-kinaesthetic feel? And does the tone-percept fade if the muscle memory fades, as when, for example, a pianist retires?

listening to the sounding phenomenon created by performers were equal to the experience of reading a musical score, as Schoenberg claimed, a culture of score-reading – similar to reading books – would have emerged a long time ago. This has never happened and is unlikely to ever happen. Listening to music is intricately connected to how performers bring about music physically; to understand music *as* performance, therefore, requires taking the experience of performing as the basis for an epistemology of music and relating the performing experience to the ways listeners come to know music, and indeed to the ways composers create it.

To establish a phenomenology of the body that performs music is a complex task: it almost certainly requires devising new methodologies, conceptualizations and perhaps even terminology. It is particularly challenging because, as Cumming has written:

> the 'quest for certainty' can have interpreters [theorists] avoiding comment on any aspect of musical content for which they cannot find an empirical foundation. Comment on such things as sound quality and its signification, or the affective connotation of a phrase, do, for example, present a greater risk to an interpreter [theorist] who wishes to project the image of secure knowledge, because the factors informing aural judgments of this kind are not always readily accessible … and they cannot be specified by reference to a score. (Cumming 2000: 46)

In this endeavour, the onus is on performers to break the mould surrounding their notorious image as inarticulate doers (Kerman 1985: 196), and bring to light what is involved in physically making music and what this entails for musicology.

References

Abbate, C. (2004). Music – Drastic or Gnostic? *Critical Inquiry* 30/3: 505–36.

Benjamin, W. (2002). The Work of Art in the Age of its Technological Reproducibility. In H. Eiland & M. W. Jennings (eds), *Selected Writings, Volume 3, 1935–1938* (pp. 101–33). Cambridge, MA: Belknap Press of Harvard University Press.

Bermudez, J., Marcel, A. J. & Eilan, N. (1995). *The Body and the Self*. Cambridge, MA: MIT Press.

Berthoz, A. (1999). *Leçons sur le corps, le cerveau et l'esprit*. Paris: Odile Jacob.

— (2000). *The Brain's Sense of Movement* (trans. Giselle Weiss). Cambridge, MA: Harvard University Press.

Brower, C. (2000). A Cognitive Theory of Musical Meaning. *Journal of Music Theory* 44/2: 323–80.

Clark, A. (1997). *Being There: Putting Brain, Body, and World Together Again*. Cambridge, MA: MIT Press.

Clarke, E. (2004). Empirical Methods in the Study of Performance. In E. Clarke & N. Cook (eds), *Empirical Musicology: Aims, Methods, Prospects* (pp. 77–102). New York: Oxford University Press.

— & Davidson, J. (1998). The Body in Performance. In W. Thomas (ed.), *Composition – Performance – Reception: Studies in the Creative Process in Music* (pp. 74–92). Aldershot: Ashgate.

Cook, N. (1999). Analysing Performance, Performing Analysis. In N. Cook & M. Everist (eds), *Rethinking Music* (pp. 239–61). New York: Oxford University Press.

— (2001). Between Process and Product: Music and/as Performance. *Music Theory Online* 7/2 (http://www.societymusictheory.org/mto/; accessed June 2008).

— (2003). Music as Performance. In M. Clayton, T. Herbert & R. Middleton (eds), *The Cultural Study of Music: A Critical Introduction* (pp. 204–14). New York: Routledge.

— & Clarke, E. (2004). Introduction: What is Empirical Musicology? In E. Clarke & N. Cook (eds), *Empirical Musicology: Aims, Methods, Prospects* (pp. 3–14). Oxford: Oxford University Press.

Cox, A. (2001). The Mimetic Hypothesis and Embodied Musical Meaning. *Musicae Scientiae* 5/2: 195–212.

— (2006). Hearing, Feeling, Grasping Gestures. In A. Gritten & E. King (eds), *Music and Gesture* (pp. 45–60). Aldershot: Ashgate.

Cumming, N. (2000). *The Sonic Self: Musical Subjectivity and Signification*. Bloomington: Indiana University Press.

Damasio, A. (1994). *Descartes' Error: Emotion, Reason, and the Human Brain*. New York: Avon.

— (1999). *The Feeling of What Happens: Body and Emotion in the Making of Consciousness*. New York: Harcourt Brace.

— (2003). *Looking for Spinoza: Joy, Sorrow, and the Feeling Brain*. Orlando: Harcourt.

Davidson, J. W. (1993). Visual Perception of Performance Manner in the Movements of Solo Musicians. *Psychology of Music* 21: 103–13.

— (1994). Which Areas of the Pianist's Body Convey Information about Expressive Intention to an Audience? *Journal of Human Movement Studies* 26: 279–301.

— (1995). What does the Visual Information Contained in Music Performances Offer the Observer? Some Preliminary Thoughts. In R. Steinberg (ed.), *The Music Machine: Psychophysiology and Psychopathology of the Sense of Music* (pp. 105–13). Berlin: Springer Verlag.

— (2001). The Role of the Body in the Production and Perception of Solo Vocal Performance: A Case Study of Annie Lennox. *Musicae Scientiae* 5/2: 235–56.

— (2002). Understanding the Expressive Movements of a Solo Pianist. *Musikpsychologie* 16: 9–31.

— (2005). Bodily Communication in Musical Performance. In D. Miell, R. MacDonald & D. J. Hargreaves (eds), *Musical Communication* (pp. 215–28). Oxford: Oxford University Press.

— (2006). 'She's the One': Multiple Functions of Body Movement in a Stage Performance by Robbie Williams. In A. Gritten & E. King (eds.), *Music and Gesture* (pp. 208–26). Aldershot: Ashgate.

— (2007). Qualitative Insights into the Use of Expressive Body Movement in Solo Piano Performance: A Case Study Approach. *Psychology of Music* 35/3: 381–401.

— & Correia, J. S. (2002). Body Movement. In R. Parncutt & G. E. McPherson (eds), *The Science and Psychology of Music Performance: Creative Strategies for Teaching and Learning* (pp. 237–50). New York: Oxford University Press.

Doğantan, M. (2002). *Mathis Lussy: A Pioneer in Studies of Expressive Performance*. Bern: Peter Lang AG.

Doğantan-Dack, M. (2006). The Body Behind Music: Precedents and Prospects. *Psychology of Music* 34/4: 449–64.

Dunsby, J. (1995). *Performing Music: Shared Concerns*. Oxford: Oxford University Press.

Friberg, A. & Sunberg, J. (1999). Does Music Performance Allude to Locomotion? A Model of Final *Ritardandi* Derived from Measurements of Stopping Runners. *Journal of the Acoustical Society of America* 105/3: 1469–84.

Friberg, A., Sundberg, J. & Frydén, L. (2000). Music from Motion: Sound Level Envelopes of Tones Expressing Human Locomotion. *Journal of New Music Research* 29: 199–210.

Gabrielsson, A. (2003). Music Performance Research at the Millennium. *Psychology of Music* 31/3: 221–72.

Galembo, A., Askenfelt, A. & Cuddy, L. L. (1998). On the Acoustics and Psychology of Piano Touch and Tone. Paper presented at the Sixteenth International Congress on Acoustics, Seattle, WA, June. Abstract: *Journal of the Acoustical Society of America* 103: 2873.

Gerig, R. R. (1990). *Famous Pianists and Their Technique*. Washington, DC: Robert B. Luce, Inc.

Goebl, W., Bresin, R. & Galembo, A. (2004). Once Again: The Perception of Piano Touch and Tone. Can Touch Audibly Change Piano Sound Independently of Intensity? In *Proceedings of the International Symposium on Musical Acoustics*, Nara, Japan. (http://www.ofai.at/cgi-bin/tr-online?number+2004-02; accessed June 2008)

Hajda, J. M., Kendall, R. A., Carterette, E. C. & Harsberger, M. L. (1997). Methodological Issues in Timbre Research. In I. Deliège & J. Sloboda (eds), *Perception and Cognition of Music* (pp. 253–306). East Sussex: Psychology Press.

Handel, S. (1991). *Listening: An Introduction to the Perception of Auditory Events*. Cambridge, MA: MIT Press.

James, W. (1884). What is an Emotion? *Mind* 9: 188–205. (http://psychclassics. yorku.ca/James/emotion.htm; accessed June 2008)

Jäncke, L. (2006). The Motor Representation in Pianists and String Players. In E. Altenmüller, M. Wiesendanger & J. Kesselring (eds), *Music, Motor Control and the Brain* (pp. 153–72). New York: Oxford University Press.

Jeans, J. (1968). *Science and Music*. New York: Dover Publications.

Johnson, M. (1987). *The Body in the Mind: The Bodily Basis of Meaning, Imagination, and Reason*. Chicago: University of Chicago Press.

Juslin, P. N. (2003). Five Facets of Musical Expression: A Psychologist's Perspective on Music Performance. *Psychology of Music* 31/3: 273–302.

Kerman, J. (1985). *Musicology*. London: Fontana.

Kronman, U. & Sundberg, J. (1987). Is the Musical Ritard an Allusion to Physical Motion? In A. Gabrielsson (ed.), *Action and Perception in Rhythm and Music* (pp. 57–68). Stockholm: Royal Swedish Academy of Music.

Lakoff, G. & Johnson, M. (1980). *Metaphors We Live By*. Chicago: University of Chicago Press.

Larson, S. (1997). The Problem of Prolongation in Tonal Music: Terminology, Perception, and Expressive Meaning. *Journal of Music Theory* 41/1: 101–36.

LeDoux, J. E. (1996). *The Emotional Brain*. New York: Simon and Schuster.

— (2002). *Synaptic Self: How Our Brains Become Who We Are*. New York: Viking.

Lerdahl, F. & Jackendoff, R. (1983). *A Generative Theory of Tonal Music*. Cambridge, MA: MIT Press.

Levinskaya, M. (1930). *The Levinskaya System of Pianoforte Technique and Tone-Colour through Mental and Muscular Control*. London: J. M. Dent and Sons.

McClelland, R. (2003). Performance and Analysis Studies: An Overview and Bibliography. *Indiana Theory Review* 24: 95–106.

Manshardt, T. (1994). *Aspects of Cortot*. Northumberland: Appian Publications.

Mason, W. (1897). *Touch and Technic: Artistic Piano Playing, Op. 44. Vols. I–IV*. Philadelphia: Theodore Presser.

Matthay, T. (1903). *The Act of Touch in all its Diversity*. London: Bosworth & Co.

Maus, F. E. (1999). Musical Performance as Analytical Communication. In S. Kemal & I. Gaskell (eds), *Performance and Authenticity in the Arts* (pp. 129–53). Cambridge: Cambridge University Press.

Merleau-Ponty, M. (1968). *The Visible and the Invisible* (trans. A. Lingis). Evanston, IL: Northwestern University Press.

Neuhaus, H. (1993). *The Art of Piano Playing* (trans. K. A. Leibovitch). London: Kahn & Averill.

Newlin, D. (1980). *Schoenberg Remembered: Diaries and Recollections (1938–76)*. Pendragon Press.

Ortmann, O. (1925). *The Physical Basis of Piano Touch and Tone*. London: Kegan Paul.

— (1929). *The Physiological Mechanics of Piano Technique*. London: Kegan Paul.

Parncutt, R. & Troup, M. (2002). Piano. In R. Parncutt & G. E. McPherson (eds), *The Science and Psychology of Music Performance: Creative Strategies for Teaching and Learning* (pp. 285–302). Oxford: Oxford University Press.

Persson, R. S. (2001). The Subjective World of the Performer. In P. N. Juslin & J. A. Sloboda (eds), *Music and Emotion: Theory and Research* (pp. 275–90). New York: Oxford University Press.

Repp, B. H. (1999). A Microcosm of Musical Expression: III. Contributions of Expressive Timing and Dynamics to the Aesthetic Impression of the Initial Measures of Chopin's Etude in E major. *Journal of the Acoustical Society of America* 106: 469–78.

Reybrouck, M. (2001). Musical Imagery between Sensory Processing and Ideomotor Simulation. In R. I. Godøy & H. Jørgensen (eds), *Musical Imagery* (pp. 117–35). Lisse, The Netherlands: Swets & Zeitlinger.

Rink, J. (2004). The State of Play in Performance Studies. In J. Davidson (ed.), *The Music Practitioner: Research for the Music Performer, Teacher and Listener* (pp. 37–51). Aldershot: Ashgate.

Sándor, G. (1995). *On Piano Playing: Motion, Sound and Expression*. New York: Schirmer Books.

Sartre, J. -P. (1978). *The Psychology of Imagination*. Westport, CT: Greenwood Press.

Saslaw, J. (1996). Forces, Containers, and Paths: The Role of Body-Derived Image Schemas in the Conceptualization of Music. *Journal of Music Theory* 40/2: 217–44.

Schaeffer, P. (1966). *Traité des objets musicaux*. Paris: Éditions du Seuil. Unpublished English translation by J. Dack & C. North.

Schechner, R. (2002). *Performance Studies: An Introduction*. Routledge: London.

Schenker, H. (2000). *The Art of Performance* (trans. Irene Schreier Scott). New York: Oxford University Press.

Sears, T. A. (1977). Some Neural and Mechanical Aspects of Singing. In M. Critchley & R. A. Henson (eds), *Music and the Brain* (pp. 78–94). London: Heineman.

Shove, P. & Repp, B. H. (1995). Musical Motion and Performance: Theoretical and Empirical Perspectives. In J. Rink (ed.), *The Practice of Performance: Studies in Musical Interpretation* (pp. 55–83). Cambridge: Cambridge University Press.

Sloboda, J. (2005). *Exploring the Musical Mind: Cognition, Emotion, Ability, Function*. New York: Oxford University Press.

Smalley, D. (1992). The Listening Imagination: Listening in the Electroacoustic Era. In J. Paynter, T. Howell, R. Orton & P. Seymour (eds), *Companion to Contemporary Musical Thought* (pp. 514–53). London: Routledge.

Snyder, B. (2000). *Music and Memory: An Introduction*. Cambridge, MA: MIT Press.

Todd, N. (1992). The Dynamics of Dynamics: A Model of Musical Expression. *Journal of the Acoustical Society of America* 91: 3540–50.

— (1995). The Kinematics of Musical Expression. *Journal of the Acoustical Society of America* 97: 1940–9.

Zbikowski, L. M. (1997). Conceptual Models and Cross-Domain Mapping: New Perspectives on Theories of Music and Hierarchy. *Journal of Music Theory* 41/2: 193–225.

— (2002). *Conceptualizing Music: Cognitive Structure, Theory, and Analysis*. New York: Oxford University Press.

Chapter 13

Motive, Gesture and the Analysis of Performance

John Rink, Neta Spiro and Nicolas Gold

'Musical gestures are musical acts, and our perception and understanding of gestures involves understanding the physicality involved in their production' (Cox 2006: 45). Arnie Cox's provocative statement serves as the point of departure for this chapter.[1] One of its main premises is that music's gestural properties are neither captured by nor fully encoded within musical notation, but instead require the agency of performance to achieve their full realization. The performances in question need not be live: recordings too have distinctly gestural properties even if the visual dimension and experiential character of live music-making are lacking.

This chapter also reverses a common tendency to assign the status of musical gestures to conventional musical motives.[2] In contrast, we regard the gestures created in and through performance as potentially having motivic functions within the performed music. Such 'motives' are defined not in terms of pitch, harmony or rhythm, however, but as *expressive patterns* in timing, dynamics, articulation, timbre and/or other performative parameters that maintain their identity upon literal or varied repetition.[3] The essential point has to do with the nature and function of the given patterns. By way of example, the following discussion focuses on select

---

[1]   The bulk of this chapter was written by John Rink; Neta Spiro and Nicolas Gold wrote Section C in Part 2 in addition to collecting and analysing the data used for the SOM study. The chapter is one of the outputs of our collaborative project on 'Analyzing Motif in Performance' in the AHRC Research Centre for the History and Analysis of Recorded Music (see http://www.charm.kcl.ac.uk; accessed 1 March 2011). The chapter develops the work described in Spiro et al. (2008) and Spiro et al. (2010), in which a number of the figures here also appear.

[2]   For further discussion, see Rink (2007). *Grove Music Online* (Macy, 2001–) defines 'motif' as follows: 'A short musical idea, melodic, harmonic, rhythmic or any combination of these three. A motif may be of any size, and is most commonly regarded as the shortest subdivision of a theme or phrase that still maintains its identity as an idea. It is most often thought of in melodic terms, and it is this aspect of motif that is connoted by the term "figure".'

[3]   Compare the discussion of 'expressive patterns' (defined in terms of tempo and 'loudness') in Widmer et al. (2003). Note that the authors do not explicitly relate these expressive patterns to physical or mimetic gestures, nor do they consider their findings necessarily to be 'musically relevant and artistically interesting' (2003: 126). Furthermore,

performances of Chopin's Mazurka, Op. 24 No. 2, including certain dance-related features characteristic of the mazurka genre as a whole.[4]

Part 1

A

Considerable scepticism has been expressed in recent scholarship about the mapping from structure to performance that was once considered to be ideal in the musicological literature. Clearly the interpretative practice of performers of Western art music involves a good deal more than translating notated symbols, theoretical constructs and analytical findings into sound, just as listening is not simply a matter of the 'structural hearing' valorized by certain authors. That does not mean that musical structure as conventionally understood is wholly irrelevant to performers or listeners – only that the relationship is far more complex and less exclusive than some have assumed.

One problem has to do with a reductivist tendency to regard musical structure as a single, seemingly static entity rather than as a range of potential, inferred relationships between the various parameters active within a work. Not only is it more accurate to refer to music's structure**s**, but the origin and dynamic nature of those structures must also be acknowledged. In this respect performers have a seminal role to play, creating musical structures or their counterpart – musical 'shapes' – in each and every performance. These go well beyond the surface-level expressive microstructure upon which much of the literature has focused to date. Indeed, the dynamic structures underlying and generated within performed music potentially operate at numerous hierarchical levels – a point demonstrated in the case study that follows.

Both shape and shaping are key concepts throughout this chapter and of signal importance to musicians more generally. One of the ways in which performers give music a sense of shape in time is by

> devising a hierarchy of temporally defined musical gestures from the small to the large scale. While playing, the performer engages in a continual dialogue between the comprehensive architecture and the 'here-and-now', between some sort of goal-directed impulse at the uppermost hierarchical level (the piece 'in a nutshell') and subsidiary motions extending down to the beat or sub-beat

---

there is no suggestion that these prototypes might be viewed as having what we describe as 'motivic' functions within given performances.

[4]   It should be noted that the structure of this chapter is homologous with that of Chopin's Mazurka – i.e. introduction, three main parts with corresponding subsidiary sections, and coda.

level, with different parts of the hierarchy activated at different points within the performance (Rink 1999a: 218).[5]

Although some of the musical materials constituting these gestures may remain invariant across performances, the scope for innovation is vast and should not be underestimated.

Such gestures may be manipulated according to strategies that performers consciously or unconsciously devise to project their musical conceptions. One of the goals of performance analysis is to infer such strategies – not in a (misguided) attempt to discern the original expressive intentions of the performer, but rather to determine how the sounding music is made to cohere. Unfortunately, analysis of this kind occasionally falls into the same trap as more traditional analytical approaches, merely assembling data about phenomena whose broader musical purpose and effect are ignored. The ensuing study of Chopin's Mazurka tries to avoid this by coupling a relatively objective analytical methodology – self-organizing maps – with an avowedly subjective one, namely critical assessment. The extent to which this combination succeeds can be judged by the reader in due course, but it should be noted that the quality and value of any music-analytical endeavour depend not only on the data that are produced but also on the cogency of their interpretation – in particular, whether or not the latter is musically convincing according to criteria that inevitably are individually determined.

B

Chopin wrote mazurkas more or less throughout his career; some seem to have originated as improvised dances, whereas others are complex, extended works. Much has been made in the literature about the putative influence of Polish folk music on Chopin's mazurka output. Here it suffices to note that although his visits to the Polish countryside in the 1820s introduced him to instruments, idioms and sonorities that he had never encountered as a student in Warsaw, Chopin inherited and perpetuated an urbanized mazurka tradition established by his immediate predecessors. One can nevertheless find in his mazurkas traces of at least three folk dances – *oberek*, *mazur* and *kujawiak*, respectively lively, joyous and plaintive in character. He also made use of modal elements – particularly the Lydian fourth – along with an associated tendency towards chromaticism. Other typical devices taken directly or indirectly from folk models include drone fifths in the accompaniment, 'tight' as opposed to florid ornamentation, obsessive repetition of small bits of material (often in changing contexts), and second- and third-beat accents within a prevailing triple metre that correspond to the foot-stamping gestures of danced mazurkas. Another dance-like feature of numerous

---

[5]   Note that 'temporally defined musical gestures' may involve any musical parameter, not just those specifically to do with timing.

Chopin mazurkas is a waltz-like accompaniment with its typical strong–weak–weak stress pattern.

In a letter to his family from 1830, however, Chopin insisted that his recently composed mazurkas were 'not for dancing [*nie do tańca*]',[6] and this is also true of Op. 24 No. 2, which was composed in 1833 and first published in 1835. Although its underlying ternary form is conceptually simple, there is considerable sophistication in the disposition of and interrelationships between constituent sections and subsections, as shown in Figure 13.1.

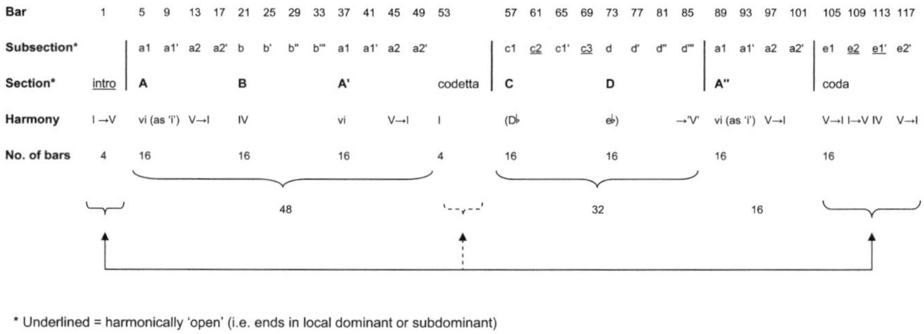

Bar	1		5	9	13	17	21	25	29	33	37	41	45	49	53		57	61	65	69	73	77	81	85		89	93	97	101		105	109	113	117
Subsection*			a1	a1'	a2	a2'	b	b'	b"	b'"	a1	a1'	a2	a2'			c1	c2	c1'	c3	d	d'	d"	d'"		a1	a1'	a2	a2'		e1	e2	e1'	e2'
Section*	intro		A				B				A'				codetta		C				D					A"					coda			
Harmony	I →V		vi (as 'i')		V→I		IV						vi		V→I	I	(D♭				e♭)				→'V'	vi (as 'i')		V→I			V→I	I→V	IV	V→I
No. of bars	4		16				16				16					4	16				16					16					16			

48 | 32 | 16

* Underlined = harmonically 'open' (i.e. ends in local dominant or subdominant)

Figure 13.1   Chopin, Mazurka, Op. 24 No. 2 – formal/tonal plan

After a four-bar introduction notable for its hemiola-like tonic/dominant oscillations, section A begins in the relative minor before re-establishing C major as tonic. This opening section itself belongs to a subsidiary ternary form, the middle of which – section B – is in the subdominant, featuring a rhythmically free, *mazur*-inspired right-hand melody over a more regular waltz accompaniment. After section A returns (i.e. A'), a brief codetta in C major paves the way for the contrasting trio section. Whereas Chopin's polonaises tend to have symmetrical (i.e. ternary) trios, his mazurkas often feature unitary or, as here, binary middle sections; what is especially distinctive in Op. 24 No. 2 is the harmonic remoteness of and inner contrasts within the through-composed trio section, which progresses through an ebullient, *mazur*-like D♭ major phase (section C) and an E♭ minor passage with the aching melancholy of the *kujawiak* (section D) prior to the reprise of section A in bar 89 (that is, A").[7] The recapitulation is foreshortened, however: section B never returns, nor the ensuing A section. Interestingly, in the German first edition this passage differs from its counterpart in the French and

---

[6]   Letter of 22 December 1830 from Vienna to his family in Warsaw (Sydow 1955: 161). Chopin's comment is unspecific but applies to at least some of the works in his Opp. 6 and 7, published in 1833.

[7]   In an unpublished book manuscript (*The Languages of Western Tonality*) Eytan Agmon describes the D♭ major and E♭ minor passages in terms of their enharmonic equivalents, i.e. C♯ major and D♯ minor.

English first editions:[8] the German print was prepared from Chopin's autograph manuscript, and when correcting the proofsheets that ultimately served as the basis of the French edition (from which the English edition was prepared in turn), he introduced variants to bars 98 and 102–3, intentionally differentiating these bars from corresponding passages by increasing closural momentum prior to the start of the coda (bars 105ff.).[9] In this final phase, material first presented in the introduction is developed as the oscillatory figuration winds down and the piece draws to a close.

A'

The foregoing analysis usefully identifies structural features of the Mazurka, but without redefinition or mediation these may have limited immediate relevance to the music as performed. It is important to consider the quite different ways in which musicians apprehend, translate into action and ultimately subsume within broader expressive strategies structural elements such as the ones just described. As suggested earlier, performers are likely to grasp or 'feel' musical structure dynamically and gesturally rather than according to spatial or architectural paradigms. Whether consciously or unconsciously, they assess the structural features they become aware of through ongoing contact with the music, weighing up the contribution of those features to the music's *process* at one or more levels and in multivalent trajectories. Process of this sort occurs from note to note, bar to bar, phrase to phrase and so on, while also involving overarching relationships between less proximate passages such as the introduction, codetta and coda in Chopin's Mazurka. As the role of the various elements is determined, decisions are also made about their relative priority within a broader dynamic conception of the music, likewise the means of projecting them accordingly.

With musical process foremost in mind, a hypothetical task list can be drawn up for a more comprehensive analysis of Op. 24 No. 2 in terms relevant to performance; to some extent this could also serve an agenda for performance-related analysis in general. Although such a menu encompasses such standard parameters as form and rhythm, these again must be understood in a manner reflecting the temporal basis of as well as the potentially infinite variety within and between performances.

---

[8]   For a discussion of the publication history of this opus and Chopin's music in general, see CFEO (2007).

[9]   The editions of this Mazurka published after Chopin's death in 1849 tend to follow either the undifferentiated version of the German first edition (see, for example, the Henle Urtext) or the varied one found in the French and English editions (for example, the *Wydanie Narodowe*). When listening to a performance of this piece one can often infer which edition(s) a pianist may have used on the basis of these and other textual idiosyncrasies. The French, German and English first editions can be viewed at CFEO (2007).

In this respect, what seems most significant about the successive formal sections that we have surveyed is their gravitational tendencies – whether processive or recessive, prospective or retrospective, and so forth. For example, the main sections depicted in Figure 13.1 could be treated more or less discretely or in a comparatively 'through-performed' manner, with less pronounced differentiation between the constituent phases. This is also the case with the introduction, codetta and coda, which conceivably could serve as structural pillars within an all-embracing framework. A further consideration concerns how the non-symmetrical middle section is handled as against the symmetrical first part and, for that matter, the non-symmetrical, foreshortened reprise. The same holds for the more general foreshortening from the first part's 48 bars (3 × 16) through the middle part's 32 bars (2 × 16) to the recapitulation's 16 bars, which engenders a sense of formal acceleration balanced out by the extended coda.[10]

Important issues also surround absolute tempo. It is interesting to note discrepancies between the metronome markings in the three first editions (crotchet = 108) and Chopin's autograph manuscript[11] (crotchet = 192), although these particular tempos are obviously not the only ones available to pianists. Further questions arise regarding the respective tempos of individual sections (are they consistent or contrasted, and to what extent?) as well as the presence of rubato (where, and what types?). The latter is of interest not least because Chopin's own playing was characterized by several different styles of rubato, including those derived from *bel canto* and folk traditions.[12] In Op. 24 No. 2 – where 'rubato' is explicitly marked in bar 29 – one may favour a more structured temporal flexibility, with a regular pulse either on the downbeat (whereby the bar length is kept constant) or on the beat (whereby the beat length is kept constant). Alternatively, or in addition, the rubato may be freer, with irregular beat lengths engendering irregular bar lengths. There is also the possibility of rubato at the level of form, such that an expected pulse defined with regard to whole phrases or sections is either stretched or compressed to produce a large-scale agogic accent.

Similar manipulations in dynamics may occur within and between individual sections as well as at an absolute level. The potential differences between performed

---

[10]   The combination of foreshortened reprise, heightened sense of cadential closure at the end of the main tonal structure, and extended recapitulatory coda compensating for the briefer reprise is found in numerous works by Chopin from the Etudes, Op. 10 onwards (for discussion, see Rink 1992, 1999b).

[11]   In fact, '108' is the metronome marking of Op. 24 No. 1; it was wrongly added to No. 2 by the engraver of the German first edition (on which the French and English editions were based). The autograph manuscript, which served as the *Stichvorlage* for the German first edition, is held by the Biblioteka Narodowa in Warsaw under shelfmark Mus. 216.

[12]   In addition to *bel canto* and folk-inspired rubato (respectively characterized by a steady pulse in the accompaniment versus freedom in the melodic line, and by a consistent pulse at the level of the bar), Chopin also indulged in 'fleeting changes of pace relative to the basic tempo ... [in] a whole section, period or phrase' (Eigeldinger 1986: 120).

dynamics and indications in the score – whether Chopin's manuscript, the first editions or later editions – also warrant consideration, likewise the contour and extent of dynamic fluctuations in a given performance, each of which contributes to the shape of the music to some degree. The respective dynamic levels of the two hands equally merit attention.

So too do the synchrony or asynchrony of the two hands and the fingers in use at any point. Analysis of the full range of articulation available to the pianist would be enlightening, not only legato and staccato but also pedalling (for example, secco and/or 'blended'/blurred), voicing (whether homophonic or contrapuntally layered), timbre and silences in the form of rests, delays, and so on. Of particular interest are notated as well as unnotated accents: not only is there scope for dynamic as well as agogic stress in performed music, but in Chopin's case a difference exists between conventional accents and so-called long accents, the functions of which vary according to context (see Rink 2005). Here one should consider not only the presence and relative intensity of accents but also whether their placement is varied or consistent (e.g. on second beats, third beats or elsewhere). Moreover, their correspondence with physical gestures characteristic of the mazurka as a dance, notably stamping of the feet, may need to be assessed. The dynamic and temporal treatment of ornamentation is yet another salient element, also whether trills, turns, grace notes, and so on, are played on or before the beat (or, in the case of some of Chopin's grace notes, played at all).[13] In certain recorded performances of this Mazurka, ornamentation of various kinds is improvised; similarly, the melodic variants that characterize different scores (including the ones discussed above in bars 98 and 102–3) may invite consideration.

Space constraints prevent consideration of all of these factors in the study that follows, although ideally each would be taken into account within any performance-related analysis, just as they are routinely (though differently) grappled with by those performing the music. Instead, we concentrate here on two parameters – tempo and dynamics – for reasons that will become apparent. Although these are often the focus of 'performance analysis', our aim is by no means conventional: instead, rather than simply demonstrating how tempo and dynamics change over time, we look at the manipulation of identifiable expressive patterns within the respective performances. Revealing these patterns and the gestural properties they project is in fact the principal goal of what follows.

---

[13] In Chopin's manuscripts, grace notes on the same pitch as a notated trill indicate a trill start on the main note, not the upper auxiliary. Generally, however, trills in his music begin on the upper note as in eighteenth-century music, just as many ornaments should be played on rather than before the beat (for discussion, see Rink 2005).

Part 2

C

The analysis of timing and dynamic information in performances typically starts by preparing note-to-note or beat-to-beat representations of these parameters. Because the accompaniment of this Mazurka has a strong and more or less constant crotchet beat, here we have used beat-level data as the basis of our representations.[14] Figure 13.2 depicts the changing beat lengths in 29 case-study performances,[15] illustrating common and varied aspects alike. In the figure, broad phrase arcs are clearly traced, and the shaping of sections and the overall similarity and other relationships between them, such as differences in the extent of beat-to-beat variance of note-length, can be discerned not only for the group of performances as a whole but also for individual ones (as will be illustrated below).

To analyse these characteristics of performance more closely, we have developed a means of identifying expressive patterns in performance which potentially can be interpreted in gestural terms. The first step in this method is to 'pre-process' the raw data shown in Figure 13.2 by converting beat-timing data from absolute values to relative proportions of the containing bar, and converting dynamic data into offsets – both positive and negative – from the previous beat.[16] We analyse patterns of relative duration rather than absolute value in order to categorize and observe the distribution of 'shape' within the performances.

Our principal analytical method in this study is based on self-organizing maps (SOMs, also termed Kohonen networks), which are a form of artificial neural network trained by unsupervised learning.[17] The maps have been used for a

---

[14]   Timing and dynamic data included in the freely available datasets produced by the CHARM Mazurkas project (CHARM 2009b) was used. Timing data in these sets is gathered by a process of human-tapping to recorded performances, followed by a data-cleaning stage using the Sonic Visualiser tool and plugins to assign timing positions to musical beats with greater accuracy (available at http://www.sonicvisualiser.org; accessed 1 March 2011). Dynamic data is similarly gathered using Sonic Visualiser plugins to measure the sampled loudness (using smoothed power curve data) for each beat (for further information, see Sapp 2007).

[15]   The 29 recordings were chosen from a total of 48 available through the CHARM Mazurkas project (see CHARM 2009b); the selection was determined by considerations of chronological and national coverage as well as general performance approaches. A discography of nearly 70 performances of this Mazurka is available at CHARM (2009a).

[16]   The maps can be trained on units of any size or musical identity. In this case we investigate patterns at the bar level (see n. 18 below).

[17]   Artificial neural networks (ANNs) are typically divided on the basis of their learning method: supervised or unsupervised. Supervised learning means that training consists of the ANN making a prediction on the basis of input data and being told whether this is correct or not. Over time, the network adapts itself to predict more accurately on the basis of this feedback. Unsupervised learning does not contain a feedback loop: instead

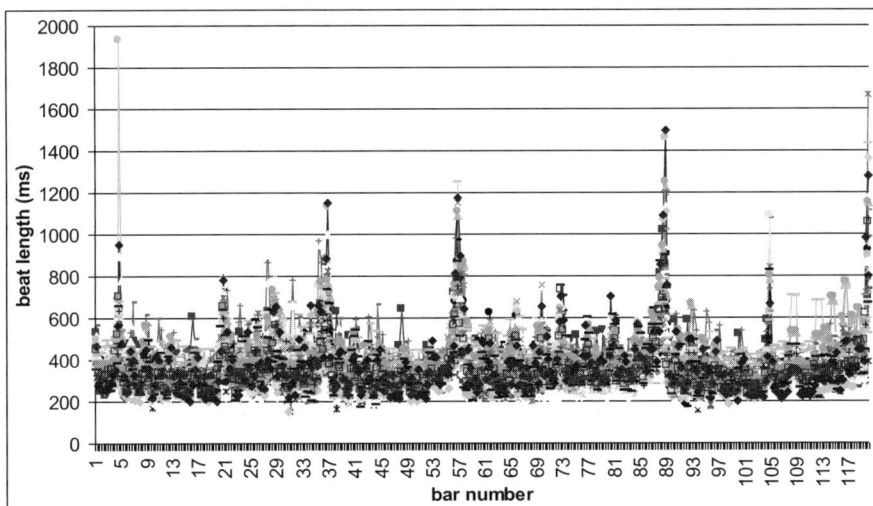

Figure 13.2   Beat length in all 29 performances

wide range of classification and clustering tasks. The key advantage of the SOM methodology for the work presented here is its ability to group patterns according to the similarity of relative beat length or dynamic nuance. Using this approach allows one to discover 'natural' similarities in timing or dynamic shapes without *a priori* determination of how many should exist or how large each group of patterns should be.

We use single bars as our units of analysis, modelling each one as a point in a three-dimensional space, either timing or dynamic.[18] After training, bars of similar temporal or dynamic shape occupy proximate areas of the vector space and, when presented in two dimensions, appear as clusters of nodes in the resulting map. A SOM-Ward clustering[19] is then applied to determine the boundaries between clusters.

---

the network adapts itself to represent some characteristic of the input data. In the case of a Kohonen network, this is the topological relationship between items of data in the input set (see Kohonen 2001).

[18]   The decision to use bars as the unit of analysis has partly to do with the mazurka genre's constructive tendencies (for analysis of four-bar units and paired timing and dynamic information, see Spiro et al. 2008).

[19]   Ward clustering is a method for clustering items based on an objective similarity measure referred to as the Ward distance (Ward 1963). Starting from each item being a cluster itself, the two closest items are combined into a new cluster. The process repeats itself until all items are in a single cluster, leaving a hierarchy of possible clusterings. The most appropriate clustering for a given task can then be determined by inspection, guided by metrics such as the lowest overall quantization error. The SOM-Ward cluster algorithm used here (as implemented in the Viscovery SOMine 4.0 software package – see http://www.viscovery.net; accessed 1 March 2011) also accounts for local similarity (i.e. proximity on the map) in the distance measure.

The mean values of nodes in each SOM-Ward cluster are extracted to provide an average shape for the bars that a given cluster represents (see Figure 13.3). Finally, the original data is classified using the trained map in order to assign cluster shapes to bars (Figure 13.4).

Using the SOM method to group into clusters those units that have similar timing or dynamic patterns, we find that across the 29 performances four clusters emerge for each of these parameters. Figure 13.3(a) shows the four timing clusters that have been identified (T1–T4); for each one, the relative proportions of the three beats within the bar are revealed. The clusters are plotted in decreasing frequency: T1 occurs in 32 percent of the bars, T2 in 30 percent, T3 in 24 percent and T4 in 14 percent. Similarly, Figure 13.3(b) displays the emergent dynamic clusters (D1–D4), for each of which the cumulative change in dynamic from beat to beat is depicted. So for D1, beat 1 is 4% quieter than the last beat of the previous bar, beat 2 is 1.5% quieter than beat 1, and beat 3 is 4.5% louder than beat 2. Again, the clusters are plotted in decreasing frequency: D1 is found in 32 percent of the bars, D2 in 30 percent, D3 in 24 percent and D4 in 14 percent.

In terms of timing, the second most common pattern (T2) has a relatively long middle beat, as might be expected in a mazurka (see the discussion above).

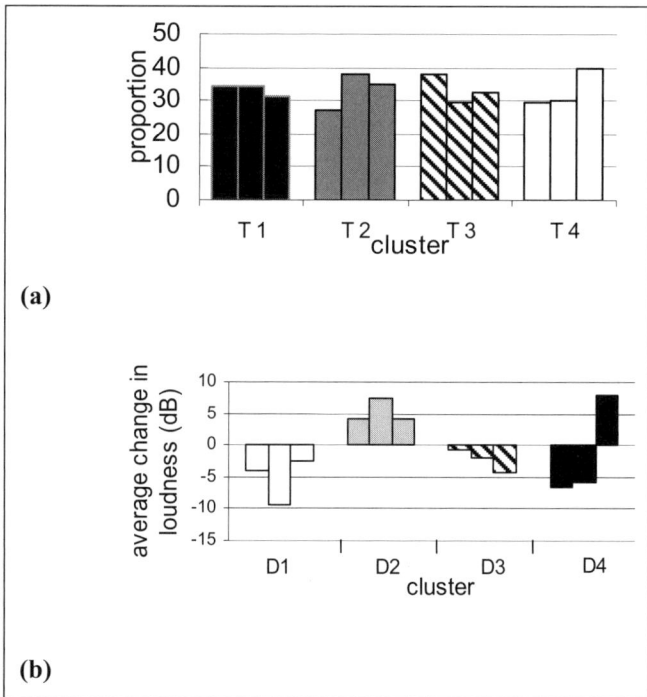

(a)

(b)

Figure 13.3   Timing and dynamic clusters in all 29 performances

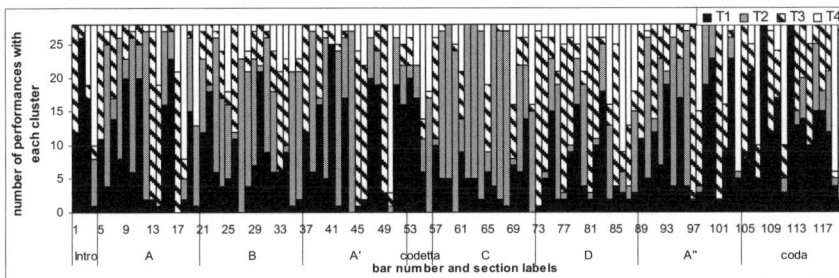

(a)

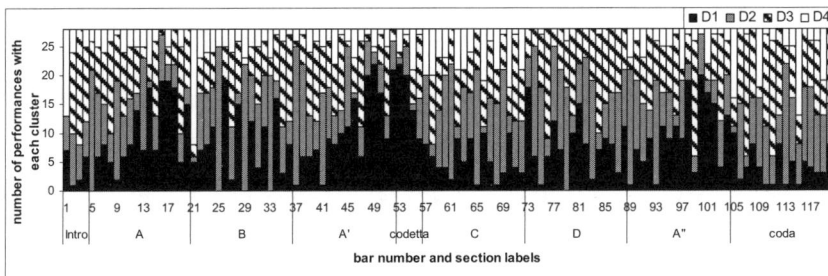

(b)

Figure 13.4   Distribution of (a) timing and (b) dynamic clusters in all 29
performances of the Mazurka. The sections of the piece are overlaid
in each graph.

T2 also has a comparatively long third beat, so the pattern could be related to
more general ritardandos. In T3 the first beat is longest, as one would anticipate in
a piece in triple metre, whereas T4 has a longer final beat, which again could be
related to slowing at the end of the bar or possibly to the third-beat agogic and/or
dynamic accents also typical of the mazurka genre. Finally, the most common
pattern (T1) is almost flat. As for the dynamic patterns, D1 and D4 have relatively
louder third beats, D2 is characterized by a relatively louder second beat, and D3
features a slight diminuendo across the bar. These patterns confirm expectations
arising from the more conventional analysis above with regard to second- and
third-beat accents.

Having identified the patterns, it is possible to investigate their distribution
through the piece (see Figure 13.4). Note that sections A and A' have a very
similar distribution of patterns. In some sections specific patterns are prevalent
throughout: for example, section C is dominated by T2 and the introduction by T1
and T3. Although the latent hemiola pattern in the introduction potentially could
be brought out, most performances have either flat patterns or agogic accents
on the initial beat (particularly in the first bar). Some patterns occur relatively

often in parts of sections; for example, T4 is common at section ends. In these ways, the music's general structural characteristics seem to be reflected in the performance patterns. However, there is by no means complete agreement across all performances, and the proportions and distributions of patterns differ even when the latter are in positions that structurally or thematically are very similar (such as section ends). This once again indicates that musical structure as conventionally understood is far from being the only determinant of musical expression.

As discussed above, broad comparison of the use of patterns by all the performers together shows that the frequency of cluster patterns reduces from T1 to T4 (see Figure 13.3). When looking at each performer individually, however, we find that the frequency of patterns is not the same within each performance (Figure 13.5). Some performances feature a dominance of T1, often keeping an undifferentiated timing pattern within the bar (e.g. Chiu 1999); others make particular use of second- and/or third-beat agogic accents (e.g. Pobłocka 1999); and others emphasize the phrase-final lengthening pattern (e.g. Ashkenazy 1981).

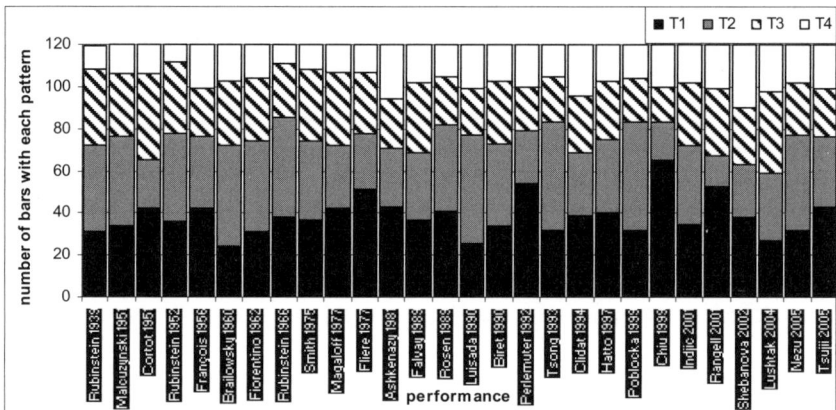

Figure 13.5   Occurrence of timing clusters in each performance

In Luisada's (1990) performance, the phrase and section ends are clearly highlighted and second beats tend to be accentuated (with a comparatively high use of T2 and T4). Conversely, whereas Chiu's (1999) performance has relatively contrasting average beat lengths across sections (see Figure 13.6), within each section there is a dominance of the flattest of the four timing patterns.

Although broad comparison of this kind usefully reveals general trends across a large number of performances (a task for which the SOM method is extremely well suited), detailed examination of individual interpretations is required to gain insight into the expressive patterning distinctive to each one. To that end, the SOMs are trained on data for individual performances rather than the group as a whole. This allows comparison both within and among performances of the patterns and their distribution. The interpretation with the smallest number of identified clusters

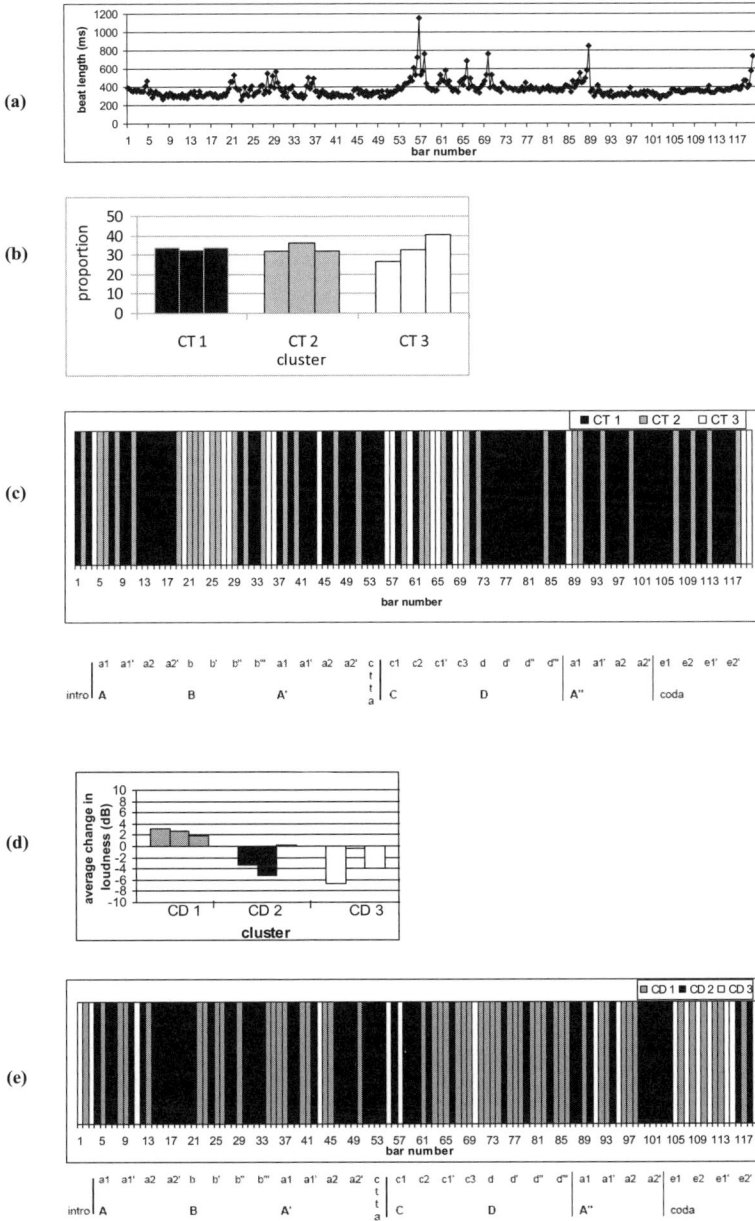

Figure 13.6   Frederic Chiu, 1999 (HMX 2907352.53): (a) beat length, (b) timing clusters, (c) distribution of timing clusters and structure of piece, (d) dynamic clusters, (e) distribution ofdynamic clusters and structure of piece

is that of Chiu (1999), with only three timing clusters, whereas the greatest number of clusters occurs in Magaloff's (1977), with 18 clusters of this type. In between, Rubinstein's (1939) performance has eight timing clusters.

A similar pattern, though less extreme, is seen in the dynamic clusters, with three found in Chiu's recording, six in Rubinstein's and eight in Magaloff's. As explained below, the number of cluster types within a particular interpretation may be significant in terms of its perceived richness and interest.

In Chiu's performance, the most common timing and dynamic clusters (CT1 and CD1) are almost flat in contour, while the others involve the following: lengthening of the second beat (CT2) and final beat (CT3); diminuendo through the bar (CD2); and a relatively loud second beat (CD3). The distribution of the clusters in this interpretation is more or less systematic: for example, CT3 occurs almost exclusively at phrase ends, whereas CT2 is found in the most characteristically mazurka-like sections (that is, B and C).

In contrast, Magaloff's performance (see Figure 13.7) has many different timing clusters, very few of which return when material is repeated. Notwithstanding the abundance of patterns, however, commonalities do occur in the form of relatively long first, middle or final beats, such that three sub-groups of patterns can be discerned (as indicated by the shadings in Figure 13.7(b)). Fewer patterns in the dynamics are identified, though more dynamic clusters can be found in this performance than in most of the others.

The timing patterns discernible in Rubinstein's 1939 performance also fall into sub-groups, which are shown by the different shadings in Figure 13.8(b) and (c). As for the dynamics, two types of first-, second- and third-beat dynamic accent can be seen in Figure 13.8, that is RD1/RD5, RD4/RD6 and RD2/RD3 respectively. Unlike Magaloff's performance, there is considerable alignment here between the repetition of thematic material on the one hand and that of expressive patterns on the other: for instance, the three A sections have more or less identical dynamic profiles,[20] just as the first phrase in sections B and C is entirely dominated by third-beat dynamic accents. Agogic and dynamic accents fall on the same beat in 31 individual bars but receive particular joint emphasis on the third beats of bars 14, 18, 28, 49, 50, 54 and 101 – that is, nearly half of the 18 bars in which

---

[20]   In the following table of the three A sections (each of which has four four-bar hypermeasures), '1' represents the presence of clusters with first-beat dynamic accents (i.e. RD1 and RD5), '2' those with second-beat dynamic accents (RD4 and RD6), and '3' those with third-beat dynamic accents (RD2 and RD3). The general consistency is remarkable, although the deviations (especially in the second and fourth hypermeasures in A'') are also noteworthy:

	Hypermeasure 1	Hypermeasure 2	Hypermeasure 3	Hypermeasure 4
A	1 3 1 3	1 3 1 1	3 3 1 3	3 3 1 3
A'	1 3 1 3	1 3 1 1	2 3 1 3	3 3 1 3
A''	1 3 1 3	2 3 2 3	3 3 1 3	3 3 2 1

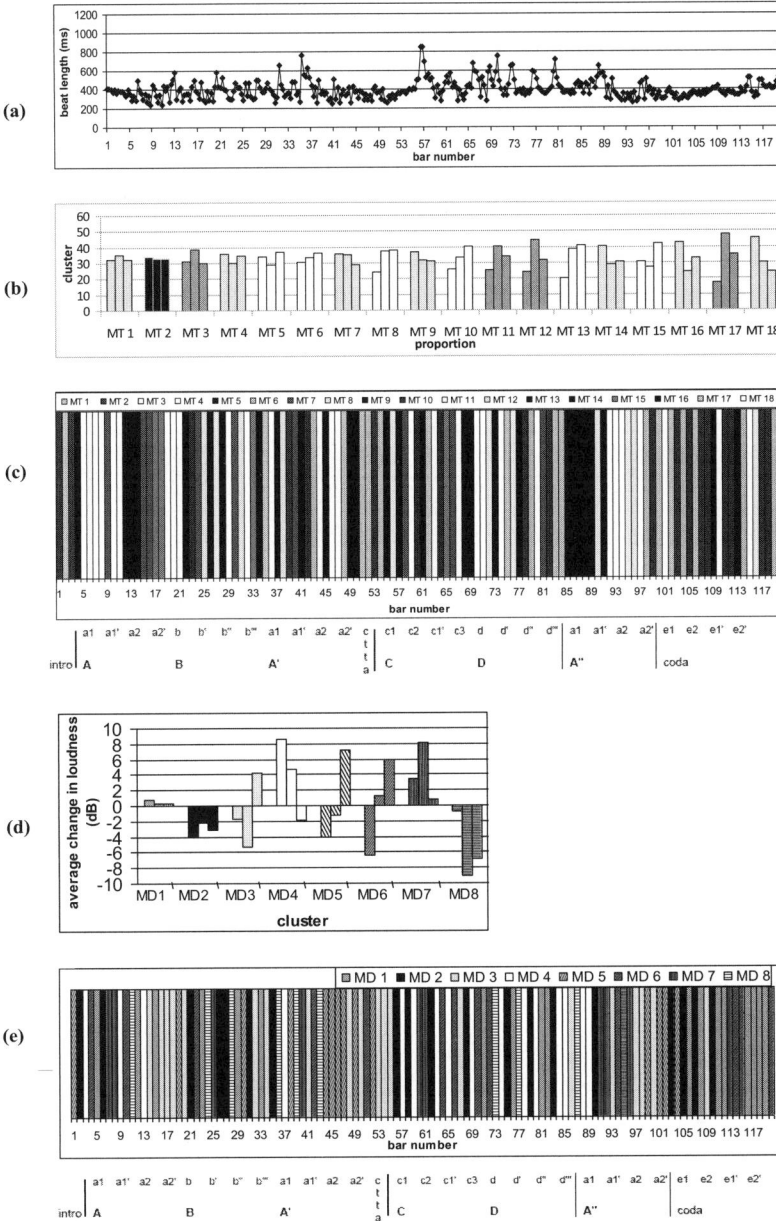

Figure 13.7   Nikita Magaloff, 1977 (Philips 426 817/29-2): (a) beat length,
(b) timing clusters, (c) distribution of timing clusters and structure
of piece, (d) dynamic clusters, (e) distribution of dynamic clusters
and structure of piece

(a)

(b)

(c)

(d)

(e)

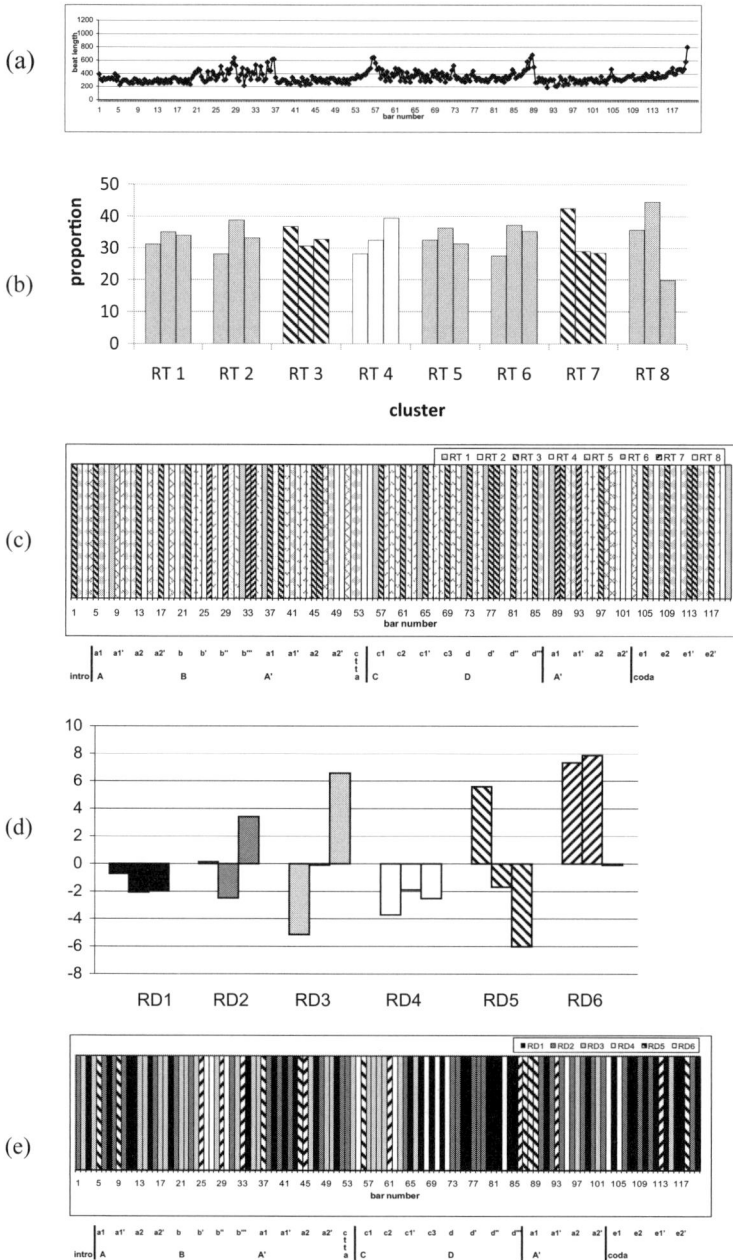

Figure 13.8   Artur Rubinstein, 1939 (Naxos 8.110656-57): (a) beat length, (b) timing clusters, (c) distribution of timing clusters and structure of piece, (d) dynamic clusters, (e) distribution of dynamic clusters and structure of piece

third-beat agogic accents appear at all. Second-beat agogic accents tend to be favoured, arising in 71 bars; however, as we shall see, Rubinstein attaches even greater weight to first-beat accents in defining the Mazurka's expressive shape in performance.

D

Just as the formal analysis towards the start of the chapter identified structural features of variable relevance to the Mazurka as performed, not all of the properties of the 29 performances revealed by the foregoing survey may correspond to how listeners hear the music and how the respective pianists conceived it in the first place. That does not mean the analysis lacks value, however, nor are the implied limitations necessarily problematic. What needs to follow here and indeed in any act of analysis – whether of performances, scores or altogether different material – is ongoing interrogation of the initial findings as well as the sort of mediation referred to earlier if relevance to actual practice is to be assured.

In this case, three questions invite our attention – the first of which applies in respect of performance analysis more generally: (1) What *musical* meaning or significance do the analytical findings have? (2) How do the expressive patterns that have been identified contribute to the coherence – that is, cohesion and comprehensibility – of a given performance? (3) How might we better understand the 'hierarchy of temporally defined musical gestures' within individual performances of this Mazurka as a result of this analysis?

The second and third questions are dealt with in the final part of the chapter, which focuses specifically on Rubinstein's interpretation from 1939. As for the first, consider the suggestion above that the number of cluster types within different performances may relate to the 'perceived richness and interest' thereof. Recall that in Chiu's (1999) recording, only three timing clusters were found, as against eight in Rubinstein's (1939) and eighteen in Magaloff's (1977); similarly, the number of dynamic clusters respectively totalled three, six and eight. Although Magaloff's interpretation might seem 'richer' on the strength of these higher counts, that is not how it comes across aurally – at least not to the authors of this chapter. For example, whereas Chiu's playing features little temporal modulation and thus sounds rather mechanical, Magaloff's is altogether unpredictable both rhythmically and metrically, with continual shifts in agogic accentuation as well as rubato more generally.[21] Although to some this flexibility might seem imaginative and vitalizing, to our ears Magaloff's approach sounds wilful and, in the context of a mazurka, disconcertingly unstable. Rubinstein, in contrast, subtly offsets rhythmic consistency (namely, a relatively steady pulse at the level of the bar and

---

[21]   It would be difficult to dance to this performance if one chose to do so (notwithstanding Chopin's intentions to the contrary): the ataxic qualities of the playing are inimical to the steady bar-level pulse typical of the mazurka genre, within which there nevertheless tends to be considerable flexibility 'contained' by the pulse.

within the accompaniment) against variegated rubato in the melodic line. As we will see, this may reflect a higher-level timing strategy on his part.

One point needs to be emphasized: it is not the presence or quantity of expressive clusters that matters most, but what use performers make of the features in question. Obviously it would be simplistic to claim that in a piece of this nature and duration, the presence of a given number of cluster types is a reliable indicator of artistic quality, likewise that fewer such cluster types are necessarily too few or many of them too many. Nevertheless, the foregoing analysis may reveal at least one contributing factor to the greater or lesser sense of satisfaction that some performances evince as compared with others. Although a listener might intuitively apprehend the relative differences between these performances, the study here demonstrates and defines them more explicitly, allowing one to make up one's own mind in response to a greater range of evidence than the ear alone can muster, even after repeated listenings.

Part 3

A''

Although the naked ear has undeniable limitations, it is almost certainly the musician's most important tool – likewise, potentially, the analyst's. Long before one prepares note-to-note or beat-to-beat representations of the timing and dynamic information in performances, it is advisable to listen over and over to a performance not only to gain general familiarity but also to decide what is interesting and distinctive about it. Admittedly, such a judgement will be subjective, but at the very least identifying the most intriguing features can act as a starting point for more thoroughgoing study. On first hearing Rubinstein's 1939 recording, for example, one might be struck by the unusually delicate articulation and relatively contained dynamic compass, the latter of which serves to highlight the music's temporal shaping,[22] especially the refined rubato used with such flair in section B. Compared with the other recordings in our sample, Rubinstein's stands out not only by virtue of these characteristics but also by achieving underlying control and improvisatory freedom in the same creative breath. That combination is surely one of the keys to playing Chopin well, at least judging by the compositional and performance aesthetic that can be construed from his music and from the accounts of those who heard him play; it may also be a hallmark of great music-making more generally.

But what is the source of that underlying control? And how does Rubinstein work within as well as against it? It is possible to answer these questions using one's aural powers and tools of verbal description alone, but application of the analytical findings presented above may be revelatory, allowing us furthermore to

---

22   This is one reason why the following discussion focuses on timing.

address the issues raised at the end of Part 2 concerning the musical significance of this sort of analysis, the cohesion and comprehensibility of the performance in question, and the nature of and interrelationships between the temporally defined musical gestures therein.

Let us start by reconsidering the beat-per-minute (BPM) data graphed in Figure 13.8(a). In Rubinstein's performance a definite progression in temporal fluctuation can be discerned across the three A sections: the first is more temporally contained, the second more varied (possibly because of the influence of the preceding B section) and the last the most varied of all. B contrasts starkly with the preceding section in terms of both absolute tempo – it is noticeably much slower – and the greater amount of temporal shaping at bar and beat levels. C, too, has a good deal of temporal flexibility, but (as we shall see) its rhythmic articulation is highly patterned and thereby foregrounded. In D, Rubinstein combines flexibility and control to a greater extent than anywhere else, achieving a concentrated temporal flow with commensurate expressive intensity. The ensuing section, A'', is heard against that background, just as its own flexibility is striking in comparison with the tightly shaped coda to follow. All of these contrasts imbue the performance with a somewhat sectionalized character – yet the sense of progression across the A sections and the referential use of the more temporally articulated section C create large-scale directionality and continuity that thwart any possible sense of concatenation. Overall, then, Rubinstein achieves an equilibrium between the definition of structure and the generation of momentum – one that is manifested in numerous dimensions.

His manipulation of tempo throughout the performance creates further momentum in part through the use of three broad tempo levels that themselves act referentially as the music proceeds.[23] Figure 13.9 shows the BPM data with superimposed tempo 'averages'[24] represented linearly. The introduction starts at around crotchet = 185 and section A follows at crotchet = c. 210. Most of section B is much slower at c. 160 beats per minute, while in A' the tempo returns to crotchet = c. 210. The codetta begins at roughly the same speed but gradually tails off, with

---

[23]   His recordings from 1952 and 1966 are similar in this respect, even though the precise tempo levels vary. There is less differentiation between the respective levels in the 1966 performance, which on the whole is slower than the earlier ones (for discussion of Rubinstein's three recordings, see Spiro et al. 2010).

[24]   Various conceptual difficulties surround the calculation of average tempo (for discussion, see Gabrielsson 1988). Taking into account the data for all beats in the performance (including those within general ritardandos that artificially depress the mathematical average for given sections), the tempos in BPM for the successive sections are as follows: introduction – 185; A – 211; B – 157; A' - 211; codetta – 146; C – 164; D – 172; A'' – 210; coda – 158. The overall average thus calculated is 182 BPM – but, as implied above, this is slower than the music actually feels; the same point applies to the tempos indicated for sections B, C and D, the codetta and the coda. In fact, the baseline tempo is probably close to the one specified in Chopin's manuscript, i.e. 192 BPM.

a less rapid tempo in section C quite close to the one in section B, that is crotchet = c. 160. The first three phrases within D are palpably faster, at just under 185 BPM, whereas the fourth phrase slows towards the recapitulation. A" has virtually the same tempo as its earlier counterparts, and the coda begins at c. 185 – like the introduction – but becomes progressively slower from the third phrase onwards.

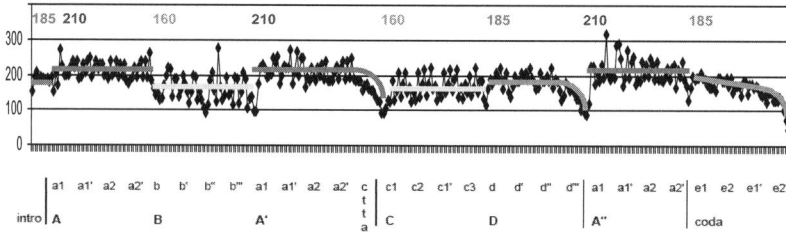

Figure 13.9   Rubinstein, 1939 (Naxos 8.110656-57): beat lengths with average tempos in the principal sections

These broad tempos act as a background to or foundation for the more immediate temporal fluctuations shown in the graph. Furthermore, they point to a distinct strategy on Rubinstein's part – one confirmed by the similar layering in his 1952 and 1966 performances (see Spiro et al. 2010). The gestural properties of these temporal layers are all the more palpable if Figure 13.9 is understood in diachronic rather than synchronic terms. One way of grasping the underlying flow is in fact through literal gesturing, in other words by tracing the different tempo layers with one's hand while mentally performing the music from beginning to end. What results is a gestural profile manifested physically – that is, a 'conducting-out' of one aspect of the music's structure, an aspect of the structure of the music *as performed*.[25] Even though Rubinstein may not have conceived the different tempos specifically in terms of physical gesture, their rendering within his performance at the very least creates a fundamental gestural energy.

Energy also arises from other gestural properties of the performance, and in this respect Rubinstein's articulation of the Mazurka's successive hypermeasures (that is, four-bar units) is noteworthy. As suggested earlier, the distribution of timing clusters reveals a preponderance of first- and second-beat agogic accents, with two out of eight clusters relating to the former and all but one of the remaining clusters pertaining to the latter (see again Figure 13.8(c)). Of the 30 hypermeasures in the piece, as many as 23 feature agogic accents on the very first downbeat; these occur within clusters RT3 and RT7, which otherwise appear in only eight bars. The preponderance of these two clusters on hypermetrical downbeats can be seen in

---

[25]   It should be noted that tempo levels like the ones here might be physically represented in precisely this manner by musicians trying to characterize the temporal shaping of their own performances.

Figure 13.10, where the thinner arrows indicate the presence of cluster RT3 in the first bar of 19 hypermeasures all told, while the thicker arrows show cluster RT7 in the same position within four more hypermeasures. Note that RT7 – the cluster with the greatest relative stress on the first beat of the bar – is strategically used by Rubinstein as an anchor for the second half of section B (where the melodic rubato is most pronounced); this is also the case in the first two phrases of the reprise. Stability is additionally conferred through the repeated use of cluster RT3 throughout sections C and D as well as the coda, where Rubinstein maintains a steady agogic rhythm at once reflecting the phrase structure of the notated music and creating its dynamic counterpart in sound.

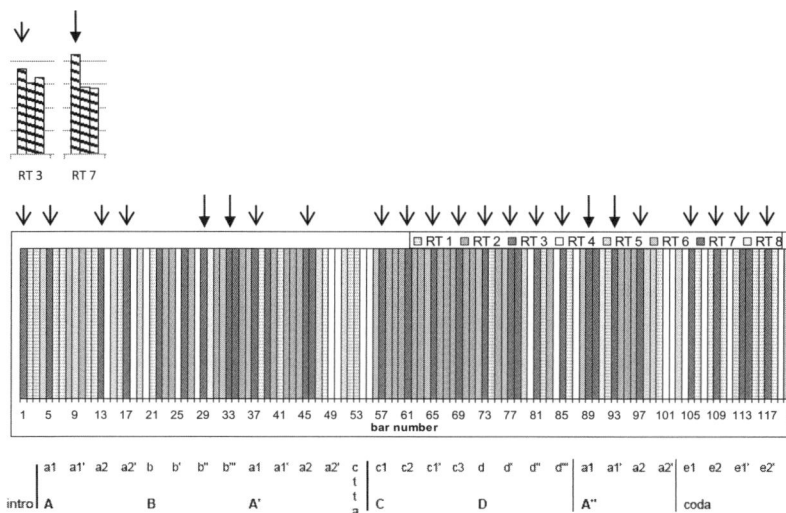

Figure 13.10   Rubinstein, 1939 (Naxos 8.110656-57): distribution of timing clusters and structure of piece, with arrows indicating where clusters RT3 and RT7 fall on hypermetrical downbeats

It would be worth exploring further this relationship between non-variant aspects of structure and those dependent upon the performer's prerogatives. Although greater stress on the first bar of a four-bar hypermeasure would normally be anticipated, likewise a longer first beat in triple metre (as noted above), the absence and, thus, irregularity of emphasis on respective beats or bars in parts of Rubinstein's performance effectively cast light on those passages where such emphasis does occur. Again, this supports the claim that musical structure as conventionally modelled is not the sole and possibly not even the primary determinant of expression; if that were the case, every first beat and every first bar would be emphasized at the relevant bar or hypermetrical level. Rubinstein's less predictable approach reflects a shaping of the music both typical in its idiosyncrasy (in the sense that no performance is ever a 'true' representation of underlying structure) and idiosyncratic in its particular non-conformance to underlying structure. In other words, the distinctive ebb and flow of first-beat/first-bar emphasis creates energy within this performance, with the irregularly regular downbeats stabilizing the music in precisely the way that a conductor's fluid but controlled gestures generate forward impulse and effect coordination at the very same time.

One conclusion to be drawn from this is that the *absence* of particular features within a performance may be as musically significant as their presence. This certainly applies to another gestural aspect of Rubinstein's interpretation, namely a dual impulse emanating from the first part of the Trio, section C, which Rubinstein treats in a remarkably systematic fashion. Indeed, the temporal regularity here so radically contrasts with the flexibility elsewhere that it ends up influencing how his entire performance comes across, possibly reflecting a conscious or unconscious strategy on his part for making the music cohere. Another look at the recordings of Chiu and Magaloff suggests just how unusual Rubinstein's approach is compared with other interpretations as well as within his own. Table 13.1 shows the timing clusters in section C within these three recordings. As the previous discussion also confirms, Chiu's displays a limited number of clusters, which may partly explain the broadly similar treatment of hypermeasures 3 and 4 (respectively CT3/2/1/3 and CT3/2/1/2 across the constituent four bars) and also the use of CT2 and CT3 in the third and fourth bars of both hypermeasures 1 and 2. In Magaloff's case, one finds certain commonalities (MT7 in bar 2 of hypermeasures 1 and 3, MT3 in bar 3 of hypermeasures 1 and 4, and MT10 in bar 4 of hypermeasures 1 and 2) but no larger-scale patterning. Rubinstein, in contrast, treats the four hypermeasures with extraordinary consistency, employing the same succession of clusters – RT3/2/2/2 – in the first and third hypermeasures, followed in the second and fourth by an identical succession closely related to the one just mentioned, that is RT3/2/2/6.[26] Recall that RT2 and RT6 feature second-beat agogic accents (see again Figure 13.8(b)), thereby revealing a fundamental similarity between the two hypermetrical patterns in use here. As we have seen, the first cluster in each hypermeasure, RT3, is characterized by a first-beat agogic accent, reinforcing the beginning of each four-bar group and thereby creating a higher-order rhythmic articulation.

---

[26]   On the whole the dynamic shape of Rubinstein's section C is comparatively irregular, despite the fact that the first hypermeasure consists only of cluster RD3 (see n. 20 above for an explanation of the abbreviations in the table):

	Hypermeasure 1	Hypermeasure 2	Hypermeasure 3	Hypermeasure 4
C	3 3 3 3	2 2 3 3	1 3 1 2	1 2 1 2

Table 13.1   Timing clusters in section C of Chiu 1999 (HMX 2907352.53), Magaloff 1977 (Philips 426 817/29-2) and Rubinstein 1939 (Naxos 8.110656-57)

Hypermeasure	Bar	Chiu 1999	Magaloff 1977	Rubinstein 1939
	57	CT3	MT14	RT3
	58	CT1	MT7	RT2
1	59	CT2	MT3	RT2
	60	CT3	MT10	RT2
	61	CT1	MT5	RT3
	62	CT2	MT1	RT2
2	63	CT2	MT11	RT2
	64	CT3	MT10	RT6
	65	CT3	MT15	RT3
	66	CT2	MT7	RT2
3	67	CT1	MT11	RT2
	68	CT3	MT13	RT2
	69	CT3	MT5	RT3
	70	CT2	MT18	RT2
4	71	CT1	MT3	RT2
	72	CT2	MT8	RT6

It is the striking regularity of section C that distinguishes it from the rest of Rubinstein's performance. In this pivotal passage, the listener is invited to re-evaluate everything that has been heard prior to the Trio, the flexibility of the earlier music standing out in retrospect against the temporal consistency in C; at the same time, one newly anticipates what will follow, with an expectation of ongoing regularity dissipating as flexibility gradually prevails once again. Thus, paradoxically, greater cohesion is achieved through contrast, and along with it a heightened sense of momentum: huge impulses are unleashed in both directions through the idiosyncratic temporal structure that Rubinstein creates, backward towards the beginning and forward towards the end.

Figure 13.11 depicts these impulses as broad gestures emerging from section C at the core of the performance – gestures that hint at the generation of both centrifugal and centripetal force. But the music's directionality is not defined only by these outwardly directed gestures: as we have seen, Rubinstein also creates forward momentum through the layered tempos reproduced in the middle of the diagram, as well as the 'irregularly regular rhythm' of the stressed hypermetrical downbeats shown at the top. This hierarchy of temporally defined gestures portrays an essential motion within the performance while also identifying how and why Rubinstein's Mazurka comes across as coherent, in the dual sense of cohesive and comprehensible. The image helps us understand what we are listening to but possibly unable to hear.

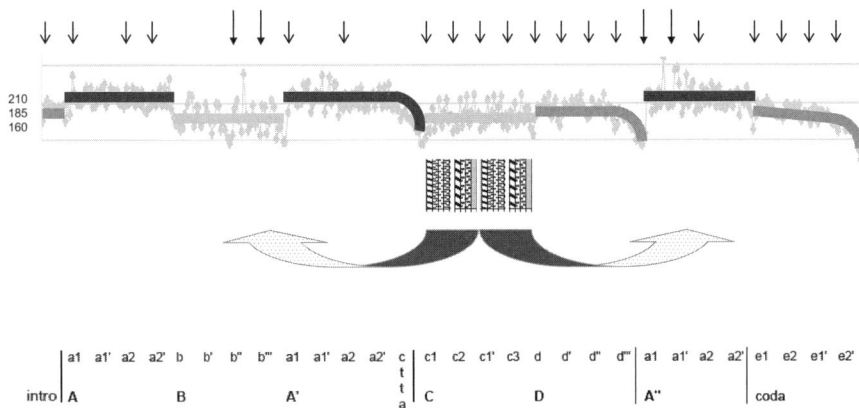

Figure 13.11   Rubinstein 1939 (Naxos 8.110656-57): hierarchy of 'temporally defined gestures, depicting the temporal shape of Rubinstein's performance'

Coda

To do full justice to Rubinstein's performance as well as those of the other pianists, one would need to focus on a broader range of parameters, if not the entire task list presented earlier. The relatively constrained focus of this analysis need not be considered a weakness, however, even if more could be said. First of all, no single analysis can ever be exhaustive: selectivity has to be exercised if only for practical reasons – and that is as true of analysis as it is of performance, in which a range of different possibilities might well be pursued on different occasions. Moreover, music generally does not depend equally upon all or even many of the parameters that constitute it: just as composers often construct comprehensive and expansive musical arguments out of limited material, performers typically conceive their music-making in simple structural terms, attaching particular expressive significance to certain elements and using them as a backbone for the unfolding music. That this is true of Rubinstein's performance from 1939 is open to debate, but it seems remarkable that his manipulation of timing in particular serves as the basis for much of what he does. In short, Rubinstein frames his performance in accordance with the key features of the mazurka genre – four-bar phrasing, bar-level pulse, agogic accentuation on downbeats (for stability) and on second beats (for vitality), and other forms of melodic rubato – although he moulds these idiosyncratically and creatively. Through our analysis we have arrived at a deeper understanding of *Rubinstein's* Mazurka as well as Chopin's Op. 24 No. 2 more generally. The fact that more work would be needed to plumb the potential of the latter in terms of all the different performances that do or could exist is not to be lamented but rather to be celebrated – by those who play the piece and by those who choose to analyse it, each in their own ways.

References

CFEO (2007). *Chopin's First Editions Online* (http://www.cfeo.org.uk; accessed 1 March 2011).

CHARM (2009a). Discography of Chopin's Mazurka, Op. 24 No. 2 (http://mazurka.org.uk/info/discography/mazurka-discography.txt; accessed 1 March 2011).

—— (2009b). Mazurkas Project (http://www.mazurka.org.uk; accessed 1 March 2011).

Cox, A. (2006). Hearing, Feeling, Grasping Gestures. In A. Gritten & E. King (eds.), *Music and Gesture* (pp. 45–60). Aldershot: Ashgate.

Eigeldinger, J.-J. (1986). *Chopin: Pianist and Teacher as Seen by His Pupils*, ed. R. Howat (trans. N. Shohet with K. Osostowicz & R. Howat). Cambridge: Cambridge University Press.

Gabrielsson, A. (1988). Timing in Music Performance and its Relations to Music Experience. In J. Sloboda (ed.), *Generative Processes in Music: The Psychology of Performance, Improvisation, and Composition* (pp. 27–51). Oxford: Clarendon Press.

Kohonen, T. (2001). *Self-Organizing Maps*, 3rd edition. Berlin: Heidelberg and New York: Springer.

Macy, L., ed. (2001–). Motif. In *Grove Music Online* (http://www.oxfordmusiconline.com; accessed 1 March 2011).

Rink, J. (1992). Tonal Architecture in the Early Music. In J. Samson (ed.), *The Cambridge Companion to Chopin* (pp. 78–97 and 305–8). Cambridge: Cambridge University Press.

—— (1999a). Translating Musical Meaning: The Nineteenth-Century Performer as Narrator. In N. Cook & M. Everist (eds.), *Rethinking Music* (pp. 217–38). Oxford: Oxford University Press.

—— (1999b). 'Structural Momentum' and Closure in Chopin's Nocturne Op. 9 No. 2. In C. Schachter & H. Siegel (eds.), *Schenker Studies 2* (pp. 109–26). Cambridge: Cambridge University Press.

—— (2005). Les *Concertos* de Chopin et la notation de l'exécution. In J.-J. Eigeldinger (ed.), *Frédéric Chopin, interprétations* (pp. 69–88). Geneva: Librairie Droz.

— (2007). Review of *Music and Gesture*, eds. A. Gritten & E. King (Aldershot: Ashgate, 2006). *British Journal of Aesthetics* 47/2: 224–6.

Sapp, C. (2007). Comparative Analysis of Multiple Musical Performances. In S. Dixon, D. Bainbridge & R. Typke (eds.), *Proceedings of the Eighth International Conference on Music Information Retrieval* (pp. 497–500). Vienna: Österreichische Computer Gesellschaft.

Spiro, N., Gold, N. and Rink, J. (2008). *Plus ça change:* Analyzing Performances of Chopin's Mazurka Op. 24 No. 2. In K. Miyazaki et al. (eds.), *Proceedings of the Tenth International Conference on Music Perception and Cognition* (pp. 418–27). Sapporo: ICMPC10.

— (2010). The Form of Performance: Analyzing Pattern Distribution in Select Recordings of Chopin's Mazurka Op. 24 No. 2. *Musicae Scientiae* 14: 23–55.

Sydow, B. E., ed. (1955). *Korespondencja Fryderyka Chopin*. Vol. 1. Warsaw: Państwowy Instytut Wydawniczy.

Ward, J. H. (1963). Hierarchical Grouping to Optimize an Objective Function. *Journal of the American Statistical Association* 58/301: 236–44.

Widmer, G., Dixon, S., Goebl, W., Pampalk, E. & Tobudic, A. (2003). In Search of the Horowitz Factor. *AI Magazine* 24/3: 111–30.

Index

References to illustrations and music examples are in **bold**.